MECCA

Desperately Seeking Paradise: Journeys of a Sceptical Muslim
Balti Britain: A Provocative Journey Through Asian Britain
The Consumption of Kuala Lumpur
The A to Z of Postmodern Life: Essays on Global Culture in the Noughties
Breaking the Mould: Essays, Articles and Columns on Islam, India,
Terror and Other Things That Annoy Me

The Future of Muslim Civilization
Islamic Futures: The Shape of Ideas to Come
Reading the Qur'an
Muhammad: All That Matters
What Do Muslims Believe?
Introducing Islam
The No Nonsense Guide to Islam (with Merryl Wyn Davies)

The Touch of Midas: Science, Values and the Environment in Islam and the West
Explorations in Islamic Science
The Revenge of Athena: Science, Exploitation and the Third World
Thomas Kuhn and the Science War
Information and the Muslim World
Hajj Studies
An Early Crescent: The Future of Knowledge and Environment in Islam
Introducing Chaos
Introducing Mathematics (with J. R. Ravetz)
Introducing Philosophy of Science

Muslims in Britain: Making Social and Political Space (with Waqar Ahmad)
Muslim Minorities in the West (with S. Z. Abedin)

Orientalism
Postmodernism and the Other
Aliens R Us: The Other in Science Fiction Cinema (with Sean Cubitt)
Cyberfutures: Culture and Politics on the Information Superhighway
(with J. R. Ravetz)
The Third Text Reader on Art, Culture and Theory
(with Rasheed Araeen and Sean Cubitt)
Barbaric Others: A Manifesto on Western Racism
(with Merryl Wyn Davies and Ashis Nandy)
Introducing Cultural Studies
Introducing Media Studies
Introducing Postmodernism (with Richard Appignanesi *et al.*)

Rescuing All Our Futures: The Future of Future Studies
Future: All That Matters

Islam, Postmodernism and Other Futures: A Ziauddin Sardar Reader
How Do You Know? Reading Ziauddin Sardar on Islam,
Science and Cultural Relations

Why Do People Hate America? (with Merryl Wyn Davies)
American Dream, Global Nightmare (with Merryl Wyn Davies)
Will America Change? (with Merryl Wyn Davies)

MECCA

The Sacred City

Ziauddin Sardar

B L O O M S B U R Y

LONDON · NEW DELHI · NEW YORK · SYDNEY

First published in Great Britain 2014
First published in India 2014

Copyright © Ziauddin Sardar 2014
Map by John Gilkes

The moral right of the author has been asserted

No part of this book may be used or reproduced in any manner whatsoever
without written permission from the publisher except in the case of brief
quotations embedded in critical articles or reviews

Every reasonable effort has been made to trace copyright holders of
material reproduced in this book, but if any have been inadvertently
overlooked the publisher would be glad to hear from them

This edition published with permission from
Bloomsbury Publishing Plc, 50 Bedford Square, London WC1B 3DP

Bloomsbury is a trademark of Bloomsbury Publishing Plc

Bloomsbury Publishing, London, New Delhi, New York and Sydney

A CIP catalogue record for this book is available from the British Library

For sale in the Indian subcontinent only

ISBN 978 93 84052 95 9

10 9 8 7 6 5 4 3 2

Bloomsbury Publishing India
Vishrut Building, DDA Complex, Building No. 3
Ground Floor, Pocket C – 6 & 7, Vasant Kunj
New Delhi 110070
www.bloomsbury.com

Typeset by Hewer Text UK Ltd, Edinburg
Printed and bound in India by Thomson Press India Ltd

For my friend, the late Ayyub Malik, architect and ceramic artist of distinction, in fond memory of scintillating conversations and good times on the streets of Mecca and Jeddah, and in my conservatory.

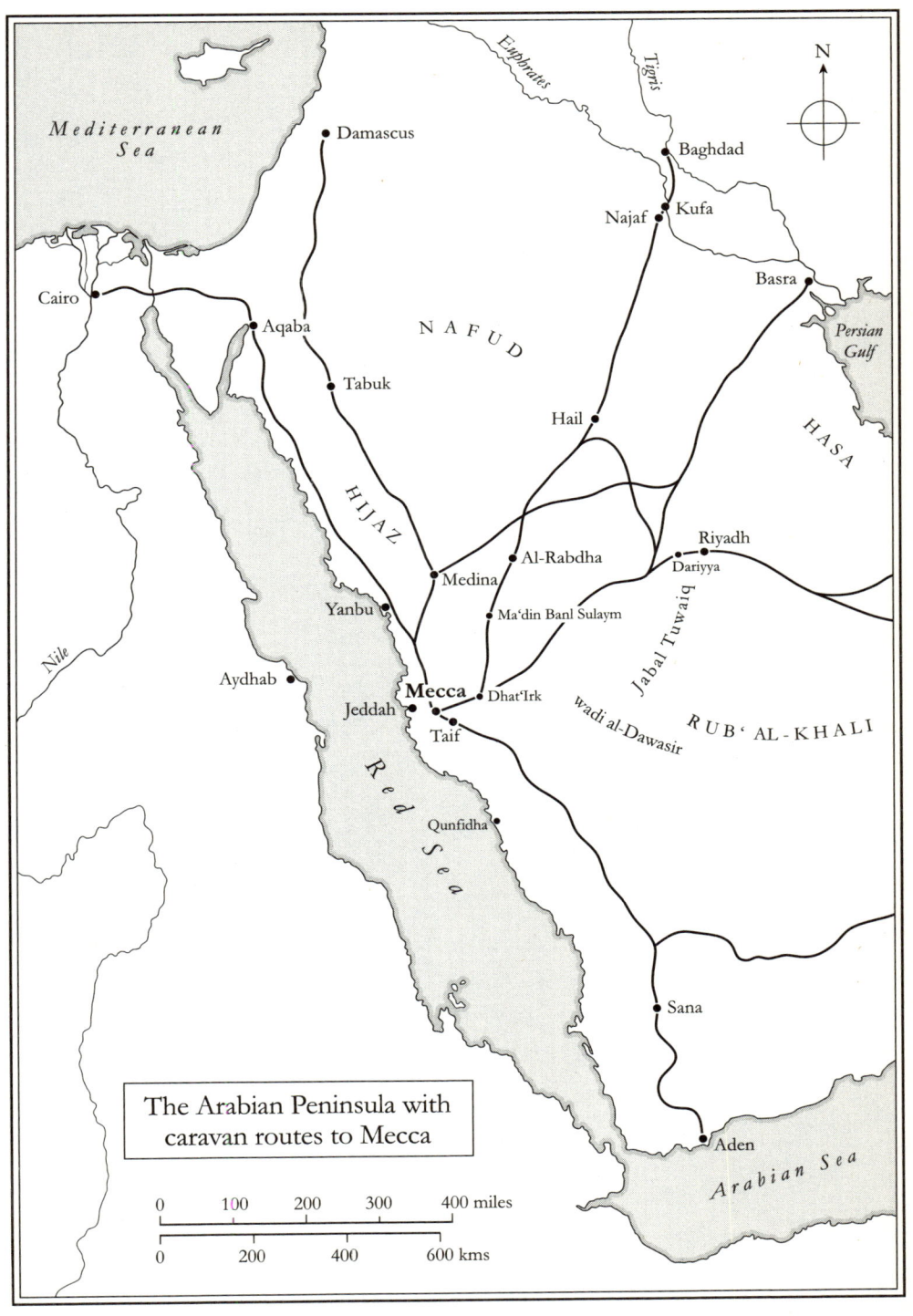

N

Mediterranean Sea

Damascus

Euphrates

Tigris

Baghdad

Najaf • Kufa

Basra

Persian Gulf

Cairo

Aqaba

N A F U D

H A S A

Tabuk

Nile

H I J A Z

Hail

Al-Rabdha

Riyadh

Medina

Dariyya

Yanbu

Ma'din Banl Sulaym

Jabal Tuwaiq

Aydhab

Dhat'Irk

Mecca

wadi al-Dawasir

R U B ' A L - K H A L I

Jeddah

Taif

Red Sea

Qunfidha

Sana

Aden

Arabian Sea

The Arabian Peninsula with
caravan routes to Mecca

| 0 | 100 | 200 | 300 | 400 miles |

| 0 | 200 | 400 | 600 kms |

Contents

Map   vii
Introduction: The Lure of Mecca   xi

 1 The Valley of Weeping   1
 2 'I Love Thee More Than the Entire World'   33
 3 Rebellions at God's Earthly Throne   65
 4 Sharifs, Sultans and Sectarians   104
 5 Love and Fratricide in the Holy City   141
 6 The Caravans of Precious Gifts   174
 7 The Wahhabi Threat   214
 8 Camels, Indians and Feudal Queens   244
 9 Western Visitors, Arab Garb   275
10 Mecca Under the Saudis   313
11 The Reconfigured Utopia   343

    Chronology   365
    Notes   373
    Acknowledgements   393
    Index   395

Introduction

The Lure of Mecca

The pilgrim bus was stuck in an almighty gridlock. Through an early morning haze I surveyed the snarled jumble extending for miles. The buses, the standard yellow American school bus variety, were distinguished by large Arabic and English lettering on their sides. Around each bus lapped a churning tide of white cloth draped over countless pilgrim souls. The only sign that this ocean contained individual forms came from the varying hues of human flesh. Male pilgrims all wear the same traditional dress – two pieces of unstitched cloth, known as *ihram* – in such a way that one shoulder is left bare. This vast seething mass of humanity, between 2 and 3 million people, is drawn from every corner of the world, all rushing at the one appointed time to this one place: Mecca.

Once gathered, pilgrims move en masse around the city and its environs progressing from one sacred site to another. This particular tide was to take them from Muzdalifah, where they had spent a night under the stars, to Mina, some three miles away, where they would symbolically humiliate Satan by casting stones at three pillars of rock. But like some powerful bore attempting to force its way up a narrow channel, the onrush had backed up, a white-crested wave as yet unable to generate any hint of forward motion. From my vantage point it was not the fluid dynamics of this impasse that fascinated me. The jostling stasis before me was becoming as traditional as the pilgrim garb has always been. Frequent congestive interruptions are modernity's answer to manoeuvring multitudes of people from place to place by the most up-to-date means. Already I found these hiatuses at odds with my exalted expectations and cherished ideas of the experience offered by this place at this time. Perhaps it was the detachment of ideal and reality that captured my mind. Perhaps it was something in the power of this place. As I surveyed the scene before me I was drawn through the myriad host to just one bus and just one face.

The bus was stuck in a colossal traffic jam. Through one of its windows, I saw one pilgrim sitting perfectly still. A wrinkled face illumined by eyes whose resolute gaze was focused beyond the horizon. Mesmerized by that look, I transported myself through the hubbub as if floating timelessly towards this old man. As I inveigled my way through the crush I understood that he was aware of me, though his gaze had not shifted nor had he made any movement. Only when I got close to the bus did he move. With the deliberation of age and infinite effort he negotiated his way against the tide to leave the bus. It seemed to take for ever. I watched each tottering step until he stood before me. Face to face, I knew what had drawn me to this one old man. Serenity emanated, a blissful calm surrounded him. Without a word, he stretched out his hand and gave me the two pieces of bed linen he had been clutching. Instinctively I took hold of his bundle and followed. He led me beyond the crowds.

At a quiet spot beyond the roadway he indicated that I should lay his sheet upon the ground. It billowed like a sail in the morning breeze. When I had smoothed it out, he lowered his frail body onto it and settled himself down. As he lay there at rest he nodded to me and I understood his gratitude. I sat beside him – I don't know for how long. We did not talk. There was nothing to say. And then I knew he had traversed the horizon. Gently, with reverence, I spread the second sheet to cover his body. Only then did I become concerned. What should I do next? What memorial, what procedure, who to tell, how to keep his body from being trampled by some sudden eddy of the crowd? I was left with questions. He had his answer, his final destination.

It was 16 December 1975. I was fulfilling one of the most important religious duties of a Muslim: Hajj, or pilgrimage, to the sacred
city of Mecca. I was excited, enraptured, and somehow connected to
over 2 million other pilgrims who were performing the Hajj. I hoped
to return spiritually uplifted. Yet the old man had come to die. I felt
that he understood the inner meaning of Hajj better than me.

Mecca, birthplace of Islam and also of the Prophet Muhammad, is
Islam's holiest city. It is a city that I, in common with almost all
Muslims, have known all my life. A once-in-a-lifetime visit to Mecca
is a key obligation. Most Muslims, however, will never see Mecca,
and yet will have learned, perhaps even memorized, its geography
from the moment they were taught to pray. The first lesson for any
Muslim child preparing to pray is to identify the location of Mecca,
and then to prostrate in the direction of the city, not once, but five
times daily.

Our house in Dipalpur, Pakistan, where I was born and spent my
infant years, had one tattered old calendar on the wall. In fact, it was
very likely the only item of decoration in our house. The calendar
had a picture – rather gaudy, I now realize – of the Sacred Mosque
that stands at the heart of Mecca with its soaring minarets amid the
encircling hills. The heart of the Mosque, the centre of the picture,
was the Kaaba. The Kaaba drew the eye. It was an abrupt, arresting
presence, a simple cuboid structure enveloped by a drapery of gold-
embroidered black cloth. If you peered intently at the picture you
could just make out that the streams of white swirling around this
focal point were a mass of pilgrims. The word 'Allah' was written in
bold Arabic letters just above the minarets.

Time has moved on, but the image of the Kaaba on our decorative
calendar is fixed, burnt into my memory. The very first picture I ever
saw confirmed in me the certain knowledge that, while God is everywhere, in some special sense the divine power is focused in this one
place; that the Kaaba is quite simply God's House. This picture so
clearly indicating God's presence formed a primal bond that I knew

connected me, inseparably, for all time to this one place. It was a childish innocence, and yet everything I learnt was to strengthen this conviction. It grew up within me as I added new layers of understanding. This sense of personal attachment is not mine alone. It is a love and devotion, a yearning and a dream that I share with more than a billion others. It is a common bond between Muslims: Mecca and I is at one and the same time Mecca for all. To be at Mecca is the taproot of individual identity and the common link of an entire worldwide community.

My first religious lessons were all about Mecca. When my mother taught me to read the Qur'an as an infant, I learned that the Sacred Text of Islam was God's Words first revealed to Muhammad at Mecca. The stories I was told about the life of the Prophet Muhammad made Mecca and its environs more familiar to me than the country in which I lived: the cave at Hira, on the outskirts of Mecca, where the Prophet received his first revelations in 611; the town of Medina, which was called Yathrib during the days of Muhammad, where the Prophet sought refuge from persecution in Mecca; and the well of Badr and the mountain of Uhad where the Prophet fought his battles. But in Islamic tradition the history of Mecca long pre-dates the seventh century. The holy precincts around the Kaaba contain stories stretching back to the very beginning of time. Adam, who in Muslim tradition is the first Prophet, visited Mecca and was buried there. Prophet Ibrahim, or Abraham, the father of monotheistic faiths, built the Kaaba with his son Ismail, or Ishmael. Every Muslim child grows up with these stories, internalizing their geography as a personal landscape whose contours and history define who they are.

But Mecca is so much more than a place where things happened once upon a time in history. Mecca matters because, as my mother often explained, it was there that God revealed to the Prophet Muhammad his guidance on how to lead a moral life. So what the Prophet taught, what he said and how he did things provided the examples that I was told I should try hard to follow in order to grow up to be a fine human being. What happened in Mecca was alive in the simplest daily activities of my life, in all the strictures with which adults seek to tame youthful exuberance and the knotty deliberations that a gregarious youngster like me encountered in determining whether I was being naughty or not so nice. There was never a doubt that I must always look towards Mecca if I was to amount to anything worthwhile in this world.

When I was sent to more formal religious lessons the supple sympathy of my mother's approach was replaced by the sterner discipline of the madrassa. The lessons I was required to master fed my fascination with Mecca. Like all Muslim children I learnt that one of the five pillars of our faith was an obligation to visit Mecca, if I was able, at least once in my lifetime to perform the Hajj, to be part of the great annual pilgrimage that is the highest expression of Muslim existence. I drank in all the details: one had to walk around the Kaaba – for real. The other stations of the pilgrimage became landmarks in my growing sense of geography: the hamlet of Mina, where the pilgrims were required to spend a few nights; the plains of Arafat, at the foot of the Mount of Mercy – here pilgrims prayed the noon prayer in unison; the parched landscape of Muzdalifah, where pilgrims spent a night under the open sky. What an adventure it would be – to cross continents and stand where the Prophet had stood, to walk in his footsteps performing the same rituals he established and be part of that ocean of brotherhood that united people of every race and nation. And ultimately to stand with this vast gathering to ask God directly for His mercy and blessing – of course I was determined, like Muslims everywhere, that one day I would go to Mecca. I would be a pilgrim, Mecca would not always be a picture: one day I really would be there.

My family did cross continents, though we bypassed Mecca as we journeyed from Pakistan to settle in London. We changed the course of our lives in many ways – but Mecca remained a fixed point. We had of course to locate it from a new direction, but it was still central to our shifting identity. Our new home raised complex new questions, from the existential to the utterly practical, in which Mecca was a vital feature of the choices we made. A moral compass does not cease to function because one's surroundings are new and strange, or else it is no compass at all.

As I grew up in London, Mecca continued to be my lodestone and objective. I studied the glories of Muslim history, I read about other cities – Damascus, Baghdad, Cairo, Fez, Samarkand, Granada and Delhi, the source of my own Mughal heritage. They encompassed the birth of science, the glories of architecture, literary achievements, subtlety of debate, the history of ideas, legacies that enriched the whole of human history as they were appropriated far beyond the confines of Muslim lands. Wherever these achievements occurred, they emerged only because of Mecca, the progenitor of their values and virtues. Obviously, this was why the Hajj existed, the perennial annual return to the source that should spiritually replenish and rejuvenate Muslims everywhere.

And then, as I dreamt about Mecca and planned to visit the city during my mid-twenties, Mecca actually came to me. It came as an offer of the job of a lifetime. This was to become part of the team at the newly established Hajj Research Centre, based in Saudi Arabia's port city of Jeddah. The Centre was located on the campus of the newly established King Abdul Aziz University, and my job was to study and research the logistic problems of Hajj, as well as the past, present and future of Mecca.

From the birth of Islam to just before the discovery of oil, Mecca would host on average 100,000 pilgrims each year, arriving on foot, by sea, or riding on the backs of animals. But that world has now vanished and modern transport links mean that up to 3 million Muslims perform the pilgrimage each year, making it the greatest gathering of humanity anywhere on earth. The sudden influx of oil wealth created the possibility of meeting this immense logistical challenge in entirely new ways. Plans were afoot to transform Mecca,

I was told. Modernization, however, brought consequential problems and threatened collateral damage. Everything was happening fast. There was little time to learn how to manage the coming change with a better understanding of the dynamics of pilgrimage and appreciation of the historic significance and environment of Mecca. How could I refuse? I would walk within the primal image I had cherished from childhood, be part of the greatest adventure I had ever conceived – and be paid for the privilege!

I was going to Mecca. And that's how I came to be in Mecca in that momentous December of 1975.

I worked at the Hajj Research Centre for some five years.[1] I took part in the Hajj itself for each of those five years, studying the comings and goings of Hajj pilgrims, and also those who would come for the year-round 'lesser' pilgrimage that is known as Umra. The rituals of Umra are a subset of the Hajj and can be performed at any time of year outside the designated Hajj season, which falls in the twelfth and final month of Islam's lunar calendar. During those years I became intimately familiar with Mecca and its environs, I watched them change, almost never according to the ground plans and advice we devised at the Centre. In those years, and since, I have travelled to and from Mecca many times, by various means to and from many places in the world. And still nothing quite prepares you for the experience. Nor is there anything I can compare to the very first time I entered the city of my heart's longing and found myself within the Sacred Mosque.

It was late afternoon. I went through the main gate, Bab al-Malik. I began to tremble as I walked through the cool shaded building upheld by innumerable archways and approached the final colonnade. The light beyond the shade rebuffed me. It was not daylight. It was some intensified glorious glow, a luminosity peculiar to this place, contained within the open plaza at the heart of the Mosque. The oxygen drained from my lungs. 'I am here.' The thought reverberated through my body with each gulp for air. 'I am here.' The words struggled to emerge from my open mouth. My head was spinning, yet my eyes were focused on the Kaaba. I stood in awe and wonder, reverence and astonishment, elation and perplexity; a profound sadness and an irresistible smile of infinite joy took possession of me simultaneously in a moment that seemed to last for ever. I felt an urge to spread my arms and embrace everyone, enfold everyone in my exultation. And yet I was blissfully unaware of other people here in this place. It was me and the Kaaba. How could it be here? How can I be here? How can it be here before me? It was beyond imagination, beyond comprehension, more than reality. It was the point at which there is only prayer.

I was rooted in humility, standing stock-still before the sight of the Kaaba, humbled by the feelings overpowering me, struggling with all my might to take hold of the sensations I felt, to keep possession of every aspect of this experience. The sight, the light – and gradually there was a smell. What was the odour of sanctity? It infused this atmosphere. I could identify the lingering grace notes of incense, mingled with a miasma of dust, the infinitesimal fine particles of airborne sand mixed with motes of woollen fluff stirred up by the throng of feet traversing a bed of carpets. This melange blended with the effusions of human bodies. And there was something else. Some edge, some sharp, acrid something. Suddenly a flight of pigeons took to the air in the open space before me. The beating of their wings startled me, jolting me back to time and place and a simple realization – the added ingredient was pigeon droppings. Out of slime we all came, the Qur'an says, and though we can ascend higher than angels the footprints of humanity remain in the mud. So why should the odour of sanctity not include the savour of pigeon droppings?

I needed no thought to know what must happen next. Automatically I took my place, merging into the flow, becoming part of the stream of people moving ceaselessly around the Kaaba. One is required to complete seven circuits, round and round that fixed point. Counting was beyond me. I could have walked for ever. I had become one with my earliest image, one with the tide of history, with all those who had walked here before me, and one with myself. 'I am here.' It is the pilgrim's phrase, '*Lab-baik.*' 'I am here.' It is the only statement that makes sense, the only thing one can say in this place at any time.

I have stood before the Kaaba many times since. I have seen it at all times of day and night in every season. It is not true of course that there are actual sharply defined seasons in Mecca. There are enormous differences of temperature and changes in humidity, which can be experienced in a day as well as over the course of a year. At the height of summer temperatures soar to well over 40 degrees Celsius. When the sun sets, the heat rapidly recedes and the nights can be chilled, even feel bitterly cold. Summer nights begin by being as warm as a hot summer's day in northern Europe, and end with a dawn that has a distinct autumnal chill. The contrast between the intense heat of the day and the cold of late evening can make you reach for a woolly jumper or wrap up in a warm shawl.

Life in Mecca, however, is regulated, not by climate, but by the rituals and rhythms of the Islamic calendar. In Ramadan, the month of fasting for example, the city sleeps during daylight hours when fasting is observed, and awakes at evening and night, when fasting comes to an end. During each Ramadan night, the Grand Mosque teems with pilgrims attending special prayers known as *tarawih* in which all of the Qur'an's 114 chapters are recited aloud over the course of the entire month. These days, *tarawih* prayers from Mecca can be watched by anyone with a TV or computer, but back then you had to be there to behold the experience.

Ramadan moves through the varying temperatures of the year, like the Hajj season. The Islamic calendar, based on the Moon, is eleven days shorter than the Gregorian, so the fixed dates in the Islamic calendar move through the seasons in a stately progress. The Hajj officially lasts for ten days in the month of Dhu al-Hijjah. However, many pilgrims arrive perhaps a month before and linger in the city for many more weeks afterwards. They have dreamed of coming to Mecca all their lives, and find it hard to say 'Goodbye' to the city. It takes time to acclimatize to the enormity of becoming a 'Hajji', the honorific title for those who have made the pilgrimage. Just as the pilgrims are transformed, so is the whole of Mecca during the Hajj. Its visual appearance and structural features are altered. What was essentially a small town is suddenly crowded with people everywhere, people in constant motion, in a hurry to be here and then there, and never a moment when everybody sleeps.

The Sacred Mosque is crowded at all hours of day and night. White becomes the predominant colour as pilgrims jostle in their enthusiasm and fervour to experience everything Mecca has to offer from the highest moment of their life to the ceaseless bustle of gathering mementoes. Bottles, even jerrycans of water from the eternal well of Zamzam are essential, as are dates, prayer beads, prayer-carpets, copies of the Qur'an; anything to take home to share the blessing; things that no matter how ordinary will have special meaning for those back home because they actually come from Mecca. There is never an end to people coming to Mecca; like the temperature the numbers just vary in intensity through the year. Nor is there any way to describe the utter diversity of colours and languages of this gathering of so many different people, rich and poor, the educated and sophisticated mingling seamlessly with simple rural peasants barely, if at all, able to read or write. A world community with all its distinctiveness and differences subsumed in a common purpose and shared euphoria. The immensity of the experience is all that does not alter.

To stand before the Kaaba is a moment beyond change. And yet, I watched Mecca, the city that surrounds it, change almost beyond recognition in the years I lived in Saudi Arabia. By the time I left, the Sacred Mosque had been expanded, almost completely rebuilt, changed utterly from the image I carried in my heart from childhood. Perhaps it was this sense of the passing away of something I had always considered enduring, perhaps it was the hippie environmentalist in me – even some tinge of the romantic that made me determined to make my fifth Hajj the old-fashioned way, on foot. The sense of detachment between ideal and reality that I had felt on my first Hajj had increased each year. More people, more congestion, more exhaust fumes, more traffic and more lags of churning stasis. I wanted to know what it must have been like in the days before motorized transport. Certainly it ought to give me better insight into the experience of pilgrims of earlier centuries.

What would it have been like for ibn Battuta, for example? The fourteenth-century author of one of the world's great travel classics had become something of a hero of mine.[2] He set off from his home in Tangier on 14 June 1325, aged twenty-two, intent on performing the Hajj. It turned out to be no return journey. Like so many great luminaries of history his journey of a lifetime lasted most of his life. He performed the Hajj five times in all. Travelling to Mecca he picked up the travel bug that was so much a part of the historic Muslim experience. Being well educated he was able to work his way not only to Mecca, but all around the Muslim world, finding employment as a judge or attached as a valued scholar to the court of one ruler or another. He stopped in Egypt on his way to Mecca and then journeyed on to the Maldives, India, Southeast Asia, Central Asia and China before eventually returning home via a detour into West Africa. I loved the sense of belonging to a borderless world that his life and writings exemplify – quite a few centuries before modern technology and communications made the term a cliché. Yet his writing also makes clear that the world was by no means all the same to ibn Battuta. He was an interested observer, curious and open to all the subtle and not so subtle differences of customs and practices of the people and places he encountered. He was a citizen of the world, his outlook a distinctive consequence of the Hajj.

The travel bug, an interest in and respect for the diversity of humanity, the urge to learn and write about one's experience – these

I regarded as Mecca's gifts, not merely to the Muslim world but to everyone. They had made ibn Battuta the man he was, and I thought that perhaps sampling something of what he experienced would do the same for me. He had made five pilgrimages, I was about to embark on my fifth, too, and it seemed like the perfect plan. I would retrace the last leg of the old caravan route that made its way from Yemen to Jeddah, from where I would set out, and on to Mecca. For me it would be a three-day walk, some eighty kilometres as the crow flies.

First, however, I needed a donkey.

Why not a camel, you might ask. A camel would have been the most appropriate way to retrace the past, but the advent of the pickup truck has made this an impossible dream. True, I worked in Saudi Arabia on an expat's salary, but I did not earn a king's ransom, and the erstwhile utility beast of burden (aka the camel) was now a pampered aristocrat whose destiny was the camel-racing circuit, changing owners for exorbitant sums. A humble donkey, therefore, seemed a more feasible choice to carry our vital water and other supplies for a modest re-enactment of a historic pilgrimage.

I had thought it should be possible to find a donkey in Jeddah or its environs, but after several weeks of diligent search and inquiry my search had proved fruitless. Then one particularly stifling afternoon, another of those days afflicted by the power cuts that, in those days, were a regular feature of the building site known as Jeddah, I made my way to my favourite cosy *quawas* (traditional coffee house) in what remained of the old town. Here the tall houses, whitewashed or painted in subdued pastel colours with their overhanging louvred window screens, were perfectly suited to the environment. Inside they allowed air to circulate and cool while the glare of the sun was filtered through the fretwork of the window screens. Outside the relationship between the height of the buildings and the narrowness of the alleyways meant one could walk around bathed in cooling shade. The old town was the coolest part of Jeddah. It was, I knew, a setting that would have been familiar to ibn Battuta – and none the less humane and friendly for being historical.

By now the regular clientele of the *quawas* knew I was set on buying a healthy donkey. An animal blessed with good health was an important qualification, as most in Jeddah were either too thin, too hungry, or covered in an even layer of whatever the external atmosphere had to throw at them. On this afternoon I was greeted warmly by the sergeant of the local police station, with whom I would often share a cup of tea and water-pipe, known locally as *shisha*.

'I was hoping you'd come along,' he said. 'I've found a Bedouin willing to sell his donkey.' Without wasting any time, I accompanied him to the Bedouin's house. Sure enough he had a reasonably healthy donkey to sell. 'How much is it?' I asked eagerly.

'Ten thousand riyals' (about £2,000), came the reply.

'It's outrageous,' I said. 'It's only a donkey.'

'For over a month,' replied the Bedouin, 'I've been hearing about this man who is desperately looking for a donkey. I figured if he's so desperate he'd pay a good price. This is a fine animal and there's much life in it.'

The old fox had me cornered, and I suspected the sergeant was getting a cut too. Nevertheless, I put in a good haggle and eventually secured the animal for half the asking price.

'There is one thing I must tell you in all honesty,' said the Bedouin before handing me the lead. He was strictly observing the appropriate Islamic etiquette that is innately the Saudi way. 'While I've fed him well, I have not been able to look after all his needs.'

'What do you mean?' I asked, somewhat confused.

'Well, there aren't as many donkeys in this city as there used to be. So it is difficult to mate the animals. I've been trying for over two years, but alas.'

At this point the sergeant cut through the Bedouin's diplomatic pretence. 'What you have here,' the policeman declared, 'is a sex-starved donkey. But as this is the only donkey there is, you may as well buy it.' There was little else I could do. I grabbed the lead of my new companion and we set off through the winding streets of old Jeddah.

The following week, on the sixth day of the Islamic month of Dhu al-Hijjah, the month of the Hajj pilgrimage, my small expeditionary party assembled in front of the Hajj Research Centre. My companions in this long walk to Mecca included my friend Zafar Malik, our Yemeni guide Ali, and our prized donkey, who we named Genghis after the great Mongol king, famed for his temper and propensity to lash out and kick people for no rational reason. Genghis, we were soon to discover, intended to live up to his namesake.

I had known Zafar from my student days in London. We were buddies, had committed most of our youthful sins together, so when the Jeddah job came up, Zafar joined me at the Hajj Research Centre working as a designer and publications manager. Zafar's distinguishing mark was (and is) a luxurious but precision-trimmed beard. This was Zafar's way of telling the world that he was neither a mindless dogmatist (who let their beards grow long and unruly), nor an extremist (who support bushy stubbles). Zafar also had an infectious sense of humour, which I thought was an essential requirement for this journey.

Our local guide Ali, in contrast, was a lean, short man in his late twenties. He lived in Sanaa. Whenever he or his family needed money he would cross the border into Saudi Arabia and work till he had collected enough for his needs, returning to his hometown. Ali had come to the Centre looking for work, and given his knowledge of the terrain, we thought he was a gift from God. Although he looked rather fragile, he had tremendous stamina and could move, as he said, 'like a lizard on sand'.

Zafar and I, prudently, took our positions at the head of our convoy, leaving Ali to handle Genghis. Initially, we walked along the Jeddah–Mecca motorway. A few miles outside the city we veered off towards the Hijaz mountain range. Every now and then we would hear Ali encourage Genghis, a grudging participant in our adventure, to move a little faster. We walked till late at night, and on Ali's advice camped in a valley.

Early the following morning we set off again and had walked over fifteen kilometres by the afternoon when Genghis started to misbehave. Ali admitted the beast was growing more and more cantankerous. At which point Zafar spotted an animal standing on top of a small hill in the distance. 'Ah,' he said, 'I bet that's why Genghis is excited.'

Ali thought it advisable to frighten off the itinerant donkey and, leaving Genghis in our care, he sped off determined to shoo away the interloper, shouting to us: 'Hold Genghis as tightly as you can.' But Ali's efforts seemed to have no effect. He hooted and yelled, threw stones, even tried to catch the beast. All to no avail. Yet he seemed not in the least crestfallen by failure when he returned. 'It's all right,' he announced. 'That other donkey is a male.'

Relieved, we loosened our hold on Genghis. The other donkey nonchalantly sauntered a little nearer. Genghis brayed with what sounded like a loud victory declaration, bucked, offloaded his burden, and ran off in ardent pursuit.

Zafar surveyed the spilled water as it rapidly spread, before evaporating into the sun-baked earth. Genghis meanwhile caught up with the object of his desires, and the two moved closer. Zafar pressed his lower lip between his teeth, looked reproachfully straight at me and said: 'I think Genghis is making inappropriate physical contact with the other donkey. I suppose,' he added, 'that the old Bedouin who sold him didn't tell you that Genghis is gay.'

I began to wonder what to do, and at the same time sensed the arrival of a strong hostile presence. Almost simultaneously, Zafar and I looked at each other; and then we both looked at a group of rather surprised Bedouins who were now surrounding us. Were we, indeed, inhabiting the past when pilgrim caravans were regularly hijacked en route to Mecca?

'What are you doing here?' asked a rugged-looking young man.

'We are going on pilgrimage,' Zafar answered.

'Pilgrimage?' The man looked puzzled. He reflected for a moment. 'You should be in a pilgrim bus with other pilgrims. This is not the way to Mecca. There are only mountains and desert patches here.'

'We're walking to Mecca,' Zafar explained. 'We're trying to trace the old caravan route and perform the Hajj as it used to be in the old days, like ibn Battuta.'

'Walking? Walking? Ibn Battuta? Ibn Battuta?' The young man neither understood nor believed what he heard. 'Why do you want to walk? The government has spent millions and millions of riyals to provide the pilgrims with transport. What's wrong with the bus? Or the car?' he demanded.

It was time, we felt, for the Bedouins to benefit from some of the Hajj Research Centre's top experts. The Hajj, we began, is a journey of spiritual enlightenment, the very word Hajj means to exert and the Hajj must be a journey of considerable spiritual exertion. The modern Hajj, in contrast we said, transports pilgrims like cattle along a complex of roads, bridges and spaghetti junctions that have ruined the natural environment. 'We would rather walk than see our holy environment bulldozed to build roads and flyovers,' we declared.

The young man turned round and looked at the other Bedouins. They were gazing at us as though we were aliens from another planet. I now decided to use a more drastic approach.

'Do you know, brothers,' I said, 'that some fifty tonnes of exhaust fumes are produced every day by all the cars and buses in Mina? Most pilgrims spend more time coughing than praying. A car or a bus takes over nine hours to cover one mile in the holy areas during the Hajj season. And the noise! Sirens. Hooters. Engines starting and stopping. The well-off pilgrims flit around in the exclusivity of their cars, seldom meeting anyone from different countries. The poor spend their time dodging cars and suffocating from the exhaust fumes. Where is the brotherhood the Hajj is supposed to express?'

The new approach seemed to work. The young man nodded as though he agreed. Encouraged, I continued.

'You see brother, our research has shown that if everyone walked there would be an orderly flow. No congestion, no pollution, the pilgrims would have the sublime spiritual impact of the Hajj as it has always been.'

'Research? What research?' An older Bedouin who had stood expressionless suddenly sounded alarmed.

I noticed the young man had disappeared.

'Do you have permission for this research from the government? Do you have permission to walk? And what are you doing with that donkey? He has abused my animal in front of my eyes. May God forgive me!' The old man roused himself to anger.

Before either of us could reply, two police cars with flashing lights and blaring sirens pulled up beside us. A helicopter loomed and hovered above us. Two policemen, accompanied by the young Bedouin, leapt out of one of the cars and demanded to see our papers. I looked at Zafar, who was smiling. He took a letter from his pocket and handed it to one of the policemen. The other policeman peered, intrigued, over his shoulder.

Quite soon the policeman turned to the assembled Bedouins and announced imperiously: 'Go back to your dwellings. These people have the permission of His Majesty to walk to Mecca.'

Seconds later the helicopter whirled off over the horizon. The Bedouins departed as silently as they had appeared. 'Good luck,' the policeman shouted as he drove off.

It took us more than three hours to track down and catch Genghis. A couple of hours later we arrived at the outer limits (the Miqat) of the holy area, known locally as the *haramain*. Knowledge of this point is important, as tradition demands that here pilgrims have to wash and put on the *ihram*, the two unstitched pieces of cloth. The *ihram*, however, is not just the pieces of cloth, it is also a state of mind. To enter the *haramain* pilgrims have to be in a condition of *ihram*: a continuous state of prayer and meditation, in harmony with and respectful of the environment and its natural and wild life, while they abstain from all worldly desires. We decided it was now inappropriate to speculate on whether this applied to Genghis and whether, or indeed how, he might have sublimated his needs and desires.

We walked late into the night and after a meal of nuts and dried fruit, we slept in the desert in a tent. We awoke just before dawn to discover we had been visited during the night by a number of snakes and lizards. The reptile population of the desert around Jeddah and Mecca is extraordinary, with over fifty species of snake, including cobras and horned vipers, and more than a hundred species of lizard. From the tracks on the sand, I deduced that a family of Saudi vipers, which resemble puff adders, were nearby. They have beautiful brown skins with round black spots. An inquisitive posse of lanky and delicate lizards, which I thought were Toad-Headed Agama, were still running around. They moved so fast that all one could see was their long tails. Zafar spotted a beautiful gecko family: grey and only three or four inches long, they seemed to be guarding and patrolling their territory.

After breakfast of bread, cheese and olives, we set off once again towards Mecca. By noon we had crossed the desert. Desert sand has the softest, finest texture. Wind-borne, almost silky, it can easily insert itself into clothing fibre. Its colour and that of the landscape changes hue with the sunlight, from the wan creamy yellow of early morning, through an intense golden glare of bright daylight to a soft peachy blush at evening. Wherever one turns the sand is sculpted into sensuous rounded forms. The only harsh lines are provided by the jagged outcrops of sunburnt rock. As if tormented by heat, these piles of stone are twisted into ungainly shapes. Their innards turn to liquid that seeps out and forms a blackened crust on the surface. They seem, literally, to have a bad case of dried skin that only in some lights gives off an iridescent glimmer, like the surface of coal.

Now we were ready for the next phase of our journey. Before us stood the rocky outcrops that litter the desert and form a mountain curtain that envelops the barren valley of Mecca. We started our arduous climb of the first peak. Genghis proved to be the slowest and most reluctant of climbers. Every few steps, Ali had to intimidate him into movement. At one point Zafar stopped and turned accusingly to Ali: 'What are you doing? We are supposed to be in *ihram*. In a state of peace, love and grace. You can't beat that donkey,' he told him. Genghis seemed to have caught the drift of this statement and now simply refused to move. He stood motionless. We tried to coax him with nuts and dried fruit. He ate the food but stood his ground. Zafar tried to pat and cajole him. It merely incited Genghis to turn and go into reverse, and he began to descend the mountain. We followed him. Once off the mountain, Genghis started running towards the motorway. We ran after him. The harder we tried to catch him, the faster he ran. Eventually he ran straight into the Mecca Intercontinental Hotel.

Located on the Old Jeddah Road on the outskirts of the city, Mecca Intercontinental was the only five-star hotel in Mecca in those days. It has a theatrical tent-like structure modelled on Bedouin marquees. There was an old well inside the front enclave of the hotel that was preserved as a site of historic interest. Genghis ran straight past the well into the crowded lobby. The staff at five-star hotels is trained to deal with any eventuality: everything from late checkouts to natural disasters. A donkey running wild in the lobby was something quite different. They dropped whatever they were doing and ran after Genghis, trying to catch him, while the guests looked on aghast. Eventually, several porters managed to overpower our rampant beast and proceeded to evict him and us from the hotel. Zafar tried to plead with them. 'It is the Hajj season, brothers. Time to show friendship and love to all creation,' he argued.

'You love the donkey if you want to,' replied the head porter angrily. 'But do it outside the hotel.'

We duly removed ourselves from the inside of the hotel and tied Genghis to the ancient well in the courtyard. I knew it was the right moment for us to part company. This latter-day Mongol marauder in donkey guise was slowing us down, caused too many problems and seemed to have no appreciation for the higher purpose of our adventure. Donkeys just don't do *ihram*. Ali suggested he should take him to our camp in Mina in a pickup truck. Making a reluctant pact with modernity seemed our only option.

We negotiated with several unwilling drivers of pickup trucks before Ali found one driver prepared to do the job at an astronomical price. 'Look at it this way,' the driver explained. 'I take up to fifty pilgrims in one trip. Now with a donkey in the back, I am not likely to get any other passengers. Who'd want to share his seat with a donkey? You must pay for the full load.' We knew we had no choice.

The pickup truck reversed into the hotel. The driver joined Zafar, Ali and myself to install Genghis; but as usual Genghis was having none of this. We pushed. We pulled. We even tried to pick him up. Genghis would not be budged. Then Ali asked all of us to stand back. 'Hajj or no Hajj, there is only one way to deal with a donkey,' he announced. He rolled up his sleeves, spat on his hands and rubbed them together. His face a picture of determination, he picked up a large walking stick and made his way to where Genghis stood. Zafar made as if to stop Ali, and then changed his mind. I became the personification of the three monkeys – simultaneously saying, seeing and hearing nothing.

A few minutes later Genghis was standing in the pickup truck. Ali sat next to the driver and waved goodbye. First slowly, and then swiftly, the truck made off towards our research camp in the hills of Mina.

As we drew a quiet breath, we reflected on our journey so far. 'Stuff ibn Battuta,' declared Zafar. 'I am going to stick to the beaten track.'

It was true: neither of us now had the energy or the motivation to get back to the mountains. I feared that without the expert guidance of Ali we might be entangled for ever in their convolutions, unable to find our way. Without further debate we started to walk alongside the motorway for the last twenty kilometres – which would take us all the way to the Sacred Mosque that houses the Kaaba. We regretted our decision almost immediately. Walking on the motorway was not just hazardous, but slower and more laborious than climbing a mountain range – with the ever-present danger of being hit by a car, bus or truck. Indeed, by the time we reached the Sacred Mosque we had had several near-death experiences. We were also out of breath and, thanks to exhaust fumes, quite dizzy.

I suppose the moral of the story is that one can never escape the times in which one lives. The only real option is to find better ways of dealing with the problems they present. All the romantic notions of our journey melted once we entered the Sacred Mosque. We joined the other pilgrims – some 80,000 of them – to go around the Kaaba. The peace and tranquillity, the contemplation and elation, the connection between past and present I'd sought in walking was and is always here, ever present. How you get here is immaterial, it's being here that really matters.

It was already dark when we left the Sacred Mosque. We walked the ten kilometres or so to Mina, avoiding the main roads. We knew Mina well but still got hopelessly lost. The place looked unfamiliar. True, the landscape was changed by the presence of the countless shops, stalls and eating places that mushroom overnight to cater to the pilgrims. Familiar spots lurked behind their awnings. And, indeed, the scene had been physically altered. A new spaghetti junction of hideous complications had appeared.

'It shouldn't be too difficult to find the Research Centre camp,' Zafar said confidently. 'It is located on the mountain right opposite the Jamarat' – the spot where pilgrims take part in a ceremonial stoning of Satan. All we had to do was find the Jamarat.

We approached a pious-looking member of the Saudi National Guard who was passing the time with his worry beads.

'Which way to the Devils?' Zafar asked.

The guard curled his worry beads in the palm of his right hand. He then swung them around his index finger. 'Devils?' he reflected. 'This is the Kingdom of Saudi Arabia. Here there are devils everywhere. There are devils even within the pilgrims. That's why they are here. To seek forgiveness. To seek Mercy of their Creator.'

'We are looking for a more specific manifestation,' I said.

'Ah!' he said. 'We have three. They are that way. Take your pick.' He pointed out the direction.

We followed his finger and eventually arrived at our intended destination. But there was no large mountain in front of the Big Devil. Indeed, there were no mountains in the vicinity at all.

I looked at Zafar, bewildered.

'They've moved our mountain,' he said, perplexed.

'Don't be daft,' I replied. 'How can they move a mountain?'

'They've moved our mountain. I tell you it was *right here*. They've moved it.'

By now I was very tired. Very hungry. And very sleepy. I suggested we lie down wherever we could find enough room.

Zafar had other ideas: 'They would have set up the research camp on the highest peak. Look for the highest peak. *That*'s where our camp will be.'

We wandered about Mina until finally we settled for the one mountain we both agreed our colleagues, following a logic similar to our own, would have chosen as the site for the research camp. It had to be on the top of this mountain.

We began to climb. It was a rugged peak, about five or six hundred metres straight up. In pitch-darkness, we moved carefully and slowly. Pilgrims were sitting, sleeping, praying or precariously hanging from every available spot. On several occasions I nearly stepped on the face of a sleeping pilgrim. On a number of occasions my foot planted itself not in the slime from which mankind emerged but the kind of slimy effluent that emerges from mankind. Further exertion was needed to maintain my dignity and modesty as the loosely attached lower half of my *ihram* frequently threatened to unravel. We perse-vered. A few steps from the top we heard a familiar sound. I took a final step, secured a foothold on the flat top of the mountain – and came face to face with Genghis. Even in the darkness, I recognized the derisive smirk on his face.

Genghis was laughing at us.

We had been climbing the wrong side of the mountain. We had climbed up the cliff, while we could easily have ambled up the gentle slope on the opposite side. Thanks to the spaghetti junction and new roads we had failed to realize we were on the wrong side of the Jamarat. This was our mountain, the site of the research camp.

The following morning was the ninth day of the month of Dhu al-Hijjah, the day when the main ritual of Hajj is performed. It is known as the 'Day of Arafat', when all 2 million pilgrims make their way to the plain of Arafat to pray together, from dawn until sunset. It is the main ritual of the Hajj. We slept late and left Mina around nine o'clock. Two hours later we were in Arafat, where a massive tent city is erected every Hajj season to accommodate the pilgrims for a day. It is a vast stretch of land, overshadowed by a small hill known as the Mount of Mercy.

When the sun passes the meridian, the pilgrims begin the ritual of *wquf*, the standing. It is a simple affair that requires nothing more than standing straight, facing towards the Kaaba, and asking God for forgiveness. Row after row of pilgrims all dressed in white, as far as the eye can see, stand together. At the time of the noon prayer, they bow down in unison. Yet, for each one of the 2 million assembled, this is the most personal, most private, most intense moment of their life. It is I, and my Lord. Here, in this vast congregation, they are no regimented crowd. Here I am known, we are each known, and know, in our inimitable individuality. There is a serenity and peace that cannot be described by words. The pure and profound simplicity of that time is the ultimate spiritual experience. This is the moment that gave the old man I saw on the bus, and who had come to die in

Mecca, his serenity, the blissful certainty with which he faced his ultimate journey.

After sunset we joined the *nafrah*: the mass exodus of the pilgrims out of the plain of Arafat towards Muzdalifah. Known as the 'Roofless Mosque', Muzdalifah is a valley between Arafat and Mina. We spent the night there, under the open sky, and walked back to Mina just after dawn next day.

The elation I experienced back in Mina was not purely spiritual. Despite all the prayers and reflection, there was still an ego not quite annihilated. I could not suppress my pride. *My* pilgrimage had been different. I had walked – as much as donkey perversity and modernity had allowed. I had connected, as much as I was able, with the likes of ibn Battuta, and the others before him, going right back to the Prophet Muhammad himself. Inside my tent on the highest peak in Mina, I sat shaving myself for the first time since leaving Jeddah. And I thought: perhaps this is what true travel is all about.

Zafar entered the tent with another pilgrim and looked at me as though he read my innermost thoughts.

'I thought you ought to meet Brother Sulaiman,' he said.

He was a tall, slim African. On his left shoulder he carried a tote bag. He leaned with nonchalant ease on a large wooden stick.

'He has come for pilgrimage from Somalia. Walking all the way. It took him seven years to get here.'

My ego evaporated. My journey from Jeddah to Mecca looked insignificant.

I realized also that I had been walking in search of two different Meccas. One of them could not be approached by physical means, or rather it did not matter what means of transport or route one took to get there. This was the Mecca I had known all my life: the Mecca that since childhood I had idealized as the fixed spiritual centre, home to God's House, the moral compass by which I set my approach to life, the Universe, and everything. The only Mecca I ever really acknowledged was a metaphysical destination, not so much a place as a state of being that was beyond time and place, beyond direction because it had to exist everywhere as an orientation of the soul and conscience. This was the Mecca beloved of all Muslims. It mattered that we turned to this Mecca, but I now understood it did not necessarily matter where this Mecca was positioned on Earth. True, pilgrims journey there from all around the world, but only to discover how little here or there matters. The pilgrim experience is a humbling of all worldly distinctions including geography before more awesome certainties. On the way to this Mecca, the donkey, the desert, the climbing had been mere distraction.

So what had been the point of Genghis? We had been walking to quite another Mecca, an entirely different place. This second Mecca is firmly rooted in time and space, a place where people have lived through history with all the twists and turns of human fortune. It is the place to which people in numbers uncounted have travelled down millennia. All of these journeys, like my own, were not timeless but products and part of the specific circumstances of moments in history. This second Mecca, inhabited by real people with all their strength and faults, is an ever-changing city caught in the rapids of time. Walking, recalcitrant donkey in tow, to this Mecca could never improve the quality of my Hajj, as the encounter with the pilgrim from Somalia had shown. It should have been about gaining a different insight into history.

What difference does understanding Mecca as a place of human habitation make to anything? To understand Mecca in all its complexity we need to see its sacred as well as profane character. This book examines what has lurked like a desert mirage on the edge of our perception, the unexplored territory amid all we think we know about our beloved Mecca, the focal point of Muslim consciousness. To know the history of Mecca is to accept ownership of what actually happened in history. And there is a great deal in the history of that piece of Earth called Mecca, it turns out, that is far from ideal, fully prey to all the ills that have bedevilled the reality of Muslim civilization down through the centuries.

Since my walking Hajj with Zafar and Genghis, I have read and reread what has been said about this most written-about destination from a new perspective. What I have learnt has often shocked me, just as it will shock any reader. Most of all it has shown how surely the confused conflation of two Meccas is not an accident so much as the means by which a false consciousness of history has become the norm among Muslims. The confusion between ideal and reality has been and is the central fault line along which so many of the problems of Muslim societies are located.

Most Muslims think, as I did, that Mecca has always been crucial to Islamic history. Yet Mecca, the fixed focal point of all Muslims' lives, has never been central to the history of Muslim civilization. How can this be true? The Sacred City has never been the capital of any Muslim society, not even that of the Prophet Muhammad himself. It was displaced by Medina before the official beginning of Muslim history and left to remain a backwater, though one with special significance. Even Medina was quickly eclipsed as the centre of Muslim history. The Umayyad Caliphate (661–750) established its capital in Damascus, the Abbasid Caliphate (749–1258) moved the capital to Baghdad, and then the focus shifted to Istanbul during the Ottoman Empire (1299–1922). In between these shifts, other great Muslim cities – Cairo, Fez, Tunis, Granada, Cordoba, Timbuktu, Samarkand, Bukhara, Delhi, Lahore – rose and fell. The culture, the learning, the achievements of all these places had little impact on Mecca. The great and the good, the powerful and the wealthy came from elsewhere to lavish largesse on the Holy Places. Then they went home. Travellers, like ibn Battuta, came, but the bulk of what he wrote concerns all the places beyond Mecca he visited as a consequence of making the Hajj.

The same imbalance is repeated in chronicle after chronicle written over the centuries. What we are told about Mecca has an endless familiarity because what concerned the visitors to the Holy City were the rituals of Hajj, which have remained the same since the time of the Prophet Muhammad. The fascinating sections of their books are not really about Mecca but the getting to and going from Mecca where the world is forever changing. Those who lived in Mecca were marginal to the chronicles written about the Hajj. The permanent residents had their own concerns, earthly, worldly concerns that they pursued in ways far removed from the sublime ideals the rest of the Muslim world was constructing around the idea of Mecca. The great ideas and achievements, science and learning, art and culture, of Muslim civilization were seldom embraced in Mecca. Great scholars and scientists came to visit, but Meccans had no interest in what they had to teach and were concerned only with narrow and often obscurantist theology. When it came to ideas Meccan scholars tended to be conservative, and their influence, such as it was, operated to constrain and denounce rather than motivate intellectual and cultural endeavours.

There is an obvious explanation why Mecca had to become such a potent idea for Muslims everywhere. On one level it signifies all that is spiritual and unworldly, though the essence of religion is how that is to be incorporated and made a motive force of earthly existence. Yet, on another level, this place became an ideal beyond time and place because in history so few Muslims were ever able to fulfil the dream of performing the Hajj. The operative phrase, when it comes to the obligation to perform the Hajj, is of course 'if you are able'. The realities of society, economy and transport meant the vast majority of Muslims throughout history were not able. There have always been pilgrims, but who they were and where they came from has changed over time. And numerically they constitute only a tiny fraction of the Muslim peoples who have occupied the world down through history. As a result, what happened in Mecca, its lived history, has always been remote and largely unknown to the rest of the Muslim world, and vice versa. Mecca busy and concerned with its own business of being the place of pilgrimage had not been much influenced by events in the rest of the Muslim world.

So this book is not about the idealized Mecca, though it explores how that idealization was constructed. It is about the peripheral and disregarded Mecca, a place where lives were lived, heroes (and villains) thrived, atrocities were committed, and greed and intolerance were the norm. It plants itself in time and place and in the extremely messy lives of those who have inhabited the city, as well as some of the people who came to perform the Hajj. Much of it makes uncomfortable reading. Even in the place Muslims idealize as sublime, human feet stand firm in mud and slime. The Meccans have had as many problems with the orientation of soul and conscience as people anywhere. The history of Mecca is as dreadful and bloody as the histories of many other cities. There's a lesson in that for us all, as well as, I hope, a few good stories worth telling.

The Valley of Weeping

A first bright glimmer of dawn lit the horizon, the cool breeze giving way to dusty heat. A man stood still in the long, loose folds of his garments, watching as a small group of people made haste towards the central part of the city. He observed them enter a circular arena containing a cubic structure surrounded by statues. He watched as they passed the idols, and, one by one, bowed down to kiss the largest, a red agate bust known as Hubal.

The man turned away from this familiar scene to resume his journey. He walked past a family, including a small child wrapped in muslin, on its way to the cemetery. He could hear the approaching sounds of a caravan bustling into the city and moved to avoid it. Camel after camel, loaded with spices and silk, wine and perfume, loped its way to the market, followed by a long line of slaves trudging in single file. The noise and the odour of aromatic liquids filled the air. The city was now stirring. The man continued on his way towards a mountain northeast of the city. In less than an hour he was negotiating its gentle lower slope. When he reached the point where the gradient rises abruptly and the climb becomes more difficult, he stopped. Standing erect, he turned and looked towards the city below, surrounded by mountains from all sides. He was looking at Mecca.

The man's name was Muhammad. He was in his early forties and of medium stature. Though his complexion was fair, where his body had been exposed to the elements he was tanned to a reddish hue. He had a slightly rounded face, a wide forehead and thin but full eyebrows. His curly hair, parted in the middle, tumbled around his neck.

Mecca has had many names. It was known as *al-Balad*: simply 'the main city', as it was a key urban centre and market town. It was known as *al-Qaryah*: a place where large numbers of people congregate like water flowing into a reservoir. And as the 'Baca' of biblical times it is mentioned in Psalms 84: 5–6:

> Blessed are those whose strength is in you, who have set their hearts on pilgrimage. As they pass through the Valley of Baca, they make it a place of springs; the autumn rains also cover it with pools.[1]

Some associate Baca with a balsam tree; a 'gum-exuding (weeping) tree'; or 'weeping wall-rocks'. The Arabic form of Baca, Bakkah, can be translated as 'lack of stream'. The valley was indeed a dry place with no vegetation. The Greeks translated Baca as 'the Valley of Weeping'. This Valley of Baca had strong associations with lack of water and 'deep sorrow', a place of lament. Yet, when the righteous passed through the valley, they could make it 'a place of springs', a source of life.

The focal point of pilgrimage in the Valley of Baca was a structure known simply as the Cube, or in Arabic, Kaaba. Forensic linguistics is littered with examples of a common phenomenon that occurs in many languages: this is the replacing, adding or subtracting of single letters in place names over time. London, for example, was originally called Londinium when the city was first established by the Romans. In the case of Mecca a shift took place from 'one labial consonant to another, from B to M, and Baca, in Arabic Bakkah, came to be called Makkah, or English Mecca'.[2]

The inhabitants of the city were once known as the 'Aribi', a term that makes its first appearance in a cuneiform account of the Battle of Qarqar (853 BCE) by the Assyrian king Shalmanesar III. It means 'nomad' or 'desert dweller'. In the sculptures dating back to this period, many discovered recently in tombs and cemeteries in northern Saudi Arabia, the Arabs have oval faces, large straight noses, small chins and huge eyes. The eyes, with dilated pupils (inlaid with black stones or lapis lazuli), hint perhaps at religious stupor. Or are they an indication, perhaps, of the widely held belief in the region that spiritual power resides in the faculty of sight? A beneficial look would induce bliss, an evil eye could kill.

Mecca was not the only major city in the region. The oasis of Taif lies sixty miles to the south, known as 'the Garden of the Hijaz' for its vines, fruits and vegetables. Just over 200 miles to the north of Mecca is the city of Yathrib, which in Muhammad's time was home to Jewish clans renowned as goldsmiths and home to scholars familiar with the Hebrew Bible and the Talmud. And around sixty miles southwest is the port of Jeddah, the gateway to the world outside. Apart from the Kaaba, Mecca had another advantage over these cities: it stood at the junction of two major global trade routes. The first went north–south, through the mountains of the Hijaz. To the south it went to Yemen, where it linked with the trade coming across the Indian Ocean from India and Southeast Asia; and northwards it went to Syria and the Mediterranean littoral. The second route went east–west. The eastern route ran through Iraq and on to Iran, Central Asia and eventually China; the western route connected to Abyssinia, the Red Sea ports of Egypt and eastern Africa.

The city's fame was based on the Kaaba. The names of things are full of associations from the straightforward, such as the Kaaba, to the complex and multilayered implications of the names attached to the Valley of Baca in which it is located. It is possible to see the subtle shifts that connect the variety of names that fix and identify this particular spot on earth. Placing them in time is a different matter. Time is a dimension of human understanding, a challenge to our assumptions, imagination and our ability to make and, on occasion, break connections. Many arguments have swirled around the

3

ancestry and age of the Kaaba and the city that grew around it.

Some modern academic critics question whether Mecca was ever an ancient pilgrimage site, as there is no archaeological evidence in support.[3] But in this instance, an absence of evidence amounts to little more than an absence of archaeology; and these are very different things.

Today's Mecca, in modern Saudi Arabia, has for the past eighty years been ruled by a family with a horror of history, of historical evidence, that includes evidence from archaeology, as well as from manuscripts. The government ensured that Mecca was washed clean of its history in June 1973 when entire districts of the city were bulldozed and its cultural property and historic sites were erased from the landscape as easily as one rubs out pencil marks on paper. The little archaeology that has been undertaken in Saudi Arabia occurs far removed from the Holy Places. As far as the Saudis are concerned Mecca has no prehistory, no history before Muhammad, and no history after Muhammad. This denial of Meccan history is based on a single reason: the Saudis do not want anyone to venerate Muhammad. The fear is that historical sites, rather than God, will become objects of worship.

Archaeological evidence, however, is not our only source of insights into history. Our window into the past includes words as well as memories, what today is known as oral history. Learning about the past from words requires a kind of detective work. Humanity's written records are a jigsaw full of gaps that need to be filled. The gaps exist for no other reason than that writers of yesteryear were not writing for today's audiences. They had their own concerns, their own reasons to write, and no requirement to answer today's questions.

While it is impossible to place the origin of the Kaaba and the city that contains it in time, the mention in the Psalms of 'those who set their hearts on pilgrimage' ought to indicate some point in time when the practice was sufficiently established and well known to be comprehensible in the poems of the Jewish people. The Psalms, therefore, certainly would be a place to start seeking a point in time, if experts could agree on when they were written.

Many of the Psalms are attributed to the Prophet King David, whose reign is tentatively dated 1040–970 BCE. Psalm 84, however, is attributed to 'the sons of Korah', believed to be either a family of religious singers or a guild of singers and musicians. Originally, the sons of Korah were appointed by David to provide songs and music during the building of the Temple in Jerusalem. However, they continued to function long after. Psalm 84 might have come into existence at any time from the era of King David up to the time when the 150 Psalms found in the Old Testament are known to have existed in written form. This spans a period from somewhere after 1040 BCE up to around 165 BCE. At one time most experts opted for a more recent date, with a preference for the third century BCE. Nowadays the consensus pushes their origin further back in time based on evidence of comparable musical and literary forms known from other cultures in the region.[4] All of this amounts to a great deal of detective work – but not exactly a result.

We can, however, agree with Edward Gibbon, the eighteenth-century historian and author of the celebrated *Decline and Fall of the Roman Empire*, that 'the genuine antiquity of Caaba ascends beyond the Christian era'.[5] Gibbon knew of claims that the existence of Mecca was known to the ancient Greeks. Diodorus Siculus, the Greek historian who lived during the first century BCE, mentions the Kaaba in his *Bibliotheca Historica*, a book describing various parts of the discovered world: 'a temple has been set up there, which is very holy and exceedingly revered by all Arabians'.[6] The city is also mentioned by Claudius Ptolemy, the Egyptian Roman citizen who wrote his classic text, *Geography*, in Greek, and lived around 90–168 CE. A mathematician and astronomer, Ptolemy's works remained the basis of learning before the birth of the modern era. In his survey of the inhabitable world he provides a list of cities in Arabia Felix.

Amongst them is 'a place called Macoraba',[7] which 'allows us to identify it as a South Arabian foundation created around a sanctuary'.[8]

History can also be traced through objects, and in particular through long-distance trade in the Middle East that goes as far back as 14,000 BCE. For example the volcanic glass obsidian is of limited occurrence and its distinctive chemical makeup allows its journeys over time to be mapped. A string of archaeological sites from modern-day Iraq to Pakistan, home of the Indus Valley civilization of Harappa and Mohenjo-Daro, provide evidence of a trade route dating back to around 3000 BCE.[9] When the Egyptian Pharaoh Ramses II was buried in 1224 BCE several peppercorns that would have originated in India or even Southeast Asia were used along with other unguents as part of the embalming process.[10] The camel, the utility beast of burden of long-distance trade, was domesticated by around 1000 BCE.[11]

In addition to land-based routes, by the first century CE there is evidence of the existence of seaborne trade linking Southeast Asia via the Arabian Peninsula to the cities of the Roman Middle East and the Mediterranean world. The *Periplus of the Erythean Sea*, a Greek periplus, describes and documents these routes. It was written around 40 CE, though it does not mention Mecca as a trading centre. But the city had all the right attributes and factors of location to play its part in connecting the well-established networks of global commerce from an early date.

As he surveyed his city Muhammad had no need to doubt the importance of trade in the life of his community. He had participated in the caravan trade himself. His success had even brought him to the notice of the wealthy widow, Khadijah, who would become his wife. But it was not the economic status of Mecca that preoccupied him. His concern, as he gazed on the valley below, was that he was looking at the 'Valley of Abraham'. As he stood there – *there* about a third of the way up Jabal al-Nur, the Mountain of Light – he could easily pick out the Kaaba, at the centre of the city. And he began to reflect on its association with Abraham.

In the stories and poems of Arabia before Islam, Mecca was the city of Abraham, biblical prophet, patriarch of Israelites and Ishmaelites, and founder of the monotheistic faiths. Indeed, there was nothing in the arid, barren valley before Abraham turned it into a place of permanent habitation. He is said to have been born in the city known as Ur of the Chaldees, now located in modern-day Iraq. His place in time and geography is not clear. Judaic sources suggest that Abraham lived somewhere between 1812 and 1637 BCE. This could mean he was born into the Sumero-Akkadian Empire of Ur-Nammur, the third dynasty of Ur. This is the majority Judaic opinion and is shown on most modern biblical maps, located below the confluence of the Euphrates and Tigris rivers in Iraq today.

Little was known of the city state of Ur before excavations began in 1922 on a vast brick mound some 230 miles south of Baghdad. No reference to Abraham was found. Then, during the digging season of 1928–9, researchers unearthed one of the most evocative artefacts of the ancient world. It was a gold and lapis lazuli statuette of an animal standing on its hind legs caught in the branches of a golden bush. It reminded the researchers of God's words to Abraham in Genesis 22:13 – 'Abraham looked up and there in a thicket he saw a ram caught by its horns' – and it was named 'the ram in the thicket'. It now resides in the British Museum. I remember I was entranced the first time I saw it. The statuette was as responsible as the wealth of information that became available about this powerful city for sealing its associations with Abraham.

However, there has long been an alternative dissenting view, both in Islamic tradition and in the opinion of the great medieval Jewish scholar Maimonides. This alternative theory locates Abraham at Urfa, the modern Edessa, now in southern Turkey. It is argued that this is a more logical starting point for a migration that took the patriarch from his native city via Haran, in modern-day Turkey, and on to the Land of Canaan, somewhere between modern-day Lebanon and the Jordan river valley. Other minority opinions opt for a variety of different locations in northern Mesopotamia. There are additional minority opinions on his dates as well: some place him in a much earlier time, as far back as 2153 BCE.

As he stood on Jabal al-Nur, Muhammad was not concerned with the historical detail of Abraham's life but with the meaning and significance of his founding of the Kaaba and Mecca. Muhammad would have grown up with stories that Abraham's father was a maker and seller of idols. As the young Abraham watched his father carve statues out of wood, he began to ask questions: questions such as, how could something shaped by human hands be an object of worship? His doubts led him not only to denounce idol worship but to dedicate his life to the one God. Muhammad knew Abraham as *Khalil Allah*, a true and intimate friend of God. And, as recent research confirms, he counted himself as a follower of those who, like Abraham, believed in One Omnipotent God, who created the heavens and the earth and all that is in between.[12]

Abraham failed in his mission to liberate his people from paganism. Incensed by his questioning and by his mockery of their gods, they punished him by throwing him onto a fire. He was saved by God; and moved, with his wife Sarah, first to Palestine and then to Egypt.

The couple wanted more children. However, unable at the time to conceive, Sarah suggested that Abraham take as a concubine her slave girl, Hagar. Soon afterwards, Hagar gave birth to Ishmael. Later, when Sarah was blessed with her own son, Isaac, she became intensely jealous of Abraham's other family and asked him to take both of them away. Realizing that it was not possible for the two women to live in the same household, Abraham took Hagar and her son and travelled south with one of the great caravans on the incense route.

They left the caravan when they reached the Valley of Baca. Abraham left Hagar and her infant son there with some provisions.

Hagar built a little hut and settled down, waiting for Abraham to pay a return visit. When the provisions ran out, she began to look for food and water but could not find any. She ran frantically between the two small hills of Safa and Marwah, and returned to find her child crying from thirst. She ran again and again, becoming more and more desperate. The valley lived up to its name: Baca, a place without a stream, 'the Valley of Weeping'. Seven times she ran between the two hills but without success. Then, as we read in the Bible:

> When the water in the skin was gone, she put the boy under one of the bushes. Then she went off and sat down nearby, about a bowshot away, for she thought, 'I cannot watch the boy die'. And as she sat there nearby, she began to sob. God heard the boy crying, and the angel of God called to Hagar from heaven and said to her, 'What is the matter, Hagar? Do not be afraid; God has heard the boy crying as he lies there. Lift the boy up and take him by the hand, for I will make him into a great nation'. Then God opened her eyes and she saw a well of water. So she went and filled the skin with water and gave the boy a drink.[13]

Hagar and Ishmael drank till they were both satisfied. The well and the spring that fed it came to be known as Zamzam. Mother and child settled in the valley, which began to be established as a place of rest and refreshment for the travellers and caravans that passed through. In exchange for the services they rendered to passers-by, Hagar and Ishmael were sufficiently provided for. 'God was with the boy as he grew up. He lived in the desert and became an archer,' the Bible tells us.[14]

Abraham visited Hagar and Ishmael from time to time. According to the Islamic tradition, on one of his visits he found Ishmael sharpening an arrow beneath a tree, close to Zamzam. When Ishmael saw his father, he stood up and greeted him. After they hugged each other,

Abraham said: 'O Ishmael, God has commanded me to do something.'

'You must do what your Lord has commanded you to do,' Ishmael replied.

'But will you help me?' Abraham asked.

'Of course,' the boy replied instinctively.

'God has commanded me to build a house here,' Abraham said, pointing towards a small rise that was higher than the land around it.[15]

Together, father and son set about their task. First they laid the foundations of the House. Then Ishmael started to gather and bring stones from the surrounding hills as Abraham placed them carefully to create a well-defined structure. As the structure grew in height, it became difficult for Abraham to raise the stones and place them on higher levels. So Ishmael brought an especially large boulder. Abraham stood on the rock and carried on the building work; so arduous was his task that his feet left an impression in the stone, a point that today, according to Islamic tradition, is known as Muqam Ibrahim (the place of Abraham).

When the cubic building was almost complete an angel brought a special stone – it had fallen from Paradise onto the nearby hill of Abu Qubays. Abraham and Ishmael incorporated the black celestial stone (*al-hajar al-aswad*) in the eastern corner of the Kaaba. The building, which still lacked a roof, was now complete. Abraham declared it a sanctuary, a place of pilgrimage for men and women to come and visit on foot and on every lean camel out of every deep ravine.

I have often wondered about both the standard biblical and the orthodox Muslim accounts of Abraham's story. Abraham, supposedly a devout servant of God, turns out to be rather cruel, happy to abandon Hagar and his infant son in an arid, uninhabitable place. Is this the example that a Prophet is meant to leave for the rest of humankind? Similarly, I wonder why it is that Sarah offers Hagar to

Abraham.[16] Yet more perplexing are the geographical locations of events recorded in the Bible and in Muslim history.

According to the Bible, Hagar wandered in the city of Beersheba, located in the Negev desert, and eventually settled in the desert known as Paran. If that is the case, then it is highly unlikely that she would turn up several hundred miles away in Mecca; or that Abraham would visit her frequently. It is possible, as recent research suggests, that Abraham and his family were located not in Egypt and Palestine, but in the Asir province, which shares its western border with Yemen, in the southwest of Arabia.[17] That, of course, would make the Muslim account more plausible. And Abraham would be able to visit Hagar and Ishmael relatively easily and more frequently.

The story of Abraham, with all its contradictions, improbabilities and different interpretations, like those of all biblical patriarchs, is history without definitive and accurate biography. It is mostly an oral saga handed down from generation to generation.[18] The absence of a factual biography does not mean that this story lacks historical roots. Abraham, Ishmael, Isaac, Sarah and Hagar are real, even if the details of their biography vary in different religious traditions. Moreover, their story is not solely a tale of how Mecca came to be. It is also a story of what Mecca means to billions, and how *this* came to be. The importance is in the meaning as much as it is in the factual detail.

Does the meaning of the life of Abraham become more pertinent if we can fix it in time and place? The moral of the story, after all, is timeless, just as its substance reaches beyond time. Abraham perceives, appreciates and is loyal to the Eternal; this is what he establishes for those who come after, whatever was his time, wherever he lived. It is also the meaning of the House he built, the Kaaba, and the city that grew around it. And yet I am fascinated by all the detective work, the sifting through the variety of available evidence, the way in which old and new evidence has been interpreted and reinterpreted as the jigsaw of the human past has been fitted together in its still incomplete current version.

Is it likely that we will appreciate Abraham and his significance
more should someone unearth definitive archaeological proof of his
existence? I am less certain, and am reminded of the discovery of the
city of Troy by archaeologists in 1868. The works of Homer are
etched in the European imagination, and it is safe to say that the
world's collective appreciation of the *Odyssey* and the *Iliad* did not
grow as a consequence of this piece of science.[19]

The biblical narrative of Abraham and his sons divides to establish
the origins of two different groups of people. The Bible promotes
Isaac, while Ishmael is treated contemptuously in the New Testament
and in Paul's letter to the Galatians. In the Muslim tradition, Isaac is
respected but not remembered. Ishmael's descendants become the
Arabs; whereas the Jews originate from Isaac and from his son Jacob.
A single patriarch and two sons eventually produce three religious
traditions: Judaism, Christianity and Islam.

Beyond Abraham, we have to rely almost exclusively on Muslim
sources. There are no other sources on ancient Mecca. The first book
to be written about Mecca was put together before 865 by a native of
the city: *Meccan Reports* by al-Azraqi.[20] Virtually nothing is known
about al-Azraqi, but we know that the work itself, 'the earliest
preserved example of a book devoted to a single city',[21] was later
edited and expanded by a student of al-Azraqi and includes refer-
ences up to 923. But *Meccan Reports* is not history as we conventionally
understand it. To begin with, it concentrates on the city monuments,
for example the Kaaba and Muqam Ibrahim, and the living quarters
of the city. What it tells us about ancient Mecca is based on oral tradition and the stories familiar to the city's inhabitants. Whereas
al-Azraqi tells us little about the social and political makeup of
Mecca, more general histories focus on the city's notables, its politics
and struggles. One of the most important of these is the monumental
forty-volume *History of al-Tabari*,[22] the ninth-century historian,
theologian and commentator. Al-Tabari (838–923), who was of
Persian origins, was an avid collector of stories; and he includes them

all, good and bad, true and false, without comment, in his work. The biographer ibn Saad (784–845), who was born in Basra, Iraq, and worked as a scribe before blooming into a writer, seemed just as open-minded. His multi-volume *Book of the Major Classes*,[23] a compendium of biographical information on famous figures regarded as one of the earliest works of biographical literature in Arabic, is full of all kinds of narrations. It is difficult, I think, to swallow them all. Other historians were more discerning. The biographer and historian ibn Ishaq (d. 767 or 761) was more discerning in what he included in *The Life of Muhammad*,[24] the first part of which deals with the ancient history of Mecca.

We can regard these narrations as 'it has been said' history, for they are based on oral narrations, traditional stories, genealogy, poetry, sagas and myths. That, however, does not mean that we can dismiss this history. What is handed down, orally or written, need not always be economical with the truth. It does mean, however, that we need to be more critical of this material, and be scrupulous when sifting through it. It is possible to produce a realistic account of the ancient history of Mecca with some careful, judicious scrutiny.

Islamic tradition tells us that on the Mountain of Light, Muhammad was struggling to answer what had darkened the legacy of his own lineage. What had happened to the teachings of Abraham and Ishmael? Where did it all go so wrong? 'Who but a fool,' he said to himself, 'would forsake the religion of Abraham?'[25] He began to climb again. It was a steep but familiar climb. A little distance from the summit he paused to take a breath. He sat on a large boulder and turned his deep, dark eyes once again towards the city as he recalled the stories he knew of its history.

The House of Abraham became a sanctuary under the guardianship of the descendants of Ishmael at the start of the second millennium BCE. People from around the region began to pay their homage to the House, and slowly it became a site of pilgrimage that attracted visitors from further afield. Ishmael's children and grandchildren worked hard to ensure that peace was maintained in the Sanctuary and the surrounding area, that the landscape was not disturbed, or trees cut down. The visitors and those living around the Sanctuary would visit the Kaaba during the day and retire to their tents and dwellings in the surrounding countryside at sunset. The temple remained solitary and silent at night.

But the Ishmaelites' role in guarding the Sanctuary would not last. Arabia was dominated by a people of Arab stock known as the Amalik (Amalekites of the Bible), who had settled in all the major regions and towns of the peninsula, as well as in Syria and Palestine. Various clans of the Amalik engaged in long-running inter-tribal conflicts. It was during one of these conflicts that the Amalik attacked the Ishmaelites. The Ishmaelites believed that violence was sinful, and therefore did not defend themselves. The Amalik drove them out of the Baca Valley and they became nomads in the areas surrounding Mecca.

Eventually, the Amalik themselves were driven out not just from Mecca but from the region of the Hijaz by the joint efforts of two different tribes: the Jurham and the Qatura. The Jurham came origi-nally from Yemen; they migrated to Baca and were seen, unlike the Ishmaelites, as 'genuine Arabs' – Arabic was their native tongue. The Ishmaelites on the other hand were seen as 'naturalized' Arabs, for they only learned Arabic after they had settled in the Baca Valley. The Qatura were the tribal cousins of the Jurham, and travelled with them from Yemen to Mecca. The Jurham, who lived on the western slopes of Baca, controlled the passage in and out of the nearby port of Jeddah, and guarded the area around the Kaaba. The Qatura occu-pied the Abu Qubays mountain to the east and monitored the entry from Yemen. Pilgrims coming from either direction had to pay protection money to these tribes. It was a precarious arrangement, and hostilities inevitably followed, leading to a clash of the two tribes. Eventually, the Jurham defeated the Qatura and became the sole religious and civil authority in the Sanctuary, although we do not know when this actually happened.[26]

The Jurham justified their rule in Mecca by claiming close ties, largely by marriage, to the Ishmaelites. As their kin, the Ishmaelites were not only allowed to live in the Baca Valley but some amongst them were given exalted positions of priesthood. The Jurham ruled Mecca for several generations. The city was relatively peaceful during most of their reign, but at the height of their power, the sources indicate, the Jurham became greedy and neglectful of their duties. Far from protecting the pilgrims, from whom they levied a tax, and maintaining peace in the Sanctuary, they started to rob the pilgrims. Worse: they stole the gifts and sacrifices that the pilgrims placed in the Kaaba.[27] Thieves would climb into the roofless building and steal whatever they could lay their hands on. The sacred nature of the precinct was also compromised. It was not unusual for couples to be caught having sex in the temple, or engaging in other unbecoming behaviour.

The leader of the Jurham, who claimed descent from Ishmael's father-in-law, was called Mudad ibn Amer, known simply as 'the Mudad'. He was concerned that the gods of the Sanctuary would punish his people for their sins. There was a clear early indication: the spring at Zamzam had begun to dry up. So Mudad collected all the treasures of the Kaaba – said to include a pair of golden gazelles and fine swords – and hid them in the empty well to save them from the marauders. Then he fled into the desert to await the judgement of his gods in Mecca.

In the distant land of Saba in Yemen, the Great Dam of Marib, considered one of the engineering wonders of the ancient world, was crumbling. It had been in a state of disrepair for over a century – from inscriptions and records, we can date this to somewhere between the fourth and fifth century CE. It was about to collapse and flood the city of Saba. Alerted by one of their priestesses, the city's inhabitants decided to escape the impending disaster by migrating north. When the refugees reached Mecca, they were met by the unwelcoming Jurham. The Ishmaelites came out to support the refugees. A pitched battle followed, and the Jurham were soundly defeated. Warriors were massacred; women were taken into slavery. The Mudad looked down upon Mecca from Mount Abu Qubays, wept, and recited the following verses:

Many a woman reciter, her tears flowing abundantly,
Her eye sockets reddened from weeping,
(said): 'it is as if there had (never) been from Hajun to Safa,
A friend or a companion to speak together in the Meccan night'
And I replied to her, while my heart
Palpitated within me, as a bird between its wings:
'Aye, we were its people and we have been exterminated'.

The eyes pour tears, weeping for a land
In which is a safe sanctuary and holy stations
Weeping for the temple where the doves are unharmed,
Where they live securely. There (dwell) also the sparrows,
And the wild beasts, untamed.
And if they leave, they would fain return.[28]

The victors had their problems too. A raging epidemic broke out amongst the invading tribes. They saw this as a bad omen and decided not to stay in Mecca. Some went to Oman, others to Yathrib, still others to Syria. Only the Sabean tribe of the Khuza decided to stay in Mecca. They wanted the Ishmaelites to return to the city and resume the guardianship of the Kaaba. However, the Ishmaelites were fighting amongst themselves; so the Khuza decided to look after the Kaaba. To remove all animosities and ensure peace, the ruling family of the Khuza, the Luhayy, made an alliance with the family of the Mudad. Through this alliance the Khuza established a flourishing state in Mecca at about the beginning of the Christian era.

Amr, the leader of the Luhayy, was an extremely generous man. He went out of his way to feed and clothe pilgrims, not hesitating to sacrifice his own camels to provide meat for the visitors. But his real fame lies elsewhere: he is said to have been the first person to introduce paganism to Mecca, and bring idols into the Sanctuary. It began when he received a statue of Hubal, an oracular deity, with arrows marked on it for divining the future, as a gift. The statue, made of agate, was damaged. Amr, an exceptionally wealthy man, had the hand of the idol recast in gold. He then placed it on top of the treasury well in the Kaaba. Other families then proceeded to place their own idols in the courtyard of the Kaaba: Manaf, the sun god; Quzah, who held the rainbow; Nasr, the eagle-shaped god. The sculptures themselves were inspired by Greco-Roman art. Manaf, for example, showed clear aspects of a Hellenized solar deity. Three, more active, divinities had a special place of honour in the Meccan pantheon, and were widely worshipped by the Arabs: al-Lat, the mother-goddess; Manat, the goddess of fate who represented the darkened moon; and al-Uzza, 'the she devil', the goddess of love, sex and beauty. These goddesses had supernatural influence on stones and trees around the region. Al-Uzza was said to frequent three trees in the Valley of Nakhla. A rock in Taif was sacred to al-Lat.[29]

The pilgrimage to Mecca now became an entirely pagan affair. The Luhayy introduced a number of rites and rituals that had to be followed strictly. The underlying emphasis was on maximizing profit. The date of the pilgrimage would be computed each year by a seer and synchronized with a series of fairs held throughout the region. Pilgrims en route to Mecca would first attend these smaller fairs and festivals before arriving at the Sanctuary for the major ceremony. A poetry competition was held in Ukaz, near Taif, where people gathered to hear poets demonstrate their skills and oral dexterity. They were treated to short verses in a four-syllable metre (called *rajaz*) that emulated the pace of a camel, or to epic poems and long odes, the *qasidah*s, which paid homage to gods, great Arabs and enchanted mistresses, or related fables and desert adventures.

Or again there might be caustic satires directed against real and imagined enemies. The seven best poems, selected by an oracle, would be written out by hand, and prepared for mounting on the walls of the Kaaba. After the contest, the poets would join the other pilgrims. The pilgrim processions, led by enchanters and sorcerers, were jolly and colourful affairs, a roving religious circus. There were camels loaded with gifts from all the leaders and rulers of the region, and consecrated camels, decorated with charms and magical jewellery, carrying the idols of various tribes. According to Emel Esin, the twentieth-century Turkish historian of Mecca:

> There were seers in a state of trance, who chirped, cooed or hissed according to the bird or snake-genie that inspired them. Sorceresses, who were believed to entangle the course of human lives by tying symbolic knots, came with their long hair flying loose behind them, uttering incantations. Musicians clashed their cymbals and tambourines. Behind them streamed the crowd of pilgrims, some of them no doubt wearing Amer's gifts of striped Yemeni robes, in the sombre tones of Arab dyes.[30]

There was no shortage of entertainment, endless supplies of local date wine, as well as the more refined wines of Syria, dancing girls, jugglers, magicians, and opportunities for gambling and sex.

The fairgrounds were the ancient equivalent of modern shopping malls. They were packed with generous supplies of local goods such as scented woods, oil and perfume, gold, silver, and precious stones from the mountains of Arabia. There were imported luxury goods: spices from India, silk from China, fine cotton from Egypt, tanned leather from Anatolia, armour from Basra, slaves from Africa and Persia. There were commodities needed for basic survival: camel loads of grain from outside Arabia and fruits and vegetables from the oases in the region. There were herbalists for the sick, wandering surgeons ready to mend broken bones or perform operations, and dentists to replace broken teeth with gold ones.

After attending fairs, poetry competitions, even drunken orgies, various pilgrim processions would all converge on Muzdalifah, an open area a few miles outside Mecca, but still just inside the sacred territory. Here they would be greeted by the Meccan nobility, dressed in long flowing robes reflecting their status and religious roles. The high priest of Mecca would light a fire. The guests and allies of the Meccan rulers would join them in their camps. The guests of the Ishmaelites would be lodged in their scarlet leather tents. Everyone else – the ordinary people, the Bedouins, those who lived too far from Mecca, the foreigners who were not noble guests, those who had been cast out of their tribes, the beggars and the vagabonds – were ushered towards the plains of Arafat, just outside the sanctified area. There they waited for a signal. Just after the sunset, when a sign was given, the massed pilgrim crowd ran towards the fire at Muzdalifah and fell on a lavish feast prepared by the Meccans. After the meal, the rites of pilgrimage continued. Homage would be given to sacred trees and stones. Lavish offerings – necklaces, earrings, nose-rings – would be made to idols. Oracles would be consulted. And sacrifices would be made at altars all the way from Muzdalifah to Mecca.

On approaching the Kaaba, the pilgrims would remove all their clothes. A few would cover themselves scantily, with fabrics bought or borrowed in Mecca, but most would be naked. Dancing and clapping, the eighth-century Arab historian Hisham ibn-al-Kalbi (d. 819) tells us, they would enter the temple, now housing 360 idols, including statues of Abraham and Ishmael, and circumambulate the Kaaba chanting:

> By Allat and al-'Uzza,
> And Manah, the third idol besides.
> Verily they are the most exalted females
> Whose intercession is to be sought.[31]

Refreshed from his rest on the Mountain of Light, Muhammad resumed his climb. It was his practice to retreat to this mountain to reflect and meditate when life in the city below became too oppressive or depressing. How much would he have known about the Jurham and the Mudad, and Amr of the Luhayy? Muhammad was 'unlettered': he could not read or write. This does not necessarily mean that he was uneducated. He was the product of an oral culture, where history and tradition were passed from generation to generation through sagas, genealogical narratives, and most importantly, poetry. He was probably well versed in the ancient history of his city: he would have heard the sagas repeatedly told, the epic poems, the odes, the satires, as well as the lament of the Mudad, and the couplets of Amr of the Luhayy:

> We became custodians of the Kaaba after Jurham
>> that we might keep it prosperous, free from every
> Wrongdoer and unbeliever
> A valley whose birds and wild animals may not be touched
> We are its custodians and we do not discharge our duties
>> dishonestly
> Nay! We were its people, but we were destroyed
> By the vicissitudes of time and stumbling fate.[32]

The history of Mecca was constantly being recited in its streets and squares, alleys and assemblies, and within and around the Sanctuary. The Meccans lived and breathed their history. In this fiercely tribal society Muhammad would, of course, have been familiar with the history of his own tribe – the Quraysh.

The Quraysh, a large tribe of Ishmael's descendants, have a special place in the ancient history of Mecca. The earliest member of the Quraysh to leave his imprint on the city was Zayd bin Kilab, who was born around 400 CE. Zayd's father died soon after his birth, and his mother Fatima was left to look after him and his brother, Zuhrah.

Soon afterwards, she met and married a man from Aqaba who was visiting Mecca on pilgrimage. Fatima's new husband took her and Zayd back to his home town, leaving Zuhrah, who was much older, in Mecca amongst his own tribe. So Zayd grew up in the ancient settlement of Aqaba amongst the Nabatean Arabs, the people of North Arabia, who controlled the trading networks between Arabia and Syria, from the Euphrates to the Red Sea, from their oasis settlements. He must have stood out as different in his mother's second family, as he was dubbed 'Qusayy', or 'the little stranger'. And it was as Qusayy that he became famous in Mecca's history.[33]

Qusayy hated being seen as a stranger and was determined to get back to Mecca. But his mother would not give him permission to travel until he was a young adult, when he joined a pilgrim caravan travelling south along the desert route. Once in Mecca, he wasted no time in finding himself the perfect bride. He asked the man who was in charge of the Kaaba and ruled Mecca, Hulayl, the chief of the Khuzah tribe, for the hand of his daughter, Hubba, in marriage. Both father and daughter were besotted with the highly intelligent and handsome young man. Qusayy married Hubba and moved into Hulayl's house. Hubba bore him four sons, each named after and dedicated to one of the gods in the Kaaba. His wealth multiplied, and the respect he received from the citizens of Mecca increased proportionately.

When Hulayl become too old to perform his rituals and gate-keeping duties at the Kaaba, he asked his daughter to take over. She, in turn, turned to her husband – much to the displeasure of her tribe. The Khuza were infuriated that a sacred duty, which they had carried out for so long, should be so capriciously handed to an upstart and an outsider. Qusayy saw himself as a direct descendant of Ishmael and, as such, someone with more right to look after the Kaaba and rule the city. He decided to expel the Khuza from Mecca. He summoned all his relatives, both Ishmaelites and Nabateans, to help. They came from near and far, riding swiftly and silently at night, in large numbers. A bloody battle took place in Mina, a short distance

21

from Mecca. It was brief and decisive: Qusayy and his relatives were victorious and agreed that an arbitrator should decide the fate of the vanquished. His verdict was that the Khuza were related to Qusayy by marriage and hence could not be expelled from the city. Nevertheless, Qusayy was now the undisputed ruler and the prime priest of Mecca. He asked all the members of his tribe, the Quraysh, scattered throughout the region, to come together and settle in Mecca. After two thousand years of exile, the Ishmaelites returned to the city of their origin.

Qusayy was as brilliant an administrator as he was a politician. Under his leadership, Mecca was forged as a proper city, united under a single tribe. Up to this time there were no houses near the Kaaba. The nearest inhabitants were located on the slopes of the Abu Qubays mountains, overlooking the valley. The well of Zamzam had been forgotten and lost. Qusayy built new houses next to the Kaaba, laid out in concentric circles. Closest to the temple, enclosing the dusty courtyard and facing the north side of the Kaaba, was his own house, followed by houses for his sons and close relatives. The rows behind were designated according to strict rules of caste and status. The more prestigious a family or a clan, the closer to the temple. There was also accommodation for tribes allied to the Quraysh, or regarded as their equal, such as the Khuza. The outcasts, the slaves, and foreigners were all located on the outskirts of the city. New wells were dug around the city to supply everyone with water. The houses themselves were modelled on the Kaaba, being cubic in shape with a single door. While most were built simply of rough local stones, some were built with baked or unbaked bricks, and a few were deco-rated with marble, coloured stones or seashells from the Red Sea. The dwellings of the prosperous even had elevated ceilings supported by pillars, or a garden with an odd palm tree growing in a courtyard. 'Along the narrow streets merchants would sell spices and perfumes, local and imported cloths, garments and sandals, water-skins, stone vessels, honey and dates, the juices of Taif grapes and the millet that was their common food. There were wells with cisterns in the town squares, and caravan camels would be brought there to kneel, deposit their burdens and to drink.'[34]

The newly built city was open for business. It welcomed those who came to perform the pilgrimage, attend the numerous fairs organized around the city, or were simply passing through with their caravans. Serving the constant stream of visitors required security and appropriate facilities. Defence was the responsibility of every tribe and clan. According to tribal laws, it was all for one and one for all. Every clan had a duty to defend not only its own members but also all taken under its umbrella as guests, including pilgrims, thrill-seekers, merchants and foreign guests, and much honour could be gained by protecting them. For all other duties, Qusayy established a number of councils: a city council that looked after the overall administration of the city, an advice council of elders, a leadership council and a council for the administration of the Kaaba. A number of important duties were divided amongst various families: some were responsible for supplying water to the pilgrims, some for collecting taxes to pay for feeding the poor pilgrims, and some were required to look after horses and camels. There was an emergency committee and ambassadors responsible for foreign affairs. The person in overall charge of both secular and spiritual affairs was Qusayy himself. He led all the ceremonies within the temple, consulted the oracles, and supervised the distribution of food and water to pilgrims. His house doubled as the city hall where council meetings were held and people came to seek his permission on all matters, including his consent to marry outside the tribe. During wars, he led the troops into battle.

The policy pursued by Qusayy had two basic components: unity and neutrality. His aim was to emphasize unity by merging several Meccan cults into one. Sacred totems and tokens of every Meccan clan were gathered in the Kaaba. He also encouraged other tribes in Arabia to bring their tokens and fetishes to the Kaaba and thus come together in a common sacredness. All the different deities from all the clans, from inside and outside Mecca, were presided over by the chief deity Al-lah, literally 'the god', who was the guarantor of the pilgrimage and unity amongst the Meccan clans.

To maintain a constant flow of both pilgrims and caravans to Mecca, the city must have a reputation for neutrality in the region, and Qusayy aimed for both religious and political neutrality. By now there were strong Jewish communities in the northern Hijaz, and Christianity was particularly strong in Yemen to the south. Indeed, the Jews had established their presence in Arabia well before the arrival of the Christians. They arrived in the Hijaz as traders as early as the first century BCE; the migration increased considerably after the destruction of the Second Temple in 70 CE, and their banishment from Jerusalem by the Romans in 135 CE. There were large Jewish communities in such cities as Yathrib, Khaibar, Taima and Fadak, working as farmers, craftsmen, goldsmiths and makers of fine armour. Over one-third of the population of Yathrib was said to be Jewish. But there were hardly any Jews in Mecca itself, although the city did have some Christians. The largest Christian community was to be found not in the Hijaz but in Najran in southern Arabia. Hijaz itself had more monasteries, established by Syrian monks, than churches. The Meccans looked up to the Christians, seeing them as learned; they had mastered the art of writing at the court of Hira, a noted Christian city on the west bank of the southern Euphrates, long before it became established in the Arabian peninsula. Also, the Christians were respected for their skills in poetry. On the east coast of Arabia, Zoroastrianism was also important. Meccans welcomed and served members of all these different faith communities – they favoured none but invited all to pass through the city and attend its fairs and pilgrimages. 'Even Christian Arabs made pilgrimage to Kaaba, honouring Allah there as God the Creator.'[35]

Geographically, Mecca was almost equidistant from three major political powers of the region. Situated midway between Syria and Yemen, it was almost as far from the Persian Sassanid Empire, which controlled what is now Iraq. Qusayy aimed to keep all these major powers at bay and maintain the neutrality of Mecca and its ruling tribe, the Quraysh. In his rise to power, Qusayy had taken advantage of Byzantine interest in Mecca: he used their help to gain full control of the city and yet remain outside their sphere of influence. He was aware that both the Romans and Abyssinians had their eyes on the Hijaz and had made forays into the region. Indeed, the Abyssinians had sent troops as far north as Yathrib targeting Jewish settlements along the trade route. Mecca was a prime target for an empire looking for quick riches, and fertile ground for monks and priests seeking converts. Maintaining neutrality was not an easy task. Yet Qusayy managed to pursue an aggressive policy of neutrality and keep control of the north–south trade that made Mecca rich. By the time he died, Mecca had acquired considerable prestige and the Quraysh were seen as a dependable tribe who valued honour and honesty.

After his death, Qusayy's duties were divided amongst his family. It was a recipe for a family feud, which followed in due course. Civil war broke out, and pitted Qusayy's sons against each other. At the end of the hostilities, the clear winners were Qusayy's twin grandsons: Abd al-Shams, 'the servant of the Sun', and Amer, who was known as Hisham, 'the bread breaker', because he distributed bread to pilgrims. The young brothers, known for their courtesy and good temper, divided their grandfather's responsibilities between them, with Hisham and his party retaining the office of providing food and water to the pilgrims.

Hisham, who was renowned for his nobility and generosity, travelled extensively in the region on business. On a trip to Yathrib, he met and fell in love with a noblewoman of the Khazar tribe called Salma. They married, and a year later Salma gave birth to a boy who was named Shaybah. Hisham did not live to see his son grow up. He died soon after the birth, on a trade journey to Gaza, entrusting his brother Muttalib to take care of his son, who was still with his mother in Yathrib.

The young Shaybah stayed with his mother until he was seven or eight, developing an ardent interest in archery. When his uncle Muttalib eventually came to take him back to his father's clan in Mecca, he feared that Salma would not relinquish her son. On arriving in Yathrib he saw a group of young boys playing under the watchful eyes of some elders. He asked if they knew his nephew. 'Yes,' they said, and pointed to Shaybah. 'This is your brother's son, and if you want to take him, do so now, before his mother finds out. If she finds out she will not let him go, and we shall have to prevent you from taking him.' Muttalib called out to Shaybah: 'Nephew, I am your uncle, and I want to take you to your people.'[36] Without hesitation, the young Shaybah climbed on his uncle's camel. When Muttalib and Shaybah reached Mecca it was early morning and the city's inhabitants were sitting in their assemblies. Muttalib was wearing fine saffron robes and the purple sash of the high-born Quraysh; the boy was dressed modestly in the clothes of an archer. The citizens thought Muttalib had acquired a new slave and gave the boy a nickname: Abd al-Muttalib, 'Muttalib's servant'. History would know him by this name.

Abd al-Muttalib inherited his uncle's duties of supplying water to the pilgrims and collecting taxes for feeding the poor pilgrims. The former duty led him to rediscover Zamzam, the well of Ishmael, whose water had been buried and forgotten beneath the sand for centuries. He also helped in establishing a confederation of tribes in Mecca to prevent feuds and bloodshed. All this enhanced his reputation and prominence so much that he became the chief of Mecca. The city was prospering. Paganism had managed to hold Christianity at bay. Meccan idolatry had also developed a compromise with Judaism, and incorporated enough of its legends to attract wayward Jewish tribes. The great growth industry was the business of idol worship. And at the centre of it all was the Kaaba, which not only provided Meccans with commercial gains but also with considerable respect and esteem.

The wealth of Mecca did not go unnoticed amongst other tribes and provinces of Arabia. Some of them, including the Ghassanis, a south Arabian tribe, built their own holy houses to attract people away from Mecca. The most magnificent building, specifically designed to divert the pilgrims away from the Kaaba, was built in Sanaa, the principal city of Yemen. It was a project of Abrahah, the Christian viceroy of the negus of Abyssinia, who ruled Yemen in the middle of the sixth century. Abrahah's magnificent church, complete with ornate furniture and elaborate statues, was called *al-Qalis*. The viceroy was convinced that his holy house would draw not just pilgrims from all over Arabia but the Meccans themselves. However, no one came. The pagan Arabs continued to see Mecca as the only city worthy of a pilgrimage. Even the inhabitants of Yemen bypassed the new monument en route to Mecca. Abrahah decided the only way to increase traffic to his church was to remove this rival by destroying the ancient site, so in the late sixth century he set off from Sanaa with a magnificent army, riding an elephant that was specially brought from Abyssinia for the occasion.[37]

Abrahah's army camped at a place called al-Mughammas, a short distance from Mecca. A number of riders were sent to seize any property belonging to Meccans they could find. They returned with some cattle and 200 camels that belonged to Abd al-Muttalib. Then Abrahah sent a message to Abd al-Muttalib: 'I have not come to wage war against you. I have come only to destroy the House. If you do not fight me then I have no need to shed your blood.' The Meccans had already concluded that Abrahah was too strong to fight. When Abd al-Muttalib announced his intention not to fight, Abrahah invited him and the other leaders of Mecca for face-to-face negotiations.

Abd al-Muttalib was a handsome, dignified man. Abrahah was impressed with his demeanour the moment the two leaders met. He came down from his throne and sat on the carpet beside Abd al-Muttalib.

'What do you need?' Abrahah asked through an interpreter.

'I need my wealth back, the two hundred camels which belong to me that you have taken.'

Abrahah was taken aback. 'I was impressed with you when I saw you,' he replied, 'but I lost my respect for you when you spoke to me. You speak about the camels that belong to you. But you say nothing about the House which is part of your religion and the religion of your forefathers, which I have come to destroy.'

'I am the owner of the camels, and I would like my property back,' Abd al-Muttalib replied. 'As for the Kaaba, it has its Owner who will protect it.'

'No one can protect it from me,' Abrahah replied, and dismissed the leaders of Mecca.[38]

On his return to Mecca, Abd al-Muttalib asked the citizens to vacate the city at once and withdraw to nearby hills and mountains. Within hours Mecca was abandoned and left at the mercy of Abrahah's fearsome army. As that army approached the city, with the viceroy at its head riding his elaborately decorated elephant, the destruction of the Kaaba and Mecca seemed imminent. But then something extraordinary began to happen.

The elephant became unruly. When they tried to make it move towards Mecca, it sat down. The animal was beaten but it refused to budge. When they told it to move in the direction of Yemen, it got up and started running. Asked to move east, towards Syria, it began to gallop. But when they tried to get it to charge in the direction of Mecca, it sat down again.

The next occurrence was even more astonishing. Abrahah's army was afflicted by a deadly disease, perhaps smallpox. The disease spread rapidly within the ranks of the army and took its toll with unbridled ferocity. Abrahah was attacked by waves of birds that showered his army with deadly stones. Abrahah was terrified by what he saw and ordered his army to return to Yemen. They fled, falling and dying as they sought a way out of the Valley of Weeping. By the time Abrahah returned to Sanaa his army had dwindled to nothing. The viceroy himself succumbed to illness and may have died. Or maybe he was killed, three years later, by a Persian general named Wahriz, who invaded Yemen. But the extraordinary events witnessed by the Meccans left their mark on the city: its reputation was enhanced and its citizens acquired an exalted status. Time was now reckoned from 'The Year of the Elephant'.

Abd al-Muttalib now turned his attention to personal matters. He wanted a large family, and pledged that if the gods granted him ten sons, he would sacrifice one to an idol. It happened that he was blessed with ten sons, so to fulfil his oath he resorted to the ancient Meccan procedure for picking a candidate: he consulted divining arrows, kept in the Sanctuary under the protection of Hubal. The short straw was drawn by Abd al-Muttalib's youngest and favourite son, Abdullah. He began to have second thoughts. Abdullah's mother and her relatives were none too pleased either. They told Abd al-Muttalib: 'By God! You shall never sacrifice him, but must get an excuse for not doing so. If it takes all we possess to ransom him we will do so.'[39] He was advised to consult a soothsayer to see if a way out could be discovered. The oracle obliged: Abdullah's life could be ransomed for the price of a hundred camels. Much relieved, Abd al-Muttalib sacrificed the camels and celebrated by taking his son to Yathrib to visit relatives.

The patriarchs who shaped the political landscape and social life of Mecca seem to have lived lives that followed the same cyclical pattern. It was inevitable that Abdullah would meet and marry a noble woman from Yathrib. Her name was Amina, daughter of Wahab, a prominent leader of the city. It was also inevitable that Abdullah would embark on a trade journey. Almost at once he went to Syria, and there, equally predictably, he fell ill. He returned to Yathrib, where he died. By this time, Amina had already conceived Muhammad, the very Muhammad whose journey to the Mountain of Light we have been following by tracing his ancestry through the course of history.

Mecca had changed from the days of Qusayy. Times were hard. The sea routes had now opened up and took much business away from the city. Caravans were few and far between. Economic hardship led some to commit infanticide. But the Meccans remained steadfast to their ancient religion, the very source of their material well-being: idol worship.

Muhammad grew up in Mecca surrounded by paganism. Like most people in the city, he became a merchant. And like his father, grandfather and great-grandfather, he joined the caravan trade and travelled on business to Syria. Through his trading and other dealings he acquired the nicknames of 'the trustworthy' and 'the truthful one', but unlike his forefathers, he did not marry a noble, younger woman from Yathrib. At the age of twenty-five, Muhammad married Khadijah, an older 'woman of dignity and wealth'[40] from Mecca, who was impressed with his business acumen and integrity. The city and its pagan ways had little attraction for him. Mecca and its citizens, however, would make their own demands on Muhammad.

When Muhammad was about thirty-five years old, the Kaaba caught fire and part of the structure was demolished. It appears that a woman was burning incense in the Sanctuary when things got out of control. The Quraysh decided to rebuild and extend the Kaaba. It was only the height of a man, which made it quite easy for thieves to steal its treasures. It had no roof, the threshold was on the ground level, and water could get in during the frequent floods. The Meccans planned to add a roof and double the building's height. It happened that a Byzantine ship was thrown ashore at the nearby port of Jeddah and the Meccans were able to salvage its wood to use for the new building. A Copt, who was a master carpenter, was visiting the city. Everything was on hand for rebuilding the Kaaba.

But before that could happen, the remaining structure had to be demolished. The Meccans feared the wrath of their gods and withdrew in awe. After some time, a man called al-Walid bin al-Mughirah came forward and declared: 'I will begin the demolition.' He picked up an axe and set to work, chanting: 'O God, do not be afraid. O God, we intend only what is best.'[41] He worked most of the day and managed to demolish small segments of two corners. Next morning he returned to continue his work. When others saw that nothing untoward had happened to him, they joined in knocking down the Kaaba.

The Kaaba was then rebuilt with alternate layers of teak and stone. The Meccan tribes shared the task amongst themselves, each tribe collecting stones and working on its own part of the structure. The work proceeded according to plan; the height of the structure was doubled and a roof added. A door was placed above the level of the ground; whoever wished to enter must in future use a ladder. Only one item remained: the Black Stone had to be put in place. The Meccans started to quarrel among themselves about who should have the honour. Swords were drawn; blood oaths were sworn. For four days the city was on edge and on the verge of serious violence.

Then, on the fifth day, when the Meccans had gathered around the newly built Kaaba in another attempt to resolve their dispute, a senior citizen came forward with a suggestion. His name was al-Mughirah bin Abdullah bin Umar bin Makhzum. Al-Mughirah urged the agitated crowd to let the first man who entered the Sanctuary decide on the matter. The assembly agreed.

Muhammad was the first man to pass through the gate of the Sanctuary. 'You are the trustworthy one,' they said. 'We agree to accept your decision.'[42] He asked them to bring him a cloak. When the cloak was brought to him, he spread it on the floor. He picked up the Black Stone with his own hands and placed it on the cloak. Then he said: 'Let each tribe take an edge of the cloak, and all of you lift it up together.'[43] This equitable arrangement met with approval; collectively they raised the Black Stone into position. Muhammad then lifted the Stone and put it in its place. The construction of the Kaaba was complete.

And so were Muhammad's reflections on his day-long trek up the Mountain of Light. The newly constructed Kaaba was just over five years old. The paganism associated with Mecca and its Sanctuary had a history going back centuries, perhaps a thousand years. It was a history that troubled him deeply. He began the last, relatively easy, portion of his climb. At its summit the mountain flattened off. He followed a path he had taken many times, coiling around and then descending to an area where a hidden cave was located. He paused at the entrance to the cave, turned, and looked towards the city for the last time. The shimmering sun was slowly sinking over the horizon. In the fading light he could just make out the outlines of the city before it was shrouded in darkness.

He entered the cave.

2

'I Love Thee More
Than the Entire World'

Muhammad re-emerged from the cave as a Prophet. 'While I was
sleeping,' he later explained, 'the Archangel Gabriel came to
me with a brocade cloth in which was writing. He said "Recite", and
I said "I cannot recite". He pressed me tight and almost stifled me,
until I thought that I should die. Then he let me go, and said, "Recite".
I said, "What shall I recite?", only saying that in order to free myself
from him, fearing that he might repeat what he had done to me.'[1]

The words Muhammad repeated were: 'Read! In the name of your
Lord who created: He created man from a clinging form. Read! Your
Lord is the Most Bountiful One who teaches by the pen, teaches man
what he did not know.'[2] The vision had become revelation.

There is no objective test for divine revelation, no forensic evidence
to evaluate. Even for the believer it is an experience beyond normal
comprehension. It is, as T. S. Eliot put it, the intersection of the timeless with time. Mortals on occasion may, perhaps, catch transient
glimpses that give intimations of this profound experience, which is
the theme of Eliot's poem *The Four Quartets*.[3] A Prophet, by definition, is not ordinary. The only material evidence for what occurred in
the cave of Hira on the twenty-seventh day of the month of Ramadan
in 611 is found in Muhammad's words – and The Word he brought
down from the Mountain of Light.

What happened in the cave altered the rest of Muhammad's life.
He would now be repeatedly visited by extraordinary, conscious-
ness-bursting experiences. The words he received in the cave are the

33

first in a succession of revelations, which came to be known as the Qur'an (literally 'The Recitation'). When asked: 'How does revelation come to you?' Muhammad replied: 'Sometimes it comes to me like the reverberations of a bell, that is the hardest for me; then it leaves me; and I have understood from it, what He said. And sometimes, the angel takes a form of a man for me; and addresses me, and I understand what he says.'[4]

Each episode of revelation he received over the course of the next twenty-three years added piece by piece to the Recitation, which repeatedly refers to itself as 'The Book'. A book presupposes an author and purposeful construction. It is the basis of Muslim belief that the origin and authorship of The Book is Divine. The very definition of being a Muslim is to believe that the Qur'an is the direct Word of God transmitted to Muhammad through the agency of the Angel Gabriel. As the Messenger bearing these words, the Prophet returned to Mecca a man charged with the awesome responsibility of communicating his direct experience of divine revelation and making it comprehensible and meaningful to his community and ultimately to the rest of humanity.

In any age belief comes down to this: accepting the word. This does not mean that faith is blind acceptance; it is a process that should or ought to be informed by reasoning. Muslims accept that the profundity and potency of the words of The Recitation in style, content and meaning all declare that they are the word of God. Muslims also accept the testimony of Muhammad, and trust his fidelity in reporting exactly the words he received. This distinction is evident in the difference between the words of revelation and the language in which Muhammad explained his experience, indeed, all the reports of his own words and deeds.

We live in an age of scepticism where the power of words as persuaders is continually and increasingly questioned. From advertising slogans and their glib promises to the endless examples of broken promises and failed utopias of political rhetoric, or indeed the murderous promises inspired and fulfilled on the basis of such rhetoric, we take words with a large pinch of reasonable doubt. We reach for alternative forms of corroboration. However, when other proofs are absent we are thrown back to the phrase that once ruled at the London Stock Exchange: 'My word is my bond'. An assessment of human nature – the quality, character and actions of a person – is what determines the probability whether verbal claims are credible. The word is indeed our last resort. In that respect we are no different from the people of Mecca who first heard the words Muhammad brought to the city and his reports of what he experienced.

How should one react to what is the most extraordinary claim? If we had lived then, or tried to imagine someone declaring their prophethood today, what would happen? The scenario has fascinated dramatists and novelists, directly and in coded form, often enough. Yet when I began to rethink all I had learnt about Mecca in my quest to discover its history as a living city I realized that fictional speculation offers little that does not occur in the historical sources. When these accounts are read, shorn of the sanctity and centuries of deference that must accompany Muslim readings of Mecca, the city comes alive. Human nature in all its foibles and ferocity, from craven self-interest and duplicity to nobility, virtue and resolute self-sacrifice in the cause of reforming society, are all there.

Behind the pious narratives I had learnt as a child, there are far more powerful narratives about real people, about identifiable humanity, warts and all, that are so much more convincing. It is the very quality that, I think, one should understand when it is said that the Qur'an speaks to Meccan society as it was. It deals with human frailties and the dysfunction of a particular kind of social order by challenging them to recognize, adapt and live according to universal and eternal moral and ethical principles in ways appropriate to their circumstances. In that sense Muhammad's mission was as profound a challenge to the status quo of his city and his time as it is to people today.

The human reaction begins with Muhammad. His experience in the cave was not a blinding flash of instantaneous transformation. When he emerged there is no hint of the swagger of a man suddenly aware he has become a power in the land. He was terrified, confused, seemingly almost dumbfounded. He rushed back down to the city struggling to make sense of what he had seen, heard and remembered. Once he reached his home he clung to his wife Khadijah, bathed in physical, mental and spiritual turmoil. It was Khadijah, the older woman, the mother of his four surviving children, the woman so impressed with the integrity and trustworthy nature of Muhammad that she herself had proposed their marriage, who comforted and counselled him. The first person to accept the veracity of this Divine revelation was the person most intimately familiar with the nature and character of the Prophet.

Commentators agree that it would be another two years (613) before Muhammad again experienced a revelation – a time filled with self-doubt, uncertainty and even despair, we are told. Yet what happened in the cave was too momentous for inaction or silence. Muhammad shared his experience with his family circle and closest friends, and clearly such an amazing story could not remain a secret. Mecca was not a large city. It had just a few thousand inhabitants, all bound by close and complex networks of family, tribal and economic ties. Meccans became aware that Muhammad now claimed to have received the Word of what he asserted was the One and Only God. It was, after all, in pursuit of this idea that he so often retreated to the mountains. However, so long as this was a private matter, a personal caprice of a respectable peaceful citizen, it could remain the stuff of gossip. It did not yet bear the hallmarks of a matter that threatened to turn the world of Mecca upside down.

But Mecca would never be the same again. When the extraordinary experiences resumed, their message was clear and precise, and Muhammad was called to proclaim publicly that the polytheistic ways of the Meccans were based on falsehood and would lead them towards self-destruction and doom. Tell the Meccans, the revelations instructed Muhammad, to 'Say, "He is God the One, God the eternal. He begot no one nor was He begotten. No one is comparable to Him."'[5] It is not the deities in the Sanctuary, the revelations announced, but God who makes 'the Quraysh secure, secure in their winter and summer journeys' – of their trade caravans to Syria. 'So let them worship the Lord of this House.'[6] The revelations asked the Meccans to treat each other with equality and kindness, not to 'be harsh with the orphan' or 'to chide the one who asks for help'; to 'talk about the kindness of your Lord',[7] to give alms and believe in life after death, the Day of Judgement, when 'angels gather together those who did wrong, and others like them, as well as whatever they worshipped beside God, and lead them all to the path of Hell'.[8] The revelations also accused the city's chiefs of ignoring the plight of the less well off – 'You people do not honour orphans, you do not urge one another to feed the poor, you consume inheritance greedily, and you love wealth with a passion'[9] – and described its inhabitants, 'the idolaters', as 'the worst of creation'.[10]

Meccan leaders were horrified. These words were not merely an affront to their dignity and sense of self-worth, but to their entire worldview and all that sprang from it. Muhammad was denouncing the gods, beliefs, practices and ancestors of his own tribe. He was also insisting that his God was incompatible with their gods – his God was One, universal and ancestral, the Creator of all Arabs. This was not only a religious but also a political statement. It meant that all the tribal divisions, based on and sanctioned by the ancestral deities of polytheism, were false. Muhammad was asking not just for a different set of beliefs but also a radically different social and political order. The emphasis on the orphans and the poor, on giving alms and shunning conspicuous wealth, suggested that Muhammad was looking for a new basis for social solidarity. He was denouncing the existing way of life founded on tribe and trade as corrupt, unfit for its purpose in this world and the hereafter. His message cut to the very roots of the sources of power that sustained the Meccan hierarchy and all those who depended upon them.

Meccan horror was somewhat tempered by the quality of what Meccans were hearing. The Meccans were steeped in poetry, and yet, even by their own high literary standards, Muhammad's Revelations were unmatched. And this took them by surprise. 'This is not poetry,' they said. It was something else. Perhaps it was sorcery; magical spells. Were these the utterances of a soothsayer, or a poet possessed by a ghost? Their speculations, rooted in the common beliefs of the time, must have seemed less far-fetched than the claims Muhammad asserted.

Muhammad began gathering people to his cause, but in a society organized according to rank and privilege those in the city's upper echelons initially scoffed at his early followers. The first converts came from his immediate family. His devoted wife Khadijah, his young cousin Ali and his oldest and truest friend Abu Bakr accepted him as a Prophet without hesitation. Not everyone in Mecca was a polytheist. The city had some noted individuals who had given up deity worship and were known as the Hanifs. They had no faith of their own but were believers in one God and called themselves the followers of Abraham or the Seekers of Truth. Some of the Hanifs had mystical inclinations. The next converts came from this group.[11] As people who stood apart from the conventions of their society, none of these converts had any positions of honour in the hierarchy of the Quraysh – most of them were poor, some were slaves. The Quraysh despised them for their poverty and they hardly constituted a challenge, let alone a threat. 'Are these the people God has favoured in preference to us?' they joked with dismissive contempt for the lesser orders.

As long as Muhammad preached in secret, Mecca's leaders could dismiss him as a man suffering a temporary aberration. When Muhammad began to openly denounce idol worship, derision gave way to concern. A group of Quraysh leaders complained to

38

Muhammad's uncle, Abu Talib, head of the Prophet's own clan, the Banu Hashim. Abu Talib dismissed their complaint politely. But as Muhammad grew more vocal about the message of Islam, Mecca's leadership became more alarmed as they realized its implications. A select group called on Abu Talib again. How could he allow his nephew to curse their gods, insult their religion, mock their way of life and accuse their forefathers of error? Abu Talib was left in no doubt: 'Shut your nephew up or we will.'

We now know that the relationship between Abu Talib and his nephew is crucial to the success of his mission and yet curiously paradoxical at the same time. Everything we know about it indicates a warm bond of affection. In accordance with the custom of his clan, Abu Talib took Muhammad in as a seven-year-old orphan. He raised and nurtured the boy, taught him the rudiments of trade and commerce, and exposed him to the wider world by taking him on trading expeditions. It is thanks to his uncle that Muhammad secured his place in Meccan society.

We learn from Muhammad's biographer the historian ibn Ishaq that Abu Talib was in no doubt that the situation was becoming serious. He summoned his nephew. 'Do not put a burden on me greater than I can bear,' he told Muhammad. 'Spare me and spare yourself.' Muhammad feared that he was about to lose his uncle's protection. With tears in his eyes, he replied: 'By God if they put the sun in my right hand and the moon on my left on condition that I abandon this course, I would not abandon it until God has made me victorious or I perish.' As he turned away from his uncle, Abu Talib called Muhammad back: 'Go and say what you please, for by God I will never give you up on any account.'[12]

Abu Talib was not declaring himself a convert. He was a fond uncle accepting the sincerity of his nephew's cry of conscience, no matter how troublesome or disconcerting that might be to the rest of society. And what is the paradox? What Muhammad preached sought to overturn, indeed to replace entirely the ethos and conventions of

39

tribal solidarity. Yet it was this very principle extended and guaranteed by Abu Talib that secured Muhammad's personal safety and hence his ability to continue his mission. It is a paradox of human dynamics, of how the progress of new ideas often rests on the survival of old ways. This paradox would be repeated through the centuries in the history of Mecca.

When the Quraysh realized that Abu Talib would not abandon his nephew, they returned with a proposition of staggering brutality. They brought a strong and handsome young man with them. 'Adopt him as a son,' they asked Abu Talib. 'You will have the benefit of his intelligence and support. And give up to us the nephew of yours, who has opposed our religion and the religion of our forefathers, so that we may kill him. This will be a man for a man.' Abu Talib replied: 'By God this is an evil bargain that you offer me. This shall never be.'[13]

Thwarted yet again, the Meccans now faced a dilemma. Muhammad they could see represented a danger to the established order. And yet paradoxically he was being protected by the very clan he sought to overthrow. The Meccan leadership could not kill him, as in return this would spark a blood feud impossible to contain. And so they looked to other means, short of murder, that would make Muhammad's life intolerable. They abused and accosted him at every opportunity, threw thorns and rubbish on his path, and pelted him with stones when the chance arose. As for Muhammad's followers, those without clan protection, they were beaten, tortured, and some were murdered.

Opposition to Muhammad came from a handful of prominent personalities in the city. Amongst Muhammad's bitterest enemies was another uncle, Abu Lahab, the oldest of his relatives and one of the Quraysh's more prominent leaders. There was also Abu Sufyan, whose wealth was Mecca's envy, and his feisty wife, Hind. And then there was Abu Jahl, the head of the tribe of Makhzum, who had ambitions to rule over Mecca. Their combined hostility to Muhammad was calculated and calibrated by their vested interests. If prophethood had to be conferred on a Meccan citizen, then why not one of them? they reasoned. Why not a man from the Meccan nobility? If Mecca *had* to be the birthplace of another faith then its leader had to come from money and influence. Anything else was unthinkable.

Then there was concern about the implications of what they saw as Muhammad's blasphemies. They believed that his criticism of their gods could lead to misfortune, famine, infertility, blood feuds and war. Perhaps most worrying of all were implications for the Meccan economy. The Sanctuary and its deities were the main source of the city's income. Visitors paid to enter the city. They had to buy the correct apparel to perform rituals in the Sanctuary. They had to pay again to acquire offerings for the gods. Mecca was not just one of the world's oldest shrines, it was a citadel for capitalism. The people who oiled the wheels of Meccan religious life were known as Hums. They were an elite group who had lived in Mecca for a long time, claiming to be the sons of Abraham, and were known for their religious austerity. But they knew how to make money. The Hums would for example create new rituals that would generate new incomes.

In Muhammad's preaching the Meccan leadership correctly detected an echo of Christianity, and this, too, would create economic problems for them. Christianity was associated with Abrahah and other invaders who had descended on Mecca from Yemen, and it was the creed of the hated Byzantine Empire, which had sought footholds in Arabia to advance its centuries-old conflict with the Persians. But it was Mecca's economy, based on attracting polytheist worshippers, that would potentially suffer most from anything that smacked of monotheism. Muhammad's sermons in the squares of the city were not just unpalatable, they were inherently dangerous.

Something had to be done not only to preserve but to strengthen the edifice Meccan society had built over centuries. The Quraysh kept casting around for new tactics and changed their means and point of attack. Instead of dealing through intermediaries it was time to confront Muhammad directly. The Meccans dispatched one of their chiefs, Utba bin Rabia, a clever, worldly man known for his tact and negotiation abilities. His approach would be a diplomatic honey trap. He found Muhammad sitting by himself in the Sanctuary and sat beside him. 'O my nephew,' he is reported to have said in an affectionate tone, 'you are one of us, of noblest tribe, and of worthy ancestry. Listen to me, I will make some suggestions, perhaps you will be able to accept one of them.' Muhammad agreed to listen, and Utba went on. 'If what you want is money, we will gather for you of our property so you may be the richest of us. If you want honour, we will make you our chief so that no one can decide anything apart from you. If you want sovereignty, we will make you our king. If this ghost that comes to you, which you see, is such that you cannot get rid of him, we will find a physician for you, and exhaust our means to get you cured. So what do you say?'[14]

Muhammad's response came in the form of a revelation: 'Say [O Prophet], "I am only a mortal like you, but it has been revealed to me that God is One. Take the straight path to Him and seek His forgiveness. Woe to the idolaters who do not pay the prescribed alms and refuse to believe in the world to come! Those who believe and do good deeds will have a reward that never fails."'[15] Utba listened; as he listened he put his arms around Muhammad and leaned on him. When Utba returned to the Quraysh they noticed that he had changed. The man charged with delivering silver words had been profoundly moved by the potency of The Word. What Muhammad recited was not poetry, he told them, it was something else. He had never heard such words before. 'Take my advice,' he told the Quraysh, 'and do as I do. Leave this man alone.' 'He has bewitched you with his tongue,' the Quraysh are reported to have told their failed envoy, and ignored his advice.[16]

As Muhammad could neither be co-opted nor killed, it was time to revert to brutal repression. The Quraysh swore that they would unleash savage violence on his followers. However, this was becoming a more complex matter. The fact that one by one new converts were being drawn to his small band infuriated the Meccan elite. Two of the city's most feared men had converted to Islam. Muhammad's paternal uncle, Hamza, a hunter and a man of military prowess, and Umar, known to the city's inhabitants for his unshakeable will, bravery and direct, unambiguous manner, had both joined Muhammad's fold. Such notables were beyond assault. The same, however, was not true for those who were poor, slaves, or without powerful protection; they could feel the full force of their rulers' vengeance. Anyone who walked through the city could hear the screams of the tortured, or witness the spectacle of public beating and displays of violence.

One such victim was Khabban ibn al-Aratt, a slave who converted to Islam and was ordered by his owner to undo his conversion or lie down over burning coal. Khabban chose the latter and his owner planted his foot on Khabban's chest so that he could not move. Still, the convert would not waver. Neither would Ammar, recently married, and beaten so severely he was rendered unconscious. When his parents tried to protect their son, they suffered the same treatment.

There are many, many accounts of new converts being tortured, including women flogged publicly. But perhaps no story has been passed more vividly through the generations than that of an Ethiopian slave, Bilal ibn Rabah (d. 641). When Bilal's owner discovered he had converted he was ordered to lie on hot sand with heavy stones placed on his chest. In the evenings, he would be dragged along the streets of the city, with a rope tied around his legs. Part of the reason why Bilal's story remains a staple for today's Muslims lies in its lesson that nothing, not even extreme punishment, is more important than belief in the one God. Each time his owner demanded that he renounce his faith. Bilal repeatedly replied with just one word: *Ahad*, in Arabic, 'One' in English.

The Meccan leadership's reign of terror gave Muhammad little choice. He advised his followers to migrate to Abyssinia, in modern-day Ethiopia. It was a sensible choice for those seeking refuge, as the migrants knew they would at least be granted temporary asylum. Though a Christian kingdom, Abyssinia enjoyed long-established commercial relations with Mecca. And so some eighty Muslims who were free to travel slipped out of the city and sailed across the Red Sea on a merchant ship.

When the Meccans heard of this escape, they were incensed. A posse was hurriedly arranged to pursue them and bring them back. Negus, the king of Abyssinia, however, was not persuaded and seemed more interested if not impressed by the monotheistic words of revelation recited to him by those he had always thought to be polytheists. He granted the migrants protection and the Quraysh left empty-handed.

Back in Mecca, the Quraysh leadership prepared its next move: this would be a boycott of all those who had any connection to Muhammad's Banu Hashim clan. Today we would call this a blockade or extreme form of 'sanctions'. Back then it included a ban on marrying into the Banu Hashim, as well as forbidding all trade and other forms of association. The pact was written down and hung on the door of the Kaaba. The boycott would continue till the Banu Hashim agreed to hand Muhammad over to the Quraysh.

Comprehensively shunned and excluded from society, members of the Banu Hashim, including Muhammad, had little choice but to leave the city. Under the leadership of Muhammad's uncle Abu Talib, who still insisted on protecting his nephew, clan members moved to a nearby mountain cave. But not everyone did. Some in the Banu Hashim, such as another of Muhammad's uncles, Abu Lahab, chose to side with the Quraysh leadership and remained in the city.

Life outside the city, without food and provisions, was harsh. Reports from the time say that the new Muslims were reduced to eating leaves. Abu Jahl, Abu Sufyan and other Meccan leaders watched like hawks to ensure that isolation was strictly enforced. The blockade continued for almost three years and became so intense that the screams of hungry children from behind the mountain pass could be heard in the streets and squares of the city. But it would not last for ever, and partly because of a response from other Meccans. Many Meccans began to be revolted by what was being done to their erstwhile neighbours and friends. Naked tyranny does that: it provokes the consciences of decent people, stirring them to mobilize and confront the powers that be. In Mecca, an elderly kinsman of the Banu Hashim is reported to have approached a young man and asked: 'Are you content to eat food, wear clothes, and marry women while your maternal uncles are in the condition in which you know them to be?' 'What can I do on my own?' the young man replied. 'If I had another man with me I would take steps to repeal it and would continue until I had had it repealed.'[17]

The awakening had begun. Other men were soon found. Together the group went to the Kaaba and addressed people worshipping in the Sanctuary. 'People of Mecca,' they said, 'shall we eat, drink, and wear clothes while the Banu Hashim perish? By God, we shall not sit until this unjust document, which severs relationships, is torn down.'

Abu Jahl was in the Sanctuary at the time. 'You lie,' he shouted. 'It shall not be torn up.'

'You are a greater liar. We did not approve of it being written when it was written,' came the reply. 'This is something which has been decided during the night, and which has been decided elsewhere than this place.'[18] A scuffle is said to have ensued. Someone went up to the door of the Kaaba to tear down the document only to discover it had been eaten by termites. Almost immediately, a group of Meccans armed themselves and went to bring the Banu Hashim back to the city.

The hardship had taken its toll on Abu Talib. Shortly after his return to the city, he fell ill. Muhammad rushed to see his old uncle, a man who had done much and suffered more to protect him. He found that Abu Jahl and others were already by his side. In a last-ditch attempt to persuade his protector to accept Islam, Muhammad

said: 'O uncle! Say: none has the right to be worshipped but Allah.'
Abu Jahl is reported to have intervened: 'O Abu Talib, are you going
to denounce the religion of [our father] Abdul Muttalib?' Muhammad
repeated his request a number of times. Abu Talib replied: 'If the
Quraysh did not think that I only said it in fear of death, I would say
it. I should only say it to give you pleasure.'[19] Abu Talib remained his
own man to the end.

Abu Talib's death opened the way for the cabal of Mecca's powerful to inflict their long-desired fatal blow against the man they
regarded as an insurgent in their midst. The realities of tribal solidarity, however, had not expired with Abu Talib. To avoid retaliation by
the Banu Hashim, the murderous assault could not be a task undertaken by a single clan. There had to be general agreement and
coordinated, concerted action. The case for action was urgent.
Muhammad was seen less and less in Mecca. He was observed hurry-
ing out of the city early in the mornings. On occasions he was spotted
visiting other Arab tribes – outside Mecca, in Aqaba and even further
afield. Rumours began to circulate that he was building alliances with
tribes in other cities. The Quraysh feared that Muhammad's message
was beginning to reach beyond the confines of Mecca. If he succeeded
in converting other tribes, what would become of the sacred and
ritualistic character of Mecca? It would staunch the flow of pilgrims;
it would drain the lifeblood of the economy. With new converts
Muhammad might incite a sudden attack on Mecca by tribes from
beyond the city.

When it was discovered that Muhammad's followers had secretly
moved their children and dependants out of Mecca the civic leaders
interpreted it as evidence of their worst nightmare: that Muhammad
himself was preparing to relocate. The plague he represented had to
be contained before it spread past controlling. Mecca was on edge; a
tense atmosphere shrouded the Sanctuary.

During the first week of June 622, the city's leaders called a meeting. The chiefs of all the clans and tribes of Mecca gathered at the Dar

al-Nadwa, the Council House of the Quraysh. Abu Jahl was there; so too were Abu Sufyan and Abu Lahab. A number of suggestions were put forward. One proposal was to bind Muhammad in chains and imprison him in a house. Another proposal was to banish him from the city, enabling Mecca to get back to normal. Both of these suggestions were rejected. Then Abu Jahl spoke: 'Let us select a dexterous and sturdy person from every tribe of the Quraysh,' he suggested, 'and supply him with a sharp sword, and all of them would strike him simultaneously. The blood feud would thus be shared by all of them; and the Banu Hashim would not be in a position to decide what to do.'[20] The Council considered and found this an excellent expedient. When all hands are bloody no one man can be blamed. It was agreed. The plan would be implemented.

Just after sunset on the night of 13 June 622, Muhammad's house was surrounded. No one entered, however. Through cracks in the door the assailants observed that women were present. Even in such extreme circumstances it was beyond the honour code and dignity of true Arab men, even assassins, to enter female quarters at night. So they waited for Muhammad to come out. They waited till dawn. Then, as the sun was coming over the horizon, they rushed into the house, swords drawn. When the red Hadrami bed sheet that Muhammad used to cover himself while sleeping was removed they found not Muhammad but Ali, his young cousin and Abu Talib's son. Muhammad had slipped out of the house in the night and was now on his way to Yathrib, a city 200 miles to the north. A party was quickly organized to give chase. The Quraysh announced a huge reward, 100 camels, for his capture. It produced no results.

Mecca's most famous son had left the city of his birth. 'O Mecca,' Muhammad had said on the night he migrated for Yathrib, 'I love thee more than the entire world, but thy sons will not let me live.'[21] The city had rejected him emphatically. He had little but hardship and persecution, and less than two hundred adherents, to show for the eleven years he had spent as a Prophet. In contrast, Yathrib received him with open arms. Its citizens came out to greet the Prophet, and sang and danced in the streets in jubilation. Yathrib even changed its name: it was now called Medinat an-Nabi, the City of the Prophet, or Medina for short. Muhammad's exile, however, did not decrease Mecca's standing. On the contrary, a series of Quranic revelations would enhance its prestige many times over.

While Muhammad preached in Mecca, the words of the Qur'an he recited in prayer referred to Mecca in the third person as 'the city' or 'the town'. In the Sacred Text, God invokes the city only when he is making a promise: 'I swear by this city – and you [Prophet] are an inhabitant of this city'[22] and 'By the fig, by the olive, by Mount Sinai, by this safe town, we have created man in the finest state then reduced him to the lowest of the low, except those who believe and do good deeds.'[23] When Muhammad is in Medina, the Qur'an now refers to Mecca as 'the mother of cities'.[24] Moreover, its position as the premier site of monotheism is acknowledged and confirmed: 'the first House [of worship] to be established for people was the one at Mecca. It is a blessed place; a source of guidance for all people; there are clear signs in it; it is the place where Abraham stood to pray; whosoever enters it is safe.'[25]

Mecca's relationship with Abraham, and all the history associated with it, now had a divine mandate. Then, in the year 633/634, Mecca attained its enduring status as the prime focus for all Muslims for all time. While in Mecca, the Muslims prayed facing in the direction of Jerusalem. Now, in Medina the Qur'an tells them to 'turn your face in the direction of the Sacred Mosque; wherever any of you may be, turn your face towards it'.[26] Mecca was not the 'city of the Prophet' – that honour belonged firmly to Medina – but it was and would be pre-eminent as the 'city of Allah'.

Mecca's polytheists received constant intelligence about the new revelations. The danger and imminent disaster of the scenarios they had foreseen seemed to be taking shape. In Medina, Muhammad became both the religious and the political leader of the city. The original inhabitants of Medina and the immigrants from Mecca had become one community of believers – some locals even shared their homes and wealth with the refugees. The number of Muslims began to swell rapidly. The Prophet built a mosque and introduced a number of rituals that gave special features to the new religion he preached, for example, the *Adhaan*, the words called from the mosque that summoned the faithful to the daily prayers. He was also actively establishing treaties with neighbouring tribes. The Meccan leadership observed these developments with horror. The most serious and obvious threat they perceived concerned their trade caravans from Syria. They had to pass by and were open to attack from Medina. The danger was particularly serious during the spring and early summer months when the bulk of the trade took place. Something had to be done.

To safeguard their trade, Meccan leaders spread false rumours about the timing or the precise routes of the caravans. Although one or two of their caravans were discovered and came under attack, most managed to reach Mecca safely. However, the news of a particularly large caravan, one of the richest of the year and said by some to have over 2,500 camels, could not be kept secret. It was led by Abu Sufyan, who had no doubt he would be a prime target. He sent a courier ahead to Mecca to summon a rescue force. When the message arrived the Quraysh were already preparing for war with Medina. It did not take them long to set out from Mecca with 1,000 men in arms, augmented by 100 cavalry. All the grandees of Mecca were there, including Abu Jahl. En route to Medina, the Quraysh learned that Abu Sufyan's caravan had passed and was safely on its way to Mecca. But at the same time Muhammad had come out to Badr, a valley near Medina, with an army of 313 Muslims.

Some amongst the Quraysh began to have doubts. The aim had been to defend Abu Sufyan's caravan and this was fulfilled. Moreover, there would be blood relatives on each side if it came to war. The son of the Quraysh commander, Utba, was in the Muslim camp.

49

'By Allah,' Abu Jahl declared, 'we shall not go back unless we have encamped at Badr.'[27] He accused the Quraysh of being cowards and reminded them of their pledge to eliminate the Muslims from the land of Arabia. This was the most opportune time to wipe out Muslim power and finish them once and for all, he announced. It galvanized the Meccan troops. They rode all night to arrive at Badr on the morning of 17 March 624. It had rained heavily the previous day and the camels and horses struggled to make speed. On reaching Badr, the Meccans discovered that Muhammad had taken possession of the spring in the valley and rendered the surrounding wells useless. The Muslim army had enjoyed a good night's rest; it was ready for battle. Still, the Quraysh reckoned the small Muslim army, with limited armour and no horsemen, was no match for them. It would be easily crushed.

The battle began, according to custom, with three Meccan champions challenging the soldiers from Medina to one-to-one combat. The three Meccans were killed; one Muslim was badly injured. The Quraysh could contain themselves no longer. The entire army charged into the Muslim ranks. As the battle raged, the Meccans noticed that their leaders were falling. Abu Jahl was killed. Utba, the commander, was also slain. Panic seized the Quraysh ranks. They found themselves running in all directions, some falling to the swords of the Muslims, others fleeing for their lives. It was all over within a few hours. Seventy Meccans had been killed, a further seventy captured.

Mecca was stunned by its crushing defeat at Badr. The Valley of Weeping was filled with the wailing of women. The men, however, refused to shed tears. Indeed, their chiefs announced that no expression of grief would be permitted. One citizen lamented: 'Life has lost all its relish.' Abu Sufyan now assumed leadership in Mecca. When the defeated army returned he swore never to dress his hair with oil or have a bath unless he had taken revenge. His earlier caravan had produced rich dividends and he now decided to use the profits to build a new military force to launch against Medina. Abu Sufyan sent

out a few poets to stir the passions of the tribes with their rhetorical
skills and fiery tongues. Words were at the base of this conflict: both
sides were backing the power of words to create or preserve the
world they wanted to maintain. It was the meaning the words
contained that was so different. Notable women of the city – amongst
them Abu Sufyan's wife, Hind, daughter of Utba, the commander of
the Meccan army, devastated at losing her father as well as her son at
Badr; and Umm Hakim, wife of Ikrama, son of Abu Jahl – would
stroll through the streets inciting men to prepare for revenge, not to
rest till they had drunk the blood of those who had slashed their sons
to death. It took a year to muster a force of 3,000 men, 200 mounted.
And there were women too! This time the Quraysh were determined
to surprise the Muslims. They marched swiftly and quietly to the
outskirts of Medina and camped near the mountain of Uhad. It was
19 March 625.

But Muhammad was forewarned of their plan. He was ready with
an army of 700 men; he had strategically placed a group of fifty archers on the high ground afforded by the mountain. The archers had
strict orders not to leave their post under any circumstances. Learning
from their experience at Badr, the Quraysh arrayed their lines with
particular care, Abu Sufyan leading the main army, with 200 horses
ready in reserve.

The battle began with the war songs of the Quraysh women. Led
by Hind, beating their drums and tambourines, they sang:

> O Ye sons of Abdul-Dar,
> O protectors of our rear,
> Smite with every sharpened spear!
>
> If you advance we hug you,
> Spread soft rugs beneath you;
> If you retreat we leave you,
> Leave and no more love you.[28]

Even before the women had finished, the Quraysh champions came forward to challenge the Muslims. The Muslim response was swift and deadly; it was led by Hamza, Muhammad's uncle, and Ali, his cousin and son-in-law. The two broke into the Quraysh ranks, sweeping off whole formations. When the Quraysh tried to advance, they came under a shower of arrows from the archers at the top of the mountain. They tried a pincer movement but were forced back by the archers. The rain of arrows forced the Quraysh army to retreat. The women encouraging the warriors ran for protection in confusion. The Muslim army thought the battle had been won, and started to secure the booty. The archers abandoned their position in jubilation and joined in.

Khalid bin Walid, one of the Quraysh commanders whose forces had suffered the most from the archers, called out to Abu Sufyan. 'Hold fast!' he shouted. 'The battle can yet be yours.' He turned his cavalry around, galloped round Mount Uhad, and came through a pass to attack the Muslims from the rear. First he attacked those archers who still held their positions. He was now able to overrun the Muslim army from the rear. One by one, the backbone of the Muslim army began to fall. In the confusion that followed, its front rank, unable to distinguish friend from foe, started to fight the rear ranks. Hamza, who was specially targeted by an Ethiopian slave of Hind called Wahshi, fell victim to his spear. The Meccan force now moved in to claim their main prize: Muhammad.

The Meccans could see that he was wounded. They rushed towards him in wave after wave. He was surrounded by eleven of his men – including Ali, Umar and Abu Bakr. Again and again, the Meccans advanced, a rolling tide, but each time they were repulsed. One well-known warrior of the Quraysh managed to get quite close to Muhammad. He struck him on his face so hard that two links of his visor pierced his flesh. The Quraysh started to fire arrows towards him. Muhammad's companions made a cordon around him, covering him with their shields. Slowly, this tight-knit group edged their way to the summit of the mountain until they were out of the reach of the Meccans. The Quraysh regrouped and charged up the hill. They were pelted with boulders and forced back.

The Meccan women now fell on the bodies of the Muslim dead, mutilating them by cutting off noses and ears. Hind and other women made necklaces of their gruesome trophies and proudly displayed them around their necks. When Hind found the body of Hamza, she is said to have cut open his belly and tried to eat his liver. But she could not swallow it and had to spit it out. Then, she mounted a high rock and shouted at the top of her voice:

> We have paid you for Badr
> And a war that follows a war is always violent.
> I could not bear the loss of Utba
> Nor my brother and his uncle and my first-born.
> I have slaked my vengeance and fulfilled my vow.
> You, O Wahshi, have assuaged the burning of my breast.
> I shall thank Wahshi as long as I live
> Until my bones rot in the grave.[29]

Abu Sufyan went as close to the Muslim position as he could and shouted: 'Is Muhammad there?' There was no reply. Then he shouted the names of Abu Bakr and Umar. Finally, he heard the retort: 'O enemy of God! We are all alive.' Abu Sufyan replied: 'There are some mutilated bodies among your dead. By God, it gives me no satisfaction, and no anger. I neither prohibited nor ordered mutilation.'[30] He then led his troops to a nearby place to recover and contemplate his next move. When he heard that Muhammad was sending troops to pursue him, he returned to Mecca.

Mecca was jubilant. The outcome at Uhad had energized its inhabitants. The news travelled fast to other tribes in Arabia – they too were motivated to attack Medina. The Meccans made a point of inciting the visiting pilgrims against their enemies. A number of tribes were thus encouraged to make sorties against Medina, but they had little impact. Abu Sufyan, who had been involved in every twist and turn of strategic planning to eradicate Muhammad, could not but feel that his task was only half finished. A much greater force, one that could not possibly be defeated, was needed to completely destroy Medina. Secret envoys were sent out from the city, hushed meetings were held at long-forgotten waterholes, secret plans were made for a decisive battle to take place the following year.

One day a small band of emissaries came to Mecca. They were from the Jewish tribe of Banu Nadir, who had been expelled from Medina by Muhammad. They wanted to know if the Quraysh would join forces with them against Medina. The Meccan leadership could not believe their good fortune. But Abu Sufyan wanted a force greater than the two tribes could provide, and other tribes were recruited. First to be approached were the powerful tribes of Ghatafan and Fazara; both were easily persuaded to join Abu Sufyan's force. Next to come on board were the Banu Asad, who had an alliance with Ghatafan, the Banu Sad, allied to the Banu Nadir, and the Banu Sulaim, who had a blood connection with the Quraysh. This coalition of the willing gathered momentum and other tribes fell in line. Soon a confederate army, said to comprise 10,000 men with 600 horses, was ready to march against Medina.

The Meccan army consisted of three main divisions. The Quraysh forces, consisting of 4,000 foot soldiers and 300 horsemen, were led by Abu Sufyan, acting as the army's general. The other two divisions were led by the chiefs of the Ghatafan and the Banu Asad. The plan was to attack Medina both from the north and the south, 'from above and below', with lighting speed. It was kept secret, and implemented silently to maintain the advantage of surprise. Moving swiftly through the desert, the confederate army reached Medina on 31 March 627.

The Arabian Desert is not good at keeping secrets, however, and Muhammad came to know of this plan. When the Meccans and their allies arrived at their destination they found that a large moat had been dug across the unprotected side of the city. A deep, wide trench prevented their entry, and was too wide to jump across. They were perplexed. 'This is a device which the Arabs have never employed,' they cried.[31] Some horsemen attempted to jump over the moat; a few managed to get across, but they were cut down as soon as they reached the other side. Unable to cross the trench, the bulk of the invading army was reduced to hurling stones and shooting arrows from a distance. Denied the real war it had come to fight, members of the Meccan alliance instead spent several days exchanging insults among themselves before changing tactics. Notable warriors were given command for a day and each tried to lead a general assault with the whole army, but none had any appreciable success. Then they tried to persuade the Banu Qurayza, a Jewish tribe of Medina, to rebel and attack the Muslims from within the city. This too failed.

The Quraysh leadership were growing restless. They had come to fight and were unprepared for a siege involving 10,000 soldiers. Provisions were running out and horses and camels began to die. At the same time, the Quraysh's tents offered little protection against the winter cold and rain. It wasn't long before the allies started to blame each other, and soon the Quraysh and Ghatafan began to fight amongst themselves. Confusion engulfed the coalition forces and Abu Sufyan began to realize that victory was impossible as long as Muhammad controlled the other side of the trench. He also knew that the Muslims were in a stronger position and could hold on for months, if not years.

Then one night the weather changed. A fierce storm brought havoc. Strong winds blew tents away, and animals ran in wild frenzy, trampling many allied soldiers. The Meccans, believing that the Medinans were about to attack under the cover of bad weather, opted to flee. Among the first to do so was Abu Sufyan, who told his men: 'O Quraysh! We are not in a permanent camp; the horses and camels are dying. The Banu Qurayza have broken their word to us and we have heard disquieting reports of them. You can see the violence of the wind which leaves us neither cooking-pots, nor fire, nor tents to count on. Be off, for I am going.'[32] He mounted his hobbling camel and returned to Mecca.

For the Meccan leadership, success from the previous battle with Muhammad's forces mattered little. They had lost what came to be known as the Battle of Trenches. Moreover, to build and maintain an army costs money, and without a win, the Meccan economy was now in tatters. The Meccans felt that nothing could now stop Medina from becoming a powerful rival city, nor could Muhammad be prevented from spreading his message, and the news that their erstwhile Jewish collaborators in Medina, the Banu Qurayza, had been punished told them that the new Muslims were not in forgiving mood. And yet, turning to the Kaaba in worship and supplication, they remained determined to thwart Muhammad's ambitions.

Perhaps the old Sanctuary was listening, because it was at this point that Mecca, effectively sidelined, would witness the start of a great revival, and from a most unexpected source. A new revelation came to Muhammad, recognizing the city as a site of pilgrimage and making pilgrimage to Mecca an obligation for believers in the new faith: 'Pilgrimage to the House is a duty owed to God by people who are able to undertake it.'[33]

In March 628 the Meccans learned from a messenger that Muhammad would be returning to the city of his birth to perform the 'lesser pilgrimage' – this involved visiting the Kaaba and walking or running the 450-metre distance between the hills of Safa and Marwah. The Meccans were perplexed. Was this a way of honouring their city? Or was it a trick, some new tactic like the trench in Medina? They decided that Muhammad could never be allowed to enter Mecca.

Preparations to defend the city began in earnest. The Quraysh summoned all their allies, who came in great numbers and camped outside Mecca. A detachment of 200 horsemen was sent to intercept the advancing Muslim procession of around 1,400 men and women. The procession stopped at Hudaybiya, a settlement fifteen kilometres west of Mecca. Muhammad sent a message to the city's leaders: he said that he had no intention of fighting, his only desire was to visit the Sanctuary, which was why he had invited non-Muslim tribes to join him in the performance of the sacred ritual. He added that if the Quraysh insisted on fighting him during the holy months, when by ancient custom a truce was to be universally observed, and if they insisted on preventing people, irrespective of faith, from visiting the Kaaba, they would find themselves isolated and condemned by all Arabs.

The Quraysh were in a quandary. Muhammad had seized the moral high ground. But even if Muhammad's intentions were peaceful, they argued, he should not be allowed to enter the city against their will with so many followers. Apart from the obvious military dangers they feared that the Quraysh would become the laughing stock of Arabia. The advance guards returned with news that the men from Medina were dressed as pilgrims and carried no weapons. Even this failed to convince, and they sent another delegation to reconfirm the improbable news. Other tribes intervened and negotiations continued for some time. Eventually, the Quraysh sent Suhayl ibn Amr, an experienced and shrewd envoy, known for his sharp mind and someone they trusted, to negotiate as their intermediary.

Suhayl went to Muhammad and the two men talked for a long time. They agreed terms that would be committed to writing as a formal treaty. Muhammad began to dictate to his cousin and confidant Ali: 'In the name of Allah, the Merciful, the Compassionate'. Suhayl, being a polytheist, intervened: 'I do not recognize this; so write "In thy name, O Allah."' Muslims protested angrily, swords were drawn, and Ali refused to cross out what he had written. Muhammad, who could neither read nor write, took the pen, asked to be shown the contested words and himself crossed out the words

'Messenger of Allah'. 'Write', he said to Ali, 'this is what Muhammad, the apostle of God has agreed with Suhayl bin Amr.' Suhayl objected again. 'If I witnessed that you were God's apostle I would not have fought you. Write your own name and the name of your father.' Muhammad started again:

This is what Muhammad bin Abdullah has agreed with Suhayl bin Amr.

They have agreed to lay aside war for ten years during which men can be safe and refrain from hostilities on condition that if anyone comes to Muhammad without the permission of his guardian he will return to them; and if anyone of those with Muhammad comes to the Quraysh they will not return him to him. We will not show enmity one to another and there shall be no secret reservations or bad faith. He who wishes to enter into a bond and agreement with Muhammad may do so and he who wishes to enter into a bond and agreement with the Quraysh may do so.[34]

It was further agreed that Muhammad would not enter Mecca that year but that the Quraysh would not oppose Muslims visiting the Holy Places the following year. Muhammad and his followers would be allowed to enter the city for three days, on the condition that the pilgrims left their arms outside the city. The Muslims saw the agreement not as a treaty but abject surrender, and they pleaded with the Prophet not to sign.

Muhammad, however, was adamant. Before he could put his signature on the treaty, a young man burst through the Meccan ranks. He was Abu Jandal, son of Suhayl bin Amr. He had converted to Islam and had been tortured and imprisoned. He rushed towards the Muslims, dragging around his ankle the links of his broken chain. When Suhayl saw his son, he got up, hit him on the face, and dragged him by his collar, saying: 'Muhammad, the agreement between us was concluded before this man came to you.' 'You are right,'

Muhammad replied.[35] Abu Jandal was handed over to the Quraysh. Muhammad now asked members from both parties to witness the contract and returned to Medina.

The Meccans were in no doubt they had made an exceptionally good deal. They had prevented Muhammad from entering Mecca – at least for a year. The Meccans who had converted to Islam and fled to Medina would be returned to them; they would hold on to anyone who came from the other side. It looked to them like a win–win situation for Mecca and a sorry reverse of fortune for Medina. A few years of peace they figured would be enough to enable their city to recover from previous battles, rebuild its economy and marshal its troops once again against Medina.

The following year Muhammad returned to perform the 'lesser pilgrimage' as the treaty specified. The Meccans could not bear to witness the spectacle and most of the Quraysh dignitaries left the city for the hills. A few watched the proceedings from the top of a nearby mountain. Muhammad was accompanied by some 2,000 Muslims. All left their arms outside the city and followed Muhammad as he went around the Kaaba at a brisk pace. The Muslims roamed around the city, the migrants to Medina showing the houses where they had lived to their companions. When the three days were over, the Meccans came down from the hills and asked the Muslims to leave.

The emergence of an 'Islamic threat' had distracted Meccans from their own inter-tribal disputes, but with no common enemy to unite against, old disputes resurfaced. The tribe of Banu Bakr, for example, who according to the Treaty of Hudaybiya had sided with the Quraysh, decided to settle old scores with their enemies, the Khuza, who had an alliance with the Muslims. The two tribes had been at war for so long that they had even forgotten how the conflict began. With the clandestine support of the Quraysh, the Banu Bakr attacked the Khuza under the cover of darkness. The Khuza sought refuge in the Sanctuary. The Banu Bakr, respecting the sanctity of the Kaaba, held back. Finally, their leader spoke. If you do not take action now you will lose this golden opportunity for ever, he told his fellow tribesmen. The Banu Bakr entered the Sanctuary and massacred most of the Khuza. Around forty surviving members escaped to Medina and related the whole story to Muhammad.

Muhammad sent a message to Mecca. The city's inhabitants, he said, had three choices. They could pay blood money for each member of the Khuza killed by the Banu Bakr. The Quraysh could give up their alliance with the Banu Bakr. Or the Treaty of Hudaybiya could be declared null and void. Without hesitation, the Quraysh chose the last option.

But Mecca's leader Abu Sufyan had his doubts, as the treaty conferred advantages on Mecca. He decided to go to Medina to see if he could persuade Muhammad not to rescind it, but Muhammad refused to see him. Abu Sufyan tried to meet whomever he could, even calling on Muhammad's daughter, Fatima. But no one would see him and Abu Sufyan returned to Mecca unsure whether or not to advise his fellow Quraysh to prepare for war.

On a chilly night in January 630, the Meccans saw the desert around the city alive with points of light. Row upon row of flaming beacons were arrayed as far as they could see. The leaders of the city hurriedly gathered in the Sanctuary. 'I have never seen such fires and such a camp before,'[36] Abu Sufyan is reported to have said, and asked a few leaders to accompany him. The 'field of light' was an army of Muslims camping for the night, and Abu Sufyan was spotted and brought before Muhammad.

'Why, O Abu Sufyan,' asked Muhammad, 'do you still deny that there is no god but Allah?'

'Had there been any,' replied Abu Sufyan, 'he should have helped us now.'

'Do you doubt that I am His Messenger?'

'As to that I still have some doubt.'[37]

Muhammad instructed that Abu Sufyan be taken to the top of a nearby hill so that he could watch the proceedings from there. A few hours later, Muhammad's mighty army, which according to some reports numbered over 10,000 men, stirred into motion.

Abu Sufyan saw tribe after tribe, each under its own banner, march towards Mecca. The flag of the Ghifar tribe was the first to be seen, followed by the tribes of Juhaina, Hudhaim, Sulaim and Saad, then the Ansar, the Muslims of Medina, splendidly equipped and ready to go into battle. 'What kind of army is this?' Abu Sufyan is said to have asked in amazement. Muhammad had in fact entered Mecca unopposed and announced an amnesty for those who would lay down their arms, those who sought shelter in the house of Abu Sufyan, those who closed their own doors or who entered the Sanctuary. Most of the city followed his advice, but a small group of the Quraysh decided to offer resistance and showered the Muslim troops with arrows. According to reports, there was a short skirmish, then all was quiet.

The streets and squares of Mecca reverberated with Muhammad's voice:

'O Quraysh! This is Muhammad . . . There is no god but Allah. He has no associates. Every claim of privilege based on blood or property is abolished by me except the custody of the Sanctuary and the watering of the pilgrims. Man springs from Adam and Adam sprang from dust.'[38]

When Muhammad had finished, the citizens of Mecca – the leaders and the chiefs, those who had conspired to murder him; those who drove him from the city, tortured, murdered and abused his followers, those who waged bloody war against Medina – all gathered in front of him.

'What do you think I am about to do to you?' Muhammad asked the crowd.

'You will do good. You are a noble brother, son of a noble brother,' people replied.

'Go your way. You are free,'[39] Muhammad said.

The Prophet had returned to his point of origin and consummated what for me is the moral heart of his mission. At the moment of his most complete triumph he asserted that peaceful coexistence is not only possible but the essential basis for doing good, for enacting ways for justice and equity as living realities for all.

There was one final act to conclude the vindication of his Prophethood. Muhammad made his own way to the Sanctuary. After performing the seven circuits of the Kaaba, he walked towards the hills of Safa and Marwah. The area was covered with 360 deities of those the Meccans worshipped as lesser gods – one on Safa, one on Marwah, and the rest covering the area between them. Using the stick he was carrying, he smashed them all, one by one, reciting the verse: 'The Truth has come, and falsehood has passed away; falsehood is bound to pass away.'[40] Some reports suggest that there was an etching of the Virgin Mary on the wall of the Kaaba. The Prophet left it untouched.

He was now approached by those Muslims forced to migrate to Medina. Their houses were possessed by the Meccans and they wanted their properties back. The Meccans knew this would happen and feared the outcome, but Muhammad persuaded his followers to forgo any such lawful claims.

The following day, Muhammad sat at an elevated place on the hill of Safa. The inhabitants of Mecca lined up to pay homage. Some swore allegiance to him according to tribal custom; others expressed their desire to convert to Islam. The Prophet asked each individual wishing to embrace Islam to promise to observe the basic rituals, behave in a morally upright manner and treat others with equality and dignity. Then he would dip his hand in a bowl of water, the convert would follow suit, and the conversion was thus solemnized. One of those who came to be converted was Hind, his tormentor-in-chief, the wife of Abu Sufyan, who had rejoiced at the Meccan victory at Uhad by disembowelling and then chewing on the raw flesh of Muhammad's dead uncle Hamza. Hind wore a veil to emphasize her class and to avoid recognition. She was defiant but respectful and Muhammad, not knowing her identity, asked if she gave her word not to associate anything with God.

'By God,' she replied, 'you lay on us something that you have not laid on the men and we shall carry it out.'

He said: 'And you shall not steal.'

She replied: 'By God, I used to take a little of Abu Sufyan's money and I do not know whether that is lawful for me or not.'

Abu Sufyan was present. He told her that what happened in the past was now forgiven. But the mention and intervention of her husband gave Hind's identity away.

'So you are Hind?' Muhammad asked.

'I am,' she replied. 'Forgive me my past and God will forgive you.'

He said: 'Do not commit adultery.'

She said: 'Does a free woman commit adultery?'

He said: 'And you shall not kill your children.'

She said: 'I brought them up when they were little and you killed them on the day of Badr when they were grown up, so you are the one to know about them.'

He said: 'You shall not invent slanderous lies.'

She said: 'By God, slander is disgraceful, but it is sometimes better to ignore it.'

He said: 'You shall not disobey me to carry out orders to do good.'

She said: 'We would not have waited all this time [in a long queue to see the Prophet] if we wanted to disobey you in such orders.'[41]

Muhammad then accepted her conversion. There is little doubt, if we read the classical sources unencumbered by the accretions of later Muslim historians, or indeed the stereotypes derived from them, that women were full participants who played essential parts in the human drama that unfolded in Mecca. From Muhammad's first wife Khadijah to Hind, along with his daughter Fatima, his later wife Aisha and other wives, we see women as active agents in the making of history.

Muhammad was born in Mecca. The city was home to his tribe the Banu Hashim and he had two houses there. He was the Prophet who proclaimed the message that made Mecca the spiritual heart of his

63

mission. Yet, much to the surprise of Meccans, the Prophet returned to Medina, fifteen days after his triumphal and peaceful return.

It would be Medina and not Mecca that would become the capital of the new Muslim state. My dwelling in life and death, the Prophet declared, will always be Medina. In the summer of 632, the Prophet announced his intention to go to Mecca to perform the pilgrimage. The news spread rapidly; people from all over the Hijaz flocked to Medina, glad of the opportunity of accompanying the Prophet on the pilgrimage. But this would not be the pilgrimage of previous times; it would mark the beginning of Hajj, the pilgrimage that remembers and celebrates the monotheistic history of the House of Worship, the pilgrimage according to Islam.

The limelight now shone on Medina. It was not just the capital but the cultural and intellectual centre of the emerging Muslim state. Mecca, in contrast, was decidedly quiescent. It remained mostly dormant throughout the year – coming alive only during the period of the pilgrimage. Indeed, Islamic history itself forgets Mecca at this stage and focuses solely on Medina. But a city with fiercely independent inhabitants was not content to remain dormant for long. Mecca had ambitions. It aimed to go beyond, far above the religious and terrestrial confines of Hajj to the realms of celestial metaphysics.

3

Rebellions at
God's Earthly Throne

The Prophet visited Mecca once more before his death. It was in
March 632, during the Islamic month of Dhu al-Hijjah. This
time he went as a pilgrim to perform his first and only Hajj, the
pilgrimage to Mecca. The 'Farewell Pilgrimage', as it is known in the
tradition, is significant for two reasons. It demonstrates how the Hajj
is performed and establishes its rites and rituals. From then on,
pilgrims have followed in the footsteps of Muhammad, and will
continue to do so. The Sermon that Muhammad gave at the climax of
his Hajj summarizes his teachings. It is frequently cited by Muslims.

The Prophet led a procession of over 90,000 people – men and
women, husbands and wives, all dressed in what became the traditional garb of the pilgrims: two simple white unsewn sheets of
cloth, one serving as the loincloth, the other draped over the shoulder. The women dressed plainly in white. On the way from Medina
to Mecca, the procession stopped at various mosques to pray.
Throughout the journey, the voices of the multitudes filled the dry
desert air with the sounds of supplication: 'At your service O God!
At your service! You have no associate! At your service O God!
Praise be to God!' On reaching Mecca, the convoy spent the night
at the edge of the city. The following morning Muhammad went
direct to the Sacred Mosque and made seven rounds of the Kaaba,
after which he prayed at the Station of Abraham. Then he ran seven
times between the hills of Safa and Marwah, and all those with him
followed.

A day or so later, on the eighth day of the Islamic month of Dhu al-Hijjah, Muhammad rode to the valley of Mina. He stayed there for a day and a night, and at sunrise the following day, the ninth of Dhu al-Hijjah, he proceeded on his camel to the Mount of Mercy in Arafat. As he ascended the mountain, he was surrounded by pilgrims as far as the eye could see. There, sitting on his camel, when the sun had passed its zenith, he delivered his sermon. His words were repeated and echoed by strategically placed criers, sentence by sentence. Tradition tells us that the crier who stood closest to him, underneath his camel, had his head covered with the foam falling from the camel's mouth.

'O people,' Muhammad began. 'By the grace of God, may a man who hears my speech retain it. Many a bearer of jurisprudence has no understanding of it . . . Know that your property and your blood are sacrosanct to you as the sacredness of this day of yours, in this month of yours, in this land of yours! And know that the hearts will not betray three things: the sincerity of Godly acts; the advising of those with authority; and the attachment to the community of Muslims. All things from the affairs of the *jahiliyya* [the pre-Islamic period] are abolished, under my feet.'[1] Then he exhorted Muslims to treat each other with kindness, neither inflict nor suffer inequity, nor do injustice to others or to themselves, to avoid usury and to reason well. He asked spouses to respect each other's rights, instructed that good care should be taken of orphans and the needy and declared that all Muslims are one brotherhood: 'Know that every Muslim is a Muslim's brother, and that the Muslims are brethren. It is only lawful to take from a brother what he gives you willingly, so wrong not yourselves.'[2]

After the sermon, Muhammad led the congregation in prayer. At sunset he rode to Muzdalifah, where he spent the night sleeping under the open sky. On the morning of the tenth day of Dhu al-Hijjah, he returned to Mina, stopping to throw pebbles against the symbol of Satan. After arriving at his tent, he sacrificed sixty-three camels, one for each year of his life, and distributed the meat amongst the poor. Finally, the Prophet shaved his head and declared that the pilgrimage was now complete.

Muhammad went straight back to Medina. He died a few months later on 8 June 632. By now Mecca had been turned upside down. From the moment Muhammad stood victorious in the central square of Mecca, everything changed. Momentous events would occur within the lifetime of those who heard Muhammad declare his amnesty in the city of his birth, or who gathered two years later to hear his final sermon during the Hajj. Yet the consequences for Mecca would be entirely counter-intuitive. In this topsy-turvy new world the very moment that sealed Mecca's pre-eminence as the focal point of the new religion began its long steady decline into a sleepy backwater. The prestige of Mecca as the city of God was secure for all time. However, the vested interests it had fought to defend for so long were overthrown. With so much happening in the world around them it would take some time before the people of Mecca would realize the decisive yet contradictory nature of the shift of fortune that was overtaking them.

The power that Mecca enjoyed during the pre-Islamic period, the *jahiliyya*, had shifted. Mecca still had a paramount religious significance: to be in Mecca is to be in the presence of God. But to be with Muhammad – that is to have earthly power and significance – one had to be in Medina, the city which had been renamed in honour of the Prophet. Medina would be the capital, the political centre of the new society he was building. It made perfect sense. Mecca had rejected the meaning of its own origins as the city of Abraham and monotheism with its determined persecution of Islam. Yathrib, which renamed itself Medina, had embraced Muhammad's message and stood resolutely behind the new spiritual and social order it proclaimed. Medina was the cradle of the new society, the seedbed of the new way of being that Muhammad's followers were about to share with the wider world. The choice of Medina as the political and strategic centre of operations confirmed the rejection of the tribal roots of social solidarity. It was an endorsement of the bonds of faith and commitment as the new basis of the community.

The Meccan elite had to swallow their pride along with their defeat. The political autonomy they had guarded and fought for over the course of centuries was at an end. The status and benefits the city's elite had derived from being the pre-eminent place of pagan pilgrimage was entirely altered. To make their way in this new world and improve their fortunes, Meccans would have to look elsewhere. To become influential in determining the course of events, they would have to leave Mecca.

The rebuff to Mecca was softened by another of Muhammad's decisions. Having accepted Mecca's capitulation and the conversion to Islam of much of the population, he appointed many of its leaders to important posts in his administration. People such as Abu Sufyan, his son Muawiya and Khalid ibn Walid, who had openly plotted against him and strenuously opposed him for so long, acquired favoured positions in the system they had resisted. It was a gesture of peace and conciliation that shocked the supporters who had migrated with the Prophet to Medina and stood firm behind him in the long struggle with Mecca.

Muslim historians emphasize that nothing survived of Mecca's pagan past: its ancient history evaporated for ever like steam from boiling water. But the attitudes and outlook of 'the age of ignorance' (*jahiliyya*) were ever-present in the city – and have remained intact. The tribal structure, with its codes of loyalty and blood ties, continued to rank as high for the citizens of Islamic Mecca as it ever did for the pagan Meccans. Outwardly, the city had become Islamic, but there was an invisible substratum of old cultural traits that were for ever present. The new converts were eager, enthusiastic recruits to the project of Islam, yet the reflexes of the old order would find ways to operate within the new system. It seems that the words of Muhammad's final sermon had little effect on the city.

After the death of the Prophet a new leader was proclaimed in Medina. Abu Bakr, the first successor, or caliph, was of course a Meccan. He ruled for just two years and was succeeded by another Meccan, Umar. Indeed, in the chain of successors for centuries to come the question of family, lineage and tribe out of Mecca would continue to matter. It was not until 1517 that the last scion of a Meccan family was displaced from the position of caliph, by the Ottoman conquest. By that time caliphs who traced their ancestry back to Mecca had long been mere figureheads, their existence conferring prestige on those who wielded effective power.

Beginning under the leadership of Abu Bakr, the caliphs' attention and concern was no longer the Hijaz and its rivalries, not merely Arabia and its turbulent tribal divisions. Abu Bakr took up the mission to bring Muhammad's message to the wider world. Within decades Muslim forces were campaigning in and had assumed control of Iraq, Persia, Syria, Palestine and Egypt and out into the Mediterranean. What did all this mean for Mecca?

Mecca must have been denuded of its leading citizens. The young, the vigorous and the ambitious left the city. Many found permanent positions administering the newly won territory. They might return for Hajj and family duties, of course, when circumstances permitted. Yet those who answered the call must have been changed men, men who saw their homes very differently from the proud defiant defenders of the old pagan order they had once been. Perhaps many were among those who settled in the newly won territories, married local women and founded new lineages that would be proud of their Meccan ancestry. The speed and the scale of the Muslim conquests make it difficult to grasp the human dynamics by which the world changed around Mecca and for Meccans. One thing is certain: from this time on what happens in Mecca and to Mecca is shaped by and within the context of this rapidly expanding Muslim world.

While the energies of so many of its citizens were focused elsewhere, those who remained in Mecca had to attend to the new importance of their age-old concern for the city of pilgrimage. It was necessary to improve the condition of the Kaaba and the Sacred Mosque. The Sanctuary had no walls and was surrounded by houses on all sides, with alleys in between serving as entrances to the Kaaba. With what would be an inexorable increase in the number of pilgrims, the compound would have to be extended. The Sanctuary was also in constant danger of flooding. Indeed, in 638, the year Jerusalem surrendered to the second caliph, Umar, the Kaaba was hit by a torrential flood. Houses adjacent to the Kaaba and the surrounding areas were purchased and demolished, and the compound of the Sanctuary expanded. Umar also built a wall – the height of an average man – around the Sanctuary and placed lamps on it for illumination. The course of the stream, Sayl Wadi Ibrahim, was altered and a high earth dam built to prevent flooding and protect the Sanctuary. The Sacred Mosque was expanded yet again by Othman, the third caliph, in 646. Additional space was acquired and arcades were introduced to provide shade for the worshippers.

While Mecca was preoccupied with the expansion of the Sanctuary, the capital, Medina, was embroiled in a bitter dispute over succession. Abu Bakr, the first caliph – the word means 'successor' – ruled from 632 to 634. He was followed by Umar, who ruled from 634 to 644, and then Othman, whose reign lasted from 644 to 656. Although the transfer of power from the first to the third caliphs was smooth and democratic, both Umar and Othman were murdered. All three were Meccan immigrants to Medina and from the tribe of the Quraysh, but each was from a different clan, and none were from Muhammad's own clan of Banu Hashim. The succession became problematic with the election of the fourth caliph, Ali, the cousin and son-in-law of the Prophet. The politics had strong religious implications and Mecca would find itself the focus of two major rebellions within decades of the Prophet's death.

Ali was elected the day after the murder of Othman. The classical Persian historian Abu Ja'far Muhammad ibn Jarir al-Tabari described Ali as 'a tawny man, markedly so, with heavy and large eyes, corpulent, bald, tending to shortness',[3] but this – rather derogatory – description overlooks the fact that the 'Knight of Islam', as he was called, was a heroic and generous spirit. He was an erudite, artistic man with mystical tendencies. During the Middle Ages he was considered the patron of Muslim painters; there are numerous miniature paintings that were clearly inspired by him. A volume of eloquent sermons, letters and sayings is attributed to him,[4] and he was also an accomplished poet. Most of his supporters were natives of Medina. The Meccans, who felt they had not been properly consulted, were unhappy with the election of the new caliph. Leading figures of the Quraysh who were in Medina at the time, including some who aspired to the position of caliph themselves, immediately returned to Mecca without swearing allegiance to Ali. When Ali appointed new governors, replacing the appointments of Othman, Mecca and Syria refused to follow his orders. Syria was governed by Muawiya, son of Hind and Abu Sufyan, and kinsman of Othman. He argued that Ali had no claim to rule until the killers of Othman, who were now siding with Ali, were brought to justice.

In Mecca, rebellion was festering. It coalesced around Aisha, the youngest wife of the Prophet and daughter of Abu Bakr. The Meccans too insisted that Othman's murderers should be brought to justice, and demanded that the question of a successor should be decided by *shura*, a consultative council involving the whole Muslim community. What happened next is an indication of the new dimensions of the Meccan world. A decision arrived at in Medina and opposed by people in Mecca was no longer a dispute between two cities. Its consequences were not confined to the Hijaz. The crucial action would take place in Iraq and have implications and ramifications that reverberated throughout the Muslim world. Aisha assembled a large force from many different tribes of the Quraysh, and in October 656 she led her troops to Basra, in southern Iraq, where she was joined by additional forces. She took the city after a short skirmish with Ali's governor.

Ali assembled a larger army, including the leaders of those who had mutinied against Othman, and set out for Basra to confront Aisha. The two sides met just outside the city. On both sides, there were close companions of the Prophet. Both armies were multi-tribal, and most tribes had members on both sides, some backing Ali, others backing Aisha. It was believers against believers. Not surprisingly, some refused to fight, declaring that they did not support either side. Envoys went to and fro, extended negotiations were conducted. Both sides hurled accusations at each other. There was a serious attempt to avoid battle. But early one morning, when it was still dark, those who had conspired against Othman mounted a surprise attack on Aisha's forces. There was total confusion, each side thinking it had come under attack from the other. By dawn, the two sides were engaged in a mortal conflict. It came to be known as the Battle of the Camel, as the epicentre of the fighting was around the camel carrying Aisha. It was a bloody encounter, with heavy casualties on both sides; an estimated 15,000 people were killed within a few hours. Eventually, Ali's forces triumphed. Aisha returned to Mecca, where she stayed for a short while, and then moved to Medina, with strict instructions from Ali to keep out of politics.

The Battle of the Camel had a traumatic effect on Mecca. Its memory was to haunt the city for centuries. The first civil war of Islam – which was basically a war within the family of the Prophet – was about much more than bringing Othman's assassins to justice. The fundamental issue was about who had the right to rule: those from the family of Muhammad or those who were elected by the whole community. After all, the Prophet had abolished claims of privilege based on blood. And it was about the treatment of women. The Meccan women, as we have already seen, were fiercely independent and, after the advent of Islam, eager to protect the egalitarian rights instituted by the Prophet. Aisha had a number of legitimate grievances. Her sister, Umm Kulthum, had refused to marry Omar 'because he was rough and harsh with women'.⁵ Women had actively participated in public life, but Umar had them confined to the household. They were not consulted on social issues and their opinions were ignored on political matters. Obey your husbands at all times, they were instructed. Even their right to property was being questioned.

Where women were concerned, it appeared that pre-Islamic customs were not only being retained but reinforced. The general dissension amongst the ranks of women was articulated and personified by Aisha. It is far too soon in Muslim history to say that the virtual house arrest imposed on Aisha sealed the fate of women. She would continue to be influential, but always from behind closed doors, a political purdah, though her recollections of the words and deeds of the Prophet would be crucial to the development of Islamic religious studies. However, it seems to me that the Battle of the Camel and its aftermath is one of those seminal moments that loom large in the consciousness of later times. She suffered the fate of all losers in history: blamed for the mayhem irrespective of the virtue of her cause. And, implicitly, she is tainted as a stereotype of a headstrong, passionate member of the 'weaker' sex, proving her unfitness to meddle in politics. As such her example is used as a not so subtle argument 'to exclude women from public life, to relegate them to the household, and reduce them to the role of silent spectators'.⁶

Victory did not secure Ali's short-lived reign. It was becoming almost impossible to govern the whole now widely dispersed Muslim community from Medina. A second step in the successive phases of re-centring the political control of the Muslim world seemed a logical response to circumstance. Each successive change of the capital city moved the centre of earthly authority and control further from Mecca, the focal point of religion. Ali selected Kufa in Iraq as his seat of power. Kufa had been established only twenty years earlier. The city grew out of the military camp used by the Muslim troops who overran the Sassanian Empire. The military outpost that became a city was intended to differentiate and separate the Muslims from the non-Muslim population they ruled. Garrison camps that developed into cities became a common pattern in the expansion of the Muslim Empire. They were supposed to insulate the Muslims from the seductions of the luxuries and distractions of customs and cultures different from their own. Of course, it did not, indeed could not work, but it gave the world some glorious new cities. The new capital was regarded as more strategically significant, a clear signal that the perspective of the caliphs and their administration was making pragmatic adjustments in adopting a more global outlook.

In Mecca, the remaining members of the old aristocracy, dissatisfied at the loss of their power, looked on the caliphs with suspicion. Their old reflexes were about to resurface. It is not hard to imagine their reasoning; it is common enough in any period of dramatic change. In a matter of twenty-five short years this radical new experiment in religion and society had drastically changed the world. The results in territorial expansion were immense – many Muslims believe it to be miraculous; the opportunities afforded were almost unlimited. However, its fruits also included chaos and civil war. Perhaps it was all just too radical. What was needed was breathing space, time for the new ideas to bed themselves in; not necessarily an abandonment of the new ways such as consultative participation in choosing a leader, but a temporary resort to tried and tested old ways, so as to establish some stability.

The Meccan elite did not have far to look for the perfect candidate, someone who could restore ties to tribe and blood. Muawiya, the son of Abu Sufyan and Hind, was ideally positioned to assume the mantle of caliph. In spite of converting to Islam late – at the conquest of Mecca – he was nonetheless appointed as a secretary to the Prophet. A quarter of a century later he was in the powerful role of governor of Syria. Commentators from nearer the time write of him as being an exceptionally astute political operator. 'He was tall and corpulent, with white skin, fat thighs, a tiny head, protruding eyes, a dyed beard and a grim expression.'[7] He had a canny ability to make the most of opportunities. He liked to argue; when losing an argument he would undermine his adversary with a humorous remark.

After quelling Aisha's rebellion, Ali turned his attention to the threat from Muawiya. In May 657, Ali marched towards Syria to confront Muawiya, who had gathered his troops and moved towards the Euphrates to block Ali's advance. The two armies met a month later near the town of Siffin, on the banks of the river Euphrates, in modern-day Syria. Neither leader had the total backing of his troops. Protracted negotiations, lasting several weeks, were conducted, but to no avail. A pitched battle followed in late July, with heavy casualties on both sides, but just as it was becoming clear that Ali's forces were gaining an upper hand, Muawiya asked his troops to hoist copies of the Qur'an on their lances. This was seen as an appeal to stop fighting; and Ali's forces withdrew from battle almost at once. More negotiations followed. Both camps agreed to the appointment of independent arbitrators, one from each side, and to accept their verdict on the issue of leadership.

Not everyone, however, was happy with this decision. A puritanical faction inside Ali's army argued that by agreeing to arbitration, Ali had removed God from the equation. Only God had the right to decide who should rule, and disputes over such matters could not be resolved by compromise. 'Decision is God's alone,' they declared. By agreeing to arbitration, Ali had not only given up his claim to be the sole legitimate leader, but had in effect become a non-believer. The adherents of this view withdrew from Ali's army and encamped on the banks of the Nahrawan in Iraq. They came to be known as the Kharijites ('the separatists').

The Kharijites were perhaps Islam's first violent extremists, though the original source of their grievance, as in the case of Aisha, was the inequality they saw all around them, which in their view perpetuated the old ways of Mecca's age of ignorance. They were appalled at the way the Arabs, some twenty-five years after the death of Muhammad, continued to see themselves as superior to all others. This supremacy found expression in the practice of 'sponsoring' non-Arab converts to Islam, effectively turning a new convert into a client of an Arab, rather than seeing the new converts as equal citizens. This was another way for the old elite to maintain their elite status, over and above the equalizing bonds of faith. The practice, however, was abandoned throughout the Muslim Empire after 750 CE – except for one region where it operates to this day. In Saudi Arabia and in several of the Gulf states foreign workers still need to be sponsored and enjoy fewer rights compared with nationals.

The Kharijites were incensed by this practice that relegated non-Arabs to an inferior position, which they argued was against the teachings of Islam. They were equally opposed to Arab-only rule, as exemplified by the first four caliphs – three of whom had come from the same tribe, the Quraysh. What perhaps angered them more was that some supporters of Ali were now attributing to him a divine right to rule. The Kharijites believed that tribe, clan or family should play no role in choosing a leader; anyone could hold the office of caliph so long as the candidate was morally irreproachable. Moreover, the Kharijites 'did not regard it an absolute duty that there should be an *imam*', a leader with both religious and political authority. Instead, 'they separated the religious leadership of the community from the political leadership'.[8] In all their views, the Kharijites were strict and absolutists and regarded those who disagreed with them as apostates and hence liable to capital punishment.

Initially, Ali chose to ignore the Kharijites and was more concerned with the outcome of the arbitration. But the deliberations dragged on and on, often degenerating into personal abuse. On one occasion Ali's representative, the Meccan Abu Musa, shouted at Muawiya's representative: 'You are like a dog which, if you attack it, it rolls out its tongue, or, if you leave it alone, it still rolls out its tongue.' Amr responded: 'You are like a monkey which carries writings.'⁹ Not surprisingly, they were unable to resolve the dispute over leadership and suggested that a larger consultative council, as recommended earlier by Aisha, should be established to resolve the matter. But they did agree on one thing: Othman had been murdered unjustly.

Muawiya, his family and his followers considered themselves vindicated and justified in seeking justice for Othman's murder, especially against Ali and his followers, among whom were those who conspired against Othman. Muawiya declared himself to be the 'Leader of the Believers' in Syria. He also had designs on Egypt, which was being ruled, badly, by an appointee of Ali and among the conspirators involved in the murder of Othman. Muawiya appointed Amr, his representative in the arbitration, to lead an assault on Egypt. Amr succeeded, almost without a fight. He was installed as ruler of Egypt and immediately recognized Muawiya as the legitimate caliph. Ali felt obliged to march against Muawiya once again.

This time, however, Ali would be weaker, as the Kharijites were openly calling Ali and his followers apostates. To be a Muslim, they declared, is to be a perfect person with no margin for committing sin. A Muslim who commits a sin ceases to be a Muslim and becomes an apostate. The only way to deal with apostates, they said, is to put them to death. Anyone who recognized Ali's leadership therefore was guilty of sin and deserved to die. The Kharijites, who had murdered a number of Ali's followers in Kufa, now chose to march against Ali himself.

Reading how Ali chose to deal with the Kharijite threat provides useful insights into his method of tackling conflict, which was to use reason and theological argument. After he had given a sermon in which he criticized the Kharijites, they leapt up from all sides of the mosque shouting their slogan: 'Authority belongs to God alone.' One of them shouted: 'It has been revealed to you and to those who were before you that if you subscribe partners to God your deeds shall be of no avail and you will be one of those who are lost.' Ali replied: 'Bear patiently, for the promise of God is truth, and do not let those who have less certainty despise you.'[10] Ali also asked the Kharijites to explain why they considered it lawful to fight against other Muslims, but the Kharijites had only one answer: prepare to die. Ali even admitted that he had made an error of judgement. 'What is your argument against a man who suffered temptation and found in us his repentance?' 'Hasten, hasten to paradise,' the Kharijites shouted in response, and launched their attack.

The battle by the canal at Nahrawan in 658 was swift and decisive. Virtually all the Kharijites, almost to a man – all 1,500 of them, including many friends and companions of the Prophet himself – were slain in a short time. It was as if death was all they desired. While Ali could not prevent the outcome, the massacre at Nahrawan compromised his moral authority to lead the Muslim community and his support eroded further. He had lost control of the western provinces of Syria and Egypt. Those Kharijites who were not present at Nahrawan took every opportunity to undermine his rule. Finally, they succeeded in murdering him while he was praying in the mosque of Kufa. In 660, Muawiya declared himself caliph in a ceremony in Jerusalem, and established the Umayyad dynasty. The Umayyads, who belonged to the Meccan tribe of Banu Umayya (Sons of Umayya), were regarded as the city's most powerful extended family. Thus, the scion of the Meccan elite that had consistently opposed Muhammad became his successor. His mother Hind would have been proud.

Muawiya of course came from Mecca, but so did many of the Kharijites, and the events at Nahrawan traumatized most of the city. There was hardly a house not mourning the loss of a loved one. Many wore black both as a sign of mourning and as a protest against Umayyad rule. Open distaste was expressed for the Umayyad fondness for luxury and pageantry. It was both reminiscent of the extravagances of the pagan days and proof that the new rulers were adopting the habits and behaviour of the empires they had displaced.

There were frequent meetings in the Sacred Mosque, often led by the Kharijites, to plan rebellions and guerrilla warfare against the Umayyads. Muawiya tried to appease his Meccan critics by developing their city. He owned most of the urban property and clearly, by virtue of his position, had the resources to invest. He paid for the city's first brick-built house – made from baked bricks and gypsum mortar. Khadija's house was converted into a mosque. However, the Meccans wanted to know by what right Muawiya was now redeveloping their city. Had he conquered it by force or by treaty? If he had acquired the city by force, then the houses were communal property and he had no right to buy or sell them. If he had become the ruler of the city by treaty, then, and only then, could the houses be bought and sold as private property. Muawiya realized that such consistent opposition made it impossible for the city of his birth to be his capital, nor was anywhere else in the Hijaz feasible.

It meant another move for the centre of political power. Whereas Ali had made Kufa his capital, Muawiya selected Damascus, the power base from which he had earlier launched his bid for the Caliphate. He made plans to convert one of Damascus's ancient churches into a magnificent mosque to rival the Sacred Mosque in Mecca. Instead of the Kaaba, the mosque in Damascus was to be furnished with a relic of John the Baptist to give it that extra celestial appeal. The plans only intensified the anger of many Meccans. A second rebellion became inevitable.

In 680, Muawiya was succeeded by his son, Yazid I, the grandson of Abu Sufyan. A number of prominent personalities refused to give allegiance to the new Umayyad caliph. Among them were the sons and grandsons of the Prophet's closest companions who believed they had more of a right to rule, notably Abdullah ibn Zubair, grandson of Abu Bakr, and Hussain ibn Ali, the son of Ali, the fourth caliph.

The rebels made their separate ways to Mecca to seek refuge and plan their next move. It is perhaps the first evidence of Mecca acquiring the role it has played down the centuries: a sanctuary for those out of favour with the ruling powers. It was an acknowledgement of the prestige and significance of Mecca as the focal point of religion, as much as a recognition that it was a remote location, a safe distance from the real centre of political power. At one and the same time Mecca was a centre that was on the periphery.

The inhabitants of Mecca now began to gather around Ali's second son, Hussain, who decided to go to Iraq and confront Yazid, His representatives in the Iraqi city of Kufa informed Hussain he would be welcome and would find support for his struggle against Yazid. Those in Mecca who supported Hussain did not trust the people of Kufa and thought taking on the might of Yazid at this stage was not a good idea. Hussain's cousin was among those who advised against this move: 'You would be arriving in a country where there are Yazid's tax collectors and leaders. They have control of the treasuries. The population are slaves to the dirham and dinar. I could not be sure that those who had promised you their help would not fight against you.'[11] Hussain did not take his advice.

With Hussain having become a contender for the caliph's role, Abdullah ibn Zubair was not sure what to do next. His desire to be caliph had soured his relationship with Hussain. However, the two were always exceptionally polite whenever they bumped into each other in the Sacred Mosque. One morning ibn Zubair told Hussain: 'I don't know why we have left things to these people and stood idly by . . . We should be in control of this government rather than they.' Then ibn Zubair asked Hussain what he intended to do. 'By God,' Hussain replied, 'I have reflected on going to Kufa. My Shia [followers] there and the nobles of these people have written to me. I am leaving the choice to God.' Ibn Zubair replied: 'If I had the same sort of followers as you there, I would not seek any alternative other than them.' He thought for a moment and realized that Hussain might suspect his motive. 'However, if you remain in Hijaz, you could pursue this matter here without meeting any opposition.' When ibn

Zubair left, Hussain said: 'Nothing in the world would please him more than my leaving the Hijaz for Iraq. He realizes that he has no share in the matter while I am present, for people will never consider him equal to me. Therefore, he would love me to go away from here so that he can have a free hand.'[12]

Hussain, like so much of Muslim history, was rather unfair to ibn Zubair. While Hussain is venerated and volumes have been written about his life and death,[13] ibn Zubair is almost forgotten. The fact is that he had greater support among the inhabitants of Mecca, who were, on the whole, convinced that Hussain's mission was doomed. A haze of impending tragedy hung over the city. People started to weep as soon as Hussain left Mecca with his army of seventy-two soldiers.

En route to Kufa, Hussain received the news that most of his supporters there had been executed on orders of Yazid and, as he had been warned, the city's people had shifted their loyalties. His small band of followers was intercepted by Yazid's troops in the city of Kerbala, about fifty miles or two days' journey from Kufa. The Battle of Kerbala, which took place on 10 October 680, is commemorated to this day through passion plays throughout the world on the occasion of its anniversary. Plays recounting the events of the battle, often blow-by-blow accounts, together with mourning rituals, are an essential part of the religious practice of many Shia Muslims. The battle itself lasted a few hours. Hussain's soldiers were no match for Yazid and the battle ended in the massacre of Hussain's entire army and the execution of his family and children.

Most of the people killed with Hussain were from the Meccan clan of Banu Hashim. Once again the tragedy at Kerbala made Mecca the valley of weeping, the place of lament. Men cried openly in the streets, women wailed, and the entire city wore black.

Mecca now rallied around Abdullah ibn Zubair, but it was not just the Meccans who supported him. 'The politics of piety that he engaged in clearly resonated with the overwhelming majority of

Muslims' who identified with the 'mainstream values that he represented'.[14] Ibn Zubair, however, was unsure of what course to follow. It was his mother, Asma, who inspired him to openly declare a rebellion against Yazid. Asma, Aisha's sister, is another of those strong women of early Muslim history – although she is all but forgotten by earlier historians. She played an important part in the escape of her father, Abu Bakr, and the Prophet from Mecca to Medina, at a time when she was pregnant with ibn Zubair. Now a wise and courageous woman in her nineties, she had lived a life full of turmoil, violence and political terror. Her son was the first Muslim child to be born in Medina; the Prophet was present at his birth and gave him his first name: Abd-Allah, or 'Servant of God'. Her husband had been one of Aisha's principal supporters in her stand against Ali. He was killed at the Battle of the Camel. Asma sought to instil a steely determination in her son, and encouraged his considerable poetic skills. Ibn Zubair, like his father before him, had fought in Egypt and also in Khorasan, on the eastern edge of Muslim expansion. He was a skilled soldier. While he did not support the Kharijites, he agreed with their concerns. Blood lines and genealogy had nothing to do with the notion of equality in Islam. The non-Arab Muslims had to be treated equally, women's rights had to be upheld, and rulers must be pious and just. Encouraged by his mother, he declared the Umayyads unworthy and unfit to rule the Muslim community – and effectively declared Mecca an independent state. It was 683.

The caliph, Yazid, son of Muawiya, sent a regiment, well equipped with huge catapults, to suppress the rebellion. The Umayyad army surrounded Mecca and attacked by hurling projectiles at the Kaaba. A number hit the target. The Meccans were so incensed by this sacrilege that all the citizens, Kharijites and non-Kharijites alike, rallied around ibn Zubair to defend the sacred site. Women came out with swords in their hands to fight and tend to the wounded. There were several skirmishes in which the women fought bravely and forced the Umayyad soldiers to withdraw. A blazing projectile hit the

Kaaba, burning the cover and the wooden structure. Another projectile broke the Black Stone into three pieces. The whole structure was in imminent danger of collapse. The invading army, nevertheless, was kept at bay, unable to enter the city, despite constant bombardment.

After two months of siege, news came from Damascus that Caliph Yazid had died. The invading army stalled, unsure what to do next. Ibn Zubair now faced a dilemma. Should he take advantage of Yazid's death, leave the city and march against Damascus? Not merely the whole of the Hijaz but the entire Muslim Empire seemed to be openly denouncing Umayyad rule. Ibn Zubair was increasingly seen as a legitimate successor to the Caliphate. On the other hand, Mecca was in need of attention; the Kaaba was in such a dire state that 'the flight of one of its doves would be enough to make it crumble'. This is another of those 'what if' moments that I cannot avoid. I know the historian E. P. Thompson called such speculation 'horse shit' – though he wrapped it up in an extremely long and imposing-looking German word – but again and again I find myself drawn to the dilemma posed by a few hypothetical moments in early Muslim history. And why is it, do you suppose, that all my heroines and heroes turn out to be doomed, like Mecca, to the periphery of the march of history? Why do they always end up suggesting the potential the future might offer to history, rather than determining the course of events? What is it we have to wake up to in making political, social, economic choices that would allow the good ones to triumph? And that's not a hypothetical question.

If he had taken the option to eliminate the despised Umayyads, it is conceivable that ibn Zubair could have changed the course of Muslim history. Someone raised from birth under the ethos of the moral and ethical principles of the new social order would have been at the helm. Surely then it would have been possible to resolve the inner tensions between old and new ways that were deforming the development of the Muslim world. Might he not have been able to steer a course of peaceful accommodation to undercut the homicidal, yet fervently seductive, intemperate puritan fundamentalism of the Kharijites, which has echoed so dismally through time? Might he not have made Mecca all I imagined and wanted it to be as a child?

Ibn Zubair decided to devote himself to rebuilding the Sanctuary and resolutely refused to leave Mecca. What he did and did not do has left a legacy. In effect, it seems to me, his chosen priorities established the two Meccas, of the centre and the periphery, as well as of the ideal and reality. Power and political authority would remain remote from Mecca and firmly in the hands of the hereditary imperial principle. The sanctity of the religious precincts of Mecca was protected and preserved at arm's length from the pressing question of who would rule. And thus a great fissure in Muslim consciousness would endure. Down the centuries religious scholars too would be wary and keep themselves aloof from rulers and potentates of all kinds; and radicals have never found an alternative way of peaceful accommodation to nurture and realize the full agenda of the Islamic principles of civic society.

The history of Mecca records that ibn Zubair committed himself to the future by embarking on a third expansion of the enclosure of the Sacred Mosque. It had been enlarged first by Umar, the second caliph, then by his successor Othman, but still was not big enough to accommodate the increasing number of pilgrims. Ibn Zubair devoted day and night to reconstructing the devastated building. Master craftsmen from Yemen were enlisted to rebuild the foundations; stones from mountains around the city were cut into shape, and bound with mortar made of Yemenite clay. The proportions of the Kaaba were enlarged. The exterior was made more accessible by the addition of two doors set at ground level, and two windows were added to the structure. The walls of the Kaaba were polished, inside and outside, with musk and the cubic structure was covered with *Qibati*, a special cloth brought from Egypt. The pathway used for performing the circuit around the Kaaba was paved with stone. The buildings adjacent to the Sanctuary were bought and the entire enclosure was expanded, the walls repaired, and new pillared porticoes built, roofed with wood. The entire complex now had a square shape. It took nine years to complete the work. There was great rejoicing and celebrations when the work was finally finished. 'Whosoever has sworn allegiance to me,' ibn Zubair announced, 'let him perform the lesser pilgrimage, whosoever is able to make a sacrifice, than let him do so.' He sacrificed one hundred camels and distributed the meat to the poor. The citizens of Mecca competed with each other to free their slaves and offer charity.

While ibn Zubair was busy rebuilding the Sacred Mosque, the Caliphate had passed on. Yazid had left an infant son as his heir. The boy could not command support and the empire was fractured along tribal lines. When Yazid's son died, in 684, he was last in the line of descendants of Abu Sufyan. The Umayya, however, were by no means finished. They selected the oldest member of the clan, the seventy-year-old Marwan ibn Hakim, as caliph. He survived only for one turbulent year before the Caliphate passed to the strong hands of his son, Abd al-Malik ibn Marwan (reigned 685–705). A brilliant administrator, the politically astute Abd al-Malik instructed his loyal commander Al-Hajjaj ibn Yusuf al-Thaqafi to suppress the Meccan rebellion. A ruthless commander, Al-Hajjaj had already crushed resistance to the Umayyad regime in Iraq and Iran. His initial intention was to besiege Mecca and starve ibn Zubair and his followers to death. When he realized the Meccans could hold out for a considerable time, he decided to change his tactics. He advanced towards Mecca in March 692, under the guise of performing the Hajj. As soon as his troops reached the outskirts he began bombarding the city with catapults. There was a brief truce during the Hajj season – May 692 – during which the two sides made gestures of performing the pilgrimage. The fighting resumed the moment after the pilgrims departed.

The bombardment took its toll on the newly constructed Sanctuary. The Kaaba was hit so often that it became shaky and fragile. Supplies in the city were running out. Some of ibn Zubair's allies, ravaged by famine, began to abandon him. Others, like the Kharijites, whose puritanism he now found intolerable, were sent away. Rather than see the Sacred Mosque ruined again, ibn Zubair decided to open the city to the Umayyad army and sacrifice his own life. When Al-Hajjaj's troops entered the Sacred Mosque they found no one there except ibn Zubair. He was praying. Finishing his prayers, calmly ibn Zubair drew his sword and charged towards the Umayyad soldiers, killing those who dared to get close to him. A brick was hurled which struck him on the face; blood gushed forth. Momentarily shaken, he was quickly surrounded by the enemy. They attacked him ferociously and he fell to his knees. 'My wounds will not be in my heels but in front,' he exclaimed, as a soldier cut off his head. Al-Hajjaj had his body crucified, upside down, just outside the city.

The citizens gathered to view the body. A companion of the Prophet Muhammad, now fragile and blind, mourned beneath the cross – personifying the grief of the city. One of Al-Hajjaj's generals, Tariq bin Amr, looked at the body of ibn Zubair and said: 'Women have borne none manlier than he.' 'Will you praise one who disobeys the Commander of the Faithful?' Al-Hajjaj asked. 'Yes,' Tariq replied without hesitation. 'He has freed us from blame, were it not for his valour we would have no excuse. We have besieged him for seven months. He had no defensive trench, no fortress, no stronghold; yet he held his own against us as an equal, and even got the better of us whenever we met him.'[15] Most heart-rending of all, it was Asma, now well over a hundred years old, who took her son down from the cross. In life he had determined to remain in Mecca. In death she took his body to Medina, and buried him near the Prophet.

On the instruction of Caliph Abd al-Malik ibn Marwan, all traces of ibn Zubair's dedication to the sacred precincts, which had distracted him from the call of earthly power, were to be eradicated. His restoration would bear all the embellishments befitting imperial glory. Al-Hajjaj was in charge – not the most sensitive appointment as the governor of Mecca. One of the two doors to the Kaaba was walled up; the other entrance was raised so it could only be reached by those privileged few granted permission to enter. The extension built by ibn Zubair was knocked down. Everything in the Sanctuary, including the porticoes round the courtyard, was covered in gold and silver slabs. Muhammad would not have approved, but this did not seem to trouble the Umayyads. They rebuilt Mecca to flaunt their earthly power. Qusayy's old house, where the city's council used to meet, was bought by the caliph and decorated with coloured stones and mosaic. Coloured glass was imported and added to the residences of the princes, dignitaries and the rich. The dwellings of the rich were illuminated by lamps, which burned all night, casting a shadow on the Sacred Mosque. Foreign princes were invited to come and live in the city. The houses of the nobility were filled with poets, painters, craftsmen, musicians and singers. It was a quantum leap beyond anything Meccans had ever seen or experienced of worldly luxuries and comfort. Manners became relaxed. Behaviour even inside the Sacred Mosque verged towards lewdness. It became necessary to separate men and women into two processions during the performance of the circumambulation of the Kaaba.

Having erased ibn Zubair from history, the Umayyads lost interest in the Holy City. They had a widening world of glorious cities to absorb their attention. They invested time and money in Jerusalem and Damascus; they built castles and palaces in Palestine, Jordan and Syria. And there were new cities to build in the new lands they brought under their control. Al-Hajjaj, in his two years as governor of Mecca, knew only too well that the Umayyads were hated by the citizens. These offspring of the Quraysh, with justification, were seen as bloodthirsty tyrants. They were content with Mecca as a sort of showcase resort at the disposal of their expanding empire.

The Umayyad dynasty lasted a further fifty-eight years after the defeat of ibn Zubair. In all they produced thirteen caliphs in the eighty-nine years from 661 to 750. They expanded the empire, establishing Muslim rule from Spain in the west to the Indus Valley in today's Pakistan to the east and into Central Asia up to the borders of China. Yet their rule was frequently prey to internal dissension and revolt. And the caliphs themselves became bywords for indulgence and luxury.

The more pious citizens of Mecca were scandalized by the behaviour of their Umayyad leaders. The Kharijites in the city had still not given up hope of destroying the 'godless' caliphs. A growing tide of revolt against Umayyad rule was brewing not just in the Hijaz but all over the Muslim world – particularly amongst the *ajam* – 'barbarians', as non-Arab Muslims were described. The decisive revolt that eventually ended Umayyad rule began in the land of the *ajam*, Khorasan, in eastern Iran. The rebellion was led by Abu Muslim, an agitator of considerable genius, who exploited a wide variety of discontent to dethrone the Umayyads. It had been fermented and orchestrated patiently by the head of the Abbasid clan. In 750, Marwar II, the last of the Umayyad dynasty, was heavily defeated at the Battle of Zab, east of Mosul in Iraq. Abu al-Abbas Abdullah as-Saffah (r. 749–54), a member of the Abbasid family, assumed the Caliphate.

Events far from Mecca were determining the fate of the Muslim world. Yet the Abbasids were again of Meccan stock. They came from the family of the Prophet's uncle Abbas ibn Abd al-Muttalib, of the clan of Hashim, and considered themselves the true successors of Muhammad. Mecca greeted the news of the succession of a new caliph, heralding a fresh dynasty, with some relief. There were high expectations from a more sympathetic regime. But first the excesses of the Umayyads had to be accounted for, and the treatment dealt out to ibn Zubair avenged.

The new caliph, whose epithet as-Saffah means 'blood shedder', was installed at al-Hira, in Iraq. The ceremony took place in 749, and as the occasion demanded, was full of pomp and splendour. The new caliph was surrounded by his kinsmen, sitting on ornately decorated chairs. The deposed Umayyad ruling family sat on the floor, each allotted two cushions. No sooner had the ceremony finished than the caliph was informed of an unexpected visitor from Mecca. 'O Prince of Believers!' a court official whispered in as-Saffah's ear, 'there stands at your gate, seeking entrance, a man riding on a thoroughbred camel. He comes from the Hijaz. He is a Negro. His face is veiled. He would not reveal his name, nor lift his veil, unless he is in your presence.' The veiled man was ushered in. He looked at the caliph and then at the Umayyads sitting on the floor. Then he recited a poem. The verses spoke of the tyranny of the Umayyad, and the treatment of ibn Zubair. The poem urged the caliph to 'beware of an error', to 'cut the accursed tree at its root and branches', to 'mow them' and 'let thy sword save thee of this impure stock'.[16]

The poem had the intended effect. As-Saffah began to tremble with emotion. Tears rolled down his cheeks. 'Criminal brood,' he shouted at the sitting Umayyads. 'I see before me the images of my kith and kin that you have murdered. And you still breathe and enjoy life.' He signalled his Khorasani guards to take care of them. The guards beat the Umayyads, one by one, with their clubs until all of the assembled guests, including the Umayyad family, were dead. When they had finished, as-Saffah asked for a carpet to be spread over the quivering corpses. A lavish dinner was placed on the carpet; and the caliph was joined by his entourage in the meal. The veiled man slipped quietly out of the court.

The pursuit and eradication of the Umayyad family continued with thoroughness. In January 750, Marwar II al-Himar, the fourteenth and last caliph of the Umayyad dynasty, fought the last battle near the river Zab, a tributary of the Tigris east of Mosul, where he was soundly defeated by as-Saffah's uncle, Abdullah ibn Ali. A few months later, in June 750, Abdullah ibn Ali invited some eighty Umayyad princes to a banquet at his fortress in Syria, where he had been appointed as governor. As the princes took their places for the feast they were set upon and massacred. Abdullah's brother, Dawud, was appointed as governor of Mecca and Medina with special instructions to exterminate the Umayyads in the holy cities. Only one prince survived the carnage. Abd ar-Rahman (731–88), known as the Falcon of the Quraysh, made a desperate escape, wandering as a fugitive before arriving in Spain, where he carved out a new empire for himself, the Emirate of Cordoba (755). The dynasty he founded became the Umayyad Caliphate of al-Andalus.

After the blood-letting, Abbasid rule brought peace and prosperity back to Mecca. A regular stream of princes and princesses came to visit the city and perform the 'lesser pilgrimage'. The annual pilgrimage caravans from Baghdad, which the Abbasids built as their new capital in 762, were often led by the caliphs themselves, or their designated heirs. Hence the road between Baghdad and Mecca was well kept and regularly improved. Caliph as-Saffah was succeeded by his brother, al-Mansur (r. 754–75). He was leading the annual pilgrimage caravan of 754 CE when he received the news of his brother's death and his own elevation to the Caliphate. Al-Mansur was the first to totally transform the Sacred Mosque, giving it monumental proportions. He redesigned the Sanctuary geometrically. His architects used 'builder's line' to set the diagonal of the new enclosure, and build new extensions on the northern and western sides, doubling the capacity of the Sanctuary. The old council house of Qusayy, the Dar al-Nadwa, was now incorporated in the enclosure, and a minaret added on the western corner of the northern façade of the Mosque. Seven new gates were built – the Gate of Banu Jamah had three arcades beneath which ran a stream. Numerous marble pillars were also added and the interior embellished with mosaics and Quranic calligraphy.

Al-Mansur's son, Caliph al-Mahdi (r. 775–85), continued the work of his father. He performed the Hajj in October 776 CE, and issued orders for further extension and refurbishment of the Sanctuary before leaving Mecca. Two new covered arcades were added to the

Mosque, and five new gateways constructed. Special marble columns were imported from Egypt and Syria and erected in the form of a grid. The Kaaba was stripped bare, drenched in perfume, and then covered with a new specially made cover – *kiswa* – which as before was made in Egypt. When al-Mahdi returned in 780 CE to examine the work and perform another pilgrimage, he noticed that the Kaaba was not centred in relation to the Sacred Mosque. So many previous extensions had decentred the Cube. Al-Mahdi called his architects and builders. After numerous calculations, they concluded that it was not possible to have the Kaaba at the exact centre of the enclosure because of the wadi and the watercourse. 'The wadi of Mecca is subject to enormous floods and is very deep,' they told the caliph. 'We fear that if we change the present course of the wadi, the water will not flow off the way we want. And beyond the wadi bottom are so many houses and dwellings that the cost would be very high and in the end the project might not be successful.'

Al-Mahdi replied: 'It must be enlarged under any circumstances to the point where the Kaaba stands in the middle of the Sanctuary, even if I have to spend the entire treasury on it.'[17] And so the Sanctuary was enlarged again. To find the central point, spears were temporarily erected on the roofs lining the wadi, from one end to the other, and the distance between their heads was measured to allocate which proportion of the area would become part of the enclosure of the Sanctuary, and which could be left to the wadi. Then al-Mahdi climbed the mountain of Abu Qubays and observed the court of the Sanctuary. He was able to determine exactly where the Kaaba would be at the centre of the complex, and was thus able to assign the houses that had to be demolished and allocate the area to accommodate the flood course of the Wadi. The extension work started in 783, but al-Mahdi died without seeing the final outcome of his 'greatest concern'. The project was completed under the patronage of his son, Caliph Musa al-Hadi (r. 785–6). As al-Hadi was also on the verge of death – to be succeeded within a year by his brother, the famed

Harun al-Rashid (r. 786–809) – the work had to be hastened. The marble columns were replaced with stones painted over with gypsum; the roof too did not live up to the precise direction of al-Mahdi. Al-Mahdi's expansion of the Sanctuary is not only the largest, it is also acknowledged to be the most elaborate and beautiful. None who followed could match his achievement.

The Sanctuary now had 484 columns. Most had gilded bases, covered with ornaments in carved teak and gilded moulds. They were painted in different colours – in red, purple, green, buff and gold. All were decorated with Arabic inscriptions – two with particular reference to al-Mahdi, written with silver in Kufic script. There were nineteen gates, which consisted of doors to the interior court and exits from the Mosque, each decorated with mosaics. A minaret stood at the four corners of the Mosque – al-Mahdi added three to the one built by al-Mansur. They were crowned with crenels. The interior of the Mosque had 272 crenels, stucco window decorations, and arched openings decorated with stucco relief and iron railings. Two new ceilings had been added: the upper ceiling of Dum wood from Yemen, and the lower in beautiful teak decorated with Quranic inscriptions, prayers of the Prophet, and prayers for the Caliph al-Mahdi himself. Specific areas within the compound, like the station of Abraham, were given special attention, and embellished with gold. The surrounds to the doorway of the Kaaba were also dressed in ornamental gold sheets. The Sanctuary – or the Haram as it is called – now had a distinctive and instantly recognizable identity. Both its interior and exterior became iconic symbols of Mecca and Islam. Not the image in the very first picture I ever saw, but its contemporary equivalent.

It was not just the Sanctuary that was transformed. Mecca too changed. It became a rich, cosmopolitan city. The Abbasids felt uneasy in Medina, where the descendants of Ali continued to live, and to claim their right to rule. An insurrection of the partisans (Shia) of Ali against the Abbasids had already taken place in Medina during

762. So they lavished their attention on Mecca, their ancestral home. The caliphs came with largesse, generously distributed amongst the inhabitants of Mecca and the visiting pilgrims. Al-Mahdi, for example, is said to have distributed 30 million dirhams, along with 150,000 garments, on his first visit to Mecca. Caravans from Baghdad, Damascus, Cairo and Khorasan brought not just pilgrims but also alms and gifts. Almost every year one of the city's squares would be adorned with a special gift. One year, Baghdad sent a throne that had belonged to the king of Kabul. The next year a statue of gold, seated on a square silver throne upon a silk carpet decorated with small gold and silver bells, was sent from China. It belonged to the king of Tibet, who after embracing Islam, sent the idol to Mecca as a present to its citizens.

A regular visitor to the city was Princess Zubaidah, the grand-daughter of al-Mansur, and the wife of Harun al-Rashid. She initiated and supervised a huge project to provide a permanent and reliable source of water for the city. It involved building underground aqueducts that brought water from the Spring of Hunayn – some twelve miles east on the road to Taif – and other sources to Mecca. The project was completed in 810 and cost an estimated 1.75 million dinars. Or, as Zubaidah herself put it: a gold dinar for every stroke of the pickaxe. She went on to build an open waterwork at Arafat – named after her, the Spring of Zubaidah – and adorned the city with a number of fountains.

The Abbasid period, described by some historians as an intellectual and cultural 'revolution',[18] saw literature, philosophy, theology and natural sciences all flourish, with fertilizing influences coming from Persia, India and the Hellenistic world. There was a strong accent on travel in search of knowledge and scholarship. Not surprisingly, given its status, and the qualitative improvements in roads and other facilities for travellers, Mecca was often the first port of call for the itinerant scholars. The indigenous population of the city was not more than a few thousand. Their numbers were swelled by a constant stream of visitors, who could all be distinguished by their dress. The Abbasids, along with their officials and administrators, wore black garments. Originally, black was the colour of the Kharijites, other pietists and the followers of Ali – the Shia – who wore black either in protest or as a sign of mourning for the Battle of Kerbala. By appropriating black the Abbasids hoped both to domesticate dissent and to keep an eye on the dissenters. The dissenters and the partisans of Ali were forced to wear green coats and turbans. Ordinary folk mostly wore white. The scholars and seekers of knowledge favoured large turbans, wide sleeves to their coats and scarves across their shoulders. Dress spoke status, profession, even ideological and political inclination.

The scholars, easily identified on the streets of Mecca, were eagerly sought. Discourses would be held in various squares of the city. The Sanctuary, always a place of worship, also became a site of learning. Scholars, travellers, mystics – all kinds of learned men came here to give or listen to sermons and lectures. Some even walked for hundreds of miles, from the Nile or North Africa, Persia and India, to perform the Hajj and then stayed on for a few years to learn or teach. Some never left.

It was an era when the traditions of the Prophet Muhammad were being collected and Islamic law was canonized. Imam Bukhari, the great collector of the sayings of the Prophet Muhammad – the hadith – was a noted visitor to the city. Born in Bukhara, in Central Asia, in 810, he came to Mecca with his brother and widowed mother at the age of sixteen to perform the pilgrimage. He stayed for a number of years before moving on to other centres of learning in the Abbasid Empire. No doubt many of the hadith in his canonical collection, *Sahih Bukhari*, were collected in Mecca.

The founders of two of the four schools of Islamic law could also be seen in the city. Imam Muhammad ibn Idris Shafii, who established the Shafi school, had a special section of the Sanctuary reserved for him. Born in Gaza in 767, he belonged to the Quraysh and traced his lineage back to Abd al-Muttalib, the grandfather of the Prophet. His father died when he was very young, leaving his Yemeni mother to bring him up. She decided that he belonged in his ancestral home, and sent him to Mecca when he was about ten to live with a relative. By the time he was twenty, Shafii, who lived the life of an ascetic, had become renowned in Mecca for his learning and his keen sense of justice. A moderate, not afraid to make an error, he disliked theology and theologians. Also visible in the city was Shafii's student Ahmad ibn Hanbal, founder of the Hanbali school of law. Although an Arab, he was born in central Asia in 780, and settled in Baghdad. A devout man, ibn Hanbal was persecuted for his views on the Qur'an by the Abbasid Caliph al-Mamun (r. 813–33). He spent his later years in Mecca before returning to Baghdad, where he died in 855. It was about the same time that Mecca produced its one and only historian of repute, al-Azraqi, the author of *Meccan Reports* (*Akhbār Makkah*), who we met in chapter 1.

It was not just the scholars who were drawn to Mecca. The city was also a magnet for mystics on special missions: to illuminate their hearts with the 'radiant lustre' of the Prophet. They came to meditate in and around Mecca and live the life of ascetics. Unlike other visitors, who could be distinguished by their dress, the mystics were not easy to spot. The man 'dressed pitifully', wandering aimlessly in the streets of the city with a crescent-shaped comb in his hand, offering to comb the hair of passers-by, might be the great mystic Mansur al-Hallaj. He was born in 858 in Fars, Persia, and made three trips to Mecca, each time staying in the city for up to a year. On one occasion, it is said, the inhabitants of Mecca took pity on his tattered condition and offered him some cast-off robes. He returned the garments reciting the verse:

> If you have met me tonight in clothing
> which is doubly that of poverty,
> Be assured that by being threadbare on my back
> this clothing has bestowed on me
> the most generous Freedom.[19]

It is unlikely that the city's inhabitants, locals or visitors, were impressed by the heterodox views of Mansur. He believed in union with God and was in the habit of losing himself in mystical intro-spection. While in this state, he would declare: 'I am the Truth.' This declaration eventually led to his long trial and imprisonment in Baghdad, culminating in his execution by the order of the orthodox jurists in March 922.

The carpenter mending a house in the poorer part of the city might describe himself as a *zahid* (ascetic worshipper), but his real name could be Sultan Ibrahim bin Adham (*c.* 730–77). A former king of Balkh, in Persia, Ibrahim was given a mirror while seated on his throne. 'I looked in it,' he is reported to have said. 'I saw only a wayfarer toward the tomb, bound for a place where there would be no friend to cheer me. I saw a long journey stretching before me, for which I had no provision. I saw a Just Judge, and myself unprovided with any proof for my ordeal. My royalty became distasteful in that moment.'[20] Ibrahim gave up his throne to live the life of a mystic and spent considerable time wandering the streets of Mecca. Another former prince in the city, frequently seen begging near the Sanctuary, was the famous Persian Sufi Bayazid Bastami (804–74), nicknamed 'the splendid beggar'. Bayazid was perpetually in a state of trance during which he made the most unmentionable – but allegedly mysti-cal – utterances: 'Glory be to me!'; 'There is no one in my garment except God';[21] and 'I am I, there is no God but I, so worship me!' Another mystic apparently meandering aimlessly in the city was Rabiah al-Adawiyah (713–801), who first entered the city by drag-ging herself all the way from Arafat to the Kaaba. Later, she lived a hermit's life in the nearby desert, existing on a meagre vegetarian diet.[22] On the whole, the Meccans paid very little attention to the mystics in their midst. Such people, however, were to become tower-ing figures in the annals of Sufism, the mystical tradition of Islam.

While Mecca had become a cosmopolitan city, brimming with theologians, historians, mystics and travellers and vibrant with debate and discussion, something important was conspicuously absent: philosophy. Hardly any philosopher of repute visited the city from Baghdad, the centre of Muslim thought and learning, or from Muslim Spain, where the last surviving Umayyad prince had founded his own Caliphate and transformed the region into a highly sophisticated and cultured civilization. In sharp contrast, Mecca was a haven for anti-rationalists. This was partly due to the influence of the puritans, the Kharijites and other conservatives who were obsessed with keeping Islam 'pure' and uncontaminated by what they called *bida* (often translated in English as 'innovation'), or the influence of foreign thought and ideas. Partly, it was the city's way of showing dissent and standing up to Baghdad, where philosophy and rationalism were not only in vogue but positively enforced as state creed. Indeed, the Abbasids 'made reason the sole basis of truth and reality and thus identified the sphere of philosophy with that of religion'.[23] The Meccans saw this as placing Islam, a revealed religion, on a par with philosophy, a product of human reasoning. It was almost as bad as associating partners with God.

Mecca's distaste for philosophy was strengthened by the *Mihna*, which also established the reputation of Ahmad ibn Hanbal as the greatest traditionalist of his time. The *Mihna* was an attempt by the Abbasid Caliph al-Mamun to impose his own theological views on his subjects. Al-Mamun, a rationalist and champion of Greek philosophy, was a highly learned and sophisticated liberal man credited with promoting thought and learning in Muslim civilization. An accomplished scholar of the Qur'an and the traditions of the Prophet Muhammad, it is said that he used to complete thirty-three recitations of the Qur'an during Ramadan. Yet this ruler who nurtured and shaped one of the richest and most fertile periods of scientific and philosophic development in human history also initiated what comes closest to the Spanish Inquisition in Islamic history. The term *Mihna* means 'testing' or 'trial'; it consisted of a series of letters written by al-Mamun to his *qadis* (judges), administrators and noted scholars, thinkers and personalities of the time in which the caliph asked a specific question. All Muslims, whatever their persuasion, agreed that the Qur'an was the unadulterated Word of God. What al-Mamun wanted to know was whether the Qur'an was created or uncreated. As a rationalist, the caliph himself believed that the Qur'an was created. Indeed, to see the Qur'an as the uncreated Word of God, he argued, was a form of spiritual tyranny that closed minds to intellectual inquiry, rational thought and philosophy. But in attempting to overturn a form of spiritual tyranny, al-Mamun himself turned tyrant. Those who gave the wrong answer faced imprisonment, flogging, dismissal from public office, even torture.

Al-Mamun's main target was a specific group of pious-minded jurists who described themselves as *Ahl al-Hadith* (People of the Hadith, or Hadith folk) and regarded the traditions of the Prophet Muhammad as the chief source of religious authority. Exceptionally conservative, they were devoted to shaping Islamic Law, or the Shariah, and argued that the Qur'an and the example of the Prophet were 'alone enough to allow a community of human beings to achieve a life of unmediated responsibility to God. This could be felt to be so if God could be found truly unmediated in the Law itself.'[24] Hence their doctrine that the Qur'an was God's eternal speech, and the Muslim community needed not reasoning but His Law, as illustrated in the sayings and actions of Muhammad. The Hadith folk stressed the importance of moral rigour, 'more emotional than intellectual',[25] and saw the attempts to rationalize their faith as an insult to God's power. Al-Mamun saw their position as obscurantist, with serious implications for the culture and civilization of Islam.

Ahmad ibn Hanbal was amongst a group of thirty-odd jurists to be brought in front of an official in Baghdad. After hearing the caliph's letter, the scholars tried to fudge the issue and pretended to be uncommitted. 'The Qur'an is God's word,' they said. When pressed further, they added: 'God is the creator of everything.' 'Is not the Qur'an a thing?' they were asked. There followed a discussion on what is a thing. 'All things apart from God are created,' they finally concluded. But this still did not answer the specific question, and they were further pressed. Clearly, they replied in unison, 'the Caliph has heard what we have not heard, and knows what we do not know'.[26] Ibn Hanbal was one of the two scholars who stated their views clearly. 'If I remained silent and you remained silent, then who will teach the ignorant?' he declared. The official faithfully reported the answers to the caliph, who ordered that ibn Hanbal should be brought before him, in chains, to defend his view. But for one reason or another, the audience with the caliph never took place. Ahmad ibn Hanbal spent twenty-eight months in prison. The *Mihna* continued after al-Mamun's death under his successors al-Mutasim (r. 833–42) and al-Wathiq (r. 842–7), and was finally ended in 861, after sixteen inglorious years.

In Mecca, the *Mihna* was seen as a titanic struggle between corrupt rationalists in hock to the state and independent God-fearing traditionalists. There was some justification for this view. While the rationalists were indeed very learned, valued philosophy and advocated freedom of thought, they also tended, on the whole, to be self-indulgent and pleasure-loving. The philosophers preached the gospel of freedom, it was thought, because they saw law and religion as an inconvenience, something that stopped them behaving as they wished. It did not help that these champions of free thought were, by and large, part of the state's apparatus or aligned with the state and its policies. The traditionalists, on the other hand, were exceptionally pious, or at least were seen as such. Ahmad ibn Hanbal, for example, demonstrated exemplary humility and contentment and a strong sense of justice and fairness. He was devoted to common people – who were looked down upon by the rationalists and the philosophers. Indeed, in the first letter of *Mihna* Caliph al-Mamun described ordinary men and women as 'insignificant', 'vulgar', folk who 'are without insight and deep reflection'[27] and do not know how to reason. In sharp contrast to the philosophers and rationalists, the traditionalists were devoted to the very things that ordinary people cherished: God, the Prophet, the Qur'an, the Traditions and examples of the Prophet, and equality of and for all. Indeed, ibn Hanbal even refused compensation for his unjust treatment and objected to his family receiving a stipend from the state.

Mecca adored the pious jurists. They could do or say no wrong. And their work on the principles of Islamic jurisprudence – *fiqh* – was idolized and eagerly studied. Shafii, who stayed in Mecca for nine years, taught his students to reject logical deduction, and steer well clear of philosophy and rational conjecture. Logical theology, he declared, was useless. Analogy was the only device that could be used to develop Islamic law; everything had to be deduced by analogy from the primary sources, the Qur'an in the first instance, but mostly the traditions of the Prophet. Ibn Hanbal taught that the opinions of the companions of the Prophet – the *tabeen* – had to be respected and followed. If the opinions of the successors of the Prophet differed, then all different opinions had to be considered valid. Imitation (*taqlid*) of the companions of the Prophet, and their successors, and the successors of the successors, was to become the norm in all matters of religion; innovation (*bida*) was to be shunned.

The veneration of the pious jurists and their tradition in Mecca had profound consequences. It set in motion the rise of the religious scholars as the undisputed authority on questions of theology and law. Pilgrims and visitors to Mecca were regaled with the stories of the piety of the jurists and returned to the various parts of the Muslim world with an uncritical love of religious scholars and tradition, and an equal distaste for philosophy, reason and speculation. Mecca became a bastion of tradition and traditionalism, in particular of the strict and ultra-conservative Hanbali school of thought. No one who lived in the city for a few months could be immune from its influence – an influence that has survived for over fourteen centuries.

And something else happened in Mecca that raised the place beyond terrestrial confines. All the suffering, the bloodshed, the sieges and rebellions the city had endured encouraged its inhabitants to feel extra-special. Mecca had to be much more than simply a city of pilgrimage, the birthplace of the Prophet of Islam and the citadel of tradition. Indeed, even the accolade of being the city where the House of God was first built was not enough. It had to be a city created not on earth but in Heaven: right at the origin of creation.

So it was that Mecca developed a new myth for itself. It began as an allegory, an interpretation of the story of Adam's fall from paradise as it appears in the Qur'an. God creates Adam, and asks him and his wife to live in the Garden of Eden. 'Both of you eat whatever you like, but do not go near this tree or you will become wrongdoers,' they are told.[28] But Satan deceives them; he lures them with lies. 'Their nakedness became exposed to them when they had eaten from the tree: they began to put together leaves from the Garden to cover themselves. Their Lord called to them: "Did I not warn you that Satan was your sworn enemy?" They replied: "Our Lord, we have wronged our souls: if You do not forgive us and have mercy, we shall be lost."' So Adam and his wife are cast out of the Garden of Eden and sent to earth, 'where they have a place to stay and livelihood – for a time'. 'There', says God, 'you will live; there you will die; from there you will be brought out.'[29]

But where on earth did Adam go after being thrown out of paradise? The Meccans had a specific answer. As reported by the historian al-Tabari, Adam fell to earth on a Friday as the sun was setting and found himself on Mount Budh, either in India or Ceylon. He missed what he used to hear from angels in paradise, and he felt lonely. He said: 'My Lord! Does this earth of yours have no one but me to live there and praise and sanctify you?' God said:

I shall have some of your children praise and sanctify Me on it. I shall have houses raised for mentioning Me on it, houses in which My creatures will give praise and mention My name and call it My House. I shall have one of those houses singled out for my generosity and distinguish it from all others by my name and call it My House. I shall have it proclaim My Greatness, and it is upon it that I have placed My majesty. Then, in addition, I, being in everything and together with everything, shall make that House a safe sanctuary whose sacredness will extend to those around, those underneath, and those above it. He who makes it sacred with My sacredness obligates Me to be generous to him. He who frightens its inhabitants there forfeits My protection and violates My sacredness. I shall have it be the first house to be founded as a blessing for mankind in the valley of Mecca. They will come to it dishevelled and covered with dust . . . shouting emotionally: At Your service! Shedding copious tears and noisily proclaiming *Allah o Akbar* [God is Great] . . . You shall dwell there Adam as long as you live. Then the nations, generations and prophets of your children shall live there, one nation after the other, one generation after the other.[30]

Adam was then commanded to go to the Sacred House, which was cast down from paradise to earth, and asked to circumambulate it, just as he had seen angels circumambulate God's Throne. The Black Stone, which was originally white, was also brought down for him. He was assisted by an angel on his journey towards Mecca. 'Whenever Adam passed by a meadow or a place that he liked, he would say to the angel: Let us stop here! And the angel would say: Please do! This went on until they reached Mecca. Every place where he stopped became cultivated land; and every place he bypassed became a desolate desert.'[31] On arriving in the valley of Mecca, Adam constructed the House. After circumambulating the House, he wandered into the wilderness of Arafat and performed all the rites of the pilgrimage. When he had finished, the angel said to him: You have performed the pilgrimage faultlessly. This surprised him. Noting his surprise, the angel said: 'Adam! We have performed the pilgrimage to this House two thousand years before you were created.'[32] Adam felt chastised.

The House was a reflection of God's Throne on earth. In the plain at Arafat, Adam was reunited with his wife. The couple lived in the vicinity of Mecca with their children. Adam died in Mecca, and is buried in a cave beneath Abu Qubays, the highest mountain of the Meccan region, by his pious son, Seth. His wife is buried in Jeddah.

In the allegory, Mecca represents the Divine Throne on earth. Just as the angels go round and round in prayer about the Throne of God in Heaven, so men go round and round the Kaaba on earth. Mecca is a reflection of Heaven; it is not just a way to paradise but paradise on earth. It may be located in a 'barren valley' but its real essence is elsewhere. Mecca is not simply a city but a metaphysical idea: that is why the angels have been performing the pilgrimage to the Sanctuary since even before Adam was created.

The allegory became the official creed and was exported enthusiastically. The Meccans took great pride in relating it to the visitors to the city – pilgrims, scholars, students and itinerant travellers. The allegory spread far and wide. For Muslims everywhere, Mecca had now become the primordial city, a place to taste paradise before death, a magnet drawing the very soul of every believer.

4

Sharifs, Sultans and Sectarians

The process of elevating Mecca to paranormal realms took at least two centuries after the birth of Islam. Mecca came to be seen not just as a source of correct Islamic doctrine and conduct, but as a heavenly place where everything, good or bad, was blessed. Of course, certain things from Mecca had always been considered blessed: the water of Zamzam, the spring that gushed forth at God's command in the barren valley to succour Hagar and Ishmael in their distress, was self-evidently a divine blessing. The Kaaba symbolized the focus of worshipful faith. But it would be a short step before this building and anything associated with it would be seen as having magical powers. Pieces of the embroidered cloth that cover the Kaaba were sold to the rich, but given free to the poor. And before long anything remotely associated with Mecca – a relic, a book, a local product – was treated with veneration. Even the soil and dirt from the city today are considered sacred and valuable.

Such elevation of Mecca raised complex questions. For example, who would decide what was or was not holy; who would decide the rules for coming and going into the city? Pilgrims would happily destroy the relics or goods they had acquired in Mecca if they feared that they might fall into the hands of non-Muslims. Some even thought that any contact with non-Muslims would invalidate their visit to Mecca and lead to contamination of some form. Not that there were any non-Muslims in Mecca; they had already been barred from the city. Jews and Christians were prohibited from entering Mecca and Medina by Muawiya, the first Umayyad caliph.

The more I think about this far-reaching decision the more I wonder if it was the outcome of a subtle Orwellian process. Was this son of Abu Sufyan and Hind, Muhammad's twin tormentors and guardian of Meccan tradition, looking for a way to institutionalize what his parents had always wanted? This idea of Meccan superiority refused to disappear when Muslim rule expanded rapidly beyond Arabia. It was evident in the client status of the new converts and the isolation of the Arab Muslim armies in garrison camps. However, the closing of Mecca was in stark contrast with practice elsewhere. The original community founded by Muhammad in Medina had been a multi-religious community comprising Muslims, Jews, Christians and pagans. This kind of heterodoxy helped to maintain Islam's great cities. Indeed, echoes can still be seen in Baghdad, Damascus, Cairo, Marrakesh, Cordoba and Tehran today. Mecca, however, was different. The closure of the city that was the portal of paradise to all but Muslims implied that paradise was the exclusive possession of Muslims.

Thus the open and inclusive message preached by Muhammad acquired new connotations. Islam became an exclusive possession of the faithful. The alternative sense of Islam as a set of values by which all human beings and their works are to be judged never disappeared; it merely became a secondary addendum to the ethos exemplified by Mecca. The negative consequences of this way of thinking are alive and well to this day. Considering how bad a press the Umayyads have received, especially among religious scholars, it is interesting that their particular legacy in closing Mecca to non-Muslims, which presages a certain closing of the Muslim mind, is never questioned, even today. Though, it must be said, making this facsimile of paradise on earth forbidden fruit has made it a source of irresistible fascination and an endless temptation to non-Muslim adventurers down the years, as we shall see later.

Various groups and sects, jostling for power and position in the city, sought to stamp their mark on Mecca, laying an exclusive claim to the paradisiacal authenticity Mecca conferred. Each sect had its own place within the Sacred Mosque, where it prayed behind its own imam or leader. After prayers, devotees would sit in front of a lamp, identified by the colour of their sect, listening to sermons and lectures extolling the particular virtues of their particular group. By the end of the ninth century, the four schools of law had become established, and the old idea that 'only what was stored in memory was truly known'[1] had been replaced with new emphasis on writing down hadith and legal judgements. The space near the Station of Abraham was reserved for the followers of Shafii. Other places were marked out for the supporters of ibn Hanbal, the hero of the *Mihna*; Abu Hanifa (699–767), founder of the Hanafi school; and Malik bin Anas (711–95), the teacher of Shafii and founder of the Maliki school. The partisans of Ali, who were collectively known as the Alids, later to be known as Shia, and miscellaneous other groups that had organized in secret opposition to Abbasid rule, some with violent tendencies, had their own specific places in the Sacred Mosque.

It was not unusual for different sects to overstep their territory, or abuse or challenge others, leading to serious disputes. Sanctity has never been insurance against the depredations of the sanctimonious, a sad truth and by no means exclusive to Islam. Around the Sacred Mosque, which had been battered by the dynastic battles over succession, full-scale brawls and fist fights over spiritual verities were not uncommon. On a number of occasions, the quarrels between different sects became so serious that the gates of the Sanctuary had to be closed to stop brawling groups from entering. During the Hajj season, every sect will have wanted to attract the attention of the pilgrims, as potential followers and ambassadors to carry their teachings to other parts of the Muslim world.

More than ever in their long history, Meccans came to see pilgrims as a religious as well as an economic resource. 'We sow not wheat or sorghum, the pilgrims are our crops'[2] is an old local saying that must have emerged during this period. Other cities, such as the port of Jeddah, received traders all the year round; and Medina, where the tomb of the Prophet is located, had a constant stream of visitors. But Mecca depended almost entirely on large numbers of pilgrims arriving at a particular time of the year. The pilgrims brought not just religious fervour but much-needed commodities for the city's permanent inhabitants and for pilgrims. Poorer pilgrims might bring some artefact or product from home to trade to offset the expense of making the journey to Mecca. Or, en route to Mecca, they might buy crafts and utensils from villagers and Bedouins to sell for profit in the city's bazaar. As well as supplies, the city pilgrims also had to bring their own basic necessities with them: honey, butter, oil, olives, rice and wheat, the sole exception being meat, which they bought in Mecca. For most of the year, the people of Mecca lived on what they bought and from the income they accumulated from pilgrims. During the Hajj itself, around half the inhabitants of the city acted as hosts and guides to the pilgrims while others looked after the Sanctuary, living off the pilgrims' largesse.

The city's population would swell several-fold during the Hajj season, which meant that Mecca had to supply other essentials that pilgrims could not provide for themselves, such as water. Not only had thirsts to be quenched, but every act of the five daily prayers had to be preceded by *wudu*, the ritually required washing that is distinct and additional to all normal ablutions. Water was a perpetual problem for Mecca, always in short supply during the Hajj season. Yet the city was also prone to frequent flooding, a concern for all who undertook alterations to the Sacred Mosque as far back as the very first works undertaken by Caliph Umar in 638. Indeed, flooding became such a problem that the Abbasid Caliph al-Mutadid (r. 892–902) ordered that the course of the wadi should be cleared out completely so that, instead of entering the Sanctuary, the flood waters would flow cleanly through the wadi. The work led to another renovation and expansion of the Sanctuary area.

The Hajj, however, was not a source of income for Mecca alone. It provided a lucrative supply of revenue for bandits and for Bedouins too, who would frequently attack and loot pilgrim caravans. The journey to Mecca began wherever Muslims lived, but caravan routes to Mecca coalesced at three main hubs where pilgrims would gather in large numbers to commence the final stage of the journey. For example, pilgrims from North and Northwest Africa joined the caravan in Cairo, thence to set off across the Sinai Peninsula, following the coastal plain and reaching Mecca in about forty days. A second great caravan assembled in Damascus, moving south via Medina and reaching Mecca in roughly thirty days. The third caravan crossed the Arabian Peninsula from Baghdad. These caravans were like small cities on the move: all human life, and all that life required, was there. Apart from transport, there were traders who managed general stores; medical facilities were available; learned men were on hand to instruct pilgrims in the many different religious rites; mystics and scholars searching for gnosis and knowledge abounded and there were musicians, singers, and all variety of entertainers. Most important of all, from the marauder perspective, there were precious goods – spices, cloth, jewellery – sent by caliphs and sultans, either as presents for Mecca or to be sold for profit in the city. Not surprisingly, such a lure was an urgent temptation, so much so that it was not unknown for caravans to pillage each other.

Indeed, towards the end of the ninth century, midway through Abbasid rule, one religious sect, the Qarmatians, made a point of attacking caravans and succeeded in inflicting humiliation and bloodshed on the Holy City. Like the Kharijites before them, the Qarmatians (also known as Carmatians) emerged as a social reform movement among Ismailis around 870 in Syria and Mesopotamia, embracing a radical agenda motivated 'as much from the social discontent of the times as from their religious message',[3] but just like their predecessors they soon degenerated into an extremist cult. What is it about visions of paradise that turns minds hellish? This enduring human conundrum is neither a hypothetical question nor one exclusive to Islam. The Qarmatians opposed the luxuries and excesses of the Abbasid Caliphate. Where the Umayyads had been a byword for adopting the excesses of Hellenized Syria, the Abbasids adopted the imperial panoply of the Sassanian court that once ruled the Persian Empire from Ctesiphon. The ruins of that city were adjacent to Baghdad, the new capital the Abbasids founded in 762. The Qarmatians were determined to undermine the Abbasids and 'felt that the old way of life was to be swept away, the privileged classes overthrown, and pure justice was to reign'.[4]

The movement was named after Hamdan Qarmat, who in 894 established a state that extended from Kufa in Iraq around the coastal areas of southern Iraq and eastern Arabia to Bahrain. With their capital in Hajr, the main city of Bahrain, the Qarmatians set about creating what they hoped would be a utopian society. For example their state was organized on egalitarian principles, with shared property and an interest-free economy. Land and property were distributed equally amongst citizens, and no one paid any taxes. If anyone became poor or fell into debt, the state treasury would step in to provide support with interest-free loans. The people elected their leader, the imam, and an advisory council of six viziers, who made political decisions by consultation. Workers were organized into guilds. Most of the citizens were strictly vegetarian, which is why the cult is sometimes known as 'the greengrocers'. They attracted the urban young, who were trained in special boot camps and instilled with a revolutionary fervour.

We read of a pious mother who went out to the desert camps to reclaim her son, who had joined the rebels. She was horrified at the defiant atmosphere of the camps, egalitarian, consciously rejecting the proprieties of established society – and demanding rigid conformity to its revolutionary norms. The emancipated son made a point of his toughness and cruelty, showing no acknowledgement of a mother's dues; the mother disowned him and returned full of denunciations of the Qarmatians.[5]

While the Qarmatians were great believers in equality and reason, they were, as is usual with utopians, messianic in their outlook. They believed in the imminent arrival of the Mahdi, the Promised Messiah. A strong militaristic and religious state was a necessary precursor to prepare for his arrival. While waiting for the promised Mahdi, they became followers of Ubaydallah al-Mahdi (r. 909–34), the founder of the Fatimid Caliphate in North Africa, whose teachings they preached fervently. History, they believed, repeated itself constantly in cycles.

When one examines what people have done in the name of religion, I find myself thinking we are indeed trapped in 'Groundhog Day', as in the title of the 1993 film starring Bill Murray, who constantly relives one day until he learns that to break out he must reform himself. If only life really imitated art. Instead consider all the sectarian and messianic movements down the ages and across religions who repeat the same repertoire of themes and ideas and, no matter how noble their ideals, end badly. Messianic fervour easily turns to violent action, totalitarian imposition and intolerance towards all who do not embrace their worldview. And invariably they challenge and often fall victim to the violent retribution of the society in which they exist. Think of the Diggers, the Muggletonians, the Anabaptists and the Levellers, the Nonconformist sects spawned by religious fervour in the aftermath of the English Civil War (1649–88).[6] Opposed to the established religion as well as to the corruption and tyranny of monarchy, their agenda for social reform was in many ways remarkably similar to that of the Qarmatians and produced its own tale of bloodshed and oppression.

The Qarmatian cult became an esoteric society, though their initiation rites, which all newcomers had to go through, were not secret. Indeed, one could argue that the Qarmatians were the first communist state in history, and also one that developed strong Stalinist tendencies. They instigated a reign of terror in Kufa that endured for almost a century. They threatened Baghdad itself, but the Abbasid generals were just about able to hold them off. However, it is for what they did in and to Mecca that they are remembered most.

The Qarmatians believed that pilgrimage to Mecca was a pagan practice. Once they had consolidated their power in eastern Arabia, they formed alliances with Bedouin tribes and began raiding pilgrim caravans. Throughout the first decades of the tenth century, they harassed the Iraqi Hajj caravans. In 906 they ambushed the Hajj caravan from Baghdad and massacred an estimated 20,000 pilgrims. In the following decades the caravans from Baghdad seldom managed to arrive in the Holy City without being looted. The caravan of 925 failed to reach Mecca altogether. Traffic from Baghdad virtually ceased because of Qarmatian terror.

Then, in January 930, under the leadership of Abu Tahir al-Qarmati, the Qarmatians attacked Mecca itself. It was the Hajj season and the city was full of pilgrims who were taken by surprise. What happened next is described by the nineteenth-century Ottoman historian Qutb al-Din:

> They entered armed and on horseback into the Haram [the Sanctuary], putting those circumambulating to the sword – all those praying and in the state of *ihram* [dressed for pilgrimage] being weaponless in their sanctified condition – and in the end they killed altogether about 30,000 people in the Haram, in Mecca and in the ravines around the city . . . Abu Tahir drunkenly charged with his sword drawn in his hand and halted before the Noble House [the Kaaba], where his horse dropped dung and urinated . . . The well of Zamzam and all the other wells and pits of Mecca were filled to overflowing with the remains of the martyrs. Abu Tahir went to the venerated door of the Kaaba and tore it out while he

cried: 'It's me, by God, and by God it's me. He creates and I exterminate them.' Then he shouted at the pilgrims: 'You asses! You say
that whosoever enters here shall be secure [Qur'an 3. 97]. So where
is the security when we have done what we have done?' A man
who chose martyrdom by giving himself up to be killed seized the
bridle of Abu Tahir's horse and said: 'The meaning of that honourable verse is not what you have mentioned, but rather that
whosoever enters it, give him security.' At that Abu Tahir turned
his horse away from him and paid no heed.[7]

The Qarmatians stayed in Mecca for eleven days, during which
they removed the dome that covers the well of Zamzam and ransacked
the treasury. When they left they took the Black Stone with them. It
was twenty years before it was returned, in 951, broken into pieces.
According to some accounts the split was into seven pieces, a coded
reference to the seven imams recognized by the Ismaili sects. Abu
Tahir is said to have died a most terrible death: 'Afflicted with gangre-
nous sores, his flesh was eaten away by worms.'[8] The valley of Mecca
neither wept nor lamented for him.

The massacre and desecration of the Sacred Mosque sent shockwaves throughout the Muslim world. Yet it was symptomatic of the
turbulence, disputes and rival claims, religious as well as political,
that Muslims found themselves embroiled in. There is a deep irony in
this situation because the Abbasid period is seen as a phase of consol-
idation. It was the era in which the characteristic institutions and
customary practices of Muslim society emerged, setting off enormous achievements. It meant there was an underlying familiarity
that allowed a Muslim to travel from one end of the known world to
the other with a sense of belonging and communality. It is a pattern
that endures to this day; one I have experienced in all my travels
around a Muslim world now divided into very different nation states.

This was also the era of a great intellectual flowering, which inaugurated the Golden Age of Muslim civilization, as remarkable and

expansive as the territorial explosion of Muslim society. Arabic was not only the language of the Recitation, of religious worship. In 696 it was declared the language of empire, of government and administration. All across the Muslim world it became the common language of ideas and learning, as much for non-Muslims as Muslims. Caliph al-Mamun is credited with founding the Bayt al Hikma, the House of Wisdom, in Baghdad, around 813 CE. It gathered manuscripts from far and wide and translated the learning of Persia, Greece and India into Arabic. Paper-making, learned from the Chinese, ensured that 'the community of The Book', as the Muslims like to describe themselves, became a civilization of books. A paper factory was established in Baghdad in 793 CE. Free libraries, with collections numbering in the hundreds of thousands of texts, became common features of Muslim cities. Scientific and learned societies proliferated. It was the age of the great polymaths, towering names in the history of ideas who contributed to the development of many branches of science, mathematics, medicine and philosophy. Technological advances saw marvellous machines and the development of new industries; there was an agricultural revolution with new developments in irrigation which enabled crops to be transplanted from one end of the empire to the other.[9]

A free public hospital, in the form we would recognize today, was founded in Baghdad in 806, where medicine and pharmacology were taught. It was copied by other cities. And gradually centres of higher education emerged where this new learning was disseminated. They became the model for Europe's early universities.[10] They were to be found in cities as far from Baghdad as Cordoba, founded in 970, and Timbuktu, founded in 989. A theory and practice of jurisprudence developed that could be worked by and through the diverse schools of law, despite their contentious differences. This culture of learning, along with the institutional forms and practice it generated, gave cohesion to Muslim civilization. The breadth and extent, the openness, of this culture is summed up in the pages of the *Fahrist of al-Nadim*,[11] published in 987. It is an annotated catalogue of the books that a buyer could have copied, for their very own, at al-Nadim's bookshop in Baghdad. It included not only religious texts on Islam but those of other major religions known to Muslims; the scripts and grammar of many of the diversity of languages of their known world, as well as Arabic; the classic texts of Greece, Persia and India as well as the science, philosophy, culture and learning produced by the scholars of Muslim civilization. This cultural vibrancy regularly visited and passed through Mecca. Indeed, it was stimulated and facilitated by the obligation to travel to Mecca. Yet, evidently, it departed from Mecca when the pilgrim travellers went home again, often by highly circuitous routes. Mecca was different. It founded no great library, no university, no hospital like the other great cities of the Muslim world. The more Mecca became part of the celestial realm the less need it had to conform to earthly norms.

On the other hand, the fragmentation of the Muslim world exemplified by the Qarmatians was by no means confined to the activities of that sect. The varying abilities and interests of the Abbasid caliphs and the sheer extent of the territory they nominally ruled has prompted many historians to paraphrase W. B. Yeats's poem 'The Second Coming' and argue that the centre could not hold.

Personally, I feel it would be entirely appropriate to continue quoting that poem to describe the Muslim world in the tenth century. In that time it seems as if anarchy was indeed let loose, and it was pretty much all the Muslim lands could expect. And how better to sum up the Qarmatian terror in Mecca than in Yeats's words:

> The blood-dimmed tide is loosed, and everywhere
> The ceremony of innocence is drowned . . .[12]

Poetry was and is the favoured Arabic art form. At the height of 'the Golden Age' of Islam, when the new-fangled universities were copied wholesale in the Christian-ruled regions of Spain, tutors despaired because their students would not give proper attention to learning Latin, being too fond of reading Arabic love poetry.[13] So it seems only fair to redress the balance by acknowledging one of the finest exponents of modern English poetry, who was of course Irish. The fracturing of the Muslim world occurred through the domestication of local power by Arab governors and tribal leaders, giving rise to a plethora of dynasties and polities. It was a continuous feedback loop spurred by weakness at the centre that continually eroded central political control and government. Often the fracturing was compounded by hotly disputed differences over religion, which inevitably found their way to Mecca. It culminated with the establishment of three rival Caliphates. And this brought an old familiar motif out of Mecca to the fore: the claims of lineage and blood.

The Umayyad Emirate of Cordoba had been founded in 756 by Abdur Rahman I, the Falcon of the Quraysh. This last surviving prince of the house of Umayyad traced his lineage back to Othman, the third successor to the Prophet. It was during the turmoil of the early tenth century, in 929, that Abdur Rahman III (r. 912–61) declared himself Caliph and Defender of the Faithful. The majority of the 'faithful' were now defined as Sunnis, or those who regarded the first four caliphs as legitimate successors of Muhammad and stressed the importance of his *Sunnah*, or example, as the basis of law. It was a bold assertion that a new defender of Sunni orthodoxy was necessary in the face of the ineffectual leadership of the Abbasid caliph in Baghdad. Both the new Umayyad caliph in Spain and the Abbasid caliph in Iraq were confronted by the growing power of the third claimant, the Fatimid caliph in North Africa, and his claim to be the one and only legitimate heir to the office by virtue of descent. It was a claim of lineage out of Mecca which was interwoven with a markedly different interpretation of religion. The Fatimids were Ismailis, a subsect of the Shia. The founder of their Caliphate was Ubaydallah al-Mahdi (r. 909–34), to whom the Qarmatians owed allegiance. He assumed the titles of Mahdi and caliph in 909 when he overthrew local Aghlabid rule to establish his power base in Morocco. The Fatimids referred to themselves as *dawlat al-haqq*, or the legitimate governmental authority. The name ascribed to them, Fatimid, derives from Ubaydallah's claim of descent from Fatima, the daughter of the Prophet, and her husband Ali, the Prophet's cousin and his fourth successor. The authenticity of this genealogy, of course, was vigorously disputed by religious scholars, keeping the issue of heritable authority over religion centre stage. It was an urgent question of blood over which blood was spilled for worldly and religious reasons. The idea of a unitary community under one governing authority seeped away into the sands from this point in time.

The Fatimids were no less ruthless and murderous than their Qarmatian acolytes. Where the Qarmatians caused havoc raiding land caravans and were geographically placed to threaten Mecca, the Fatimids had a navy that gained control over the sea routes of the Mediterranean, thereby posing a direct threat to Umayyad Spain. The Fatimids captured Sicily, raided the coasts of France and Italy and plundered Genoa. Their great objective, however, was Egypt, a prize they captured only on their fourth attempt in 969. Once in place they built themselves a new capital, Cairo – al-Qahira, meaning the victorious. By this time the Abbasids were caliphs in name only. Effective control in Baghdad had passed to the Buyids, fierce highlanders from Daylam, a region southwest of the Caspian Sea, who served as mercenary troops in the service of the Caliphate. With instability everywhere and weakness at the centre, in 945 a Buyid force seized control in Baghdad. Caliph al-Mustakfi (r. 944–6) was rooted out of his hiding place to cede them supreme control. The Buyid leader and his three sons acquired imposing titles as Chief Amir, and respectively 'strengthener', 'pillar' and 'support' of the state. Having ennobled a new hereditary dynasty to wield effective power, the luckless Mustakfi was blinded and deposed. To prove that true anarchy was now in charge, the Buyids were Shi'ites who issued orders in the name of the Abbasid commander of the Sunni faithful, a practice they retained throughout the Buyid suzerainty, which lasted till 1055. The hapless notional caliphs were mere humbled figureheads given pocket money for their upkeep. And they did not fare much better when the Seljuks displaced the Buyids as the power behind the throne.

Rival and notional caliphs were a matter of religious concern. The turmoil across the Muslim world was a practical issue that could not be avoided. It had multiple consequences and meaning for Mecca. The cultural flowering of Muslim civilization might pass through Mecca and leave the city little stirred. The consequences of political anarchy and the disruption it caused had real and direct impact. The Qarmatian terror may well have been the high tide, and the most egregious example, of events in the wider world sweeping into Mecca, but it was not the last. So long as instability prevailed, no amount of raising Mecca to celestial realms could deflect events in the wider world being visited on the city and the life of its people. The rival powers seeking allegiance from all Muslims on both religious and political grounds posed a profound problem for the city. And, as always, the welfare of the city depended on the ability of Muslims to beat a path to this place of pilgrimage. Over the course of a very long century the fate of the city ebbed and flowed, borne on the current of events in the wider Muslim world that frequently rendered life in Mecca anything but a taste of paradise.

When the great Persian traveller Naser-e-Khosraw arrived in Mecca during August 1050, he discovered a sparsely populated city in need of extensive repairs and in the grip of a famine. 'I reckoned', he writes, 'that there are not more than two thousand citizens of Mecca, the rest, about five hundred, being foreigners or travellers.'[14] Wheat was scarce and expensive, and, as a result, many citizens had left. In fact, the city had shrunk: the entire city measured 'only two arrow-shots square'.[15]

Born in Tajikistan, Naser-e-Khosraw (1004–74 or 88) provides us with one of the earliest eyewitness accounts of life in Mecca. He was an official in the Seljuk administration. The Seljuks were Sunni Muslims of Turkish origins who gradually adopted Persian culture and ruled the vast stretch from Anatolia to Persia from the tenth to the early fourteenth century. Naser's main duties included tax collection, but his first love was poetry and philosophy, which inevitably led to wine and women. In 1045 he had a spiritual crisis and gave up his job and wealth to lead a life of devotion. He converted to Ismailism and started to travel, both to quench his spiritual thirst and to preach the Ismaili doctrine. From northeastern Persia he journeyed to Azerbaijan, Armenia, Anatolia, Syria, Palestine, Egypt and Jerusalem, and naturally ended up performing the Hajj in Mecca. Naser visited Mecca three times between March 1046 and October 1052. A man of considerable culture and curiosity, he was a shrewd observer and recorded what he saw in detail. The end product is his *Book of Travels*, which is rightly seen as one of the great works of Muslim world literature.

Naser was not too impressed with the pilgrims he met in Mecca. He is rude and apparently racist about pilgrims from Yemen, who he says 'generally look like Hindus: they wear *lungis*, have long hair and plaited beards, and carry Qatifi daggers called *kattara* at their waists, like Hindus'.[16] He mistakenly thought that the name for the Indian double-pronged dagger, called *katar* in Hindi, was derived from the Arabic word *qattalla*, meaning murders. So the poor Yemeni pilgrims end up being portrayed as killers and murderers of Indian origin. But he was more objective in his description of Mecca itself and its monuments and rituals.

The Sanctuary was situated in the middle of the city, and:

the city lanes and bazaars were built around it. Wherever there was an opening in the mountain a rampart wall has been made with a gate. The only trees in the city are on the western gate to the Sacred Mosque, where there are several trees around a well. On the eastern side of the Sacred Mosque, a large bazaar extends from south

to north. At the south end is Abu Qubays. At the foot of Abu
Qubays is Mount Safa, which is like a staircase, as rocks have been
set in such a fashion that people can go up to pray ... At the other
end of the bazaar is Mount Marwa, which is less tall and has many
edifices built on it, as it lies in the midst of the city. In running
between Safa and Marwa the people run inside the bazaar.[17]

There were hospices for the natives of every region, from Khorasan
to Iraq, but 'most had fallen into ruination', as had the 'beautiful
structures' built by the Abbasids. 'All the well water in Mecca is too
brackish and bitter to drink'; there were many large pools built to
catch rainwater from the hills, but 'they were empty'. Even though
underwater conduits had been constructed to bring water to Mecca,
little reached the city. 'Therefore a pool had been made to collect the
water, and water carriers drew the water and brought it to the city to
sell.'[18] He managed to find some grapes and water melons in the
bazaar.

The Sanctuary, the enclosure containing the Sacred Mosque, Naser
writes, 'runs lengthwise from east to west, and the breadth is on a
north–south axis. The walls, however, do not meet at right angles, for
the corners are rounded so that the whole is oval shape, because
when the people pray in this mosque they must face the Kaaba from
all directions.' As such, the enclosure is narrower in some places and
wider in others. 'Around the mosque are three vaulted colonnades
with marble columns. In the middle of the structure a square area has
been made. The long side of the vaulting, which faces the mosque
courtyard, has forty-five arches, with twenty-three arches across the
breadth. The marble columns number 184 in all.' Naser tells a story
associated with the columns, which were brought from Syria by sea:
'the story goes that when these columns arrived in Mecca, the ropes
that had been used to secure the columns on board ship and onto
carts were cut and sold for sixty thousand dinars. One of the columns,
a shaft of red marble, stands at the spot called al-Nadwa Gate; it is

said to have been bought for its weight in dinars.' The Sanctuary had eighteen doors, 'all built with arches supported by marble columns, but none is set with a door that can be closed'.[19]

In the middle of the courtyard is the Kaaba, which has a door 'towards the east', made of teak. It has the Black Stone set in one corner 'at about the height of man's chest'. 'The face of the door contains inscriptions and silver circles. The inscriptions are done in gold burnished with silver and contain the following Qur'anic verse: "Verily the first house appointed unto man to worship in was that which was in Becca."'[20] There are also two large silver rings attached to the doors 'such that no one can reach them' and a large silver lock.

Naser observed the ceremony of opening the Kaaba door. It is opened, he tells us, only during the months of Shaban, Ramadan and Shawaal (just before and after the period of ritual fasting), on Mondays. The chief with the keys to the Kaaba arrives with an entourage of six people. As he approaches the structure, stairs are brought and placed in front of the door. 'The old man mounts and stands at the threshold, and to open the door, a man on either side of him holds back the brocade covering as though holding a great robe with which he has been vested.'[21] When the door opens, all the gathered pilgrims raise their hands and shout the praise of God – and the entire city realizes that the doors of the Kaaba have been opened. The chief enters the Kaaba alone and offers his prayers. Then 'both wings of the door are opened' and the chief delivers a sermon. After the sermon, the pilgrims are allowed inside the Kaaba.

The opening of the Kaaba is much the same to this day. The opportunity to enter the House of God is considered a great privilege, and Naser clearly found the experience awe-inspiring, though I must admit I was much less impressed, when invited to go inside the Kaaba in 1987. Turning to the Kaaba is my point of orientation in life and towards the Divine. Where do you turn when you are inside, at the centre point of a compass? A dot has no direction. So, as much as I appreciated the honour, I could not for the life of me understand the enthusiasm it generates. The effect on me of entering the Cube was in no way comparable to the awe I felt every time I stood outside and gazed upon the Kaaba.

Inside the structure, Naser describes the floor as paved with white marble, and there 'are three small cabinets like platforms, one opposite the door, and the other two on the north side'. The interior columns, he observes, 'are attached to the ceiling, are made of teak wood and, except for one round one, are carved on all four sides'.[22] The walls have multicoloured marble, and one, on the western side, has six silver niches – mehrabs, which in an ordinary mosque indicate the direction of Mecca – 'each one in a man's height and elaborately worked in gold and burnished in silver. While inside the Kaaba, pilgrims face the door during prayer.'

Naser-e-Khosraw moved on from Mecca to Taif, and then to Basra, after performing four pilgrimages. He left a city that was in dire need of stability and strong governance. The security of the pilgrims had to be increased and the power of the Qarmatians checked. The city was squeezed between contending powers, the declining Abbasids in Baghdad and the emerging Fatimids in North Africa. Worst of all, and nearer at hand, was an old rivalry: the rulers of Medina were constantly threatening to take over Mecca. 'The City of the Prophet' became the capital of the Hijaz during the time of the Prophet and remained so as the caliphal capital moved further and further away. Medina had provided the leadership of the Hijaz for the past three hundred years. Mecca was keen to be the dominant force in the region. It wanted its old independence, and a strong ruler who could stand up to the two Caliphates.

Numerous sectarian and tribal groups jostled for power within Mecca. Each group tried to rally support and looked for an opportunity to take over the city. The strongest were the Alids, the descendants of Ali, the fourth caliph. It had been their traditional duty to provide security to pilgrims, and in these troubled times they used all their influence to secure temporary agreements to offer safe passage for the caravans. The members of the Prophet's family and clan, in the earlier times, had used Mecca as a base to launch campaigns against the Umayyad caliphs in Damascus and the Abbasids in Baghdad. Now the city asked them to provide strong leadership and a way out of the bloody rivalries dynastic politics were visiting on the wider Muslim world as well as on Mecca.

As a matter of policy, the Umayyad and Abbasid caliphs had tried to appoint a descendant of the Prophet's family as the governor of Mecca. But being a member of the Prophet's family had different meaning and significance over time. Originally, during the days of the second caliph Umar (r. 634–44), close members of the Prophet's family were awarded a special pension. Things became complicated during the reign of his successor, the third caliph Othman (r. 644–56), when various groups claiming to be related to Muhammad's family demanded extra entitlement. After the Abbasids came to power in 750 they redefined what it meant to be related to the Prophet Muhammad: they limited his immediate family to the descendants of Ali or those who claimed kinship with his great-grandfather Hashim. However, the Shia preferred to regard only the descendants of Ali and his wife Fatima, the daughter of the Prophet, and their sons, Hassan and Hussain, as the sole true family of the Prophet. This definition became widely accepted in the Hijaz by the end of the ninth century. The emerging rulers of Mecca, who would be known as sharifs, thus had to be direct descendants of Ali and come from a very narrow family base.

The word *sharif* itself has gone through several etymological transformations. It was commonly used during the seventh and eighth centuries to describe a 'man of importance'. A sharif was someone with unimpeachable integrity and open-mindedness born of learning. Later, the term came to imply inherited nobility; and by the time it was used as a title, in the second half of the ninth century, it symbolized the legitimate claims of 'the People of the House' of the Prophet: noble descendants from Ali and Fatima. Thus the (rather un-Islamic) idea of the nobility of blood became incorporated in the title. No one else was allowed to call themselves sharif. Wherever one turned, it seemed, the old Meccan concern for the question of lineage simply would not fade away. Indeed, it endures to this day. Around the world there are legions of people whose names include the honorific 'syed' or 'sayyid' (male) or 'sharifah' (female), denoting descent from the Prophet. When such people, who can come from different corners of the world, meet, it is seldom the warm embrace of family feeling one observes. On the contrary, a wary tension usually fills the air and they will sit wrapped in conversation, sometimes for hours, tracing abstruse and intricate points of their genealogy to demonstrate to each other how their forebears got from Mecca to Indonesia or West Africa or any points beyond. Honour and precedence acquired by birth matter enormously when they confer no earthly benefit. Naturally, the stakes were higher, but in my view in no way heavenly, when real power and riches were available as the inheritance for possessors of the right blood line.

The citizens of Mecca were much exercised on the subject. They held regular meetings to discuss who would be an appropriate ruler for the 'divine throne of Earth'. But the first sharif of Mecca did not emerge from the city itself. He came to Mecca with the pilgrim caravan from Cairo and took over the city without anyone noticing. Jafar ibn Muhammad al-Hassani, a moderate Shia, did have Fatimid troops with him, but if it was a conquest it was one that even the historians did not spot, or regard the transfer of power as important enough to record the exact date. It happened in 965, 966, 967 or 968; but the period between 951 and 961 is also mentioned. It is likely that the first sharif of Mecca began his rule between 965 and 969, which would coincide with the Fatimid conquest of Egypt.

Jafar, an independent man, despite arriving in the company of Fatimid troops, managed to make Mecca autonomous by successfully playing off the rival interests of the Fatimids and the Abbasids. The dynasty he established, known by his name – Hassani – succeeded in improving security for the pilgrim caravans, which returned in greater numbers. Jafar was followed by his son, Isa, who ruled for fourteen years. Like his father, Isa refused to pay homage to the Fatimid caliphs, and in return the Fatimids tried to starve him into submission. They stopped all imports from Egypt and their troops prevented supplies from other regions reaching Mecca. Isa was forced to concede. From now on he was required to mention the name of the Fatimid caliph in Friday sermons at the Sacred Mosque, with appropriate salutations and praise. Honour and precedence will have their way. The rival claimants to caliphal dignity were seeking the allegiance of all Muslims. Mecca would ever be the pre-eminent place to publish proof of the predominance of one earthly power or another.

Paradoxically, the concession to Fatimid power enabled Mecca to retain some degree of independence. In 994, Isa was succeeded by his younger brother Abdul Futuh ibn Jafar, who ruled Mecca for some forty-five years. Qarmatian influence was by now on the wane. They had developed significant differences with the Fatimids, which led to conflict. They were expelled from Iraq in 985 by the Buyids and their Bahrain territory was no more by 1077. Mecca was relatively secure and prosperous. Fatimid rule, however, was still on the march. It was extended to include Palestine and Syria. The new Fatimid caliph, al-Hakim (r. 996–1021), was only eleven years old when he acceded to the Caliphate. He quickly showed signs of bizarre behaviour, including propagating what Muslims regarded as heretical beliefs. He believed he was not only a divinely appointed caliph, with religious and political authority, but a 'cosmic intellect', the main link between God and creation. He was seen as demonstrably mad in Mecca.

Sufficiently confident in his own position, the sharif, Abdul Futuh, felt the time was ripe to save the Muslims from these heretical beliefs, and in the process establish himself as a caliph. He was probably encouraged in this endeavour by Abdul Qassim al-Maghribi, the son of the murdered vizier of Caliph Hakim, who was anxious for revenge. Having escaped from Cairo, Abdul Qassim, pursued by the caliph's forces, had taken refuge with Bedouin tribes in Syria. The Bedouins not only stopped al-Hakim's forces but were successful in driving them from their lands. Abdul Qassim then persuaded the Syrian Bedouin tribes to give their allegiance to the sharif of Mecca, who was invited to come and declare himself the new caliph. Abdul Futuh marshalled a huge army of his Meccan clansmen and travelled to Syria. To bolster the legitimacy of his claim to be caliph, he took the legendary sword of Ali and some relics of the Prophet along with him. However, the caliph in Cairo was not as mad as the Meccans had thought. Fully aware of Abdul Futuh's plan, he had already sent considerable sums of money to each of the Bedouin chiefs who had pledged allegiance to the sharif of Mecca. When Abdul Futuh arrived in Syria he discovered, as others had before him, that money was a better currency for buying allegiance than sacred relics or lineage. Meanwhile, back in Mecca, one of his relatives had taken over and declared himself sharif. Abdul Futuh managed to return just in time to reclaim power and restore order in the city.

The al-Hassani dynasty ends with Abdul Futuh's son, Muhammad Shukr. Shukr, who became sharif in 1039, ruled for twenty-two years. A warm and generous man, his first love was poetry; he wrote under the pen name of Taj al-Maali. Unusually for the time, he died without a male heir. Inevitably, a squabble over succession broke out within the family, with the usual outcome for Mecca. One of Shukr's slaves took over as ruler and tried to restore order. This only intensified the family quarrel. Members of the al-Hassani family even started confiscating precious metals and ornaments in the Sanctuary for their private use. The political situation in Mecca became so bad that the Yemeni ruler, Muhammad al-Sulaihi, had to intervene. In 1063 he came for pilgrimage and stayed to restore order and security in the city. The intervention of an outsider seemed more palatable to the al-Hassani family than fighting amongst themselves. They asked al-Sulaihi to decide and appoint who amongst them should be the ruler of Mecca.

Al-Sulaihi chose Muhammad ibn Jafaar, a descendant of the Prophet's grandson, Hassan, who was duly proclaimed the new sharif. He was popularly known as Abu Hashim (probably because he had a son called Hashim) and became the first ruler of the new dynasty of Hashim in 1063. During the early years of his reign, Abu Hashim had to wage a protracted struggle against his kith and kin, many of whom still harboured political ambition. When the opposition had been silenced, Abu Hashim set about making his mark.

The vital decision, of course, was which way to look: towards Baghdad and the Abbasids, towards Cairo and the Fatimids, or towards the new rising power, the Seljuk sultans who in 1055 had displaced the Buyids as the effective masters of the eastern empire. Abu Hashim unashamedly offered his allegiance to the highest bidder. His allegiance would come complete with special mention in the Friday sermon (*khutba*), to which Abu Hashim had added a few extra rites involving further honourable mentions. He even suggested that the name of the winning bidder could be included in the *Adhaan*, the call to prayer. It seems that the Abbasids won; the then caliph, al-Muqtadir (r. 1075–94), was content with a mere glowing mention in the *khutba*.

When Hashim dropped the name of the Fatimid caliph from the Friday sermon, and replaced it with their Abbasid counterpart, the Meccans knew what to expect. Almost at once, the Fatimids stopped all imports from Egypt, just as they had done before. Abu Hashim was forced to buy supplies at much higher prices and to raise the extra cash needed by selling ornaments from the Sanctuary. The Abbasid caliph came to the rescue with a gift of 30,000 dinars. However, the money did not last long and the official mention of the Fatimids in the *khutbas* was reintroduced. In fact, changes were made so many times that the Seljuk sultan, Adud ad-Dawla Alp-Arslan (r. 1063–72), who wielded more effective power than the

Abbasid caliph, or the Fatimids, decided to end the comedy. The sultan sent a regiment of Turkoman soldiers to Mecca. They came to perform the pilgrimage and stayed in and around the city, taking every opportunity to harass and humiliate Abu Hashim; eventually they drove him out of Mecca.

The ill-feeling between the sharif and the Seljuk sultan caused a great deal of suffering for the pilgrims. The arrival of the Hajj caravan from Iraq, so eagerly awaited in Mecca, now rang alarm bells in the city. It was a signal for the citizens to arm themselves. The leadership of the caravan had passed from the Alids, the descendants of Prophet Muhammad's cousin Ali and his daughter Fatima, to Turkish officials and soldiers. Abu Hashim himself did not hesitate to attack and plunder the caravan. The animosity and raiding of pilgrim caravans continued till both Sultan Alp-Arslan and Caliph al-Muqtadir had died, and Abu Hashim turned back to the Fatimids in 1075.

The rule of the Abu Hashim dynasty in Mecca was nothing if not turbulent. As the holiest city of Islam and the site of pilgrimage, it was natural for the caliphs and sultans of the Muslim world, members of fading as well as emerging dynasties, to try to influence the city. To preserve its sovereignty, Mecca had to perform a continuous political juggling act. However, the anarchy was exacerbated by the unbridled greed, covetousness and plundering of the sharifs themselves. The Hashims considered they had a natural, God-given right to rule Mecca. As descendants of Ali, they could do as they pleased and would always have the support of the city's people. It seems to have been a well-founded presumption. The citizens of Mecca looked up to the Hashims and supported them loyally, with few qualms about their excesses. In 1091, Abu Hashim was succeeded by his son Qasim, who managed to rule until his death in 1132. At the very beginning of his reign, Qasim took on the Seljuk soldiers and defeated them in a battle at al-Usfan, some fifty miles north of Mecca on the caravan route. His first act after taking full control of Mecca was to impose a heavy tax on the pilgrims. The sharifs also appointed a band of ferocious young Bedouins, fiercely loyal to them, as their permanent guards. They used them to terrorize the pilgrims and, when needed, to impose order in the city.

In the midst of such widespread disorder and jostling for power it is hardly surprising that in 1095 no one in Mecca or the wider Muslim world took careful note of an event in distant Clermont in France. Europe was beset by its own problems, with internal violence and jostling for power among its turbulent and rapacious feudal elite. A solution, however, was at hand. Pope Urban II, as the head of Western Christendom, called on Christians to take the Cross and set off to reclaim the Holy Land where Christ had walked on earth from the infidel Saracen, defend their beleaguered co-religionists and in return receive remission of their sins. It was the beginning of the movement that would become known as the Crusades. His call stirred a mass response from peasant and prince alike. In a blood-soaked march, beginning with pogroms against Jews in Europe, the First Crusade made its way to its objective: Jerusalem, which was captured in 1099. A new complexity, which would last nearly two centuries, was added to the landscape of the Middle East; a Latin kingdom had been planted in the midst of the contending Muslim powers. Momentous as the fall (or liberation) of Jerusalem might seem at first, it made little difference to the ongoing anarchy in either Christendom or the Muslim world.

For the next quarter of a century, respective sons succeeded their fathers as rulers of Mecca. Given that most of them were called Qasim or Hashim (the Meccans were rather unoriginal in their choice of names) and were constantly involved in fighting the Iraqi caravan leaders, it is not easy to distinguish between them. There were so many skirmishes with the Iraqi caravans and encounters with invaders that the ruling family decided to build a castle for extra protection. It was built on Mount Abu Qubays, overlooking the city. The family retreated to the castle to defend themselves from attack or when the city became politically unstable. Regular payments to the Bedouin tribes, some of whom they kept as a standing army, were increased, as were the numbers of Bedouin guards, noted for carrying large spears and referred to as 'the spearmen'. The extra security measures did not turn out to be all that useful. In 1175, when Mikhthar bin Isa was the ruler, the leader of the Iraqi pilgrim caravan, who had developed an intense dislike for the sharifs, decide to displace him. After a bloody fight, Mikhthar was defeated; the castle on Abu Qubays was seriously damaged. Mikhthar was replaced by the emir of Medina.

For Meccans this was a fate worse than death. They would have preferred a pagan ruler rather than someone from Medina. The citizens rose en masse and made the life of the imposed ruler from Medina hell. Finding that it was impossible to rule Mecca, the emir of Medina withdrew, salvaging what little honour he had left. He had lasted less than a week. Mikhthar eventually returned to power. His first act on resuming power was to impose a heavy tax on the pilgrims.

By now the political landscape of the Middle East had changed radically. The last vestiges of Fatimid rule in Egypt had been extinguished by the new dynasty of the Ayyubids, established in Egypt in 1169 by al-Malik an-Nasir Salah-ad-Din (depicted in English history as 'Saladin'). Here enters a true hero, not just mine, for remarkably in the midst of all the black propaganda pumped out to support the Crusades in Europe, Salah-ad-Din alone seems to have been exempt.[23] Sometimes heroic nobility transcends all boundaries. He promoted a strongly orthodox Sunni religious and educational policy. In 1173, the Ayyubids invaded Yemen, partly to destroy the troublesome Ismailis and partly to control the trade route to India. Much of southern Arabia – Aden, Hadhramaut, the Tihāmah, and the districts south of Sanaa – were now under the control of Salah-ad-Din, who had introduced a centralized administration into the region. Salah-ad-Din was also vigorously waging a *jihad* against the Crusaders; at long last he managed to weld together armies of Turks, Kurds and Arabs in the common cause. The Meccans, however, were quite oblivious to the battle cries of the Crusades reverberating throughout the Middle East. They were much too busy fighting amongst themselves, defending themselves from the Iraqi caravans, and fleecing the pilgrims.

Mikhthar's harsh tax inflicted a crushing burden on the pilgrims, most of whom came with little more than the basic costs of their journey. Some arrived in the Holy Land after being robbed and looted en route. Those who could not pay the tax would be imprisoned by the sharif. Torture of poor pilgrims was not unusual: 'amongst the various inflictions devised was hanging by the testicles'.[24] In the hands of the sharif, the pilgrims 'would suffer the most grievous oppression, with no remission of its rigours'. The Meccans seemed to take pleasure in 'seizing most of the provisions of the pilgrims, robbing them and finding cause to divest them of all they have'.[25]

The news of the excesses of the sharifs, the constant political upheaval in the city and the oppression of the pilgrims at their hands reached Sultan Salah-ad-Din in Cairo. The sultan sent a letter to Sharif Mikhthar. 'We and you', said the sultan, 'are charged with the well-being of the pilgrims. Reflect on this noble task and generous aim. The benefits of God are twofold for him who benefits His servants, and His bounteous care reaches him who exerts his care for them.'[26] The sultan abolished the pilgrim tax, replacing it with an annual subsidy from Cairo, plus regular consignments of grain from Egypt as well as numerous other gifts. The sharifs were restrained. Peace and stability was established and Mecca was transformed within a few years.

So when the Holy City was visited by ibn Jubayr, in 1183, over 130 years after Naser-e-Khosraw, he found a prosperous, thriving city. The son of a civil servant, ibn Jubayr was born in Valencia, Spain, in 1145. He excelled in the Qur'an and the traditions of the Prophet as well as in law and literature and was regarded as exceptionally pious. After spending some time as secretary to the governor of Granada, at the time one of the wealthiest and most splendid cities

of the Muslim world, he took up the pilgrim staff and began his journey towards Mecca on 3 February 1183. Embarking on a Genoese
ship, he made his way to Egypt, which he explored thoroughly, and
after numerous adventures travelling down the Nile, across the desert
and the sea, he arrived in Mecca. Ibn Jubayr was a keen observer with
a keen eye for detail, and kept copious daily records of his journeys.
The Travels of Ibn Jubayr thus provides us with the most trustworthy and precise, not to say reverent, account of Mecca in the late
twelfth century.

Crossing the Red Sea on a fragile vessel, ibn Jubayr entered the
holy lands via Jeddah during the reign of Sharif Mikhthar. He found
the land he longed to visit to be very different from his homeland.
Most people in Jeddah, he observed, 'lead a life so wretched as to
break the hardest stone in compassion. They employ themselves in
all manner of trades, such as hiring camels should they possess any,
and selling milk or water and other things like dates which they
might find, or wood they might collect.'[27] Ibn Jubayr entered Mecca
through the al-Zahir gate, the biggest of the three main gates, used by
travellers from Jeddah, Medina and Syria. Al-Zahir was also known
as the Umra Gate: it marked the point where those performing the
lesser pilgrimage – the *umra* – had to bathe and change into their
ritual dress before entering the city. Places for bathing were provided,
and there was a long bench with a row of drinking mugs, and tubs
filled with water for ritual ablutions. The entire area was shaded and
surrounded with gardens. The procedure has not changed and is just
as my friend Zafar and I performed it when we made our pilgrimage
with the pestiferous donkey Genghis.

In common with all who write about pilgrimage to Mecca, ibn
Jubayr gives a meticulous description of the Sacred Mosque. Indeed,
it is often the case that the most interesting part of these travel books,
a distinct genre within Muslim letters, is to be found in the sections
about getting to and going from Mecca. When speaking of the city
itself there is a formulaic and repetitive feel to the descriptions of the

Holy Sites. It is understandable, I suppose. The writers are bearing witness to a portal of the celestial realm, the ideal of Mecca. And they are writing for those who may never have the chance to visit the city themselves. The verbal portraits of minute detail are designed to fix the city of their hearts and souls in the minds of Muslims everywhere.

Ibn Jubayr stands out for the more rounded depiction of time and place that he provides. The most significant information to be gleaned from him is the improved condition of the city compared with the time of Naser-e-Khosraw. And his detailed description has some wonderful juxtapositions which, whether intentional or not, have a telling edge. 'The Sacred Mosque is encompassed by colonnades. Against the whole length of this colonnade are benches under vaulted arches where sit the copyists, the readers of the Qur'an, and some who ply the tailor's trade.'[28] Along the walls of the colonnade, ibn Jubayr saw students sitting in circles around their teachers – each sect forming a different circle.

He reports that the door of the Kaaba, on the side facing east, was close to its principal corner, which contained the Black Stone. It is made of silver gilt and is a work of exquisite craftsmanship. He notes a gold engraving on the door, 'with graceful characters long and thick, that hold the eye for their form and beauty', which declares: 'This is amongst those things erected by the order of servant and Caliph of God, the Imam Abu Abdullah Muhammad al-Muqtafi Amri Ilah, Prince of the Faithful. May God bless him and the Imams his righteous ancestors, perpetuating for him the prophetic inheritance and making it an enduring word for his prosperity until the Day of Resurrection. In the year 550 [1155].' The door was also decorated with two leaves on which someone had written: 'Is this wise?'[29]

Of the Black Stone itself ibn Jubayr writes that its four broken pieces are now joined together. 'It is said that it was the Qarmatians – may God curse them – who broke it. Its edges have been braced with a sheet of silver whose white shines brightly against the black sheen and polished brilliance of the Stone, presenting the observer a striking spectacle which will hold its look.' Then with the genuine intensity of the pilgrim he adds: 'The Stone, when kissed, has a softness and moistness which so enchants the mouth that he who puts his lips to it would wish them never to be removed.'[30] At the Maqaam (or place of) Abraham, where the Prophet Abraham stood to build the Kaaba, ibn Jubayr says he could clearly make out the imprints of the feet: 'the water of Zamzam was poured for us into the imprint of two blessed feet, and we drank it . . . the traces of both feet are visible, as are the traces of the honoured and blessed big toes'.[31]

After visiting the Sanctuary, ibn Jubayr explores the city. He discovers that it has two baths, named after noted jurists of the time. At the summit of Abu Qubays he finds an asylum for the needy and a mosque that overlooks Mecca. Also at the top of the mountain 'are the remains of a lofty stucco building which the emir of the land, Isa, father of Mikhthar, had taken as a stronghold, but which the emir of the Iraq pilgrimage, because of a dispute with him, destroyed and left in ruins'.[32] Observing Mecca from Abu Qubays, he realizes that the city possesses a special ability, a 'manifest miracle': an ability to expand and accommodate all the pilgrims that gather to pay their homage to the Kaaba during the Hajj. The city, 'which lies in a valley bed that is a bow-shot or less in width', he writes with some surprise, can adjust and expand to accommodate 'multitude beyond count' – 'its enlargement for the newcomers is that of a uterus for the foetus'.[33] The same can be said, he notes, for Arafat and other sacred sites around Mecca.

The pious traveller visits many shrines and sacred sites in Mecca and the surrounding area. He begins – naturally – with the birthplace of the Prophet, where a mosque had been built, 'being for the most of inlaid gold', which was opened to visitors every Monday during the Islamic month of Rabi al-Awwal, during which the Prophet was born. He moves on to see the house of Khadijah, and the birthplaces of Fatima, the daughter of the Prophet, and his grandchildren Hassan and Hussain. 'These holy places which are locked and guarded were built in a manner fitting to them.' He spends some time in the House of Khayzuran, where the Prophet worshipped in secret with his early companions, as well as the house of Abu Bakr, and marvels at the dome of Umar, between Safa and Marwah, 'whose centre is a well, where he sat in judgement'. He even visits the place where al-Hajjaj crucified the body of ibn Zubair.

Talking to pilgrims, new and old, ibn Jubayr discovered that the city was unexpectedly free of crime: 'we found that all the settled pilgrims there, those who had come before or whose stay there had been long, spoke as a matter of wonder at its freedom from thieves who once had robbed the pilgrims, snatching what was in their hands, and being a plague in the noble Haram. No one could neglect their belongings for the twinkling of an eye or they would be taken from his hand or girdle with amazing cunning and astonishing smoothness.' Moreover, 'the pilgrims also spoke of the many goods in Mecca this year, and the mildness of their prices, which was contrary to their earlier experience'.[34]

Indeed, the bazaar in Mecca was 'overflowing with good things, and fruits such as figs, grapes, pomegranates, quince, peaches, lemons, walnuts, palm-fruit, watermelons, cucumbers, and all the vegetables like egg-plant, pumpkin, carrot, cauliflower, and other aromatic and sweet smelling plants'. He particularly enjoyed the watermelon, which had an 'exceptional merit in that its odour is the most fragrant of smells and the best. When someone approaches you with one, you find the fragrant odour coming first to you so that from the enjoyment of its sweetness you almost abstain from eating it.'[35]

But the markets were not just overflowing with fruits and vegetables. As the pilgrims, 'from east and west', were able to travel in relative safety and without being robbed, they, and the traders and businessmen who accompanied them in the pilgrim caravan, had brought all kinds of commodities with them to sell in Mecca: 'precious objects such as pearls, sapphires, and other stones, various kinds of perfume such as musk, camphor, amber and aloes, Indian drugs and other articles brought from India and Ethiopia, the product of industries of Iraq and the Yemen, as well as the merchandise of Khurasan, the goods of the Maghrib, and other wares such as is impossible to enumerate or correctly assess'. Indeed, Mecca saw so many goods and commodities that year that immediately after the Hajj, the day of the festival, the Sacred Mosque itself was turned into a great market where everything from flour to agates, wheat to pearls, was being sold. Flour was sold in the Dar al-Nadwa, the House of Council. But 'part of the market was in the colonnade', where slaves were being sold. Being a pious man with knowledge of Islamic law, ibn Jubayr was not pleased with the sight. 'That this is forbidden by divine law is known,' he tells his readers.[36]

However, he is enthralled by the pomp and ceremony of the Friday sermon and prayers, and seems to approve of the ritual innovations and additions the sharifs had made both to introduce an element of mystique in the process and as an ostentatious display of their power. A preacher's pulpit, on four wheels so that it can be easily moved, was kept at Maqaam Abraham. During prayer times on Fridays, it is brought to the side of the Kaaba that faces the Maqaam and propped against the Kaaba. The preacher enters the Sanctuary through the Gate of the Prophet. 'He wears a black dress, worked with gold, a black turban similarly worked, and a *taylasan* [a green cloak, worn by distinguished scholars] of fine linen.' Walking calmly and stately, 'he slowly paces between two black banners held by two muezzins of his tribe. Before him goes another of his people bearing a red staff, turned on a lathe, and having tied to its top a cord of twisted skin, long and thin, with a small thong at its tip. He cracks it in the air with so loud report that it is heard both within the Haram and without, like a warning of the arrival of the preacher. He does not cease to crack it until they are near the pulpit.' When the preacher finally reaches the pulpit – which seems to take an eternity – he turns to kiss the Black Stone.

Then he goes to the pulpit, led by the Zamzam muezzin, who is the chief of the muezzins of the noble Haram and also dressed in black clothes. He bears on his shoulders a sword which he holds in his hand without girding it. The muezzin girds the Khatib [preacher] with the sword as he ascends the first step, which then, with the ferrule of his scabbard, he strikes a blow which all present can hear. He strikes it again on the second step and on the third. When he reaches the top step, he strikes the fourth blow, and stands facing the Kaaba praying in low tones. Then he turns to the right and left and says: 'Peace be upon you, and the mercy and blessings of God.' The congregation returns the salutation and he then sits. The muezzins place themselves in front of him and call the azan [the call to prayers] in one voice. When they have finished, the Khatib delivers the address, reminding, exhorting, inspiring, and waxing eloquent. He then sits down in the conventional sitting of the preacher and strikes with the sword a fifth time. He then delivers a second *khutba*.[37]

It was this second sermon that had been the subject of conflict and over which various caliphs and sultans had fought. Who is mentioned in this sermon and where they fit in the pecking order was a matter of consequence. Those vying for the allegiance of all Muslims had no better place to broadcast their status and claim their right to precedence to the entire Muslim world. The Khatib begins with the obvious:

multiplying prayers for Muhammad, and for his family, begging God's favour for his Companions and naming in particular the four Caliphs [Abu Bakr, Umar, Othman and Ali], praying for the two uncles of the Prophet, Hamzah and Abbas, and for al-Hassan and Hussain, uniting to all the words: 'May God hold them in his favour'. He then prayed for the Mothers of the Faithful, wives of the Prophet [and] begged God's favour for Fatimah the Fair and Khadijah the Great.

It is at this point that political power enters the equation. Ibn Jubayr says: 'He then prayed for the Abbasid Caliph Abu l'Abbas Ahmad al-Nasir, then for the Emir of Mecca, Mukthir ibn Isa', whose entire genealogy going back to Abu Hashim is mentioned to emphasize his right to rule Mecca. The congregation remains silent up to this point. Then, ibn Jubayr tell us, the Khatib prays 'for Salah ad-Din Ayyub and his heir and brother Abu Bakr ibn Ayyub. At the mention in the prayers of Saladin, from all sides tongues quivered in emotion as they cried "Amin" to that.' My hero was everyone's hero, by popular acclaim. During the entire proceedings, 'two black banners are planted on the first step of the minbar [pulpit], and held by two muezzins. On the side of the minbar are two rings in which the banners are placed.'[38] When the Khatib ends the prayers, he leaves with as much pomp and ceremony as he arrived.

On several occasions, ibn Jubayr caught sight of Sharif Mikhthar in the Sanctuary. He would enter the Sacred Mosque from the Gate of the Prophet, accompanied with his entourage, including Qur'an readers and his spearmen, 'who, spear in hand, whirled in front of him'. Dressed in white, with a turban of fine white wool, and with a girded short sword, he appeared 'modest, calm and dignified'. When he reached Maqaam Abraham, a linen carpet was spread for him to pray. After kissing the Black Stone, he would start his circumambulation of the Kaaba. When he had completed his first circuit, a young boy of not more than eleven years, dressed in his best clothes, and who had climbed the dome of Zamzam, would praise the sharif in an enchanting voice. He would begin with the words: 'Grant this day, O God, to our Lord the Emir everlasting happiness and all embracing favour.' This was followed by 'a gifted discourse in rhymed prose full of invocations and eulogies, and then, concluding with three or four verses of poetry in praise of the Emir and his noble ancestors and the excellence of Prophecy, came to silence'.[39] But he remained silent only as long as the next circuit, when the whole process was repeated – indeed it went on till he had performed all seven circuits.

Sharif Mikhthar may have been 'dignified', but judging from his actions he was not 'modest', as ibn Jubayr discovered himself. His obsession with luxury and pleasure-seeking appalled even his supporters in Mecca. He was happy as long as the promised share of the sultan's largesse arrived in Mecca. If it was delayed or failed to arrive for one reason or another, he turned on the pilgrims. He ordered, as ibn Jubayr tells us, that 'pilgrims should guarantee each other for payment and might then enter the Sacred Mosque. Should the money and victuals due for him from Salah ad-Din arrive it would be well; otherwise he would not forgo his dues from the pilgrims. Such was his speech, as if God's Haram were an heirloom in his hand and lawfully his to let to the pilgrims.'[40] Moreover, his guards – the spearmen – took every opportunity to terrorize the inhabitants of Mecca to keep them on message, and frequently engaged in a bit of rape and pillage on the side. Sultan Salah-ad-Din was fully aware of the emir's behaviour.

In January 1184, Mecca was abuzz with the news of a distinguished visitor from Egypt. Sultan Sayf al-Islam (who was also known as Taghtakin), brother of Sultan Salah-ad-Din, was on his way to the Holy City. 'As for the reason of his journey,' writes ibn Jubayr, 'men said that he was on his way to Yemen because of some disputes that had risen there, and because of a rebellion raised by its emirs. But into the minds of Meccans entered a dreadful apprehension, and fear fell upon them.' Sharif Mikhthar came out of the city to greet him, but 'in truth to make submission to him'. There was a great commotion when Sultan Sayf al-Islam entered the Sacred Mosque: 'voices of men in prayer for him and his brother Salah ad-Din rose so high as to deafen the ear and confound the understanding. From his high post on the Zamzam the muezzin raised his voice in prayer and praise for him; the voices of the people rose above the muezzin's; and great was the awe of the scene to look upon and hear.'[41]

In contrast to the pomposity of Sharif Mikhthar, whose body-guards were always ready with their spears and unsheathed swords, and who insisted on fine clothing for his entourage, Sultan Sayf al-Islam demonstrated humility. 'Swords were sheathed', 'fine clothing was cast off', and he showed 'humbleness'. His troops hurled themselves into the Sacred Mosque 'with the impetuosity of moths at a lamp. Humility had bowed their heads and tears bathed their moustaches.'

Sultan Sayf al-Islam stayed in Mecca for several months, and performed the pilgrimage of 1185. By this time ibn Jubayr had left the city and was on his way back to Granada. Sharif Mikhthar, realizing that he had no control over the city, retreated with his followers to the ruined fort at Abu Qubays. The sultan's initial idea was to abolish the Sharifat altogether, but he seemed to change his mind. Instead, he reiterated Cairo's support for the pilgrims and emphasized that the annual subsidy and regular consignment of grain from Egypt would continue. Then he summoned the sharif's Bedouin bodyguards, the spearmen, who were responsible for a reign of murder and looting in the city. As the impotent sharifs watched, he had them executed in the public square. No one, he declared, is above the law – not even the sharifs and their bodyguards. Finally, he had coins struck in the name of Salah-ad-Din and introduced them as a legal currency in the city.

Even the mighty Ayyubid sultans could only improve the situation of Mecca temporarily. As soon as Sultan Sayf al-Islam departed, the ruling family descended from the fort and returned to the city. Mikhthar resumed his rule and stayed in power till 1200. The people of Mecca, who always valued loyalty to the clan more than justice and the fair treatment of pilgrims, rallied around Mikhthar and celebrated the freedom of their city. A more exorbitant tax was imposed on the pilgrims. All the erstwhile customs of the Meccans, including occasional looting of pilgrim caravans, resumed.

However, the dynasty established by Abu Hashim was approaching its final days. A revolution was brewing elsewhere in the Hijaz. Soon, Mecca was to have new rulers. The beginning of the thirteenth century saw political power in the city move to a new branch of the sharifs – and remain there for the next 600 years.

5

Love and Fratricide
in the Holy City

During the first year of the thirteenth century, Meccans were in a celebratory mood. There was a great deal to celebrate. Towards the end of 1195, a black wind appeared from nowhere and engulfed the city. For days red sand rained from the sky. Some in the city thought it was the end of time and Judgement Day was upon them. But the wind disappeared as suddenly as it had arrived, leaving the Sanctuary shaken, with only minor damage to the Kaaba. This was a second deliverance; a decade earlier the city had narrowly escaped the onslaught of the Christian soldiers.

For most of the inhabitants of Mecca, the Crusades were a distant phenomenon. The focal point of the Muslim world was peripheral to the centre of the action; it revolved around Jerusalem, which was considered the centre of the earth by Christians. The stone they called the 'navel of the earth' was located there, in the Church of the Holy Sepulchre. Medieval European map-making, an art that was more a graphic representation of biblical history than geographical, told the same story with Jerusalem as the central point.[1] News of battles and victories against the Christians reached Mecca regularly through pilgrims or visitors from Egypt. There were fervent prayers in the Sacred Mosque when Salah-ad-Din succeeded in liberating Jerusalem in 1187. He immediately restored it to the status of an open city where once again Muslims, Jews and Christians could live side by side,[2] as they had done during the preceding four and a half centuries of Muslim rule; the way that was common in all the other great cities of the Middle East. Under the eighty-eight-year rule of the Crusaders, Jerusalem had been closed to all but Christians.

Salah-ad-Din's triumph came just two years after his brother had liberated Mecca from the scourge of the Bedouin spearmen who served the sharifs. No one in Mecca thought the Christian heathens would actually enter the Hijaz. It was unthinkable. This territory had been closed to all but Muslims for more than four centuries, ever since the time of the first Umayyad caliph. Mecca, the earthly facsimile of the celestial realm, was inviolable.

The French knight Reynaud de Châtillon (1125–87) had other ideas.[3] A poor knight, he had fought in the Second Crusade, and stayed on to seek his fortune. The Latin Kingdom of Outremer which the Christians had planted in the Middle East was a genuine frontier society, a land of opportunity for those knights who were willing to take the risk and go on Crusade. Reynaud rose to prominence thanks to two fortunate marriages. Outremer seemed to produce an abundance of rich heiresses in need of husbands. By his first marriage he became prince of Antioch. Reynaud was then ambushed and taken prisoner by Muslim forces. He spent fourteen years as a prisoner before being ransomed, during which time he learnt Arabic and Turkish. Once free he found himself a widower in need of another wife. His second marriage brought him land in Outrejordan, indeed the most extensive seigniory in the Latin Kingdom. It contained the castles of Montréal and Kerak, east of the Dead Sea. Strongly fortified castles dominating the surrounding territory were the means by which the Crusaders exerted control over their conquered land and its people. Reynaud was now in possession of two of the finest examples, strategically located astride the pilgrim route to Mecca. From his strongholds he could impede and raid pilgrim caravans with impunity.

Secure in his territory, Reynaud operated as an independent agent, rather than a liege of the king of Jerusalem. He conceived a daring plan. He would attack the heart of Islam itself: the holy cities of

Mecca and Medina. The idea was to ransack the cities and steal the body of the Prophet Muhammad from Medina and the treasures of the Kaaba from Mecca. Reynaud began his campaign in 1181 by looting the pilgrim caravan that passed by the castle of Kerak, breaking a truce with Salah-ad-Din, who was 'so outraged by these actions that he vowed never to forgive him'.[4] The Meccans' previous notions about the Crusades being a distant concern were blown away.

Muslim historians describe Reynaud as a bloodthirsty marauding pirate, which he was, as perfidious to his co-religionists as to his enemies. One of his favourite pastimes was to throw prisoners from the battlements of his castles and watch their bodies break on the rocks below. But he was also an accomplished strategist. He conquered the port of Elat on the Gulf of Aqaba in a surprise attack. Then he took ships from a port in southern Palestine, dismantled them, transported them by camel across the desert, and rebuilt them in Elat. Slowly he mustered an armada of galleys; manoeuvred by oars, these were faster and more mobile than the sailing vessels of the Arabs. He was now able to cut off communication between small Arab ports, capture merchant ships and block transport. During most of 1182, Reynaud's troops plundered and ravaged villages up and down the Red Sea at will. Further south, they sacked the port of Aydhab, which was an important staging post for pilgrims travelling from the Nile to Mecca. It is even suggested that he thought of sailing beyond the Bab al-Mandab and seeking the spice route to the Indies.[5] Then Reynaud's galleys destroyed a large pilgrim ship on its way to Jeddah. Salah-ad-Din responded in January 1183, by sending a fleet under a commander known for his naval prowess. He put an end to Reynaud's activities in the Red Sea within two months, burned three of his galleys and captured most of his troops. But a small battalion of Reynaud's army fought its way inland and was now marching towards Medina.

Estimates vary, but it is thought there were around 300 well-armed men, who were guided towards Medina by the Muslims they captured.

After marching across the desert for five days, and camping on a hill-top a few miles from Medina, they were met by Adil ibn Ayyub, the younger brother of Salah-ad-Din. The battle was swift. Around 170 Crusaders survived the encounter and were taken as prisoners. Some were executed at Muna in front of a huge crowd of Meccans. Others were taken to Cairo and humiliated in public. While in Alexandria, it was the first thing that ibn Jubayr saw: 'a large concourse of people came forth to gaze upon Rumi prisoners being brought to the town on camels, facing the tail and surrounded by timbal and horn'.[6]

Reynaud himself, who had come to be known in the Muslim world as 'the Demon of the West', came to a similar end. Captured in the disastrous rout of the Crusader forces at the Battle of Hattin in 1187, he was brought before Salah-ad-Din. Despite being known for his magnanimity, in this instance the sultan made an exception, and personally beheaded his arch-enemy.

There were other things to celebrate apart from Mecca's escape from the Crusaders. Selecting the anniversary of the completed rebuilding of the Kaaba by ibn Zubair, the inhabitants of Mecca decided on a day of celebration. It would begin with *umra* (the lesser pilgrimage), on the 27th of the Islamic month of Rajab 597, corresponding to 2 May 1201. The date was significant for another reason: the day commemorated Prophet Muhammad's 'Night Journey', a vision in which he travelled first to Jerusalem and then ascended to Heaven. To perform the *umra*, the residents of Mecca had to go to a station outside the city (called the *miqat*, which marks the boundaries of the holy area), change into pilgrim dress and, after a ritual ablution, re-enter the city as pilgrims. The whole population of Mecca left the city and made their way to the *miqat*. When they returned as pilgrims, they discovered to their utter amazement that Mecca had been seized by a warrior prince. The city now had a new ruler. His name was Qatada ibn Idris.

A descendant of the Hashims, Qatada was said to be a tall, slim and honourable man, known for both his devotion and his bravery.

It is possible that he had participated in the rout of Reynaud's soldiers near Medina, and after the battle he simply marched with troops to an empty Mecca. He had just turned seventy. There was an obligatory attempt by Sharif Mikhthar's son, with the help of the emir of Medina, to regain the city. It proved futile. The new ruler of Mecca was a man of considerable political skills and his ambitions were not limited to Mecca. He wanted to rule the entire Hijaz and make the region an independent territory as so many other parts of the Muslim world had done over the course of time. Within two years he had reduced Medina to obedience and captured Taif and other towns in the region. He turned out to be a strong and fiercely independent ruler, and the ancestor of all later sharifs. Qatada brought peace and prosperity to Mecca for ten years.

That the city was in a state of relative calm was exceptionally fortunate. It had a renowned visitor who needed amity and quiet for his extraordinary works. Muhyi Din ibn Arabi was already known as al-Sheikh al-Akbar (The Supreme Master) throughout Muslim lands when he came to perform the Hajj in 1202. Born in the Andalusian town of Murcia in 1165 and educated in Seville, he is said to have gone into seclusion when he was sixteen. By the time he was in his mid-twenties, he had acquired a reputation for intense spirituality and commanding imagination. His three years' stay in Mecca provided the inspiration for many of his works, including the monumental thirty-seven volumes of *Meccan Revelations*,[7] which attempts to unearth the mystical mysteries of the Hajj and develops (yet another) metaphysical edifice around the city.

Ibn Arabi was a visionary in the literal sense. He had visions, and lots of them. His deeply textured writings tend to be both a product and an exploration of his visions. Rich in symbolism, ibn Arabi is an allusive and complex writer, sometimes almost impossible to fathom, often taxing the interpretative skills of the most accomplished scholars. In Mecca he had a number of visions, the most important his encounter with the Kaaba. In this vision, ibn Arabi saw himself going around the

Kaaba when he noticed that the Kaaba 'was pushing me with itself and pushing me away from circumambulation of it and threatening me with words which I could hear with my ears'. He was so alarmed that he could not move. Then, 'gathering its tail and getting ready to rise from its foundations and into itself', the Kaaba began to speak. It said to him: 'Advance so that you can see what I will do to you! How you lower my power and elevate the power of the Banu Adam [humanity]. You prefer the agnostics over me. Might belongs to the one who has might. I will not let you circumambulate me.' Alarmed, ibn Arabi tries to hide and shield himself. 'When I saw it leap from its place, gathering its garment about it, it also seemed to me that it drew its veils onto itself in order to attack me and it was in a moving form.' The mystic tries to appease the Kaaba by writing some verses in its praise: 'It showed happiness at what I let it hear until it reverted to its previous state.'⁸

The vision leads ibn Arabi to conclude that the true symbolism of the Kaaba, the Sacred Mosque, various rites of the Hajj and the significance of Mecca is not appreciated by the vast majority of Muslims. They come in their hundreds of thousands to the Sacred City but they do not visit it. They do not see what they come to gaze at. They do not feel what they have come to experience. They remain untouched by the true celestial dimensions of the city. The point is illustrated in a long story told from the perspective of an ordinary pilgrim who encounters a saint. The saint asks him:

'Have you looked at Mecca?' 'Yes,' I replied. He further asked: 'Has a state from The Real looked at you by your looking at Mecca?' 'No,' I admitted. He said: 'You have not looked at Mecca.'

'Did you enter the Masjid al-Haram?' 'Yes,' I replied. He said: 'When you entered the Masjid al-Haram, did you believe that you had left every forbidden thing?' 'No,' I said. 'You did not enter.'

'Have you seen the Kaaba?' 'Yes,' I said. He asked: 'Did you see what you intended?' 'No,' I replied. He said: 'Then you have not seen the Kaaba.'

'Have you removed your garment?' 'Yes,' I replied. He asked me: 'Have you stripped yourself of everything?' 'No,' I replied. He replied: 'You have not removed them.'[9]

The story takes us through all the sites of Mecca and every single ritual of the Hajj to illustrate that the actions of most Muslims are mechanical and without spiritual significance. In the rest of the book, ibn Arabi reveals the multiple layers of meaning and significance of each site and rite, and explores the symbolism of the Hajj at great length. Thus, the circumambulation of the Kaaba is like going round the Throne of God. The Black Stone is the right hand of God on earth; to touch it is to touch the Real and be changed for ever. Running between the hills of Safa and Marwah is an act of supreme compassion; it is running 'from God to God with God by God'.

After one has gone through countless allegories, numerous abstract poems, elusive prose, and been perplexed and dazzled by an elaborate system of coded imagery, ibn Arabi suggests that visiting Mecca and the Sacred Mosque is like visiting your own house. The House of God in Mecca, he writes, is like yours, and:

of your genus, that is, it is created. So His directing you to the House is His directing you to yourself in His words: 'Whosoever knows himself knows His Lord.' Therefore when you make for the House, you make for yourself. When you reach yourself, you recognize who you are. When you recognize who you are, you recognize your Lord, and at that you know whether you are He or you are not He. There you acquire sound knowledge.[10]

To look at Mecca, ibn Arabi seems to be suggesting, is to look into a Divine mirror: it reflects the divinity within you and the reflection can guide you towards becoming a 'perfect' person with true knowledge of God. For ibn Arabi the image of the mirror is of fundamental importance; it is an integral part of his overall philosophy of the

Unity of Being (*wahdat al-wujud*), in which God and His creation are united and the only truth within the universe is God.

Not everyone in Mecca was impressed by ibn Arabi's symbolic, speculative and visionary analysis. The four schools of Islamic legal thought were well represented in the city and they took exception to his 'Unity of Being' thesis. There were murmurs of heresy. Some traditional scholars made their feelings known by deliberately mispronouncing his name, effortlessly slurring their way from Muhyi al-Din (the reviver of religion) to Mahi al-din or Mumit al-din (the eraser or slayer of religion). Ibn Arabi himself was above such banalities. Besides, he had other preoccupations. Before arriving in Mecca, he had spent virtually all his life in spiritual occupations and pursuit of divine love. The city had so profound an effect on him that later scholars were to divide his life into pre-Meccan and post-Meccan periods. In Mecca, he not only wrote *Meccan Revelations* but also the first chapters of his other masterpiece *Futūḥāts* and sections of numerous other books. And in Mecca he found love of a more earthly nature. He became infatuated with the beautiful daughter of his host. Naturally, she became his personification of beauty and wisdom and inspired him to produce a whole volume of poetry. *Interpreter of Desires*[11] is a wonderful work, less opaque than his mystical outpourings; it pays homage to the tradition of early Arabic poetry. It had most of the trade-mark symbolism of ibn Arabi but much use was made of customary Arabic imagery of the desert and numerous names for the beloved:

> O Marvel! A bower amidst the flames,
> My heart is now capable of every form,
> A meadow it is for gazelles, for monks a monastery;
> A shrine for idols, for pilgrims the very Kaaba;
> The tables of the Torah, the book of the Qur'an.
> Love is my faith. Wherever its camels may roam,
> There is found my religion, my faith.[12]

The young and flirty on the streets of Mecca, not too concerned with *Meccan Revelations*, devoured *Interpreter of Desires*. And they read and enjoyed it, to the dismay of ibn Arabi, purely in secular, physical terms. Indeed, they were programmed to do so. For behind all the political turmoil and violence that charts the course of history, Mecca had a thriving cultural scene with love poetry at its core. When ibn Zubair was defending the city from Yazid's troops, Mecca was in the midst of another revolution. Pre-Islamic poetry was being transformed into something radically different. A whole new genre of love poetry known as *ghazal*, consisting of rhyming couplets and a refrain, with each line sharing the same metre, was being invented. The chief architect of the new genre was the Quraysh poet Umar ibn Abi Rabia (d. 712).[13] Umar's unrestrained poetry was the rage of the city; later, he was to acquire such a reputation that the adjective 'Umari' was used to refer to uninhibited Hijazi *ghazals*. The form travelled, adopted in languages and cultures far from Arabia that looked to Mecca for inspiration. It is the glory of Urdu poetry, on which I was raised. *Ghazals* eventually found their way into Bollywood movies of the classic era, the 1950 and 60s, when renowned poets provided the lyrics for the essential musical interludes and in the very best films made them constructive elements in the storytelling rather than the mindless ditties that seem to be in favour these days.

Umar, whose *ghazals* were largely based on his own experiences, was not interested in the longing of hopeless lovers – the classic theme of *ghazals*, developed by his contemporary Hijazi poet, Jamil (d. 701). In Jamil's poems hopeless lovers pine for each other, seldom meet or consummate their love, and frequently end up dying of unfulfilled desire. This is a general theme not just of Arabic poetry but also of Persian, Turkish and Urdu *ghazals*. For Umar there was already too much pain and sorrow in Mecca. He was much more interested in the joy of love, the unbridled embrace of lovers leading to consummation of their love. In classical Arabic poetry the story is always told in the past tense. For Umar love exists in the present, it is a game with many hurdles, but with forbidden – and hence more desirable – rewards.[14] Meccans may look up to jurists and religious scholars, but the city, as Umar emphasizes, has other heroes: young men looking for sexual conquests. He is often the hero of his poems, the handsome young man no woman can resist. When on rare occasions lovers actually meet in classical Arabic poetry, the scene is closed at their meeting and the rest is left to the imagination. In contrast, Umar has his characters stripping, revealing the play of two young lovers, and goes on to show how they avoid being caught and manage to escape undetected after their meeting:

> Behind me they dragged the hems of their garments,
> of soft material,
> so that the footsteps should not be discovered.[15]

Apart from the two lovers, the narratives often have a third person, the confidant who shares the secret, arranges the meeting, and helps them break out of precarious situations. In one of his poems, the collaborator is his lover's maid, who aids his escape disguised as a woman. The Hajj caravans brought pilgrims to Mecca; but they also brought young women. And Umar and his young companions were often found 'standing on the corner, watching all the [pilgrim] girls go by'. Once they spotted their mark, they would follow them:

> I spotted her at night walking with her women between the shrine
>   and the [Black] Stone.
> 'Well then', she said to a companion, 'for Umar's sake let us spoil
>   this circumambulation.
> Go after him so that he may spot us, then, sweet sister, give him a
>   coy wink.'
> 'But I already did,' she said, 'and he turned away.'
> Whereupon she came rushing after me.[16]

Clearly, Umar's poetry had a direct appeal to young men in the Holy City. Their popularity was considerably enhanced by their conversational tone and accessibility. The city's young men were eager to follow the example of Umar. Since his popularity endured it was inevitable that young men tried to read ibn Arabi's more opaque offerings in the same vein. The problem he faced was not simply that this constituted an unholy reading of *Interpreter of Desires*. It was that, just like the *ghazals* of Umar, it was set to music.

By the time of ibn Arabi, the theory of music was highly advanced in the Muslim world. It was their interest in mathematics that led Muslim philosophers and thinkers to music, and for many it was not just a source of entertainment but had a medicinal purpose: it could be used to calm the soul and temper the spirit. Learned men in Mecca were well aware of studies on music by al-Kindi (d. 873), the Iraqi who is known as 'the First Arab Philosopher', who wrote on the cosmological aspect of music; and the other great philosopher of Baghdad of this era, al-Farabi (d. 950), whose *The Grand Book of Music (Kitāb al-musīqī al-Kabīr)* provides a comprehensive account of the principal melody instruments then in use and the scales produced by them.[17] Students in Mecca were also poring over the work of the great Persian polymath ibn Sina (d. 1037). His *Canons of Medicine* contained a masterly section on the therapeutic properties of music.[18] A musical treatise by his student ibn Zola (d. 1048) was being circulated in the city. So educated young men in Mecca appreciated both the theory (*musiqa*) and practice (*ghina*, the art of singing) of music.

Great musicians were an integral part of the Umayyad and Abbasid courts. They incorporated influences from Byzantine and Persian musical practice, and quite a few of these virtuoso singers and instrumentalists – who are known to us only by their names: ibn Misjah (d. 710?), ibn Muhriz (d. 715), ibn Surayj (d. 726), Mabad (d. 743) – came to perform the Hajj and stayed for some time to give performances in the houses of wealthy Meccans. Often they left students behind who in turn became master musicians performing on the outskirts of the city for rich patrons. Away from the Sacred Mosque, Mecca had a vibrant and energetic music scene. Umar's poems were regularly and playfully performed at such gatherings. Now, ibn Arabi's *Interpreter of Desires* became part of the repertoire. It was being sung by famous musical interpreters, and given a decidedly secular tone. This was nothing short of a scandal, and the traditional scholars used it as an argument to denounce ibn Arabi's mystical philosophy.

Horrified by the abuse of his poem, ibn Arabi was forced to write a detailed commentary on *Interpreter of Desires*, showing that each line had multiple layers of meaning, and pointing out that his 'beloved' was nothing like Umari's lovers but served as a symbol of divine beauty. Just to prove his point he abandoned the pursuit of the daughter of his host and married another Meccan woman, Fatima bint Yunus.

Despite the scandals and accusations of heresy he faced in Mecca, ibn Arabi was totally enamoured with the city, around which he built a grand metaphysics and philosophy that still enthrals people today. He was smitten by the Meccans: 'The land of Mecca is the best land of God,' he wrote, and the best land of God could only produce the most worthy of all people. Meccans are 'the neighbours of God and the people of his House, and they are the closest creation to the firsts of the places of worship. So God gives them a Self-disclosure in His name, The First, and only the people of the Haram obtain this self-disclosure. They rival in that according to the principle of worthiness.'[19]

Given his passionate attachment to the city, it is not surprising to find ibn Arabi arguing in *Meccan Revelations* that the dispute between Mecca and Medina about which city is the most worthy is rather trite. Both are virtuous cities. But Mecca has no parallel:

O Medinan! The excellence of your land is above the lands
    but the excellence of Mecca is greater,
A land which contains the Sacred House as a qibla
    for the worlds to which the mosques turn.
He made a Haram of its land and its game
    although game is lawful in every land.
There are all the waymarks, signs and practices
    and mankind travels to its excellence . . .
So seek your emir and visit him and do not attack a city
    which is immense, and it is better for you to be warned.
God drives rain to the valley of Mecca
    and you are slaked by it and it drops to Medina.[20]

The problem with mystics is that, drunk on Divine Love, they tend to roam about with their eyes closed. Mecca may have been worthy but Meccans were something else. And, as things had been, so they would be again. I have to admit that the deeper I venture into the history of the real place rather than the idealized city of the celestial realm, the more sympathy I have for the Qarmatian theory of never-ending unreformed groundhog days. Mystics intoxicated by their beautiful visions might come and go; the city they left behind would live on in the old familiar pattern. Qatada might have succeeded in his policy of ruling Mecca in splendid isolation but for two things: his treatment of the Iraqi pilgrims and his sons. There were incidents between the Meccans and the Iraqi pilgrims in 1210 and again in 1212.

Accompanying the pilgrim caravan of 1212 was Rabia Khatoon, sister of Adil ibn Ayyub, and the mother of Salah-ad-Din. In Muna, during the ceremonial throwing of stones, Ismaili assassins – who had been active in the region for several decades, murdering various leaders and personalities in pursuit of their religious and political goals – surrounded a sharif, a cousin of Qatada, who resembled him. Believing him to be Qatada, they killed him. When Qatada heard the news, he was incensed. He gathered his African bodyguards, climbed the hills on either side of Muna and began to catapult and shoot arrows. The next day he looted the pilgrims. There were casualties on both sides. The leader of the caravan was advised to move the pilgrims from Muna to the usual pilgrim camping ground near to one of the main gates into Mecca, the al-Zahir Gate. This move was interpreted by Qatada as a sign that the pilgrims were about to fight; he launched a pre-emptive attack and killed hundreds of pilgrims. 'As I was meant to be killed I will not leave one of them alive,'[21] he declared.

The desperate caravan leader took them to the safest refuge he could think of: the camp of Rabia Khatoon. She summoned Qatada and asked imperiously what crime he supposed the pilgrims to have committed. Or was he using the murder of his relative merely as an excuse to loot the caravan? Confronted by a matriarch of the Ayyubid dynasty, Qatada agreed to cease hostilities, but only if the pilgrims paid him 100,000 dinars in compensation. Around 30,000 dinars were actually collected for him from the pilgrims, with a significant contribution from Rabia. Hundreds of people remained around her tent for three days to be sure of her protection, 'being many of them hungry, wounded, naked, and some of them dying. Qatada was convinced that the assassination had been planned by the Caliphs, and so he swore to kill any pilgrims from Baghdad the next year.'[22]

Despite his oath, or perhaps because of it, the following year Qatada sent his son Rijal to Baghdad with an apology. The caliph forgave his transgression and sent a great quantity of gifts and money. Qatada was invited to visit Baghdad. In fact he went as far as Kufa before having second thoughts and returning to Mecca – sending another apology, this time in verse, to the caliph.

The entire thrust of centuries of religious fervour, thought and poetry had been to convince Muslims that Mecca was different, a place not so much apart as exalted above all others. There was, however, one regard in which Mecca was neither different from the rest of the Muslim world nor a place showing any inkling of divine peace: the quest for power. Here indeed Mecca was a mirror, a reflection of earthly realities. Nothing demonstrates this better than the period that ended Qatada's rule, in 1220, and its aftermath. By now he was ninety, and his health was failing rapidly. The succession was disputed by all of his eight sons, although Qatada himself favoured Rijal. However, it was the eldest, Hassan, who took the initiative. First, he murdered an uncle, who might have been a rival. Then, he smothered his father with a pillow. Another brother who was in Yanbu was invited to Mecca and murdered. All the remaining brothers fled the country – except Rijal.

Next Hassan killed the emir of an Iraqi pilgrim caravan and hung his head from a waterspout in the Sacred Mosque on suspicion that he had come to support his brother Rijal. But Hassan's ambition to rule Mecca was thwarted by the Ayyubid prince al-Masud (also known as Aqsis), who was then the viceroy of Yemen. While Hassan was murdering and driving his brothers out of the Holy City, al-Masud intervened and attacked Hassan inside the city. Hassan fled and the viceroy of Yemen remained in the city for seven years. When al-Masud died in 1228, one of his lieutenants established his authority. Hassan, who had gathered an army from Yanbu, attacked the Yemeni forces in Mecca in an attempt to regain the city, but he was defeated, retreated to Baghdad and died there without ever returning to Mecca.

It was now Rijal's turn to try and regain his father's inheritance. His first attempt in 1229 failed. He was successful in 1232, but had to flee again the following year. For the next two decades, the ruler of Mecca changed on an almost yearly basis, with Egyptians, Syrians, Yemenis and the sharifs all vying with each other for control of the Holy City. It must have been the rulers of Mecca who, a century later, inspired ibn Khaldun, the Arab historian and founder of sociology, to produce his grand theory. History repeats itself in cycles, ibn Khaldun wrote in his seminal work *Introduction to History*;[23] every cycle repeats and replicates the folly of what went before – a far more elegant and sophisticated statement of the groundhog principle.

Despite political turmoil, the city had a constant stream of visitors who observed and recorded these follies. Fortunately, not all the visitors to Mecca were preoccupied with the Machiavellian politics of the city or its obscurantist religious rituals. When the Persian ibn al-Mujawir visited Mecca, between 1226 and 1230, he was more concerned with people than politics. Ibn al-Mujawir was probably from Khorasan, knew the eastern provinces of the Muslim world well and harboured literary ambitions. Unlike most Muslim travellers of this age, he was not a scholar, a jurist or a deep religious thinker. He was clearly a very devout person. His main interests were trade and commerce, and apart from performing the Hajj he had no interest in the religious significance or rituals of the city. He focused his attention on the social customs, markets and currencies, and stories about magic and the bizarre. A man with a wicked sense of humour, ibn al-Mujawir described himself as a 'historical geographer'. The account of his travels, *Tarikh al-Mustabsir*,[24] written in rhymed prose, provides a fascinating insight into social life in the Holy City and its surrounding areas during the first half of the thirteenth century.

Unlike ibn Arabi, ibn al-Mujawir found the Meccans to be people of little integrity. The inhabitants, he tells us, are 'dusky people since most of their partners are black slave girls from Abyssinia and Nubia. They are physically tall, speak correctly, are poor but belong to numerous families and tribes and are content.'[25] It is the anthropological detail of his account that fascinates and tantalizes. For example, he notes that the attire of the Meccans is made of fine Nishapuri cloth of silk and linen and that their womenfolk wear bonnets. Given the perennial debate about what constitutes *hijab*, often referred to as the veil, or otherwise the form of headdress that fulfils the contentious question of appropriate 'Islamic' dress, it would have been useful if ibn al-Mujawir had given a clearer indication of just what he meant by 'bonnets'. He was more concerned to inform his readers that far from being beautiful, Meccan women have large buttocks 'since they increase them in size on purpose' and because they are 'constantly being on all-fours'[26] – one presumes, scrubbing the floor or gratifying the desires of the generations who followed in the footsteps of Umar ibn Abi Rabia.

In a town a couple of miles from Mecca called al-Mahalib, ibn al-Mujawir discovers women who only wear leather: 'the woman takes two pieces of leather and stitches them together, cuts a round hole in it and puts it on. When she walks, the whole of her body can be seen, above and below.' This would be consistent with his comment about people being poor. However, it also throws light on the opinion of classical commentaries on the Qur'an. The recitation asks women to 'draw their head-coverings over their bosoms',[27] leading to the interpretation that the objective is to cover their nakedness, rather than to shroud themselves in the all-concealing black shroud, the *abaya*, that is familiar to us today. The problem of women achieving modest attire, seemingly, was still evident in the thirteenth century.

Throughout *Tarikh al-Mustabsir*, ibn al-Mujawir uses two imaginary characters – Zayd and Amr – to illustrate the customs of the people and tribes he encounters. So he tells us that 'When Zayd becomes engaged to the daughter of Amr' in Mecca, 'all those getting married go into their wives publicly and making a show.' And why is this? We learn that because the population of Mecca are all involved with the pilgrims, their social lives are suspended during the period of Hajj. It is when the pilgrims leave that people continue their engagements, family festivals and marriage celebrations. The grooms can't wait, so they have sex at engagement – before they are actually married. A marriage begins with agreeing the amount of dowry to be paid to the woman. Ibn al-Mujawir tells us that it is the man who 'dyes his hands and feet in a decorative manner' to signify the forthcoming marriage. I had always thought this practice was specific to women. It is certainly so in the Indian subcontinent, where the *mehndi* ceremony is preceded by a gathering of women where the bride sits patiently while intricate designs are drawn on hands and feet with henna. She then sits even more patiently waiting for them to dry.

The families of the bride and groom gather, and each member brings a piece of paper on which is written the name of the guest, together with the weight and number of everything they intend to present to the bridegroom, 'each according to their situation and financial means. The women do the same.' The bridegroom then goes to the Sacred Mosque, performs the circumambulations and other rituals, and with a candle in his hand goes to 'the house of the bride and she is revealed to him. He consummates the marriage and remains with her for seven days.' On the seventh day he leaves, collects all the money he has been promised, and uses it as a working capital: 'immediately he opens a shop from which he can earn his living'. This customary practice is familiar in many parts of the world. It is what anthropologists call mutual reciprocity, and as such is an essential part of tribal solidarity. The bridegroom is not receiving largesse, he is obligated to repay his relatives at the time of their marriage 'the same amount which they gave to him or even more'.[28]

In nearby al-Mahalib, the marriage customs are stranger.

If Zayd asks for Amr's daughter in marriage and the later gives a positive response, Zayd goes into Amr's daughter and deflowers her, remaining with her all night. In the morning he departs, leaving his shoes in the daughter's room, so that Amr knows that Zayd finds her pleasing. The marriage contract is then drawn up. But if he puts on his shoes and leaves, Amr knows that Zayd is not pleased with his daughter. This happens even now amongst the most distinguished of them.[29]

While there is no reason to doubt ibn al-Mujawir's description, it is clear that he does not have a very high regard for the inhabitants of

Mecca. Compared with the sophisticated cosmopolitanism of Baghdad (he uses the appellation 'al-Baghdadi' to indicate he lived in the city for some time) or the cultured ways of Persia, he finds the Meccans to be philistines, mired in their tribal customs and lacking in basic decencies. Sometimes he is direct in his condemnation. 'There is no one in the whole world more foul-smelling, more negligent, more sinful and viler than these people in taking the wealth of the pilgrims,' he writes. They call pilgrims 'God's begging bowl!'

> If you say to one of them, 'God cut off your sustenance which you have which is unlawful,' he will reply, 'No, rather God cut off any sustenance which you have which is lawful. You can see the only goodness we have is these black mountains; we have no agriculture, no livestock, no income and nothing to give away . . . So God has given us the advantage over you in this region, so that we get back what is just for the pilgrims among you and a third of what is unjust.'[30]

Somehow it seems that the spirituality of living in a celestial realm is lost on the inhabitants of Mecca.

At times he brings out the devious practices of the Meccans by simple statements of facts, like his observation that the standard of measurement used in the city changes slightly during the time of pilgrimage to the benefit of the Meccans. And sometimes he subverts his observation by sly commentary, often told as a story. Just outside Mecca, he tells us, is a place called Maqtalat al-Kalib (meaning place where dogs are killed). 'The reason for this name is that there was a dog belonging to a certain Bedouin and the dog attacked a man of the village, bit him and made him blind in one eye. So the man killed the dog. Whereupon the owner of the dog assembled his paternal relatives, while the man bitten assembled his people and war broke out between the two parties. They continued fighting until they were all killed. So the place became known as Maqtalat al-Kilab.'[31]

It is possible that the place where dogs were killed did not actually exist. Ibn al-Mujawir may be using the story as an allegory for the political machinations in Mecca. Despite the sacred nature of the city, there was nothing hallowed or commendable about the political and social behaviour of its inhabitants. The sharifs were anything but what their title suggested: noble and humane. One ruler after another invaded Mecca, forced out the incumbent, ruled by force and terror, and, after a short period, was driven out himself by a new sharif. Rijal was ensconced as the ruler of Mecca on no fewer than eight separate occasions. Forget musical poetry, this was political control as an often bloody game of musical chairs. Political stability, after a fashion, was introduced in 1254 when Muhammad Abu Nomay acquired power. Abu Nomay I, as he came to be known, was a stocky man with a dark complexion who was highly respected by the Meccans for his five qualities: honour, generosity, patience, courage and poetry. He preferred the desert to the mosque and ruled Mecca firmly but justly, sometimes in cooperation with his son and sometimes in alliance with the emir of Medina, for nearly fifty years. Mecca needed the steadiness he brought.

He came to power at a crucial time. In the middle of the thirteenth century the entire world of Islam changed drastically. In 1258, news reached Mecca of the sacking of Baghdad. The Mongol horde, under the command of Hulagu Khan, swept out of Central Asia like an immense force of nature, devastating everything in their path. It was a human tidal wave of destruction that had worldwide ramifications. Mecca greeted the news with mixed feelings. There was shock at the collapse of the Caliphate in Baghdad, at reports that the caliph and his sons were killed and that the entire city was in flames. The obvious fact that no pilgrims would now be coming from Iraq was of specific concern – indeed, the pilgrim caravan from Baghdad did not come for the next nine years. However, given the antagonistic relationship Mecca had enjoyed over the years with Baghdad there was also some relief at the demise of the Baghdad Caliphate. The Iraqi caravans, when they resumed, would no longer be of political significance.

A political earthquake had also taken place in Cairo, where power passed from the Ayyubids to the Mamluks. Egypt was now ruled by former slaves, who had served as professional soldiers both in the Abbasid as well as the Ayyubid regimes. And of particular interest for Mecca was the news that az-Zahir Rukn-ad-Din Baybars al-Bandaqdari, the Mamluk king of Egypt (r. 1260–77), was coming to perform the Hajj.

Baybars was a towering figure.[32] Tall, with a commanding voice, he was highly energetic, very fond of travel and always on the move. Born in the Crimea, he was bought as a slave when a young boy. His first master quickly sold him because he was said to have had a minor defect, possibly a cataract, in one of his blue eyes. He grew up to become a bodyguard to an Ayyubid ruler and went on to become the commander of a Mamluk army. He was responsible for the crippling defeat on the Seventh Crusade of King Louis IX of France. The Crusaders had determined to confront the centre of effective power in the Middle East by attacking Egypt directly. Landing at Damietta on the Nile, Louis was eventually captured after the Battle of Fariskur in 1250, where his army was annihilated. Ransomed for a huge sum of money, he withdrew to Acre, before returning to France. While Louis was to take the Cross once again in 1270 in the abortive Eighth Crusade, his confrontation with Baybars is seen as sealing the demise of the Latin Kingdom of Outremer. Its cities fell one by one: Antioch in 1268, Tripoli in 1289 and the last outpost, Acre, in 1291.

Almost two hundred years of conflict had made a decisive impact on Europe. The Crusades were not separate military adventures but an all-embracing social and cultural movement that shaped Europe's view of itself and the wider world. It was a period of intense exchange when accurate information about the learning of the Muslim world passed into Europe. The universities, an idea borrowed from the Muslims which spread across Europe, taught the works of the great Muslim scholars whose names became familiar in Latinized form. Supporting the idea of Crusade in Europe was a sophisticated work of propaganda that also disseminated an immense amount of disinformation about Islam, its Prophet and Mecca as the common currency of popular literary works and understanding. The legacy of these perverse views did not evaporate with the end of the Latin Kingdom or Europe's military adventures into the Middle East: their cultural fallout is with us still. In the thirteenth century it fuelled the animosity that made the enemy of one's enemy seem a potential friend. Christian missionaries were dispatched to try and make common cause between the Crusaders and the Mongols, though effective coordination was never attained. Again it was Baybars, leading the vanguard of the Mamluk army, who is credited with halting the advance of the Mongol horde at the Battle of Ain Jalut in 1260, the year he assumed the Sultanate of Egypt.

When he visited Mecca, in 1269, Baybars was at the height of his power; indeed, the most powerful ruler in the Muslim world. He arrived with immense largesse, distributed generously to the inhabitants of Mecca, as well as pilgrims. He also brought a new cover for the Kaaba – the *kiswa* – with his name embroidered in it. It is said that flowers were brought from Egypt every day during his stay. Baybars tried his best to patch up the differences within the ruling family of the Holy City. He regarded Abu Nomay as an energetic and competent ruler and was happy to leave the government of Mecca in his hands. So while swathes of the Muslim world were still reeling from the upheavals caused by the arrival of the Mongol terror, Mecca was insulated by its peripheral location. Indeed it was a beneficiary of the power and bounty that marshalled the Muslim riposte to the Mongol invasion.

Despite all his qualities, Abu Nomay I also had, by some accounts, thirty rather bad features: his sons. Just before his death, he abdicated in favour of two of them: Humaidha and Rumaitha. The old man died peacefully – a rare occurrence amongst Meccan rulers – at the age of seventy, in 1301. He was buried in a Meccan cemetery that was established as the burial place in the city for the sharifs. No sooner had a cupola been built over his tomb, than war broke out between his sons.

Of Abu Nomay's thirty sons, four actually ruled Mecca at one time or another: Abul Ghaith, Utayfa, Humaidha and Rumaitha. The story of the conflict between brothers is rather complex, but simply put, this is what happened. Humaidha was not too happy to share power with his brother Rumaitha, according to the arrangement made by their father. He was also concerned about challenges from his siblings. So in 1314 he killed Abul Ghaith. He took the body, it is reported, to his own house and invited all his brothers to dinner. When they arrived and sat down for dinner a slave bodyguard stood behind each with sword drawn. The main dish on the menu was the body of their brother, Abul Ghaith, cooked whole. Some of Humaidha's brothers got the message and fled the Hijaz. Some regrouped and vowed to kill Humaidha. In the end, Humaidha himself had to flee.

He took refuge with the Mongol ruler in Iraq. By now the Mongols had converted to Islam. The old familiar Meccan lure, the promise of a mention in the Friday *khutba* to confer and publish a mantle of legitimacy before the whole Muslim world, was all that Humaidha needed to obtain his support. So, in 1318, Humaidha returned to Mecca with a Mongol army and took over the city. Immediately, the name of the Mamluk king of Egypt, al-Nasir Nasir-ad-Din Muhammad, was dropped and replaced with that of Abu Said Khurbandr, the Mongol in Baghdad. As one would expect, it did not please Sultan al-Nasir. He dispatched an army to arrest Humaidha, who managed to escape from Mecca just in time. This left a vacancy in Mecca which was instantly filled by Utayfa, who had been in Egypt. The sultan's army eventually caught Humaidha two years later, in 1320, and executed him. Utayfa, honouring the wishes of his father, agreed to become co-ruler of Mecca with Rumaitha. The two ruled peacefully for a few years.

Once again, Mecca thrived, thanks largely to the rivalry that unleashed the generosity of kings and emperors rather than their wrath. Abu Said Khurbandr tried to regain the favour of the Meccans. He showered the city with gold and cash. Not to be outdone, al-Nasir increased the supply of wheat and corn, which were particularly welcomed during a time of famine. Then, in 1325, came Mansa Musa, the emperor of Mali in West Africa, who outshone all the rest in munificence. Mansa Musa's kingdom, with its capital in Timbuktu, a city noted for its scholars and learned men, controlled trade with the goldfields that supplied the bulk of that precious metal circulating in the Western world.[33] He travelled across Africa to join the pilgrim caravans in Cairo, and arrived in Mecca to a sensational welcome. He is said to have taken as many as 60,000 fellow pilgrims with him, along with hundreds of camels loaded with gold.

Exactly how much gold is much disputed amongst scholars. 'Some say 100 camels laden with gold, or no camels but 150 kilograms of gold, or 500 slaves carrying 6 pounds of gold each, plus 300 camels with 300 pounds of gold, or 500 slaves each carrying a rod of 2 kilograms of gold.'[34] However much gold Mansa Musa had with him, his generosity knew no bounds and he treated everyone, Meccans and pilgrims, ruler and ordinary citizens, with equal respect and dignity, showering them with gifts. The behaviour and politeness of his black followers made a special impression on the Meccans. They were particularly taken aback by his appearance: he had a pale complexion, which to the Meccans appeared almost red and yellow, giving the African monarch a distinctive look. And, unlike most other monarchs who visited Mecca, Mansa Musa had no political motive. He was there simply to perform the pilgrimage, and when he had fulfilled his religious duty, he left – considerably lighter in load, but accompanied by an Andalusian poet he had met in Mecca and to whom he had become attached. More importantly he also recruited an Andalusian architect to return with him to Mali. The grand palace the architect constructed is no more, but the Djinguereber Mosque he also built stands to this day in Timbuktu.

Such was the golden bounty distributed by Mansa Musa that the value of gold depreciated for a decade in the region from Cairo to Mecca. News of this golden pilgrimage spread not only throughout the Muslim world but was carried into Europe as well, where it gave birth to the legend of the golden city of Timbuktu. This fabled city in the heart of Africa stirred European adventurers almost as much as the lure of the forbidden city of Mecca. The mystery of its location was not resolved until the latter half of the nineteenth century, when the mud-brick buildings of this ancient university city proved not to be roofed in gold after all.

The bounty of Mansa Musa was a hard act to follow. The following year Abu Said Khurbandr tried a different tactic. He sent an elephant to Mecca. It was given a guided tour of the Sanctuary, and persuaded to perform all the rites of the Hajj, including the ritual circumambulation. Then, it was sent off to the City of the Prophet to visit his Mosque and tomb, and the poor animal died at the gateway of Medina.

In the wake of the elephant from the 'Tartar king' and Mansa Musa came the renowned Tunisian explorer ibn Battuta. He visited Mecca five times, between 1325 and 1354, performing the Hajj on each occasion, and spending up to a year in the city. During his first visit, he tells us in *Travels (Rihlah)*,[35] Mecca was ruled by two brother sharifs: Rumaitha, who thought of himself as 'the Sword of Religion', and Utayfa, who described himself as 'the Lion of Religion'. Utayfa lived near the Sanctuary in a house by the hill of Marwah, while his older brother, Rumaitha, lived in a convent in the outskirts of the city near the Gate of Bani Shayba. Every morning, drums were beaten, for a considerable length of time, at the doors of the two rulers. Ibn Battuta found Mecca to be 'a large town, compactly built and oblong in shape, situated in the hollow of a valley which is so shut that the visitor to her sees nothing of her until he actually reaches her'.[36]

Ibn Battuta confirms many of the observations of ibn Jubayr, made exactly 142 years earlier, particularly about the Sacred Mosque and the ceremonies surrounding the Friday prayers and the *khutab*. In sharp contrast to ibn al-Mujawir, he found 'the citizens of Mecca are given to well-doing, of consummate generosity and good disposition, liberal to the poor and to those who have renounced the world, and kindly towards strangers'. The inhabitants are elegant and clean in their dress, and as they mostly wear white their garments always appear spotless and snowy. They use perfume freely, paint their eyes with kohl, and are constantly polishing their teeth with twigs of green arak-wood.

So generous are the Meccans, ibn Battuta tells us, that even if they only have one loaf, they would happily give away a third or a half, 'conceding it cheerfully and without grudgingness'. He is impressed to observe the behaviour of the orphan children who find employment in the bazaar. When the townsfolk of Mecca come to the bazaar to buy grain, meat and vegetables, they pass their purchases to one of the boys, who puts the grain in one of his baskets and meat and vegetables in the other, and takes them to the man's house, so that his meal may be prepared from them. Meanwhile the man goes about his devotions and his business. There is no instance related of any of the boys having ever abused their trust in this matter – on the contrary he delivers what he has been given to carry, with the most scrupulous honesty. 'They receive for this a fixed fee of a few coppers.'[37] Moreover, unlike ibn al-Mujawir, who found the buttocks of the Meccan women rather forbidding, ibn Battuta thinks that 'the Meccan women are of rare and surpassing beauty, pious and chaste'. They do, however, make much use of perfume, to such a degree that a woman will spend the night hungry and buy perfume with the price of her food. On the eve of Friday, the day of the congregational prayer, groups of women gather to perform the circuit of the Kaaba.

They 'come in their finest apparel, and the Sanctuary is saturated with the smell of their perfume'.[38] Indeed, ibn Battuta finds nothing to complain about except the heat, which is so intense that the stones in the Sanctuary burn his feet.

The peace between Utayfa and Rumaitha did not last. The brothers started quarrelling again. They were ordered by Sultan al-Nasir to appear before his court in Cairo. While in Cairo, Utayfa was detained and died in prison in 1343. Rumaitha was allowed to return to Mecca and rule, assisted by his son Ahmad. Indeed, Sultan al-Nasir was so fed up with the political turmoil in Mecca that he considered exterminating all sharifs once and for all. But the religious scholars advised him against such drastic action. They might be a corrupt and murderous lot, but they were still descendants of the Prophet. Exercising the ultimate sanction against the sharifs might lead to disturbances amongst the sultan's subjects. Al-Nasir was persuaded. Rumaitha too realized that the sharifs were verging on the brink of extinction. He decided to modify his ambitions and behaviour.

Indeed, Rumaitha was sensible enough to hand over authority to his son Ajlan in 1344, two years before his death. Ajlan, who was often referred to as 'the Swift', became ruler of Mecca at the age of thirty-seven and lived to seventy, ruling with the obligatory disputes and intervals for twenty-five years. During this time there was peace and stability in the city and he was able to devote considerable time to its development. He built several water cisterns, almshouses and schools in the city, and a number of forts around it. To appease all the reigning monarchs in the Middle East, he allowed the name of the Mongol sultan to be mentioned in the Friday *khutba*. He is most noted for his harsh treatment of the Zaidis, the Shia sect that gave allegiance to Zaid ibn Ali, grandson of Hussain ibn Ali. The Zaidis, who are theologically much closer to Sunni Muslims than other Shia, were the dominant group in Yemen. They had a small but active presence in Mecca, and participated in many of the outbreaks of political unrest and rebellions the city had witnessed. Their ultimate allegiance belonged to their own imams and spiritual leaders.

Many of the sharifs themselves were originally Zaidis – it was the creed of their forefathers. But by now the dominant orthodoxy in Mecca – and much of the then Muslim world – was the Shafi school of thought. Ajlan had many notable Zaidis in the city tied to posts and whipped in the public square. One Zaidi muezzin was flogged so ruthlessly that he died. But rather than give up their faith, most Zaidis endured the persecution; some managed to flee to Yemen.

Ajlan's son, Ahmad, continued the policy of his father. The city had now become quite developed and, thanks to the riches bestowed on her by visiting monarchs, rather wealthy. Political stability brought its own rewards. Ahmad became so powerful that even the sultan in Cairo felt threatened. The 'Meteor of Religion', as Ahmad ibn Ajlan came to be known, was invited to visit Cairo several times, but he always managed to find an excuse for staying in Mecca. Towards the end of his reign, which lasted from 1360 to 1386, Ahmad became convinced that the Egyptians, or his relatives, would assassinate him. He started wearing chain mail, which made it quite impossible for him to perform either the lesser or the proper pilgrimage. Even performing the circuit around the Kaaba was problematic. Ahmad's fear was justified. The chain mail, however, was redundant. He was poisoned in 1386. A few days later his young son, Muhammad, was stabbed at Muna during the Hajj. Inevitably, political turmoil followed. During the next twelve months, Mecca had no fewer than five rulers – three ruling concurrently.

Two of Ajlan's sons (mercifully he only had five) managed to rule quite successfully. Ali ibn Ajlan ruled for seven years – from 1387 to 1394. When Ali was killed, his brother Hassan took over and managed to survive in conjunction with various co-rulers till 1425. During his long rule, Hassan established a regular army of mercenaries, which was passed from one ruler to another, to defend Mecca. He was also able to persuade the Egyptian sultan to award him the title of 'deputy of the sultan' for the whole of the Hijaz. But unlike his father, Ajlan, who was an independent ruler, Hassan could not escape the influence of the Mamluk sultans in Egypt. He functioned more as their vassal than as an independent sharif.

The arrangement proved beneficial for the city itself. Mecca was in urgent need of political stability. In 1399, the western side of the Sacred Mosque was burnt down. The fire started in a school that was connected to the Mosque through one of its doors. It spread quickly; over a hundred columns turned into ash and part of the ceiling collapsed. Then the fire spread to the northern side, damaging two sections of the porticoes. It could have easily engulfed the whole Sanctuary, but a flash flood stopped the fire from spreading. The citizens were gravely concerned; they wanted their ruler to give all his attention to rebuilding the Sacred Mosque. By now the Sanctuary had expanded so much and had grown so complex that it was a task beyond the means and capability of the Meccans. As 'deputy of the sultan', Hassan was able to get the full support of the Mamluk Sultan al-Nasir Farah bin Barqaq, who sent an accomplished architect, al-Amir Bist al-Zahiri, to oversee the rebuilding of the Sacred Mosque. Most of the city was involved in the reconstruction. Stone was cut from the mountains around Mecca. Columns were built and used to replace the 130 damaged marble columns. The building of the roof was delayed until the right wood could be brought from abroad. When it was finally completed, chains of lamps, carved with ornamental designs, were suspended from the ceiling.

During this period, three of Hassan's sons disputed the succession. To avoid any future bloodshed, the Egyptian sultan, al-Zahir Sayf-ad-Din Jaqmaq, chose Barakat and made him co-regent during Hassan's life. There was a good reason for his choice. Mecca had many schools and educational institutions; there were always scholars in the city looking for students. The education available in Mecca, however, was different from the curriculums that had become the norm elsewhere. Scholarship in the city was devoted almost exclusively to theology and law. To be properly educated in philosophy and rhetoric, astronomy and mathematics, medicine and geography, music and literature, one must go to Cairo, Damascus or Baghdad. It was a custom of well-off Meccans to send their sons abroad to acquire a more rounded education. Barakat ibn Hassan was educated in Egypt, where he became renowned for his literary knowledge. He became a sought-after teacher, with students from all over the world coming to study under him. While he was in Cairo, Sultan Jaqmaq personally invited the most distinguished scholars and literary men in Egypt to meet him. Barakat was thus close to the sultan. When his father died in 1425, Barakat faced little difficulty in succeeding him and was able, with slight interruptions, to rule Mecca until his own death in 1455.

Barakat was known not only for his literary prowess but also for his intellectual ability, genuine piety and good works. Indeed, he was probably the only sharif that Mecca had seen so far whose honesty and integrity the citizens could swear by and who did not kill anyone to gain power or flog anyone for holding beliefs different from his own. He dressed modestly – only his turban distinguished him from the other citizens of Mecca. Despite being a ruler, he was addressed in simple and direct fashion by the inhabitants of the city. He spent a great deal of time repairing public buildings and constructing new ones – a mosque and several guest houses – which were so well built that they were still in wide use towards the end of the eighteenth century.

But Barakat I ruled only as a representative of the Egyptian sultan. By now neither the ruler nor the citizens were too concerned about the ever stronger political influence from Egypt. Mecca longed for peace, and the Egyptian influence not only brought peace to Mecca but also enhanced the spiritual prestige of the sharifs. Every year, the sultan would send a *kiswa* and a *khila*. The *kiswa*, the black cover for the Kaaba, arrived with great fanfare and ceremony during the Hajj season, when the old one was removed and replaced with the new one. The *khila*, a robe of honour, arrived at the same time. It signified the sharif's designated authority and legitimate rule. While there was clearly a great deal of trust and rapport between the sultan and the sharif, the sultan did not want to take any chances. He placed a permanent garrison of fifty cavalrymen in the Holy City. They had in fact arrived as engineers to undertake the rebuilding work in the Sanctuary, but stayed on as soldiers. Their commander, known as the 'Inspector of the Holy Places', ostensibly took his orders from the sharif, but he reported directly to the sultan on the political and economic situation in Mecca. To handle financial matters, as well as to oversee the collection of taxes, the sharif appointed a vizier – usually an educated foreigner. The revenues of Mecca thus became stabilized. Many of the customs introduced by Barakat I for collection and dissemination of *zakat* (the obligatory religious poor tax), Hajj tax and other financial matters endured for several centuries.

Sharif Barakat I clarified the matter of his successor before he died. The agreement of the sultan had been obtained. His representatives in the Hijaz and Mecca approved of the choice. So the transfer of power from Barakat to his son Muhammad was smooth and peaceful. Muhammad ruled for four decades, continuing the good works of his father. He added new buildings in and around Mecca. In particular, he built a mosque of great beauty in Maymuna, near Mecca. It was the site where the Prophet married his twelfth wife, Barra bint al-Harith. The Prophet gave her the nickname 'Maymuna', meaning blessed, as his marriage to her marked the first occasion when he re-entered Mecca after his migration to Medina.

Muhammad son of Barakat had been the ruler in Mecca for three years when news came of the fall of Constantinople, the ancient capital of the Byzantine Empire. While Europe quailed, Mecca was overwhelmed with joy. The entire population rushed towards the Sacred Mosque to offer prayers of thanks. The more perceptive and educated citizens perceived that a major shift of power within the Muslim world was in the offing. The Ottoman Sultan Mehmet II, known as al-Fatih ('the Conqueror'), had achieved, in May 1453, what the Abbasid caliphs and Mamluk sultans could not. Indeed, his victory over Byzantium was the culmination of a project that had eluded Muslim forces ever since the first direct assault on the city made by Yazid, the son of Muawiya, the first Umayyad caliph, in the year 670.

What Ottoman ascendancy would mean for Mecca time would tell. In the meantime the city remained under the influence of the Egyptian sultans. When he came to the throne in 1468, the Mamluk Sultan al-Asharaf Sayf-ad-Din Qu'it Bay became the main benefactor of Mecca. From Circassia, Qu'it Bay had grown up as a slave. His extraordinary intelligence was noticed by Sultan al-Zahir Sayf-ad-Din Jaqmaq, who adopted him as a protégé. He rose rapidly through the ranks, finally acquiring the throne himself. Over the next decade, he had almost every monument in the Holy City cleaned and repaired. The Muzdalifah mosque was limewashed, the wells at Arafat cleaned, and the interior of the Kaaba roofed. Long-forgotten water channels were reopened. The quarters for the Egyptian pilgrims were renovated and extended. Old almshouses were repaired and new ones built. And four new schools, one for each of the traditional schools of thought, Shafi, Hanafi, Hanbali and Malikki, were built. In 1479, Sultan Qu'it Bay himself came to perform the Hajj, accompanied by his entire court. In fulfilment of a dream, he washed the interior of the Kaaba, watched by the nobles and religious scholars of Mecca. The relationship between the sultan and the sharif was so close that Muhammad named one of his sons after Qu'it Bay.

Sharif Muhammad son of Barakat died in 1495, leaving his own sixteen sons. The best-known was Barakat ibn Muhammad, who like his grandfather had become renowned for his learning and piety. He too was educated in Egypt, and had been a student, unusually, of a number of prominent female jurists. He had impressed Sultan Qu'it Bay, who approved his appointment. But his brothers Hamza and Jazan had other ideas. A period of war and obligatory caravan looting followed. Barakat II made several attempts to capture Mecca, involving a number of battles with his brothers. On one occasion, he was even arrested by the commander of the Egyptian troops and was taken in chains to Cairo. But he finally succeeded in gaining control of Mecca. Indeed, he became the ruler of the whole of Hijaz. His brother Qu'it Bay and his young son Ali became co-governors of Mecca.

The political landscape of the Middle East, however, was ready for another major transformation. In 1517, the Ottoman Sultan Selim annexed Egypt, putting an end to the Mamluk dynasty. The Hijaz, including Mecca and Medina, became part of the Ottoman Empire. The ageing Barakat II immediately sent his thirteen-year-old son, Muhammad Abu Nomay, to the court of Selim. The purpose was not just to pay homage to the new ruler, but also to secure some independence for Mecca. The Ottoman sultan was pleased to receive the young envoy from Mecca. Abu Nomay may have been a teenager, but he was very articulate. He regaled Sultan Selim with stories of the Holy City and gave him a detailed account of the political situation in the Hijaz. The sultan acknowledged the right of the sharifs to rule Mecca, confirmed the independence of the Holy City, and even agreed that the sovereignty of the sharifs should extend beyond Mecca to Medina, Jeddah and the whole of the Hijaz. There was only one condition. The supremacy of the 'Sublime Porte' – the symbolic term for the Ottoman Empire – had to be recognized.

Young Abu Nomay returned to Mecca with a *firman* – an edict from Sultan Selim. It was read out in the public squares of the city as well as in the Sanctuary, and put on the cloaks of honour that the sultan had sent to the sharifs. The Friday *khutba* now contained only one name: that of the Ottoman sultan.

6

The Caravans of Precious Gifts

Selim I attended the Friday prayer in the Grand Mosque of Aleppo after defeating the Mamluks in 1517. It was after this that his sovereignty over Mecca was openly acknowledged. During the sermon in the presence of al-Mutawakkil III, the last Abbasid caliph, the imam declared that the sultan was now the 'Ruler of the Two Sanctuaries' (Mecca and Medina). Recognizing the greater power of the Ottomans, the imam had deliberately avoided mentioning the term 'Protector of the Two Sanctuaries', the title adopted by the Mamluks. The sultan, however, was quick with his own correction. I am only the 'Servant of the Two Sanctuaries', he said.[1] 'This was more significant than his bearing the title of caliph, a title then in use by every Muslim ruler.'[2] But whatever the sultan's title and its significance, Mecca was now obliged to look towards Constantinople, which later became Istanbul, rather than Cairo or Baghdad, for protection and financial support. No wonder protection was urgently needed. No sooner had Selim I left Aleppo for Cairo than he heard the news that a Portuguese fleet had entered the Red Sea with the intention of attacking Jeddah and Mecca. The citizens of the Holy City were pleading for help.

The Muslim world turns to face Mecca while the fate of those who live in the city is determined by what is happening elsewhere in the wider world. Once again the dynamics of the wider world had changed. For centuries the seat of power had been moving further and further from the city. The legitimacy of claims to power had long ceased to be a matter of ties of lineage and blood to the Holy City;

they were expressed in terms of responsibility and power over the Holy City. To effectively rule, protect or serve Mecca it was necessary not merely to support the people of the city but also to secure the routes along which the pilgrims, who were the lifeblood of the city, travelled. As the Mamluks had already learnt to their cost, disrupting the Hajj and threatening Mecca was an objective of the Portuguese because they wanted to monopolize the spice trade of the Indian Ocean.

The arrival of the Portuguese signalled not merely a change in the internal dynamics of the Muslim world, but what in time was to become a profound shift in global power structures. The Red Sea was a major artery of the trading network of the Indian Ocean. Since antiquity, driven by the regular shifting pattern of the monsoon winds, the sea routes of this ocean brought spices, textiles and other products of the Indies to Arabia and Egypt. From there the goods were traded throughout the Middle East and onward to Europe. To 'secure their trade supremacy, the Portuguese began a campaign to destroy Muslim trade'.[3] Along these trade routes Islam spread around the Indian Ocean and its sea lanes brought pilgrims to perform the Hajj. The Portuguese determination to attack Mecca presented the Ottomans with a profound challenge, not because they were unfamiliar with the threat it posed, but because they were strangers to the Indian Ocean world. To effectively serve and protect Mecca, the Ottomans embarked on a journey of nearly half a century of intense military, diplomatic and intellectual endeavour to learn and become involved with parts of the Muslim world about which they knew little. In many ways these Ottoman endeavours mirrored the 'discoveries' of the Portuguese interlopers.

The arrival of the Portuguese had been long in the making. Their journey started in 1415 with the capture of Ceuta, a port on the coast of Morocco.[4] There they had hoped to lay claim to and siphon off the legendary gold of Mansa Musa. The goldfields, however, were not in Morocco. Undeterred, the Portuguese crown licensed privateering ventures that pillaged and plundered as, year by year, their ships inched their way down the coast of West Africa in search of gold, a sea route to the fabled spice islands of the Indies, and potential allies who could mount a rearguard challenge to Muslim dominance of the European economy and the expansion of Ottoman power.

The Portuguese voyages, like those of their Spanish neighbours, were authorized and legitimized by Papal pronouncements couched in the terms, rhetoric and conventions of the Crusades.[5] The trouble was that the navigators of neither nation had any clear idea of how to get to the Indies and precious little information beyond the myths and legends of antiquity about what they would find there. It took nearly a century before Vasco da Gama finally sailed his small fleet into the Indian Ocean in 1498. And what he found, while not exactly a Muslim sea, was a well-ordered trading world with Muslim states, communities and merchants flourishing everywhere from the Indonesian archipelago to the east coast of Africa. The seaborne pilgrim routes that were made for the Red Sea were an integral part of this system. Exactly how many pilgrims came to Mecca by this route as compared with the land-based pilgrim caravans is part of history's work in progress. The considerable extent and value of the seaborne trade has never been in doubt, while the spread of Islam and the growing size of the Muslim populations aspiring to make the Hajj remains a grey area. What we do know is that with the arrival of the Portuguese the defence of both trade and pilgrim travel became matters of concern.

As Selim I laid his plans to protect Mecca, he was well furnished with information about these European ventures. Just weeks after his arrival in Egypt one of his sea captains personally presented the sultan with a copy of a world map full of the details of Portuguese and Spanish 'discoveries'. Originally drawn in 1513, the map of Piri Reis, or Captain Hajji Ahmed Muhiddin Piri (c. 1465–1554), is remarkable. Probably born in Gallipoli of a family from Anatolia, Piri Reis was the nephew of the noted admiral of the Ottoman fleet

Kemal Reis. Like all Ottoman sailors, Kemal and Piri are often described dismissively as 'corsairs', with the implication that the Ottoman navy was little more than a collection of pirates. No one gives the lie to that self-serving piece of historical inaccuracy more conclusively than Piri Reis. The Ottomans devoted considerable attention to training their sailors in the latest skills of seamanship and navigation, and under Sultan Mehmet II (1451–81) they began to take a keen interest in maps and map-making. The world map of Piri Reis was lost for centuries in the archives of the Topkapi Palace. Its rediscovery in 1929 caused a sensation. It is one of the earliest known maps anywhere to show the coastline of the newly discovered lands of the Americas.[6] According to a margin note this information was copied from the chart of one 'Colombo', or Christopher Columbus. Altogether it is evident from the marginal notes that Piri was well versed in the undertakings on behalf of the crowns of Portugal and Spain. He also knew of the Treaty of Tordesillas, brokered by the Pope in 1493, assigning exploration and exploitation of the eastern part of the globe to Portugal and the western part to Spain.

The purpose of Piri Reis's map was to synthesize all available information and depict the entire world on the same scale. It owed more to the latest conventions of European map-making than to those of Arab geographers. However, perhaps the most remarkable aspect of the map is that most of its information for 'Hind, Sind and China', which would mean the Indian Ocean and beyond, came from maps 'just drawn by four Portuguese'.[7] The portion of the map covering the Indian Ocean is lost. Historians speculate that it was cut out by Selim himself to aid in making his planned response to the latest threat to Mecca.

As the career of Piri Reis demonstrates, when the Ottomans assumed responsibility for the defence of Mecca they were a major naval power in the Mediterranean. As it happens, they learnt more about the Indian Ocean from their enemies than from the extensive information on the region, its peoples and navigation which had been an Arab speciality for centuries. With the patronage of the sultans a flurry of translations of the key works of Arab geography and travel literature were added to the Ottoman archives before Piri Reis, who throughout his long life seems to turn up in the thick of events at the most crucial moments, would reappear to confront the Portuguese in the Indian Ocean. When he was not at the centre of the action he retired to Gallipoli, where he wrote his grand opus *Kitab i Bahriye* or *Book of Navigation*, the first edition completed in 1521 with a second edition in 1525.[8] It presents a comprehensive synthesis of information from Arab, Spanish, Portuguese, Chinese, Indian and older Greek maps. The first section deals with types of storms, techniques of using a compass, methods of determining direction by use of the stars, detailed charts of coastlines, the characteristics of major oceans and the lands around them. It is an immense work of scholarship rather than a pirate's handbook.

The Portuguese arrived determined to oppose Muslims wherever they encountered them. It quickly became evident this would include trying to attack Mecca and disrupt seaborne pilgrim travel. The Portuguese records are full of mention of the 'abomination' of the House of Mecca and their aspiration to capture the tomb of Muhammad which, in keeping with old legend, was still believed to be suspended in air within the city. And Vasco da Gama did make one major discovery that would forward these plans – unlike the Portuguese ships, the trading vessels that plied these waters were unarmed.

Vasco da Gama returned, in command of the third annual Portuguese fleet, in 1502. He levied tribute in gold on the East African coast where he had found the Muslim pilot who had actually guided him on the final leg of his supposed 'voyage of discovery' to India. He then sank a pilgrim ship, the *Meri*, belonging to the Mamluk sultan, with the loss of all 300 passengers. The Mamluk sultan, Al-Asraf Qansuh al-Gawri (r. 1501–17), had to respond, and began to build a fleet at Suez. The trouble was that the Mamluks lacked the necessary resources. To mount an effective naval response they relied mainly on their rivals the Ottomans for military aid and ordnance. As a Mediterranean power the Ottomans were not only practised in gunpowder technology but also leaders in the field. Piri Reis served in the convoys to Egypt transporting the wood and especially the cannons for the construction of this Red Sea fleet.

In 1505, before the fleet could be launched, Francisco de Almeida arrived to take over as viceroy of the Portuguese king, who now described himself as 'Lord of the Conquest of the Navigation and Commerce of Ethiopia, Arabia, Persia and India'. Almeida was a man shaped by the Reconquista, the rolling back of Muslim rule in Iberia. He participated in the Fall of Grenada in 1492. Piri Reis had been there too, very much a part of the fleet the Ottomans sent to defend the last outpost of the once mighty Umayyad Caliphate of Spain. After the fall of Granada, Piri returned to Spain twice more, helping to evacuate Jews and Muslims expelled by the Spanish Crown and take them to safe haven in Ottoman lands.

With twenty-one ships under his command, Almeida's mission was to establish fortresses at key locations around the Indian Ocean and above all to deny Muslim shipping access to the Red Sea, the gateway to Mecca.[9] He set about his work with gusto, sacking towns on the East African coast, burning Mombasa with the loss of 1,500 lives, attacking Aden, sailing into the Red Sea before attacking other ports along the coast of the Arabian Peninsula, bombarding Calicut in India and preying upon all the shipping that came his way. He captured the ship carrying the gold and silver collected by Indian Muslims which, every seven years, was sent as a gift to the sharif of Mecca. In 1507 he occupied Muscat on the Arabian coast.

During the same year, the Suez fleet was finally ready to sail. It was less a Mamluk response than a coalition effort of the mutually concerned. An envoy from Diu, an island off the coast of Gujarat, had already come to Egypt proposing an alliance against the inter-lopers. Venice, whose dominance of European trade with the Middle

East was threatened, took part in the alliance, as did an important contingent of Ottoman sailors. Stopping first to fortify Jeddah, the fleet launched a surprise attack on the Portuguese off the port of Chaul on the west coast of India. During the attack Almeida's son was killed. Almeida had his revenge in 1509 when he defeated the Mamluk fleet in the waters off Diu. The costs of mounting this unsuccessful challenge to the Portuguese further weakened the Mamluks. Riven by internal dissension, they were clearly reliant on the help of other powers to fulfil their responsibility to protect the Holy Places, and their supremacy was in terminal decline.

Almeida was succeeded by Alfonso de Albuquerque, the real architect of the implementation of Portugal's grand strategy to monopolize the Indian Ocean. The first priority was a permanent base for their fleet. This was established in 1510 in Goa on the Malabar Coast of India. It was to remain a Portuguese enclave until the 1960s. From this headquarters of their Estado de India the Portuguese calculated that they needed just three other key possessions to secure dominance over the Ocean: Malacca on the Malay Peninsula, Hormuz at the mouth of the Persian Gulf and Aden at the mouth of the Red Sea. Albuquerque began with Malacca in 1511. In 1513 he laid siege to Aden. If this became a secure Portuguese possession the way to Mecca would be blocked. The Mamluk alliance fleet engaged the Portuguese in a day-long battle. They only managed to dislodge the siege, the Portuguese ships taking refuge on the Kamaran Islands inside the Bab al-Mandab, from where they harried Red Sea shipping before they withdrew. The following year Albuquerque succeeded in capturing not only the city of Hormuz but the small desolate Hormuz Island that was to become their richest trading post in the Indian Ocean. Only the subjugation of Aden remained one of their prime targets. The Portuguese sent annual fleets to blockade the Bab al-Mandab, and while they never succeeded in choking off all traffic through this strait at the mouth of the Red Sea, Mecca had good cause for concern when it turned to its new Ottoman masters.

The Ottomans had to construct their own Red Sea shipping to send annual fleets to counter the Portuguese threat, and they had to build up their knowledge of the region. By 1538 they were ready to launch a major offensive. They sent 100 ships and 20,000 men down the Red Sea into the Indian Ocean. The plan was for a major assault on Goa in conjunction with Bandar Shah, the ruler of Gujarat. When the Ottoman fleet arrived Bandar Shah had already been killed by the Portuguese, prompting his heir to concede an alliance with the Europeans. After an unsuccessful siege of Diu the Ottoman fleet turned back. On the voyage home they conquered most of Yemen and took Aden. The Portuguese responded to this attack by laying siege to Jeddah, harrying Red Sea shipping and once more establishing their position in Aden.

Ten years later the Ottomans mounted a second major expedition under the command of the new admiral of the Indian Ocean fleet, Piri Reis. He succeeded in recapturing Aden, then moved on to liberate Muscat from the Portuguese before sailing for the Persian Gulf with the intention of taking Hormuz Island. He gained possession of the town but was unable to subdue the citadel. Turning aside, Piri Reis captured the Qatar peninsula and Bahrain. At this point Piri took his fleet to Basra in Iraq, a country the Ottomans had annexed in 1534. Leaving the fleet for reasons that are entirely unclear, he then returned to Suez. The vizier of Egypt was not amused. Now aged ninety, Piri Reis, one of the most extraordinary men of an extraordinary era, and 'arguably the Ottomans' most distinguished cartographer', was publicly beheaded because he 'had lost ships to the Portuguese in the Persian Gulf'.[10] The story is so reminiscent of what happened in later times to the British Admiral Byng,[11] who declined to take his ships into a hopeless encounter with the French and was executed '*pour encourager les autres*', that one can only presume there is some common irrational logic that haunts the exercise of empire.

The saddest reflection is that Piri Reis's expedition of 1548–52 was in many respects a success. It marks the turning point, the time when the

Portuguese implicitly relinquished the struggle to monopolize all trade in the Indian Ocean and settled for becoming domesticated as part of that network. They also continued what has been called their 'simple protection racket' of insisting vessels pay for a *cartaz*, a licence available only from the Portuguese, to trade and travel or risk being blown out of the water. It was an inconvenience the Indian Ocean could live with, and maintaining the flow of trade and travel was in everyone's interest. It did not mean an end to bloodcurdling calls for the capture of Mecca or regulations from Portuguese legislative and religious councils demanding a halt to all Muslim pilgrim travel. In practice, however, there is a wonderful phrase Spanish officials in the New World developed to cover such situations: *obedezco pero no cumplo* – I obey but I do not comply. There was still conflict in the Indian Ocean, as well as further incursions by other European powers in the future, but for the remainder of the sixteenth century a certain kind of stability ensued which secured both Mecca and the seaborne pilgrim traffic.

Thanks to their navy the Ottomans fulfilled their obligation to protect and serve the Holy City. In the process they had mastered and integrated a huge body of new knowledge of both East and West. They were truly a world power now: established in the Indian Ocean, they had opened relations with various rulers in India including the new rising power, the Mughals, conquered virtually the whole of North Africa, the Levant, Iraq and Arabia, and had stood at the gates of Vienna spreading terror across Europe. There was no better place to exhibit and display their power than in the Holy City whose security, and that of its pilgrim traffic, they had assured. In the time of their glory the Ottomans lavished largesse and put their distinctive imprint on Mecca. The city, perhaps as it always had, served as a stage where the condition of the Muslim world or, more precisely, the condition of the dominant Muslim power, could be seen enacted.

With the arrival of the Ottomans, Mecca entered a century of peace and prosperity. For almost the first time since the death of the Prophet Muhammad, the city seemed to be at ease with itself. The young Abu Nomay, who regaled Selim I with stories of Mecca, succeeded his father Barakat II at the age of nineteen and came to be known as Abu Nomay II (r. 1524–84). Under Ottoman protection the territory ruled by the sharifs was greatly extended. It reached as far as Khaybar in the north and Hali in the south, and east into the region of Najd. 'The Ottoman administration' plied the city with largesse and 'paid out between 15,000 and 17,000 gold pieces to the Bedouins residing in the vicinity of the caravan routes; a sizable share, however, was handed over in the shape of silver coins. Thus the Bedouins were able to purchase certain goods in urban markets, such as arms and textiles.'[12] The young sharif devoted himself to improving the condition of Mecca and its citizens: he built numerous schools, courts, almshouses and residences for pilgrims, and repaired the Sanctuary. The Ottoman sultans, members of the royal family, viziers, statesmen, wealthy merchants and popular foundations competed with each other to build mosques, fountains, schools, public baths, libraries and hospitals in the Holy City. Mecca was at last beginning to catch up with the kind of infrastructure that had been commonplace in Muslim cities for centuries. Gulnus Sultan, wife of Sultan Muhammad IV (1648–87), established a health clinic in the city, followed by two hospitals. Historic and cultural property, such as the house where Prophet Muhammad was born, was repaired and renovated and brought under the protection of the sultan. The old city walls were repaired and the Ottomans built a series of forts along the caravan routes to provide protection for the pilgrims.

Mecca was transformed. It is rightly said that the city was never happier than in the time of Sharif Abu Nomay II, who ruled for sixty years until the ripe old age of eighty. Its architecture acquired a distinctive flavour: Mecca began to take on the appearance of an Ottoman city. Town houses gained verandas for family living projected over the street and courtyards to achieve rooms as rectangular as possible. This resulted in vistas of cantilevered rooms jostling down the streets. Foundations were normally built of brick and stone; upper floors were of timber with brick and wattle and daub infill in the interstices. It was not unusual for many of the houses in the city to have gardens. Wooden lattices, classical façades, cupolas and tall, delicate minarets were scattered throughout the Holy City. Egyptian marble was now replaced with flower-patterned Turkish ceramics. The fashions of Istanbul found a strong echo in Mecca, which was now anything but a 'barren valley'.

The rapid physical development of Mecca was made possible not just by the largesse of the Ottoman administration but also by the creation of a special institution: the *surre* of the Holy Cities. The Turkish word *surre* means precious gifts. These were gifts of money and goods collected with a single aim: to be distributed to citizens and visiting pilgrims in Mecca and Medina. They were donated not just by the sultan and the dignitaries of the state but by all the citizens of the Ottoman Empire, every year, and sent to Mecca during the Hajj season. Many foundations – known as Awqaf al-Haramain (Pious Foundations for the Holy Cities) – were established in Anatolia and other regions to fund projects and institutions in Mecca. These foundations had specific purposes: some raised money solely for the poor of Mecca, others for restoration of religious sites, still others for the salaries of librarians, teachers, technicians, doctors, nurses and cleaners. Guilds of artisans devoted some of their time during the year to making specific products for the Holy City; Orders of Chivalrous Young Men who had sworn to protect the poor spent much of their free time collecting money for the needy of Mecca; Turkish ladies made special crochet coverings for the shrines in the Sanctuary. At an allotted time during the year, all these gifts from the Empire were collected. Appointed officials visited every neighbourhood in all the major cities to collect the gifts from the public – the details of each gift and its donor were recorded in a special register in the presence of witnesses. On the twelfth day of the Islamic month of Rajab, three months before the Hajj, the *surre* caravan left Istanbul on its long journey to Mecca.

The whole of Istanbul would turn up to bid farewell to the caravan, witness the spectacular ceremonies that were staged before its departure, and partake in the lavish feast that accompanied the occasion. Each ceremony was performed according to an elaborate plan, guided by protocol officers. The Ottomans were nothing if not sticklers for proper etiquette and protocol. The Chief of Protocol would describe the gifts, products and money donated. The donations would then be counted in the presence of the sultan; and the *surre* purses and records of donations would be secured with the sultan's seal and handed over to the *surre* officer, along with a letter to the sharif of Mecca. The gifts would then be loaded on the *surre* camels and, accompanied by recitation of the Qur'an as well as songs and poems in praise of the Prophet, the caravan would leave the Topkapi Palace for its destination. The caravan called at sixty different locations en route to Mecca. It spent the fasting month of Ramadan, which follows Rajab, in Damascus. Each stop along the way was well maintained and well guarded. On its arrival in Mecca, the *surre* purses would be handed over to the sharif in another elaborate ceremony.

Apart from money and gifts, the *surre* caravans brought another invaluable resource: scholars, intellectuals, mystics, architects and artisans. They came to Mecca not to make a living but to serve the city. Many came with stipends from pious foundations, and offered their services to the citizens, pilgrims and city authorities for next to nothing. Indeed, some scholars came with large sums of *surre* money to be distributed among their students. Not surprisingly, many scholars, particularly jurists, had huge numbers of students who came to the Holy City from all over the Muslim world knowing that it was a place generous to young men seeking knowledge. The Sacred Mosque now functioned as much as a university as a site of pilgrimage and prayer. It had residences for visiting scholars as well as students, and a magnificent library, which received new acquisitions year after year; books were among the gifts brought by the *surre* caravan.

The city itself had many madrassas, which functioned as institutions of higher learning with primary and secondary schools attached, and libraries. The oldest madrassa in the city was designed by the great Turkish architect Mi'mâr Sinân Âğâ (1489/90–17 July 1588), the Michelangelo of Islam, known simply as Sinan, at the beginning of the sixteenth century, during the reign of Sultan Suleiman 'the Magnificent' (r. 1520–66). It was not one but in fact four madrassas, as there were four buildings, each catering for one of the four schools of Islamic thought. Other madrassas carried the name of those who built them, such as the madrassas of Murut II and Dawud Pasha, or of the group or movement that helped finance them, such as the Mahmudiya. The curriculum at these institutions included the study of the Qur'an, the life of the Prophet Muhammad, logic, mathematics, medicine, metaphysics and natural sciences. Mecca was indeed coming into line with the intellectual culture of the Muslim world.

The professors of the madrassas, who often led the congregation at the local mosques, were held in high esteem – so much so, indeed, that they had to fight to maintain their reputations: there were public disputations where professors from different madrassas argued and debated with each other. A visiting professor had to establish his credentials by giving an inaugural lecture before he could acquire students and debate with other professors. Classes were usually held in mosques where the professor sat on a small stool (the professorial chair), while students sat cross-legged on the floor, forming a small arc around him.[13] The city's noted jurists and professors of law, who included many women, held their own *halqa* (a circle of listeners sitting in a mosque around a teacher) in specific parts of the town where they issued juristic rulings and fatwas, the considered legal opinion of an individual scholar on a specific topic.

The 'guests of God', as the community of learning was known, included many mystics who came to hide from the harsh realities of the world. They hid in the cloisters, hospices and shrines of the city,

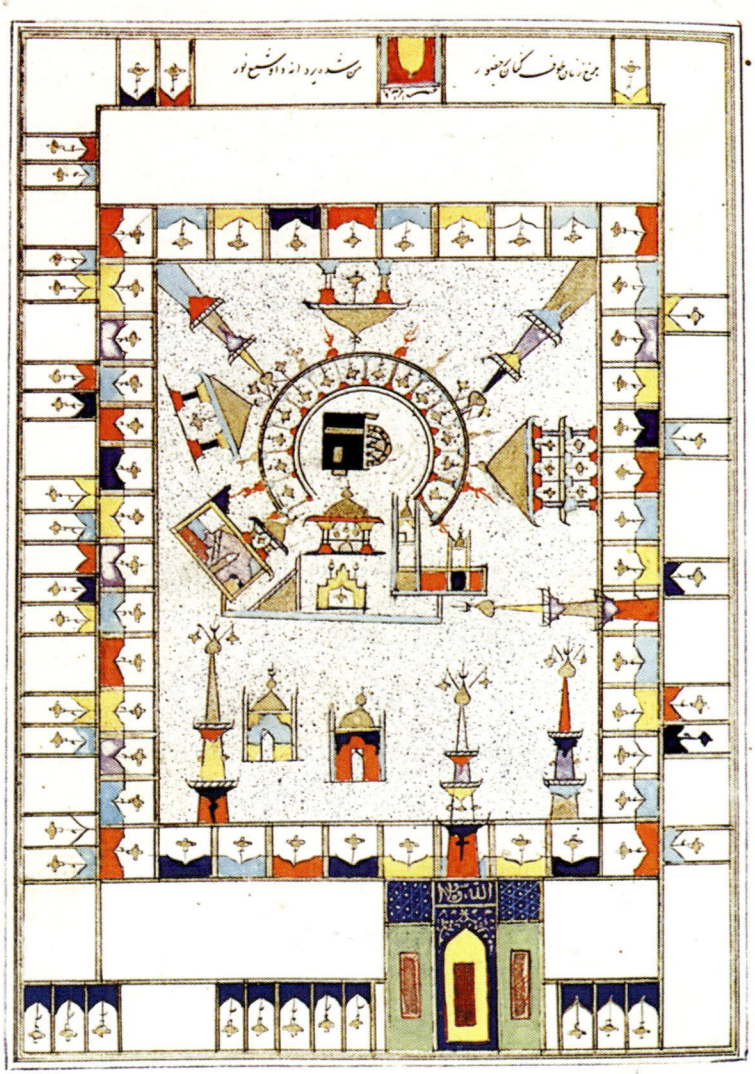

A schematic representation of Mecca by the sixteenth-century Indian
painter Muhi al-Din Lari, from his book *Conquests of the Two Sanctuaries*

The Kaaba with two angels by the sixteenth-century Turkish artist Abdullah
Lutfi from the illustrations for *The Life of the Prophet Muhammad* by the Sufi
writer Mustafa Dariri Erzeni, who completed the epic book *circa* 1388

A seventeenth-century Turkish tile with a bird's-eye representation of the
Sacred Mosque in Mecca; the Kaaba in the centre is surrounded by various
other clearly identified structures. The poem inscribed at the top of the tile
reads: 'Whoever has the fortune to visit the Kaaba, God forgives him and
the one who is invited to the house is for certain the beloved'

Opposite
An encampment of the North African caravan of pilgrims from
The Pilgrim's Companion by the seventeenth-century artist Safi ibn Vali

Pilgrim caravan by the thirteenth-century Iraqi artist Yahya ibn Mahmud al-Wasiti
from an illustration for *The Assemblies of al-Harari*, a collection of anecdotes
and stories in lyrical prose written at the beginning of the twelfth century

Pilgrims praying at the Kaaba, painting by the
fifteenth-century Persian artist Kamal al-Din Bihzad

Opposite
The door of the Kaaba, partly shrouded with the *kiswa*,
the special cover that is replaced every year

View of Mecca by the French painter Etienne (Nasreddine) Alphonse Dinet,
depicting the Kaaba and the old city of Mecca in 1918

The streets and traditional houses of Old Mecca during the mid-twentieth century

The Haram as it was during the 1976 Hajj, when the author performed his first pilgrimage

Close-up of the intricate and graceful Ottoman arcades, one of the
oldest parts of the Haram, going back to the seventeenth century

The Ottoman arcades before the first Saudi expansion

preferring their own company. Some Sufis favoured meditating in absolute darkness, secluded in a shrine or underneath a black mantle. Both mystics and the mausoleums where they were usually to be found were highly revered. Special care and attention was given to the repair and maintenance of mausoleums, which were extensively decorated and furnished with lavish carpets. The *surre* caravans always brought specific gifts and items for the decoration of the shrines and earmarked funds for the upkeep of the mausoleums and looking after the mystics.

Many Turkish mystics followed in the footsteps of the poet and Sufi Yunus Emre,[14] a grandee of Turkish literature, who came to Mecca at the beginning of the fourteenth century, long before Ottoman control of the city. He is said to have walked to Mecca along the caravan route with his head bowed, arms crossed on his breast as a token of humility. On reaching Mecca, Yunus wrote a poem that is still sung in Turkey as a hymn:

> I left the Roman land apace,
> A candle I became that melted.
> Blessed be God that I could there bow my head,
> Lord Apostle, how fair were the ways of the Kaabah.
> The moon rose as I started on the road,
> I chanted benedictions.
> Oh come with me, let us wander together,
> Lord Apostle, how fair were the ways of the Kaabah.
> The peaks come close;
> Fain would one drink a drop, for it is hot.
> The man who dies on the wayside has no mourner,
> Lord Apostle, how fair were the ways of the Kaabah.
> The mountains tower over the Kaabah,
> The spring that saw the Epiphany ever flows.
> Yunus the loving remembers and weeps,
> Lord Apostle, how fair were the ways of the Kaabah.[15]

The Ottomans transformed Mecca into a lively and thriving cosmopolitan centre. Although the city was still dependent on Cairo for grain, the markets were overflowing with goods and the citizens were prosperous. The sharif and his family received half of the taxes collected in Jeddah as well as a generous stipend and pensions from the sultan. There was no need to inflict burdensome tax on the citizens, who were seriously outnumbered by 'guests' and foreign professionals and scholars. We have a good idea of the population of the city during the later sixteenth century, as both the Ottoman bureaucrats, who had to make payments to individual households, and the nobles of the city made a list of its total inhabitants. This included 'all occupied houses and all inhabitants of the city apart from merchants and soldiers – that is, women, children and servants in addition to the adult male population, a total of 12,000 persons'.[16] Pilgrim numbers also rose substantially – from around 80,000 in the middle of the thirteenth century to 150,000 by the beginning of the sixteenth century. And there was a constant stream of visits by Turkish princes and princesses who, naturally, insisted on full pomp and ceremony. One princess arrived with a caravan of 400 camels, each bearing identical palanquins so no one could tell in which one she was riding. Later, it is said, she committed suicide because she could not throw off legions of unwanted and persistent suitors. Different races, classes and sects, including men and women, all mingled to create a vibrant multicultural and intellectually engaged society.

There were, however, tensions. The Ottomans insisted on intervening in the administration of justice. Traditionally, the chief judge of the city was a *qadi* belonging to the Shafi school of thought, which had become dominant in Mecca. The office had remained in one family for centuries. Now the chief *qadi* was appointed and sent from Istanbul, much to the displeasure of most of the Meccans. The Ottomans, who were strictly Sunni, did not look with favour on the Shia. In 1501, the newly crowned Safavid Shah Ismail I (r. 1501–24) had proclaimed himself Shahanshah of Iran and declared Shi'ism to be the religion of his state. A protracted power struggle ensued between the Ottomans and the Safavids, periods of open warfare interspersed with constant tensions that defined the eastern limits of Ottoman territorial expansion. The tensions of the wider world were reflected in serious disputes between Sunni and Shia scholars and jurists in Mecca, each accusing the other of heresy.

Later, the Ottomans would have an opportunity to bring the two main branches of Islam, the orthodox Sunni and the Shia, together and settle the disputes. Nadir Shah, king of Persia (r. 1736–47), successor to the now defunct Safavids, approached the Ottoman sultan with a rather enlightened proposal. Known as much for his military brilliance as his 'love of women' and 'drinking parties',[17] Nadir was of Turkish origin and held the Ottomans in high regard. Although a Shia, he systematically 'weakened the Shia *ulama* [scholars] by confiscating properties, abolishing clerical positions in the government, and cancelling the jurisdiction of religious courts'.[18] He would recognize the sultan in Istanbul as caliph, Nadir Shah said, if the sultan would grant the Shia equal standing with other sects in Mecca, and accept it as the fifth school of Islamic thought. Then, in effect, the sultan would be caliph of both Sunni and Shia communities. Regrettably, the Ottomans declined the offer, fearing that their own population would convert to Shi'ism. Thus a great opportunity to unite Islam and end centuries of enmity and tragic feuding was lost.

While resolving the dispute between Sunnis and Shias was of little concern to the Ottoman sultans, they were unconditionally devoted to improving the holiest city of Islam. This was seen as an act of charity, perhaps a substitute for the fact that none of them ever visited Mecca and performed the Hajj. Many major projects were undertaken; in keeping with earlier works the Ottomans tried to keep the Sanctuary in the centre of the city. Before embarking on any project, great care was taken to consult the local scholars, jurists and prominent figures. When it came to Mecca, no expense was spared, and a great deal of effort was spent on public relations to improve the standing of the Caliphate and to gain the confidence and praises of the Meccans as well as the pilgrims. Clearly, in the era before mass communications, Mecca was unchallenged as the place to establish and publish one's credentials before the entire Muslim world. The long distance and travel time between Mecca and Istanbul, the lack of engineers and skilled workers, the difficulty of finding and shipping construction material best suited for the Sanctuary, the time involved in effecting intricate ornamental work with gold and silver, as well as the harsh climate of Mecca, meant, however, that realizing grand projects often took decades.

The fact that development work in Mecca would be arduous became evident in 1557 when Mecca once again suffered from a serious lack of water. Zubaidah's gift to the Holy City in 810, the elaborate network of aqueducts, had dried up. The sharif sent a request for urgent help to Sultan Suleiman (r. 1520–66), who apart from being 'the Magnificent' was also 'the Lawgiver', and son and successor of Selim I. The cost of the work was estimated to be 35,000 dinars; the sultan's sister insisted that she would fund the project. An Egyptian treasurer in the sultan's office, Ibrahim Bey, was appointed to supervise the work. Within a few months he was in Mecca with over 400 Mamluk soldiers and a band of engineers from Anatolia, Damascus and Aleppo, and most important of all a purse filled with 50,000 dinars sent by the sultan's sister. The engineers decided to dig a canal as far as Zubaidah's well. No sooner had they started than they came upon a rock that proved almost impossible to cut. Attempts were made to dissolve the rock by burning huge quantities of fuel. Ten years later, little progress had been made despite exhausting work and the consumption of all the firewood in Mecca and the surrounding areas. The engineers were worn out; a number of workers had died of heat and exhaustion. The people of Mecca were disappointed.

The sultan appointed a new supervisor, Muhammad Bey Akmal Zadi. He received an even bigger purse from the sultan's sister, yet he too failed, dying in the attempt. There was still not much water in the Holy City and the citizens were beginning to show their frustration. The sultan placed the task on the joint shoulders of Qasim Bey, the governor of Jeddah, and a Meccan judge belonging to the Maliki School of Thought, called Hussain. It was Hussain who finally managed to complete the project, just months after the death of Qasim Bey in 1571. Water in abundance had finally arrived in Mecca; the whole city had a massive party. The final cost of the project was estimated to be 500,700 dinars – all of which came from the sultan's sister, who went on to finance the construction of a string of fountains in the city.

Sultan Suleiman himself was more concerned with extending the Sanctuary to accommodate the rising number of pilgrims. Orders were given for Sinan, who, at that time was working on Istanbul's magnificent Suleymniye Mosque, to go to Mecca and produce a plan for extending the Sacred Mosque. The sultan was particularly keen to see the roofs of the arcades replaced with domes. Sinan finished the Suleymniye Mosque in 1558, and arrived in Mecca a year later. We don't know how much time he spent in the city, but it was long enough for him to do some remedial work, restore a few aqueducts to improve the water supply while the canal was being built, and produce a detailed plan for the restoration and expansion of the Haram. But he had too many projects to finish in Anatolia, particularly the Selimiye Mosque in Edirne, widely considered to be his masterpiece, to undertake active work in Mecca. His plans for the city would not come to fruition during his lifetime. However, during the reign of Sultan Suleiman, the ceiling of the Kaaba was altered, the paving within the Sanctuary (an area known as al-Mataf) relaid, and a new high minaret was constructed. The sultan also sent an inlaid marble pulpit (minbar) to the Sacred Mosque.

It was left to Sedefhar Mehmed Aga (1540–1617), Sinan's student, to translate his teacher's plan into reality. Aga, as accomplished and renowned as his teacher, was highly skilled in a variety of art forms, as well as being an accomplished musician. Apart from the Blue Mosque in Istanbul, he also built the Mosque of Murad III in Manisa in the Aegean region of Turkey, a splendid walnut throne encrusted with mother-of-pearl and tortoiseshell, and a bridge over the Tunca river in Edirne. The *Sedefhar* ('worker in mother-of-pearl') element in his name was a title he acquired because he originally trained as an inlayer. Aga, who became the chief imperial architect in October 1606 and was 'one of the few Ottoman artists to be honoured by a full-scale biography during his lifetime',[19] was dispatched to Mecca by Sultan Selim II (r. 1566–74). He used Sinan's plan to renovate and extend the courtyard of the Kaaba, with the help of highly skilled Egyptian builders specially sent by the sultan. The nineteen gates of the Sanctuary were renewed but kept in the same place. New ones were added – now there were a total of twenty-six doorways to the Mosque: five on the eastern side, six on the western, seven on the southern, and eight on the northern. The existing columns at the entrance were replaced with marble, and yellow stone columns were set between them to help support the stuccoed stone arches and cupolas that had been substituted for the old wooden ones. A total of 881 arches supported the arcades that surrounded the Mosque, in addition to the smaller arches at the back. The flat roof of the Sanctuary was now replaced with 152 small domes on the four sides of the court. Sinan must have seen and approved some of this work, as in 1583, at the age of ninety-four, he came to Mecca for the second time to perform the Hajj.

When Mehmed Aga had completed his work, Selim II commissioned an accomplished artist to work on the interior of the Sanctuary. He decorated the interiors of the cupolas with calligraphic compositions and gold motifs. The artist was Abdullah Lutfi. We know that he stayed in Mecca after finishing his work on the Haram to make sketches of the Holy Land, during which beautifully designed lamps were hung on the columns within the Sanctuary and candle-holders

in the shape of date palms were placed in the courtyard. The seats of
the teachers of the four schools of thought were replaced with new
ones in the stylish shape of Turkish kiosks. The call to prayer now
began at the 'Caliph's minaret' – the tallest and slimmest of the seven
minarets, which was constructed with three balconies in the distinctive Ottoman style – and was echoed by the muezzins in the other six
minarets. The Sacred Mosque now had a strong imprint of distinctive Ottoman architecture and style.

By the time Abdullah Lutfi returned to Istanbul, Selim II had
been replaced by Murad III (r. 1574–95). At the behest of the new
sultan, Lutfi began turning his sketches into stunning miniatures.
The paintings were in fact done to illustrate *The Life of the Prophet
Muhammad* by Mustafa Dariri Erzeni, a blind scholar and Sufi
who came to Mecca around 1370.[20] Known amongst the Meccans as
'the blind man of Erzerum', he had a substantial following in the
city. His biography of the Prophet was widely known and read
there, and Lutfi, who was mystically inclined, was no doubt influenced by Erzeni.

It took Lutfi almost two decades, and the assistance of scores of
other artists, to complete the work: 814 miniatures in six volumes,
one of the first and complete visual portraits of the life of Prophet
Muhammad. The paintings are highly stylized, rather bold yet elusive
in character. The landscapes are bare, the figures drawn sharply, and
the details are always scanty. One shows Mecca with the Kaaba on
Abu Qubays mountain, with a rectangular building in front, and
angels on horseback and in the air. There are only five figures in the
painting illustrating the birth of the Prophet: the infant Prophet is
enveloped in a golden cloud; his veiled mother sits to the right, with
three angels in attendance. Another painting has the young Prophet
being breast-fed by his wet nurse (nipple quite visible), with his
mother and eight other women sitting observing the proceedings.
The Prophet always appears with a veil on his face; but his companions are drawn with full faces.

Lutfi's style differs sharply from earlier Persian miniatures of the Indian painter Muhi Al-Din Lari (d. 1526), about whom we know even less than about Lutfi. Lari's paintings illustrate his book *Conquests of the Two Sanctuaries (Futuh al-haramayn)*,[21] which is a guide to performing the Hajj. In sharp contrast to Lutfi's painting, Lari provides much more detail, giving us 'schematic representations' of the Sanctuary.[22] For example, his widely reproduced painting of the Sacred Mosque, in gouache heightened with gold, which shows the Kaaba in the middle enclosed by a circular arcade, indicates the places of worship assigned to different sects, as well as the location of the well of Zamzam. The doors surrounding the Kaaba have their names inscribed on them. Four minarets appear at the corner of the courtyard, with several small structures and minbars. There is an entrance gate to the compound leading to a large courtyard surrounded by two rows of colonnades with oil lamps hanging between the columns. Lari clearly used his personal experience of Mecca, 'executing architectural details with care and using brilliant colours to enliven the scene'.[23]

Both Lari and Abdullah Lutfi would go on to influence generations of artists after them; their paintings were copied by contemporary and later artists, right down to the nineteenth century. Almost all the classic illustrations we see in books on Islamic art and Hajj are either their paintings or inspired by them. Yet nothing has been written about these two pioneering artists.

Murad III did not live to see the final product of Abdullah Lutfi's monumental efforts: the work was finished on 16 January 1595, a few days after the death of the sultan. Sharif Abu Nomay II did not live to see the new extensions to the Sanctuary either. He died in 1584, while on business in Nadj, around ten days' march from the city. As the city had been transformed under Abu Nomay's rule, it was little wonder that Meccans had come to adore him. His body was brought from Nadj and the entire city joined his funeral procession. The valley was filled with the sound of women weeping as the procession entered the city from one side, while the new sharif, who had been working in Yemen, approached from the other side.

Abu Nomay II was succeeded by his son, Hassan ibn Abi Nomay, who was fifty-nine when he acquired power. He continued in the style of his father but also devoted considerable time to his great passion for poetry. Poets flourished under his reign, and the Holy City was immersed in music and culture. He built a special palace, known as the 'House of Happiness', where poets, musicians and other artists gathered to display their skills. He seemed to associate culture with urbanism and considered nomads and desert-dwellers uncouth. Consequently, he is said to have been rather severe, even despotic, in his relations with the Bedouin. Later, the Meccans would regard him as the last of their talented and skilful rulers and his reign as the 'golden age' of Mecca. Certainly, Mecca continued to be happy and prosperous for the next four decades. When Sharif Hassan died in 1602, his son Idris, known as Abu Aun, was unanimously chosen as his successor. Abu Aun decided to rule in partnership with his brother and nephew. Even though Mecca now had a triumvirate of rulers, it was still a politically stable city. The situation changed rapidly a few years after the death of Abu Aun in 1624.

The chain of events started rather innocuously. The sultan had appointed a new governor, Ahmad Pasha, to Yemen. He arrived in Jeddah with the usual pomp and ceremony. Unfortunately for Mecca, one of the pasha's ships, carrying most of his personal belongings, sank near the port in relatively deep waters. In Mecca, Sharif Mohsin, Abu Aun's nephew, had now taken over. The pasha sent a message to Sharif Mohsin asking for two divers to help retrieve his luggage. The divers duly arrived, but after repeated attempts over many days found nothing. The pasha grew suspicious. He came to the conclusion that Sharif Mohsin, who had not come to Jeddah to greet him, must have instructed his divers not to try too hard. The pasha's opinion was influenced by Ahmad ibn Talib, a scheming and ambitious relative of Sharif Mohsin. Ahmad Pasha arrested and executed Sharif

Mohsin's messenger, provided money and troops to Ahmad ibn Talib and instructed him to take over the reins of power in Mecca. But before Ahmad could march on Mecca the pasha died, probably poisoned by the relatives of the messenger he had executed. Ahmad took the opportunity this afforded him to commandeer all the Turkish troops garrisoned in Jeddah to accompany him to Mecca. As Ahmad and his army approached Mecca, Sharif Mohsin prepared to engage in battle. However, the Meccans, now rather used to prosperity, persuaded him to avoid bloodshed. Sharif Mohsin had no option but to abdicate. Ahmad ibn Talib marched triumphantly into the city.[24]

Sharif Ahmad ibn Talib's rule lasted only two years. His first act on entering the Holy City was to arrest and execute the mufti of Mecca, with whom he had a long-standing grievance. He accused the mufti of preventing his marriage to a princess, and during her marriage to another man, making disparaging comments about him – indeed, describing him as the Devil incarnate. Furthermore, when Ahmad's brother died, the mufti had come dressed in white, rather than black, to give his condolences. If that was not enough, the mufti had issued a fatwa against him, a written copy of which had been discovered underneath a cushion in Sharif Mohsin's palace.

The mufti probably had a point. The Meccans, who loved their jurists, were horrified at his execution. They despised the new sharif, quite ready to see him as the Devil himself. Secret messages were sent to the sultan in Istanbul, and the citizens began to gather around potential successors. Soon a new governor, Qunsowa Pasha, was on his way to Yemen. He arrived in Jeddah in 1630 and announced his intention of visiting the Sacred Mosque. When Qunsowa Pasha and his large army neared Mecca, Sharif Ahmad went out to meet him. The sharif was enthusiastically greeted along with his entourage and asked to inspect the soldiers and the marines who accompanied the pasha. The military band played as the sharif inspected the troops, all lined up in front of their tents. Afterwards, Qunsowa Pasha invited

Sharif Ahmad to his tent for a game of chess. The game lasted till sunset. When it was finished, Qunsowa Pasha excused himself. A group of Turkish marines entered the tent, and quietly throttled the sharif. The rest of his party were told to return to Mecca and spread the news.[25]

For the next few years, Mecca witnessed a rather monotonous struggle for supremacy between various members of the sharif family. One ruler followed another. No one lasted more than a year, even with the support of Turkish officials. Meanwhile, the city was facing an urgent problem. While the Sanctuary was being redesigned, renovated, extended and beautified, the most important object within its compound remained largely untouched: the Kaaba. It had become obvious since the time of Sultan Selim, at the beginning of the sixteenth century, that the Kaaba was falling apart. Patchwork would not do; it needed total reconstruction. The *qadis* of the four schools of thought in Mecca, as well as the Sheikh al-Islam in Istanbul, were of the opinion that the work was necessary. The citizens of Mecca supported their senior jurists and agreed that the Kaaba needed to be rebuilt without delay. But there was a serious problem: the Shia imam of Mecca had declared that it was unlawful to demolish the Kaaba. Only if it fell down of its own accord could it be rebuilt. The controversy lasted years, almost decades. Finally, the matter was settled in 1629 by an act of God. The sky opened up and torrential rains flooded the Kaaba, demolishing the eastern and western wall and the ceiling. Around 500 citizens of Mecca lost their lives. Even this was not enough to convince the Shia imam. When a second flood caused further damage the whole structure was on the verge of collapse. At last, the imam conceded; it was unanimously decided to pull down what remained of the Kaaba. Excavation work, carried out under the watchful eyes of the city's inhabitants, continued till the foundations of Abraham were reached. It was decided to build the new Kaaba on these foundations, using most of the masonry that had survived from the time of ibn Zubair.

Sultan Murad IV (r. 1623–40) sent his personal chamberlain to supervise the rebuilding work. A pious man from the Caucasus, the chamberlain was fearful of the Meccans. Convinced that they would find faults with his efforts, he prayed extensively before giving any order. He was guided by architects from Istanbul, Ankara and other Turkish cities. The Black Stone was placed under the special care of an Indian architect. Just as in previous reconstructions of the Kaaba – during the time of the Prophet Muhammad and ibn Zubair – the entire city took part in the rebuilding. The leaders of the four schools of thought, the Shia imam and the members of his clergy, the jurists and judges, the bureaucrats and administrative officials, citizens and visitors, men, women and children – all took turns in finding and carrying stones. As the reconstruction went on the Qur'an was recited constantly.

Inside the Kaaba, the old columns were strengthened, coated with a preservative solution of saffron and gum Arabic, and then covered with gold. The silver door, a present to the Kaaba from Sultan Suleiman, was reinstalled. Another gift from Sultan Suleiman, a pulpit in elaborate woodwork, was set in place. A new golden gargoyle, inlaid with inscriptions set in blue enamel, sent from Istanbul, was placed on the roof of the Kaaba. Two portable silver staircases, a gift from India, were added to provide access to the door. The whole of the Kaaba was then covered with two *kiswa* curtains, one red and one black. Finally, the sands in the courtyard were washed. The 'House of God', the prime symbol of the faith of Abraham and Muhammad, was now complete: rebuilt to last thousands of years.[26]

Mecca was now under the rule of Zaid ibn Muhsin (r. 1631–66), who, although only twenty-five, had already proved his skill in numerous battles. A man of considerable cunning and few scruples, he grew up amongst the Bedouin tribes in south Hijaz, where he acquired courage and confidence in equal measure. Zaid was also the first amongst the sharifs of Mecca to use firearms, which had now appeared in the Hijaz. The new weapon in the hands of his army proved decisive and he was able to subdue most of the warring tribes and clans in and around the city and restore a modicum of peace to the region. But the political and religious disputes Mecca had faced during the past decades were nothing compared to what now befell the city.

After dispensing with Sharif Ahmad, Qunsowa Pasha had moved on to Yemen. But his expedition there failed miserably and the pasha decided to sail back to Egypt, leaving his rather unruly army to return by land. Sharif Zaid received a message from two of the generals of this army, Mahmoud and Ali Bey, asking to stay in Mecca en route to Egypt. We need to rest and refresh ourselves both physically and spiritually before we recommence our arduous journey, they declared. Sharif Zaid was in two minds. He called the Meccans together and asked for their opinions. The overall consensus was that the generals could not be trusted. They might turn out to be polite, seem amicable and behave impeccably, and then quietly throttle the sharif – like one of his predecessors – or, indeed, take over the city. It was a defeated army with many grievances. The sharif agreed. He refused the generals permission to enter Mecca. He also ordered all the wells from Mecca to Qunfidha, where the armies were camped, to be filled.

The generals were taken aback by his inhospitality, which they took as a declaration of war. They decided to enter Mecca by force. The sharif gathered his own troops and asked for help from the Turkish governor of Jeddah, who rushed to support him. As the sun rose on the morning of 18 March 1631, Sharif Zaid's troops met the armies of Generals Mahmoud and Ali Bey just outside Mecca at a place called Wadi al-Abar. What followed was one of the bloodiest battles Mecca had seen in its recent history. Over 500 Meccan soldiers were killed, including many members of the sharif's family and clan. The Turkish governor of Jeddah also died of exhaustion. Few were left standing; and even a number of spectators watching the battle from a safe distance were killed. Zaid alone managed to escape to Medina. Mecca was now at the mercy of Generals Mahmoud and Ali Bey, who made a victorious entry into the city.

Carnage followed. The soldiers killed anyone who could oppose them, seized food supplies and looted the entire city. Women and young boys were raped. Rich and wealthy citizens were tortured to reveal their hoards of wealth. Plunder and rape continued for a week. When they had finished with Mecca, the rebel soldiers turned to Jeddah, which suffered the same fate. Seeing Mecca descend into lawlessness and anarchy, the tribes in the surrounding areas took the opportunity to engage in their age-old sport of attacking and looting caravans to the Holy City. Mecca was in the depth of despair.

In Medina, Sharif Zaid tried to regroup and made plans to rescue his city. He sent desperate messages for help to Egypt and to Sultan Murad IV in Istanbul. The sultan acted quickly and dispatched seven generals, each with an impressive army, along with a robe of honour for Sharif Zaid. Within a few weeks the sultan's army was in Medina, where Zaid was invested with the ceremonial robe in the Prophet's Mosque, signifying his legitimate rule of Mecca. The sharif joined the march against the rebel soldiers in Mecca.

When Mahmoud and Ali Bey heard of the massive army marching against them, they fled along with their rebel soldiers. They were pursued to the borders of Najd, where their armies were decisively defeated. The two generals, however, managed to find refuge in a castle. They sent a message: we will surrender if our lives are spared. Zaid, who had entered Mecca unopposed and without bloodshed, called a council of war. The citizens of Mecca, along with the Turkish soldiers, the scholars and jurists of the city, gathered in the Sacred Mosque to discuss the fate of the plunderers and abusers of the Holy City. Zaid favoured a pardon for both, particularly for Ali Bey. It transpired that during the looting of Mecca, Ali Bey had been respectful towards the women of the sharif's clan. He had gone out of his way to protect female members of Zaid's family from marauding soldiers, and visited them daily to ask if they needed anything. The gathering, however, demanded vengeance and punishment for both. After a heated discussion, it was decided that Ali Bey would be pardoned if he arrested Mahmoud and brought him to Mecca. Ali Bey duly delivered Mahmoud to Mecca, and was allowed to return freely to Egypt.

Mahmoud 'was beaten and tortured, then paraded naked, strapped on a camel, face upward, head to the tail for greater indignity, through the streets of Mecca'.[27] After this ritual humiliation, he was crucified just outside one of the gates of Mecca. While still on the crucifix, cuts were made in his arms and shoulders, pieces of cloth soaked in oil were inserted in the cuts, and set on fire. He was taken down a day or two later, still alive, and moved to the cemetery, where he was nailed by his right hand and left foot to a post next to his grave. He screamed constantly in his agony, cursing Mecca and its citizens, abusing the sharif and the scholars. He finally expired two days later.

Meanwhile, a court of scholars and jurists heard cases against a group of Meccans who had collaborated with the rebel soldiers, and members of the sharif clan who had tried to usurp power. At the end of each case, the scholars were asked for their verdict – which was always the same: 'the judgement of God'. Once the sentence had been pronounced, the accused were immediately executed by the sword and their severed heads displayed in public.

Finally the lust for vengeance was satisfied and political stability was re-established. Mecca experienced a few years of peace and prosperity before Sultan Murad IV asked Sharif Zaid for a special favour. The Shia, he said, had been particularly troublesome: they 'claimed one third of all subsidies sent to Mecca',[28] had delayed the important work of rebuilding the Kaaba for decades, and the Persian Shias were not too favourably inclined towards the Sublime Porte. Therefore, would the sharif expel the Shia heretics from the Holy City and prohibit them from performing the Hajj in future?

Sharif Zaid was not impressed by this order. Neither he nor the upper class in Mecca wanted to expel the Shias, who were largely skilful professionals much needed in the city. The Shia pilgrims brought money and goods to Mecca, two resources of which it could never have enough. And expelling the Shias from the city would also provide the unruly tribes in the region with a pretext to plunder well-to-do Persians. The sharif, however, was in no position to openly oppose the sultan. Not only would open violation incur his wrath, the sharif and people of Mecca might themselves be labelled heretics. Zaid felt compelled to accept the sultan's order, but availed himself of the classic 'I obey but do not comply' strategy. As soon as the Turkish governor of Mecca ordered the Shias to leave the city, the sharif quietly gave them permission to stay and take part in the pilgrimage.

To make matters worse, the sultan appointed a Turkish official as the Inspector of the Holy Places. Sharif Zaid was incensed. He saw this as a clear attempt to increase Turkish control of the Holy City. He was now more determined than ever to maintain his authority not just in Mecca but the region as a whole. He embarked on a clandestine campaign against the Turkish officials in the Hijaz. On his orders the Turkish Inspector of Jeddah was murdered by a Bedouin. He was, one suspects, also behind the murder of the Turkish *qadi* in Medina. While travelling from Taif to Jeddah, Mustafa Beg, the Turkish Inspector of Jeddah, had to ride alone in a narrow valley and lost his escort. A Bedouin came down from the mountain, ran towards him and stabbed him with a poisoned dagger. Mustafa Beg died within three hours. The Turkish *qadi* of Medina was ambushed on his way to night prayers. As he rode with his companions and passed the office of the Accountant General, a Bedouin emerged from the darkness, sliced him with his sword, and escaped. The horse, with the dying *qadi* clinging to his neck, went on into the Prophet's Mosque right up to the prayer niche of Othman, the fourth caliph, where the assembled congregation gasped and took his body down.

For the Turkish Inspector of Mecca, Sharif Zaid must have had a similar plan. But another death, not in the Hijaz but in Istanbul, proved rather beneficial. The sultan had appointed an Abyssinian called Bashir Agha as Inspector and sent him to Mecca with astonishing powers. Sharif Zaid knew that if the Inspector was allowed to operate in Mecca, his own authority and autonomy would be reduced to a cipher. The very idea of showing deference to an Abyssinian, albeit a Turkish official, was also anathema to him. So when Bashir Agha landed at the port of Yanbu, the sharif did not go to welcome him. Instead, a deputy was sent, entrusted with the extra responsibility of providing intelligence on the size and weapons of the agha's army. The deputy gathered the necessary intelligence but also came up with a vital piece of news: the agha had just received a letter from Istanbul informing him of the death of Sultan Murad IV, a fact he was eager to conceal. On receiving the news an emboldened Zaid abandoned the idea of holding a reception for the agha, or arranging and furnishing special quarters for him and his mission. When the agha approached Mecca, the sharif went out to greet him. They rode together towards the Holy City, but Sharif Zaid kept spurring his horse so that he was always a little ahead of the agha. When they reached the gate of the city, Sharif Zaid turned his head back towards the agha and shouted: 'May the sultan rest in peace.' Bashir Agha realized at once that Sharif Zaid knew the sultan had died, and his mission was now buried with the sultan.

Sharif Zaid went on to rule Mecca for another quarter of a century. He is remembered mostly for his efforts to thwart Turkish attempts to interfere in the affairs of Mecca and the Hijaz, in which he was backed by his influence over the Bedouin tribes amongst whom he grew up and who came to trust him implicitly. He was the founder of the Dhawi Zaid, a new branch of the sharif clan that would spend the next three centuries fighting against the Dhawi Barakat, established by Barakat ibn Hassan during the mid-fifteenth century.

Sharif Zaid died in 1666. There was the customary feud amongst his sons for succession. The two main claimants, Saad and Hamud, started firing at each other's houses. There was hand-to-hand fighting amongst their supporters and a number of skirmishes in the market and around the Sacred Mosque. After three days, Saad prevailed, largely because he had the support and approval of the caliph. Sharif Saad, a man of medium height, brown complexion and a thin moustache, was regarded as generous, though in point of fact he was an exceptionally ruthless man. He forced his brother Hamud out of the Holy City. However, Hamud was not defeated and was unwilling to give up the struggle for the throne of Mecca. He started raiding caravans and took every opportunity to frighten and terrorize the Meccans. His men would slip into the city during the night to rob and kidnap citizens. For three years, terrorism was the norm in Mecca.

Nor did the problems stop there. A timeless place is not immune to history. Global changes were undermining the prosperity and eventually the autonomy of the Muslim world. In 1600 two new powers entered the Indian Ocean: the Dutch and British East India Companies. They came to challenge the Portuguese monopoly of the direct sea route to Europe. These merchant companies were very different in organization and effect to their predecessor. Over the course of the seventeenth century they had a growing impact on the structure of global trade. Seaborne trade gradually began to undermine the economic viability of land caravans, diverting the revenues the caravans generated away from their traditional beneficiaries and subtly shifting the distribution patterns of goods. Even pilgrims to Mecca travelling the sea routes of the Indian Ocean were more and more likely to travel on English or Dutch or French or Danish vessels. And from the newly found lands across the Atlantic that Piri Reis had charted came a silvery stream whose riches were deceptive. In 1545 the Spanish happened to discover a mountain made of silver at Potosí in what is now Bolivia. The annual shipments of silver and gold from the New World gradually glutted the world economy. The value of the Ottoman dinar depreciated accordingly. The constant wars on several fronts swallowed up the vibrancy and wealth of empire. In 1529 the Ottomans were at the apex of their power and expansion as they laid siege to Vienna. In 1683 they were repulsed at the Battle of Vienna. A long slow stagnation was under way, with creeping repercussions across the whole Muslim world.

Life in Mecca moved with the tide of history. Trade caravans became scarce. In 1667 the city was in the grip of a severe famine. The markets were empty; people started to sell their possessions for food. Bread was being made out of chickpeas and broad beans. The poor attacked the houses of the rich in desperate attempts to find food. Others turned to cats, dogs, bats, rats – anything that could be eaten. Soon there was nothing left to eat. People started dying in the streets. Sharif Saad made desperate pleas to the sultan. Finally, just before the pilgrimage season, ten shiploads of grain arrived from Egypt and the citizens of Mecca breathed a sigh of relief.

It is not just the economic and political fate of the city that seems to lurch dramatically, tossed by history. The fate of knowledge and cultured civilization itself followed the same pattern of high and low points. Now it was claimed that the plight of Mecca was reflected in the heavens. One morning in June 1668, two hours after sunrise, a very strong beam of light, coming from the sun, appeared in the sky. Blue, yellow and red in colour the 'beam extended to the west, and whoever looked at it was temporarily blinded'.[29] For most of the citizens of Mecca it was a bad omen: a clear sign, a warning from God about the *fitna* – rebellion and strife – that engulfed the Holy City. More knowledgeable people in the city recognized the stellar visitor as a comet. The most notable among them was a Moorish astronomer by the name of Muhammad ibn Sulaiman Maghribi. He had been part of the last expulsion of Muslims from Spain, ordered by King Philip III in 1614. Most of those expelled from Andalusia sought refuge in Morocco, or the lands of the Ottoman Empire in Algeria and Tunisia. Maghribi chose Mecca, and spent some time in the city erecting a sundial in the courtyard of the Sacred Mosque. The comet appeared on the same day the astronomer was inaugurating his sundial. The two events were naturally connected by the uneducated and ignorant citizens of Mecca. A campaign to demolish the sundial emerged overnight and a group of citizens asked the sharif to remove the sundial and expel the astronomer. The sharif consulted the *qadi* and the two agreed that the sundial should be removed. Muhammad ibn Sulaiman appealed to Sheikh al-Islam, the head of Muslim scholars in Istanbul. The Sheikh declared that astronomy was an essential science and the sundial was an important and necessary instrument. It was restored but it did not last long.[30]

Another notable person in the city was the Ottoman traveller Evliya Celebi, a highly educated and refined man. Celebi, motivated by the Quranic verses 'there are signs in the heavens and the earth for those who believe'[31] and 'travel throughout the earth and see how He brings life into being',[32] had travelled all over Anatolia, Syria, the Caucasus, Azerbaijan and Armenia, visited Iraq, Iran and Russia, explored Greece, Hungry, Austria and the Crimea, and concluded his global explorations with a pilgrimage and sojourn in Mecca. He was pained, he says, at the denial and neglect of knowledge, the ignorance and passivity he witnessed in the Holy City. His journeys are described in ten volumes of *Seyahatname* or *The Book of Travels*.[33]

Celebi found that most Meccan men tended to be unsociable, ignorant and haughty. 'They are rough spoken in their trade dealings and in conventional discourse,' he says. 'They are not much versed in the crafts, and do not have the ability to work with heavy loads; rather, most of them are merchants, while another class get by on the charity of the Sultan.'[34] They spend most of their day idling around, dressed in their fine clothes, with henna in their beards and feet, 'they go from coffee house to coffee house, then go home with a coffee mug in one hand and biscuit in the other, and fall asleep on their pillow sipping coffee and munching on biscuits'. The women, on the other hand, 'are known for their beauty and grace; with fairy faces and angel looks, like the moon at mid-month or like garden peacocks;

and with gaits like skipping partridges'. But they are also 'slow and heavy', not to say lazy, and 'never do any work, never wash laundry or spin yarn or sweep the house'. Like ibn Battuta, Celebi notes that Meccan women drown themselves in perfume: 'If a woman passes by a man of God, his brain is suffused with the perfumes of musk and ambergris and civet.' The city also hosts a plethora of 'Ethiopian slavegirls, actually singing-girls, who set hearts aflutter. Some dance in public in the coffee houses. They all wear light-blue stockings and blue slippers.'[35] On the whole, Celebi concludes, the people of Mecca are 'very extravagant', 'not much engaged in learning' – the city has no physicians – and their favourite pastime, apart from loitering about, is fighting each other.

Not surprisingly, the sultan in Istanbul, now Muhammad IV (r. 1648–87), was exasperated with the feuds and fiascos in Mecca, and the ways of its citizens. In 1669 he sent one of his trusted generals, Hassan Pasha, to bring a modicum of political stability to the city. Hassan Pasha came as the head of the Hajj caravan, but even before he reached Mecca, a rumour spread in the city that he was coming to dispose of the sharif and bring the Hijaz under the control of the sultan. The rumour was started deliberately – in Medina, where such news was most welcome. Sharif Saad and his family decided to entrench themselves in Mecca, and refused to leave even to perform the necessary Hajj rituals in Arafat and Muna. Hassan Pasha was treated with total contempt; the shopkeepers refused to serve his men, and Mecca closed its gates when he reached the city. In contrast, Hassan Pasha was exceptionally polite and asked for a council to be called where he would openly declare that he had not come to dispose of the sharif, so that the rumour could be put to rest.

For a few days the Meccans forgot Hassan Pasha as they rejoiced at the arrival of the Shah of Persia's caravan, bringing vast treasure which was distributed amongst the family of the sharif, his army and bodyguards and a few selected citizens. The mood of the sharif changed and he came out of the city to witness the ritual of stone-throwing in Muna. The three-day ritual proceeded smoothly, but then there was a disturbance. Hassan Pasha went to investigate, became embroiled in a scuffle, and bullets began to fly. The pasha was wounded and was taken to a place of safety by his men. Sharif Saad returned at once to Mecca and gave orders to prepare for war. The Hajj continued. When the necessary rituals were complete, Hassan Pasha and all the pilgrims came to the city to perform the last circumambulation of the Kaaba, which signals the completion of the Hajj. The pilgrims were allowed into the Sacred Mosque, but then the gates were closed. What happened next was witnessed by Celebi.

> The attendants of the Sharif had by this time climbed Mount Qubays, while Sharif Saad had occupied the seven minarets of the Holy Mosque with his marksmen, who started to fire on the belea-guered pilgrims and troops from them and from the adjoining seminaries, wounding seven hundred and killing two hundred persons in the precincts of the Shrine. Nothing like this bloody massacre at the Shrine itself had occurred before, even in the days of ibn Zubair . . . The fighting lasted one day and one night . . . The courtyard of the Shrine was heaped with corpses, Hassan Pasha himself was hit by bullets, and the property of the pilgrims and troops looted.[36]

When the pilgrims and troops finally left the city, on their return journey they were set upon by Hamud and his men. Many were speared to death, others cut down with swords. Hassan Pasha himself died of his wounds near Gaza.

When the news of the massacre in Mecca reached Istanbul, the sultan was incensed. He lost no time in dispatching a battalion of 2,000 hand-picked soldiers, along with battalions of 3,000 troops each from Egypt and Syria. The army, led by Hussain Pasha, arrived with the pilgrim caravan and camped at Wadi Fah, two stages from Mecca. All the nobles of the city came to pay their homage to Hussain

Pasha – the scholars, the leading businessmen and the notable members of the sharif clan. Each received generous gifts from the pasha. There was one conspicuous absence: Sharif Saad. Everyone knew that this time the pasha really did come with orders to dispense with the sharif.

On entering the city, Hussain Pasha performed his religious rites and went straight to meet Sharif Saad. The two exchanged pleasantries and gifts, and Hussain Pasha invited the sharif to honour him with a visit the next morning as his majesty the sultan had sent him a robe of honour and a royal *firman* (decree). When Sharif Saad arrived at the appointed place, he was again honoured with praise and gifts. He was confirmed in his office, and everyone went to Muna and Arafat with much pomp and ceremony. All of Mecca's inhabitants came out to join the ceremony, which continued for four days.

As soon as the pilgrimage was over, Hussain Pasha acted. He occupied the water supply in Arafat and placed troops on all roads leading to Mecca. Sharif Saad knew what awaited him and chose to flee, leaving all his belongings. The pasha entered the city, along with all the pilgrims, and called for a public meeting. The whole of Mecca came to the meeting where the inhabitants were asked to choose their next sharif. Much discussion ensued, but Hussain Pasha himself was inclined to listen to the most learned man in the city: the Moorish astronomer Muhammad ibn Sulaiman. The two knew each other. Ibn Sulaiman, known as 'Muhammad the Moor', had left Mecca, disgusted with its citizens, and became teacher to the grand vizier in Istanbul. He taught astronomy to Ottoman officials in the capital and gave lessons to Hussain Pasha himself. He had returned to Mecca with the pasha as his adviser and mentor.

Ibn Sulaiman suggested that Barakat ibn Muhammad, the great-grandson of Barakat II, who was known for his integrity and learning, should be appointed as the new ruler of Mecca. The pasha obliged. But the astronomer from Andalusia was not happy simply to replace a corrupt and ruthless ruler with an honest, knowledgeable one. He recommended that certain reforms should also be introduced in the city. Mathematics and astronomy should be reintroduced in the madrassa curriculum. There should be a proper accounting system, particularly in the religious bequest offices. Drum-beating and dancing in the seminaries of the Dervish orders, the practice of astrology, and sexual excesses in shrines and certain quarters of the city should be banned. Inappropriately dressed women drenched in perfume wandering alone in the city in the middle of the night should be discouraged.

Barakat ibn Muhammad turned out to be a wise and capable ruler, not least because ibn Sulaiman was always by his side and ever ready to dispense knowledge and wisdom. During his eleven-year reign peace returned to Mecca. But turmoil followed, by inveterate logic, in the wake of his death in 1682. He was succeeded by his son Said, who managed to squash several rebellions masterminded by family members. The Meccans themselves had had enough of mathematics and astronomy and longed to return to astrology, drum-beating and sexual escapades in the dark recesses of shrines. They began sending poisonous messages about ibn Sulaiman to the sultan. By now, the astronomer had lost most of his friends in Istanbul. The sultan ordered Sharif Said to exile the astronomer to Jerusalem. The sharif tried to conceal and delay the order, but the citizens, eagerly awaiting the development, discovered the royal *firman* and insisted that it should be implemented without delay. The sharif was forced to comply. A year later, sickened by the behaviour of his followers and the inhabitants of his beloved city, overwhelmed by the anarchy and disorder within its walls, Sharif Said himself gave up and migrated to Damascus.

Chaos followed. There was open warfare between Dhawi Barakat and Dhawi Zaid, leading to untold bloodshed. During the next hundred years, numerous sharifs came and went. Few managed to cling to power for more than four or five years. By now the sultans in Istanbul had come to the conclusion that it was almost impossible to govern the warring tribes and unruly Bedouins of Mecca. The best they could do was to keep the natives occupied in obscurantist rituals. At the dawn of the eighteenth century, formal celebrations to mark the birthday of the Prophet Muhammad were introduced by an edict of the sultan. On the appointed day, a procession would form in the courtyard of the Sacred Mosque. It would leave the Kaaba after evening prayers with the devotees carrying candles and banners, and make its way to the Mosque of Nativity, built in 1547 on the site where the Prophet was said to have been born. Poems and hymns would be sung in praise of the Prophet at the Mosque of Nativity. The ceremony would end late in the night with a solo performance of a poem. The gathering would start to swing as the singer began with the words:

On that night of the twelfth Rabi al-Awwal,
The Lady Aminah, the mother of Muhammad . . .

becoming more animated when the singer moved on to describe the hour of the Prophet's birth, and would finally join the chorus in a state of ecstasy:

Hail to Thee, O Moon of Splendour, hail to Thee!
Hail to Thee, O Helper of the Forsaken!
God bless our Lord Muhammad, the Prophet of the Portionless.[37]

But such ceremonies brought only temporary relief for the citizens. Economically the city was in decline. Political mayhem often saw the city being looted and ransacked, and the citizens harassed, attacked or murdered. Racism and xenophobia, never far beneath the surface in Mecca, came to the fore and the citizens turned on those who were seen as outsiders. The city nobles persuaded the sharif (it was the time of Abdilla bin Said, who ruled from 1723 to 1733) to expel all resident foreigners. They are taking our jobs and posts, the

Meccans claimed. The foreigners were in fact employed as clerks, government officials, scribes, administrators, teachers, doctors – jobs that Meccans themselves were not qualified to hold or were unwilling to take. An order was issued for all foreigners to leave the city. Most of the Moroccans and Egyptians left. The Indians, Persians and Uzbeks were more reluctant, but were forced out in the end. Only a few Turks were left in the city as the sultan's staff in charge of running the caravans. The sharif issued further orders: there should be no smoking in public, and on the insistence of religious scholars, all tobacco shops and coffee houses were closed. Mecca ground to a halt. Soon it became a ghost town.

The sharifs had little control now. Order could be restored only when the Turkish army was in the city to support the sharif. On 12 July 1770, Abdullah ibn Hussain, of the Dhawi Barakat, was proclaimed sharif of Mecca, and the Dhawi Zaid candidate was defeated. But Sharif Hussain stayed in power only as long as the Turkish army backed him. As soon as the Ottoman forces left, Ahmad ibn Said, the Dhawi Zaid candidate, attacked the city with the support of local Bedouin tribes. Entering the city after a fierce battle, he ordered all the Dhawi Barakat houses to be burnt. The city was looted so badly that the citizens had virtually nothing to eat and a famine ensued. A few members of the Dhawi Barakat branch managed to escape to Jeddah, where they were given protection by Ahmad ibn Said's representative, Yusif Al Qabil. Incensed, Sharif Ahmad sent his soldiers to Jeddah and ordered that Al Qabil be brought to him in chains.

Once again Mecca produced a dashing young man who came to the rescue of the city in a time of grave peril. He was Sarur ibn Masaad, the nephew of Ahmad ibn Said. Sarur may have been only seventeen, but already he was a skilled warrior with a strong sense of justice. He was infuriated with the appalling behaviour of his uncle. When he heard the news that orders had been issued for the arrest of Al Qabil, he slipped out of Mecca in the deep of night and rode as fast as he could to Jeddah. When Sharif Ahmad's soldiers arrived to arrest Al Qabil they found Sarur standing in front of him, sword in hand. Al Qabil, he declared, was now under his protection. But Sarur and Al Qabil were seriously outnumbered, so a compromise was reached. Sarur agreed to let the soldiers take Al Qabil to Mecca, but only if he accompanied them, and on the added condition that no punishment was to be given until they had reached the Holy City. However, en route to Mecca, Sarur and Al Qabil managed to slip away from the soldiers and took refuge in a place called Wadi al Marr. From there, Sarur wrote to his uncle informing him of his intention to fight him. Ahmad bin Said replied pointing out that he was one of the Dhawi Zaid, to whom he owed his loyalty, and in any case a mere teenager was in no position to take on the sharif of Mecca.

Sarur spent a few months gathering his young friends and making his plans. On 5 February 1773, leading an army of 300 horsemen, he met his uncle's army at Wadi al Minhana. The battle lasted a mere two hours. A little later, Sarur entered Mecca as the new sharif.

At about the same time, a 'long-tailed star-like' object, 'a lance in length', was seen in the sky. The comet stayed from sunrise to sunset. It upset and frightened the inhabitants. Special prayers were said in the Sacred Mosque. And, as they had done before, the Meccans saw the comet as a bad omen. Had the astrologers not predicted imminent doom following the emergence of a celestial sign? It warned, they declared, of the arrival in Mecca of a new, dangerous infidel in the guise of a Muslim.

This time they were correct.

7

The Wahhabi Threat

Sarur ibn Masaad began his reign by removing capricious taxes and improving the administration of Mecca. The Meccans started admiring his generosity, his passion for justice and his sense of forgiveness. His reputation and prestige were enhanced when he married the daughter of the sultan of Morocco in 1779. The whole city participated in his wedding and gifts from Morocco were generously distributed to the inhabitants. Yet while Sarur's reign brought much-needed peace to the Holy City, the sharif himself did not have a peaceful life.

He had to deal with two specific enemies. Although he had been decisively defeated, his uncle Ahmad had not given up on his ambition to rule Mecca. A group of his supporters remained there; they persistently agitated and conspired to effect his return. Delegation after delegation tried to persuade the Turkish representative in Mecca to move against Sarur. The official, who personally favoured the young sharif, refused Ahmad's supporters on explicit orders from Istanbul. On one occasion, Ahmad's supporters surrounded the sharif's house and opened fire. Sarur, however, was able to suppress them easily. Ahmad managed to recruit a new army, and using Taif as his base, attacked the Holy City. Once again Sarur defeated him and deported him, along with his followers, from Mecca. The battles between nephew and uncle continued for six long years, with no fewer than fifteen engagements. Eventually, Sarur was forced to imprison Ahmad, along with his sons and most prominent followers. Exhausted by his repeated attempts to recapture Mecca, Ahmad died in prison in 1780.

Almost at once a new enemy appeared. It was the ferocious and fiercely independent tribe of Harb, which controlled a large area around Medina. As the Hajj caravans had to pass through their territory, the Harb took every opportunity to attack and loot them. There was little doubt that Medina itself was collaborating with the Harb and actively encouraging the tribe to attack the caravans and take Meccans hostage. Sarur felt he had no option but to attack Medina. The Prophet's City put up stern resistance, but after a battle lasting a week Sarur was able to take the city and release several hundred Meccans the Harb had taken hostage. The Harb fled the city and melted into the countryside. Sarur now faced a daunting prospect: his return journey to Mecca would take him through Harb land where an ambush was inevitable.

In Medina, he announced his intention to travel through the Harb country. In fact, he took a more circuitous route, going east through the desert to Taif. En route, he ran out of water and was saved by some friendly nomads. On reaching Taif, he heard that the Harb had attacked and retaken Mecca. They had also captured the port of Yanbu and taken his governor hostage. Another major clash seemed to threaten.

The young sharif persuaded a number of different tribes to join him in a hasty campaign against the Harb. Leading a massive army of 12,000 soldiers and tribesmen, with 150 craftsmen and engineers, requiring 7,000 camels to carry all the baggage, Sarur made his way to Harb territory. It was a tough trek through the desert; there was much grumbling and complaining among the tribesmen. Eventually, camel-drivers belonging to the Hudhail tribe refused to go any further. A brawl followed; shots were accidentally fired in the direction of Sharif Sarur, one bullet missing him by inches. Panic broke out amongst the Hudhail. Convinced that the sharif would seek vengeance, they decamped en masse. Sarur tried to assure them that he was not interested in vengeance but to no avail. Instead, the Hudhail announced their intention to attack and ransack Mecca.

Sarur was forced to abandon his campaign against the Harb to pursue and defeat the Hudhail. They begged for mercy, which Sarur, ever magnanimous, readily granted.

The Harb continued their campaign of looting and terror. Sharif Sarur planned his second assault on the Harb carefully, taking more time. After assembling an even greater army than before, he managed to inflict heavy losses on the unruly tribe. But the Harb were not totally defeated. They would regroup and reappear. Meanwhile, Sharif Sarur fell sick 'shortly after a particularly brilliant circumcision party for his son and nephews'.[1] He was poisoned, probably by one of his uncle's supporters, and died on 20 September 1788. He was just thirty-four years old. The Meccans would remember the name of this brave and handsome sharif, who showed so much promise, with admiration and reverence for decades to come.

While Sarur was leading his campaigns against the Harb, a storm was brewing elsewhere in Arabia. His contemporary, Muhammad ibn Abd al-Wahhab (1703–92), a religious scholar from Najd, was laying the foundations of a revivalist movement in central Arabia. Muhammad ibn Abd al-Wahhab belonged to a sedentary tribe; his family had produced a number of religious scholars but was not particularly wealthy. He 'lived in poverty with his three wives. He owned a bustan, a date garden and ten or twenty cows.'[2] He followed the footsteps of his ancestors and travelled to Basra and Medina to study and seek his fortune. He was influenced by scholars belonging to the Hanbali school of Islamic jurisprudence. Like Imam Ahmad ibn Hanbal, who was persecuted for his defence of traditionalism by Caliph al-Mamun, ibn Abd al-Wahhab too was a staunch traditionalist.

In eighteenth-century Medina, an intellectual tradition was in vogue and 'sweeping the Indian Ocean's Muslim rim: the revival of Hadith [reports about the Prophet Muhammad] studies and a concomitant desire to bring the practices of Sufi orders into conformity with rules of Islamic law'.[3] Ibn Abd al-Wahhab was probably influenced by the movement. In any case, he believed that Muslims had grown corrupt, superstitious and degenerate and it was necessary to purify Islam from all contaminations. What his followers of today call 'innovations' – practices that amounted to idolatry – had crept into Muslim beliefs. He was appalled at what he had seen in Mecca. The inhabitants were more devoted to the shrines of saints than to their daily prayers. Dancing and music were common in the city, and many men and women had become addicted to smoking. Islam needed to be purified; Muslims must return to the theological purity of the Prophet's teachings. He began a reform movement in Najd with the aim of changing Muslims. Initially, ibn Abd al-Wahhab did not want to change their social, cultural or political conditions. His revivalist movement aimed solely to purify the faith, purging what he saw as heresy and intrusions in Muslim beliefs, and enforcing correct doctrines on the followers of Islam.

For ibn Abd al-Wahhab, the Muslims had degenerated to the condition of ignorance prevalent in pre-Islamic Arabia. The original and authentic meaning of the cardinal belief of Islam – 'I bear witness that there is no god but God and Muhammad is the messenger of God' – had evaporated. An individual does not become a Muslim simply by uttering this statement, although it is mandatory. To be a true and authentic Muslim, one must devote all forms of worship, with no exception, to God and only to God.[4] It followed that Muslims who had made the declaration of faith but practised idolatry, or did not strictly follow the example of the Prophet Muhammad, were unbelievers (kafirs). Those who prayed to saints or used charms violated the Unity of God and had gone astray from true faith. Such individuals should be invited back to faith; if they refused, and persisted in their deviant ways, then the death penalty could be applied to them. Moreover, it was the duty of the state to ensure that Muslims followed the correct and authentic path of Islam in all aspects – political, cultural and social.

At first, ibn Abd al-Wahhab's teachings were strongly opposed. Even his own father and brother rejected his call. He managed to attract a few followers in the town of Uyayna, where the ruler warmed to his ideas and closed a few shrines, levelling the grave of a companion of the Prophet. Neighbouring tribes reacted violently to this and threatened to kill the reformer. Forced out of Uyayna, ibn Abd al-Wahhab sought refuge in the neighbouring city of Dariyya. It was an apt choice. The two brothers of the ruler of Dariyya, Muhammad bin Saud, had been students of ibn Abd al-Wahhab. They welcomed him to their city and persuaded the ruler to enter into a pact with the reformist scholar. An 'irrevocable alliance' was forged:

> Muhammad bin Saud pledged himself and his family to uphold and spread the Wahhabi persuasion of Islam. In return, ibn Abdul Wahhab promised him dominion. The Sword and the political power that went with it would be the realm of Muhammad bin Saud and his descendants. The Book [the Qur'an] and accompanying religious, moral and educational authority would be the domain of Shaikh Muhammad ibn Abdul Wahhab and the Al al-Shaikh, as his descendants came to be known.[5]

The partnership between Muhammad ibn Abd al-Wahhab and the House of Saud was sealed in 1747, and marks the birth of the Wahhabi movement. When ibn Abd al-Wahhab died in 1792, Wahhabi forces were on the move and had declared jihad against Muslims they regarded as non-believers and apostates – including the Shia, the Sufis and various other sects of Islam. 'The corollary of identifying Muslims other than Wahhabis as *mushrikin* (polytheists, or those who associate other with God) was that warfare against them became not simply permissible but obligatory: their blood could be legitimately shed, their property was forfeit, and their women and children could be enslaved.'[6] Their first foray was directed against Iraq. By 1799 they had reached the gates of Baghdad and obliged the Ottomans to conclude a treaty with them. Two years later, they sacked Kerbala, the holy city of the Shia. Now they turned their attention towards Mecca.

The Meccans regarded the Wahhabi puritans as dangerous fanatics, infidels who came disguised as Muslims. The *qadi* of Mecca had, on a number of occasions, denounced them as non-Muslims, who should not be allowed to enter the city. The Ottomans compared the Wahhabis to the ninth-century Qarmatians (chapter 4), as well as to the Kharijites (chapter 3). Whenever the Wahhabis asked permission to make the pilgrimage, they were sternly refused. When the Wahhabis approached Sarur, he granted them permission on one condition: they would have to pay exactly the same as the Persian pilgrims, and in addition send a hundred camels a year to Mecca. It was a polite way of saying 'no' – the Wahhabis got the message.

Although the Wahhabis had made their presence felt under Sarur and his predecessors, it was his successor Ghalib bin Masaad who saw the movement sweeping towards Mecca like a flood. While he succeeded his brother Sarur without trouble, in 1788, Ghalib's reign began in the conventional Meccan way with intrigues against him and his brothers. Even his twelve-year-old nephew, Abdullah ibn Sarur, conspired against him. Ghalib was a giant of a man, described by those who met him as 'skilful', 'engaging' and 'sweet and circumspect'.[7] While refined and cosmopolitan himself, he had great respect for the Bedouins of the desert amongst whom he grew up.

The Swiss explorer John Lewis Burckhardt (1784–1817) met Sharif Ghalib during his stay in Mecca. Burckhardt was employed by the British African Association ostensibly to find the source of the Niger river. This was a new era of exploration, when adventurers were dispatched from European capitals to explore various corners of the world supposedly in the name of science, though more than disinterested knowledge invariably followed in their footsteps. In preparation for his journey, which was to take him across the Fezzan, the inhospitable desert in the south of what is today Libya, and on to West Africa, Burckhardt travelled to Egypt. He studied Arabic and Islamic law, so that he could perfect the disguise of an Arab merchant when he joined the Fezzan caravan in Egypt. There is speculation that his assumed persona as a Muslim was more than a disguise, though his family always denied he had actually converted. He travelled around Egypt, Nubia and through the Levant, rediscovering the ruins of the ancient Nabatean Arab city of Petra – 'that rose-red city "half as old as Time"' – in modern-day Jordan. At each stage of his journey he scrupulously sent his notebooks and letters back to his London employers.

For all his elaborate and extensive preparations, Burckhardt died of dysentery and fever without ever joining the Fezzan caravan. His last excursion, before returning to Cairo, was to make the Hajj to Mecca. While in Mecca, he observed that Ghalib was exceptionally polite to the Bedouins and referred to them as father, mother and brother. When the Bedouins visited Mecca, they stayed at one of his houses. His government 'was lenient and cautious: he respected the pride of the Meccans, and seldom made any attempts against their personal safety or even fortunes of the individuals . . . He permitted his avowed enemies to live peacefully in the bosom of their families, and the people to indulge in bloody affrays among themselves, which frequently happened.'[8]

Ghalib's leniency, however, did not extend to the Wahhabis, whom he saw as violent extremists. When they approached him seeking permission to visit Mecca and to perform the Hajj, Ghalib not only refused categorically but announced his intention to wage war against what he called 'the Wahhabi threat'. By now the term 'Wahhabis', originally coined by the Ottomans 'to suggest that the movement fell outside the mainstream Islam and was focused upon ibn Abdul Wahhab rather than God',[9] was being widely used to describe the followers of Muhammad ibn Abd al-Wahhab. Ghalib's first expedition against the Wahhabis was led by his brother, Abdul Aziz ibn Masaad, in 1790. It lasted six months and was fairly successful. The second campaign was led by Ghalib himself. His use of field guns ensured the success of the raid. Despite these successful manoeuvres, the Wahhabis were not deterred. Their armies were large and fought with ferocious intensity. The Wahhabis 'came on like locusts or streams out of the hill after rain'[10] and inflicted heavy casualties on Ghalib's forces. The sharif was able to keep them away from Mecca but could not inflict a decisive blow. The Wahhabis for their part began to harass the pilgrim caravans, and levied increasingly heavy taxes on the pilgrims who passed through their territory. Within a few years, the caravans ceased to reach Mecca.

In desperation, Sharif Ghalib turned to the Ottoman sultan. He sent an urgent message to Istanbul in 1793 and again in 1798, asking for ammunition and support. But the Sublime Porte saw the Wahhabi threat to Mecca as a little local difficulty in comparison with the problem the Ottomans now faced: wrestling with the profound implications of the expansive plans of a major European power and what this signified for the future. Instead of support, Mecca received orders, at the end of 1798, to fortify itself and prepare for a possible invasion by the French. The entire city was galvanized; citizens queued up for sessions of military training, which were held every evening, and prepared for the imminent arrival of the French armies. The sharif was informed that the outer cover of the Kaaba – the *kiswa* – would not be coming from Egypt as was the custom. It would now be made in Istanbul, where the entire courtyard of the Sultan Ahmad Mosque was cordoned off to weave the cover from black silk thread. It duly arrived.

The shifting fortunes of Europe were pressing in on the Muslim world. Mecca would not be immune. The full impact of the age of colonialism was in the making, an age when rivalries between European powers would be fought in terms of possession of foreign lands and domination over non-European peoples. From their small and seemingly insignificant entry into the trading world of the Indian Ocean in 1600, the northern European powers had garnered enormous profits. Over time the balance of the global economy had shifted. Since the victory of their East India Company over the nawab of Bengal and his French allies at the Battle of Plessey in 1757, the British merchant company, acting as the agents of the Mughal emperor, effectively ruled over a large Muslim population. Year by year they rolled forward their hold over ever more Indian territory. The French were increasingly locked out of India. And the riches of empire were changing Europe society. In France the calls for change led to the bloody revolution that brought the military genius of Napoleon Bonaparte to prominence. Fearful of the might of the British navy, Bonaparte turned away from plans to invade Britain in favour of striking at a vital link in their communications with India: Egypt.

Napoleon landed his army at Alexandria in July of 1798 and in two swift battles subdued the Mamluk armies that defended this province of the Ottoman Empire. But his plans were disrupted by the very British navy he had sought to avoid. In August all but two of his vessels were captured or destroyed by Admiral Horatio Nelson in the Battle of the Nile. Instead of paving his way to India, Napoleon turned aside to conquer the Holy Land. Not the Muslim land of the Holy Sanctuaries, as the Meccans had feared, but the biblical Holy Land that had been sought by the Crusaders. He marched into the Ottoman province of Damascus, taking Arish, Gaza, Jaffa and Haifa, but could not take Acre and retreated back to Egypt, where he defeated an Ottoman army at Abukir. He then left his army and returned to France, where the following year he mounted a *coup d'état* and became First Consul. Five years later France's Senate would make him emperor.

The Ottomans were increasingly embroiled in the machinations of the European powers as the Napoleonic Wars swept across the continent. European nations now thought and planned their conflicts in global terms. They were contending for possessions in far-flung parts of the world, and the negotiation of peace involved further exchanges of foreign lands under European rule. The Ottoman

Empire would loom large as a factor in European strategy. The Sublime Porte was more and more concerned with how to make the best of shifting alliances among the European powers to preserve not only its expansive territory but also its autonomy. The more European pressure bore down on the Sublime Porte the more internal dissension threatened to fracture the Ottoman Empire. And internal strife created new openings for European powers to exert influence and gain control over Muslim lands. The Servants of the Holy Sanctuaries were not immune to this wider geopolitics. Effectively they would subcontract the protection of Mecca to their Egyptian underlings as they scrambled to make an alliance – with the French. Alliances with enemies seemed the order of the day.

And so, a year after Napoleon's Alexandrian adventure in 1798, Mecca sought a hasty truce with the Wahhabis. This permitted the arrival of the Hajj caravan in 1799, which brought the *kiswa* from Istanbul in 1800. The caravan came under the personal escort of Saud ibn Abdul Aziz Muhammad ibn Saud, the crown prince of the Saudi state and protector-in-chief to the followers of ibn Abd al-Wahhab. Much to the displeasure of Mecca's citizens, the Wahhabis were allowed to make the pilgrimage. They took the opportunity to consolidate their position: they captured the Red Sea port of Hali, sacked Kerbala for the second time in 1802 (attacking precisely on the Islamic date of 10 Muharram, the day the Shia mourn the martyrdom of Hussain at Kerbala), and attacked the Persian caravan. Saud had a particularly good network of agents and informers, and he was well informed about Sharif Ghalib's intentions and moves.

Ghalib managed to recapture Hali only to lose it again in 1802. Deciding that the best option was to negotiate a new truce with the Wahhabis, he sent his brother-in-law Othman al-Madhaifi to open talks about a possible truce with ibn Saud. This was a serious mistake. Al-Madhaifi had his own designs on Mecca. Rather than negotiate a truce, he made a secret agreement with ibn Saud: in return for his support, ibn Saud would make him the sharif of Mecca and emir of

Taif. Encouraged and aided by ibn Saud, Othman wasted no time in attacking Taif. He was thwarted by Ghalib's brother, Abdul Muin, who was then the governor of Taif. Shocked by Othman's treachery, Ghalib did not know which way to turn. Calculating that Othman would return with a bigger Wahhabi army for a second attempt on Taif, he decided to take the initiative. He would attack Othman on his own ground, in the castle in Al Abaqla, near Taif, where Othman had retreated. Taking a large force to Al Abaqla meant exposing Mecca to Wahhabi attack. Nevertheless, he joined his brother Abdul Muin and marched against Othman. Before he reached his destination news of Wahhabi troops gathering in the Hijaz in preparation for an assault on Mecca forced him to return. Othman, strengthened by fresh troops, was able to take Taif relatively easily, though with great slaughter. Virtually everyone in the city, even those who took refuge in the Friday Mosque, was killed. He then moved quickly to capture the port of Qunfidha, south of Jeddah, where he left fewer than 200 people alive. Encouraged by Othman's success, ibn Saud now moved towards Mecca.

Panic broke out in the city. Scholars and jurists gathered in the Sacred Mosque to discuss the imminent invasion. They agreed that it was the first invasion of the city from people outside the Hijaz since the pre-Islamic Battle of the Elephant, when Abrahah, the Christian viceroy of the negus of Abyssinia, attacked the Holy City. The gathering proclaimed jihad against the Wahhabi puritans. Town criers were dispatched to all parts of the city to announce the jihad and recruit volunteers for the sharif's army. The sharif himself tried to persuade the leaders of the visiting pilgrim caravans to lend him their support and join the jihad. The pilgrims, however, were only interested in completing their rituals and leaving the city as fast as they could. Sharif Ghalib was left on his own.

The joint forces of ibn Saud and Othman arrived near Mecca, making camp at Al Hussainiya, where rich Meccans had their summer houses. The Wahhabi troops stopped traffic coming into and out of the city, and cut off the sweet-water supply from Arafat. They made occasional raids into Mecca itself. But on the whole they waited and stayed out of the city. Sharif Ghalib resisted bravely. He laid mines in and around the city to prevent a full-scale invasion.

After two months, the city began to suffer from lack of drinkable water. Even the brackish water from the well of Zamzam had to be rationed. Food began to run out. Provisions for Ghalib's army dried up. The sharif felt he had no alternative but to leave the city. He burnt what he could not carry, and slipped out one night with his family and soldiers to seek refuge in Jeddah.

At dawn one morning in early May 1803, the Wahhabis entered Mecca. In Taif, the Wahhabis had 'killed some two hundred of its people, in the market places and in their homes';[11] the people of Kerbala had suffered a similar fate. So the citizens expected a mass slaughter; people locked themselves in their houses. But to the astonishment of the inhabitants of the Holy City, the Wahhabis entered in an orderly fashion. Ibn Saud announced that no harm would come to the inhabitants, and ordered shops to be opened and normal life to be resumed. Then the scholars and jurists of the city were assembled in front of him. He told them that he had seen the Prophet Muhammad in a dream, a rather clever tactic to get them on his side. The Prophet had warned him, he said, not to mistreat the people of Mecca. His task was only to reintroduce the pure teachings of Islam to the city. So he ordered shrines to be closed, banned men from wearing gold or silk, and prohibited mention of the sultan's name in the Friday sermon, as was the custom. Smoking and mixing of men and women in public were also banned. Water pipes, known as *shisha*, were confiscated and burnt in front of ibn Saud's office and tobacco shops were closed. It was obligatory for everyone to attend the five daily prayers and absentees were to be beaten severely in public.

The Wahhabi occupation of Mecca lasted only two months. Ibn Saud knew that as long as Ghalib was alive it would not be easy to hold Mecca, so he turned his attention to Jeddah, where Ghalib was busy regrouping his troops. He moved swiftly to lay siege to the city. By moving to Jeddah Ghalib had secured supplies and communication through its port from Egypt, Yemen and India. He was now much stronger and his troops fought bravely. After a siege lasting eleven days, during which he suffered some losses, ibn Saud decided to retreat. He retired to Najd.

Almost at once, Ghalib re-entered Mecca. The small garrison of Wahhabi soldiers ibn Saud had left behind surrendered without much of a fight. The city rejoiced, and among other things the tobacco shops reopened to do brisk business. But Ghalib knew that he was now at the mercy of the Wahhabis. They had taken Medina and introduced a strict regime of prayer and austerity in the Prophet's City. Shrines were closed and the Prophet's Mosque stripped of its treasures. The Wahhabis had also closed the caravan routes; no pilgrim caravans came to Mecca after 1803. Insecurity and uncertainty prevailed everywhere outside Mecca, and the sharif was now powerless to stop the Wahhabis coming for Hajj.

They arrived in force for the pilgrimage during the following years. The Spanish noble Domingo Badia y Leyblich, who used the *nom de plume* of Ali Bey al-Abbasi, was in Mecca and witnessed the arrival of the Wahhabi pilgrims. Unlike Burckhardt, Ali Bey was a Muslim, although he too was probably in the pay of a European power. Travelling through North Africa, he arrived in Mecca in 1807 just in time for the Hajj. He was in the main street of Mecca about nine o'clock in the morning when he saw a crowd of Wahhabis entering the city:

What men! We must imagine a crowd of individuals, thronged together, without any other covering than a small piece of cloth round their waist, except some few who had a napkin placed upon their shoulder, that passed under the right arm, being naked in every other respect, with their matchlocks upon their shoulders, and their *khanjears* or large knives hung to their girdles. All the people fled at the sight of the torrent of men, and left them the whole street to themselves . . . I saw a column of them defile, which appeared composed of five or six thousand men, so pressed together in the whole width of the street, that it would not have been possible to have moved a hand. The column was proceeded by three or four horsemen, armed with a lance twelve feet long, and followed by fifteen or twenty men mounted upon horses, camels, and dromedaries, with lances like other; but they had neither flags, drums, nor any other instrument or military trophy during their march. Some uttered cries of holy joy, others recited prayers in a confused and loud voice.[12]

The Wahhabi pilgrims continued their march right up to the Sacred Mosque. By this time most of the adults had left the city, with only children remaining. The children guided the Wahhabis around the Sacred Mosque and the Kaaba. When the first party of puritan pilgrims started their circumambulation of the Kaaba, the Wahhabi crowd

began pressing towards the Black Stone to kiss it, when the others, impatient no doubt at being kept waiting, advanced in a tumult, mixed amongst the first; and confusion being soon at its height, prevented them from hearing the voices of their young guides. Tumult succeeded to confusion. All wishing to kiss the stone, precipitated themselves upon the spot; and many of them made their way with their sticks in their hands. In vain did their chiefs mount the base near the stone, with a view to enforce order: their cries and signs were useless, for the holy zeal for the House of God which devoured them, would not permit them to listen to reason, nor to the voice of their chief. The movement of the circle increased by mutual impulse. They resembled at last a swarm of bees, which flutter confusedly round their hive, circulating rapidly and without order round the Kaaba, and by their tumultuous pressure breaking all the lamps which surrounded it with their guns, which they carried upon their shoulders.[13]

Then the Wahhabi pilgrims rushed en masse towards Zamzam. The very sight of this horde coming towards them terrified those who were employed to look after Zamzam. They abandoned their posts and ran for their lives. Within moments, the buckets, the ropes and pulleys were ruined. The Wahhabis jumped into the well, and, 'giving each other their hands, formed a chain to descend to the bottom, and obtained the water how they could'.[14]

The presence of the Wahhabis during the Hajj signified a serious decline in Ghalib's power. The Wahhabis roamed around the Hijaz freely and attacked whomsoever they wished. The very mention of their name was enough to reduce a Meccan to jelly. Sharif Ghalib appealed again and again to the sultan in Istanbul for help, pointing out that the Wahhabis presented a danger to the Ottoman Empire itself. But the Sublime Porte, too preoccupied with wars in Europe, remained inactive. Only when the Wahhabis attacked Damascus in 1810 was the sultan stirred into motion. Muhammad Ali (1769–1849), the Ottoman viceroy and pasha of Egypt, was instructed to provide assistance. Orders were sent to Cairo to rid Mecca and the Hijaz of the Wahhabis.

Muhammad Ali, a native of Kavalla in Ottoman Macedonia, had risen to prominence in the Kavalla Volunteer Contingent. In 1801 his unit joined the Ottoman force that reoccupied Egypt following Napoleon's withdrawal. A skilful politician, Muhammad Ali managed to play off the not totally defeated Mamluks and the Ottoman forces against each other. Manipulating the anarchy and with the backing of the religious scholars, he became governor of Egypt in 1805. His aim was autonomy and to construct a modern state in Egypt, one capable of matching the advances of European nations. He was responsible for introducing a new form of government and economic system, industrialized the country, extended irrigation and modernized bureaucracy, building on earlier Mamluk reforms and making considerable use not only of European ideas but also of European, notably British, 'advisers'. As such, he is seen both as 'the Last of the Mamluks'[15] and as 'the Founder of Modern Egypt'.[16]

As soon as Ghalib heard that Muhammad Ali had been ordered to invade Hijaz, he started a secret correspondence with him. The sharif assured the governor of Egypt of his willingness to work with him to subdue the Wahhabis and provided information about ibn Saud's army, the Wahhabi temperament, and the best lines of attack. In return, Ghalib wanted assurances that his authority in Mecca and the Hijaz would be respected and that the custom duties from the port of Jeddah, a major source of his income, would remain in his hands. Muhammad Ali, giving little credit to Ghalib's assurances, agreed to his requests. However, the political situation in Egypt was far from stable, and he was reluctant to be absent from his seat of power for too long. In turn, he demanded guarantees from Istanbul that Egypt would not be occupied in his absence. Meanwhile the sultan was being advised that 'if you grant Muhammad Ali the world he will still not go to fight in the Hijaz'.[17] In the end, Muhammad Ali decided to send an expedition against the Wahhabis under the command of his son, Tousoun Bey.

Like Sarur, and before him Abu Nomay II, Tousoun Bey was an unusually accomplished teenager – only seventeen and battle-hardened. His father thought it prudent to support him with someone more experienced who could provide wise counsel in time of need. He chose Ahmad Agha, one of his treasurers, who had served Muhammad Ali loyally. Agha was known equally for his bravery and ferocity. He started as the treasurer (khezendar) of Muhammad Ali and went on to become a successful commander, leading campaigns against the Mamluks and Arabs in Egypt. His military successes and utter ruthlessness had earned him 'the surname of Bonaparte, which afforded him much delight, and by which he was universally designated in Egypt'.[18] The two arrived with their fleet in Yanbu in October 1811 and captured the port from the Wahhabis. In Mecca, the news was received with much jubilation, and the capture of Yanbu was declared a major victory against those they regarded as the fanatics from Central Arabia. The cavalry arrived a couple of weeks later by land without meeting much opposition from the tribes, as most had already been bought off with large sums of money. But Tousoun soon discovered that not all tribes were as anti-Wahhabi as Sharif Ghalib had indicated to his father. In particular, the ferocious Harb were in awe of ibn Saud. Their dislike of the Wahhabis, and eagerness to participate again in pilgrim trade, did not mean that they were ready to join the Turks against ibn Saud. Tousoun Bey spent several months negotiating with the tribes, trying to make an alliance against the Wahhabis.

Even Sharif Ghalib was not too keen to join the Ottoman army. What if Tousoun Bey failed to subjugate the Wahhabis? They would take a terrible revenge on him and Mecca. So he sat on the fence. He wrote letters of support to Tousoun while excusing himself from joining his force. My army is rather small, and I cannot leave Mecca exposed, he told the pasha. The sharif was also approached by ibn Saud, who reminded him that the Turks had a habit of replacing the ruler of Mecca. Would it not be better for him to join the Wahhabis against the Turkish invaders? Ghalib gave similar excuses to ibn Saud. He hoped that the two parties would exhaust each other, and he would be able to stand against the victorious army.

Tousoun contemplated moving his troops to Mecca but changed his mind. The sharif, he thought, would be forced to declare his allegiance one way or the other – and there was always a chance that he would come out for the Wahhabis. His attempts to gain the support of Bedouin tribes had been fruitless. He decided to capture Medina, six days' march from Yanbu, without wasting any more time. The Prophet's City was the stronghold of the Wahhabis and their gateway to the Hijaz.

During January 1812, Tousoun Bey began his advance towards Medina. The Meccans held their breath. They heard that after a brief skirmish, Tousoun had entered Badr, the site of the famous 624 battle between the Prophet and his enemies. Medina was only a couple of days away.

Badr was in Harb territory. It is located at the entrance to a mountain range; to reach Medina, it is necessary to pass through the mountains. Tousoun expected resistance from the Harb who controlled the passage. He left a small garrison at Badr and marched his army for eight hours to reach Safra, a Harb market town. The Harb fought fiercely but were overcome. Four hours from Safra was the oasis of Judaida, the main city of the Harb. The road from Safra leads through a narrow valley, fifty to sixty yards wide, sandwiched between steep and rocky mountains. It was an ideal spot for an ambush. As the Turkish army marched through the gorge, the Harb appeared suddenly. Tousoun had expected this and was prepared. There was a short sharp skirmish and the Turkish army, believing it had the Harb on the run, pursued them. They were led deep into the ravine. Tousoun was not ready for what followed. Thousands of Wahhabi troops, commanded by Abdullah and Faisal, sons of ibn Saud, descended from both sides of the mountain and fell on the Turkish army.

Shocked and surprised, the Turkish infantry fell back. Ordered to cover their retreat the cavalry joined the battle. Out of the mountains emerged several hundred Wahhabi horsemen and camel riders. The Arabs were nimble and swift, and easily outran the Turkish troops on the rugged mountains. They poured volley upon volley of bullets into the Turks. Panic broke out in the Turkish ranks and the soldiers started to run for their lives. Only the young Tousoun held firm. He tried to rally his troops, and cried out to his soldiers to stand by him. Around twenty horsemen came forward to protect Tousoun. The cavalry rallied, and the Turks were able to retreat under cover of their protection. The Wahhabis came down from the mountains, but did not pursue the Turks. Rather, they concentrated on seizing the booty. The pasha lost 12,000 men. He retreated to Badr, from where, exhausted and downhearted, he returned to Yanbu.

The news of the Turkish defeat in Judaida sent shockwaves through Mecca. The Meccans feared that their success would spur the Wahhabis to turn on the Holy City. The fact that Othman al-Madhaifi and his army were lurking near Mecca made matters worse. Sharif Ghalib felt that he now had no option but to openly support the Wahhabis. He went to Badr and joined his erstwhile enemies. Emboldened, the Wahhabis now believed they could defeat the Turks any time anywhere in Arabia. The victory at Judaida enhanced their reputation and they imposed tributes and taxes on Bedouin tribes as far as Baghdad and Damascus.

Tousoun too was disheartened by the defeat. But a letter from his father restored his morale. Do not be discouraged, Muhammad Ali wrote, 'war is an entertainment and the smell of gunpowder to my nostrils is as the smell of aloes and roses . . . I have fought the British and the French and the Egyptian princes and defeated them with the help of the Almighty and have raised our name and increased our station.'[19] Muhammad Ali also sent a great deal of money to distribute amongst the Bedouin tribes. Tousoun spent the next eight months preparing for a second assault on Medina. One by one, he won the allegiance of a number of tribes in exchange for huge sums. He devoted special attention to winning the Harb to his side, and eventually succeeded in persuading a number of their clans to join him in exchange for exceptionally large bags of gold. Fresh troops and ammunition were arriving regularly from Egypt. By October 1812, Tousoun Bey was ready to march again on Medina.

Sharif Ghalib's conversion to the Wahhabi cause meanwhile appeared to be insincere, a temporary alliance of convenience. We know this because he wrote desperate letters to Tousoun assuring him of his loyalty and insisting that he had only joined the Wahhabis at Badr out of fear and in an attempt to dissuade them from attacking

Mecca. Tousoun seems to have understood this, as he reassured the sharif that he had no hard feelings.

The Turkish army made Badr its headquarters. Tousoun gave command of the troops to Ahmad Agha Bonaparte, who advanced through the valley where the Turkish army had faced defeat without any problem. He left a large garrison in Judaida and made his way to Medina. The Prophet's City was well equipped and stocked with provisions, ready for a long siege. The Wahhabis came out to the suburbs to make their defence, but this time they had no real advantage and were forced to retreat deep within the city. The centre of Medina was protected by high strong walls, with a fortified castle located several hundred yards from the wall. The Turks tried to blow an opening in the castle with mines, but the Wahhabis prevented them from getting too close to the wall. A second chance arose when the Wahhabis were busy with the midday prayers. Part of the wall was blown up and the Turkish soldiers poured in. Stunned by the turn of events, the Wahhabis fled towards the castle. Over a thousand were butchered in the street.

Around 1,500 managed to get inside the castle. Built of solid rock, it was impossible for the Turks to penetrate. They satisfied themselves with surrounding the castle and waited for its provisions to run out. Three weeks later, the Wahhabis surrendered on the promise that they would be given safe conduct out of the city and that camels and provisions would be provided for those who wished to return to Najd. However, when the defenders emerged from the castle, they were stripped and killed. A mere handful was allowed to return to Najd to spread the news of their terrible defeat.

Having conquered Medina, Tousoun Bey and Ahmad Bonaparte turned their attention to Mecca. A force of 1,000 horsemen and 500 foot-soldiers arrived there in January 1813. Othman al-Madhaifi, the commander of the Wahhabi force camped outside Mecca, thought it wise not to engage the Turkish troops and left for his stronghold in Taif. Sharif Ghalib came out to greet the troops and ordered a city-wide celebration. A few weeks later he joined the Turkish troops in a campaign against Taif. Once again the Wahhabis were decisively defeated.

For Sharif Ghalib there was still some unfinished business. His errant son-in-law, Othman al-Madhaifi, was still at large. The sharif hatched a plan for his capture. He announced a reward of 5,000 dollars for his seizure, and among the first to rise to the challenge were the desert Bedouins. It wouldn't be long before al-Madhaifi was caught, disguised as a poor nomad, and brought in front of the sharif in chains. He was subsequently sent to Cairo, from where he was transferred to Istanbul as a present for the sultan, and beheaded soon after his arrival.

And thus the whole of the Hijaz was once again under the Turks. Ottoman flags flew over Mecca, Medina, Jeddah, Taif and Yanbu. Ahmad Bonaparte was asked to return to Cairo. Tousoun Bey was appointed pasha of Jeddah and pilgrim caravans resumed. Life returned to normal, or as normal as it had ever been, in the Holy City. But elsewhere Ottoman power was weakening as Egypt's ruler Muhammad Ali sought to extend his rule into the Sudan and then into the Levant, even threatening Istanbul. Muhammad Ali declared himself khedive, or viceroy, of Egypt, founding a ruling dynasty that remained in place until 1952.

Its misfortunes notwithstanding, and despite the destruction meted out to its monuments and shrines by the Wahhabis, Mecca was still 'a handsome town', relatively wealthy, with few families in 'moderate circumstances'.[20] That's what Burckhardt thought anyway. The Swiss traveller may have been a spy, but he was also a keen scholar of all things Meccan and had a very sharp eye for detail. He provides us with one of the most comprehensive accounts of the city, its people and their preoccupations during the early nineteenth century. Unlike most other European travellers, Burckhardt is relatively and mercifully free of anti-Arab bias and sense of superiority.

According to Burckhardt, Mecca had broad streets, lofty houses, palaces, madrassas and colleges, traveller's lodges and public baths. The houses were built of stone and had numerous windows with elaborate frameworks and commanding views of the outside. Most of the houses were divided into apartments, separated from each other, to provide accommodation for the pilgrims. But incessant wars and looting had taken their toll, and many of the houses and buildings in the Holy City were in an acute state of disrepair. The streets were unpaved, and became muddy and waterlogged when it rained. The city had no police or administrative system to look after citizens' basic requirements. There was no means to light the streets at night and little attention was paid to the security of merchants. Rubbish from houses was thrown in the streets, where it stayed to draw flies and vermin. Beggars, infirm and poor pilgrims littered the streets asking for alms and a drink of sweet water. The post, however, was regularly collected and delivered.

The Swiss scholar found Mecca to be a highly cosmopolitan city, inhabited largely by those he called 'foreigners'. The Quraysh, the original residents of the city, had become almost extinct. Burckhardt could find only three Quraysh families. The only people in significant numbers who could claim lineage going back to ancient times were the sharif clans. The citizens of Mecca now were from Yemen and Hadhramout, India, Egypt, Syria, as well as Turks and Moroccans. There were also small communities of Persians, Tartars, Kurds, Afghans and people from Samarkand and Bukhara. Most of them had come as pilgrims, married local women, and settled in the city to do business. And each community tried to preserve the customs and traditions of its native region. New pilgrims from all over the Muslim world added to their numbers. The natives tried to distinguish themselves from the new citizens by tattooing their faces with three long cuts down both cheeks, and two on the right temple. The ritual would be performed on children when they were forty days of age, and ensured that outsiders could not claim the honour of being born in the Holy City.

Mecca may have been an international and multi-ethnic metropolis, but it was also, not uncommonly, a segregated town. The city was divided across class, professional and ethnic lines. Most of the Arabs lived in the El Shebeyka district. One of the cleanest and airiest quarters in Mecca, it had some of the best houses in the Holy City. Sharif Ghalib had a house here where most of his immediate family lived. Religious scholars and jurists lived in the rich quarter of El Shebeyka near the Sacred Mosque. The pilgrim guides – called the *mutawwafs* – lived in several streets by the Sacred Mosque in a quarter called Haret Bab al-Umra, which was also the favourite area for Turkish pilgrims. Many of the poor, including the sharif's household servants, occupied the half-ruined houses in an area called Haret al-Jyat, located towards the mountain. The poorest, including some Bedouins, lived next to an old and discarded cemetery, where few shops and amenities were available.

Most of the jewellers in town were from India, largely from Surat; they bought and sold gold and silver and jealously guarded their part of the city. These rich merchants lived in the Modaa district, where they conducted their business from their splendid homes. Poorer Indians lived in the district of Mesfale, which once had well-built houses but was now dilapidated. These Indian merchants, rich and poor, scrupulously performed all religious rituals, but were seen by many Arabs as somewhat deficient in their knowledge of Islam. 'Much prejudice' reigned, says Burckhardt, against the Indians. Similar prejudice was experienced by the Chinese and people from central Asia. The city's Chinatown was located between Modaa and Mala. Buildings here were in extremely bad condition and the narrow streets exceptionally dirty: 'the filth is never removed, and fresh air is always excluded'.[21]

One of the least respectable quarters of the city was Shab Aamer, home to a number of 'public women'. Heavily decorated, they would never appear in public without a veil. A substantial number were Abyssinian slaves, their former masters sharing the profits of their vocation. Sharif Ghalib had imposed a tax on these sex workers, increased several-fold during the Hajj season when their services were much in demand. In contrast, the slave market was located in the highly respectable district of Soueyga. The slaves for sale came mainly from Abyssinia, and they served as an instrument for showing off wealth. Almost all wealthy Meccans had slaves, and it was not uncommon for female slaves to serve as mistresses. However, if a slave gave birth to a child, the master was obliged to marry her. Otherwise he faced the censure of the citizens. Buyers would sit on stone benches to view the goods. But not everyone wished or could afford to buy. Many pilgrims, young and old, pretended to 'bargain with the dealers, for the purpose of viewing the slave-girls, during a few moments, in some adjoining apartment'.[22]

The main street of the city was located between the hills of Safa and Marwah in a neighbourhood known as the Messa quarter, where the pilgrims run to perform one of the rituals of Hajj. Full of shops, and noisy, it resembled, says Burckhardt, a 'Constantinopolitan bazaar'. It was full of Turkish shops selling dresses, fine swords, good English watches and beautifully illuminated copies of the Qur'an. 'Constantinopolitan pastry-cooks sold here pies and sweetmeats in the morning; roasted mutton, or kebabs, in the afternoon; and in the evening, a kind of jelly called *mehalabye*. Here, too, are numerous coffee-houses, crowded from three o'clock in the morning until eleven o'clock at night.' But coffee was not the only beverage served: 'in two shops intoxicating liquors are publicly sold during the night, though not in the day-time: one liquor is prepared from fermented raisins, and although usually mixed with a good deal of water, is still so strong, that a few glasses of it produce intoxication. The other is a sort of bouza, mixed with spices, and called *soubye*.'[23] The shops are 'generally magazines on the ground-floor of the houses, before which a stone bench is reared. Here the merchant sits, under the shade of a slight awning of mats fastened to long poles.'[24] This street was also home to special craftsmen who made tin bottles for carrying Zamzam water. All the houses in this district were rented out to pilgrims. The district boasted many fine public buildings, including a large public school, with seventy-two different apartments, and a huge library. On Fridays, the Messa quarter became the site of public punishments where convicted offenders were beheaded.

The best structure in the city was a public bath in the district of Haret Bab al-Umra. It was, like other baths in the cities, used largely by foreigners and pilgrims. The coolest part of the city was in the Soueyga quarter, where tall buildings on the sides of the streets provided shade and the streets were covered with high vaulted roofs of stone. It was usually crowded during midday and was a sought-after site in the evening for smoking pipes. In the district of Moabede, located in the eastern extremity of the city on a narrow passage that leads to Wadi Fatimah, was the garden of the Sharif Ghalib. Lined with date and fruit trees, and furnished with fountains, it was enclosed by high walls and towers. The houses within the compound were mostly in ruins, but the garden was open for anyone, rich and poor, who wished to visit it.

Throughout the city, the birthplaces of its most noted inhabitants were marked with buildings, small mosques or shrines. A building that consisted of 'a rotunda, the floor of which is about twenty-five feet below the level of the street, with a staircase leading down to it'[25] stood on the birthplace of the Prophet Muhammad in the quarter named after it, Mauoud al-Nabi. It had a small hole on the floor where Muhammad's mother was said to have sat when she delivered him. Another building, made of stone with a staircase that led down to the floor, which was some way below the street level, marked the birthplace of Fatima, daughter of the Prophet. Adjacent to it was a small mosque dedicated to Abu Bakr, the Prophet's closest companion and the first caliph. It was situated opposite a stone that marked the spot where he used to salute the Prophet when their paths crossed in public. Located not too far from the Chinese quarter, the street with these two buildings was called – not surprisingly – the 'Street of the Stones'. Another small mosque marked the spot where Ali, the cousin and son-in-law of the Prophet and the fourth caliph, was born, located in the quarter of Shab Ali. Near the sharif's house in the district of Mala was the tomb of Abu Talib, the uncle of Prophet Muhammad. The large burial ground of the Mala contained the tomb of Khadijah, the Prophet's first wife. It was very simple, consisting of little more than four square walls and a tombstone inscribed in the Kufic style of calligraphy. A short distance away was the tomb of Amina, the mother of the Prophet, equally simple but with a marble slab. The Wahhabis had demolished both tombs but the Turks had restored them. Indeed, the puritans from Central Arabia had destroyed most of these shrines; but all, except the tomb of Abu Talib, were restored either by the sharif or by the Turks.

Peace and tranquillity did not last long in Mecca. The Wahhabis might have been defeated in the Hijaz, but they roamed the deserts of Najd, from where they made their presence felt. Indeed, the whole of Najd acknowledged the supremacy of the House of Saud. When an opportunity presented itself, the Wahhabis attacked and harassed the Turkish troops. And whenever the two armies skirmished, the Turks came off worse.

Muhammad Ali felt the Wahhabis presented a serious future threat to Mecca and the Hijaz and it was necessary for him to subdue them totally. Once all of Egypt was under his control, he would personally lead a campaign against the puritan sect in their own territory and strike a fatal blow. He arrived in Jeddah in September 1813 with 2,000 infantrymen and an impressive corps of cavalry. A train of 8,000 camels, carrying equipment and provisions, came by land at about the same time. Sharif Ghalib went to Jeddah to greet the pasha and was received cordially by Muhammad Ali. The sharif's first concern was to ensure that the customs and taxes from Jeddah, which he was claiming for himself rather than sharing them with the Turks, should remain his. Muhammad Ali agreed. The two made a pact to support each other and to do nothing that would compromise the interests or safety of either. Muhammad Ali also asked the sharif to secure the several thousand camels he needed to transport provisions and equipment during his campaign. The sharif asked for a considerable sum for the task, which was granted to him.

Muhammad Ali was on his first visit to Mecca, so after performing the necessary rituals, he sought to gain the favour of the city's jurists and religious scholars by distributing presents amongst them. He also opened his treasury to the poor and the needy and devoted as much time as he could to repair and renovate the Sacred Mosque. But he was more eager to move on with his campaign against the Wahhabis and transport his supplies from Jeddah to Taif, a task that urgently required thousands of camels.

But the sharif reneged on his pledge. The pasha urged him again, and 'although a second advance of money was demanded from the Pasha, no camels appeared'.[26] Perhaps the Bedouins in the Hijaz were not too keen to part with their beloved beasts of burden, even for large sums of money. Perhaps Ghalib was reluctant to fulfil the request. But the outcome was that Muhammad Ali grew suspicious of Ghalib's motives. The sharif's constant complaints that despite all the promises the custom duties from Jeddah were being withheld from him did not endear him to the pasha either. Muhammad Ali also became aware that the Bedouin tribes around Jeddah saw the sharif, particularly after the capture of Othman al-Madhaifi, as their protector both against the Wahhabis and the Turks. He concluded that far from being an ally, Sharif Ghalib was an obstacle that had to be removed if he was to launch a successful campaign against the Wahhabis.

Muhammad Ali decided to move against the sharif and effectively had him put under house arrest. The sharif was entrenched in his palace, called Bait al-Sade, located on a hill slope and well fortified. It was a fort in all but name, its numerous spacious courts and chambers surrounded by very high, solid walls. The sharif had in fact attempted to destroy it by fire when he fled the Wahhabi occupation of Mecca, but the palace was too well built. It was now well guarded by soldiers. The palace was connected through secret underground passages, which also served as a communication channel, to the Great Castle on the summit of Mount Abu Qubays. The castle had been extensively repaired by Sarur, and Ghalib had strengthened it considerably and mounted heavy guns on its walls. Indeed, it was generally believed that its bomb-proof walls made it impregnable. A garrison of around a thousand men was permanently stationed in the castle. It was well stocked with provisions, with an abundant water supply provided by subterranean aqueducts.

There were also a number of other forts to consider. Ghalib had built a fort not too far from his palace, on a small hill, flanked by two towers mounted with guns. Yet another fort, repaired by Ghalib, existed on the opposite hill, called Jabal Hindi, also fully provisioned and equipped with heavy guns. In all, the sharif commanded an army of 15,000 soldiers, and could call upon more troops from Jeddah and Taif. He was constantly protected by a garrison of fiercely loyal warriors and a dozen heavy guns. Muhammad Ali was forced to conclude that a full-frontal assault on the sharif would be a bloody and probably fruitless affair. If the sharif entrenched himself in the castle on Abu Qubays, the siege could last months. The pasha was also convinced that the inhabitants of Mecca would side with the sharif, and the Bedouins around the city would rise up against him. The sharif had to be isolated from his men, and arrested quietly without public attention.

A cat-and-mouse game ensued between Muhammad Ali and Sharif Ghalib. When Ghalib had to visit Muhammad Ali on administrative business, he came to his office, a large school near the Sacred Mosque, surrounded by several hundred soldiers. But on the whole the sharif was reluctant to leave his palace except for Friday prayer. Muhammad Ali tried to put him off his guard by visiting him with only a few personal assistants in the vain hope that the sharif would follow his example. But the sharif did not return the courtesy visits. Frustrated, the pasha considered arresting the sharif in the Sacred Mosque during the Friday prayers, but the *qadi* of Mecca dissuaded him, concerned about public reaction.

Days turned into weeks. Eventually, Muhammad Ali devised a cunning plan. He asked his son, Tousoun Bey, to come to Mecca late at night on a specified date. Protocol required the sharif to go and greet the visiting pasha of Jeddah. To violate such a requirement was not only a serious breach of etiquette but, according to Turkish protocol, a declaration of war. Ghalib, aware that a failure to greet Tousoun Bey could be used as an excuse to attack him, decided to visit him early in the morning when it was still dark. He came to Tousoun's house with a handful of his soldiers, intending to return before sunrise. The move had been anticipated. When Ghalib arrived the attendants conducted him and his men to a room. He was informed that Tousoun, tired from his journey, was resting in his chamber. The sharif was asked to visit him in his bedroom, and his men were directed to stay put. As soon as Ghalib entered the pasha's room, Turkish soldiers hiding in the house came out and surrounded Ghalib's men. Tousoun greeted the sharif warmly and the two talked. When Ghalib stood to take his leave, Tousoun informed him that he was now a prisoner. He was ushered to the window and ordered to tell his soldiers, gathered below, to return to their barracks, as no harm was intended either to him or to his men.

Mecca woke up to the news of Sharif Ghalib's arrest. The city feared a bloodbath. His two sons and his army barricaded themselves in the castle and began preparation for defence. But Ghalib remained calm. Muhammad Ali asked him to write a letter to his son ordering surrender. He hesitated at first. Then, fearful of the violence that would befall the Holy City, and faced with threats to his own life, he agreed to the demand. Next morning the Turkish army entered the castle. Ghalib's men dispersed – some went back to their tribes in the neighbourhood of Mecca, others joined the Wahhabis.

When the *qadi* began to make an inventory of the sharif's property, he found that Ghalib had accumulated a fortune beyond measure. Huge bundles of notes, gold and silver in various shapes and forms, along with trading contracts and documents were found hidden in numerous secret places. The sharif was actively trading in India and owned two ships, each of 400 tonnes, and several small vessels that he used in the coffee trade in Yemen. He seemed to have his finger in every kind of business in the region and was a major player in the Red Sea trade.

The sharif was kept imprisoned in Mecca for a few days. Then he was transferred to Jeddah, from where he was sent by ship, along with most of his accumulated wealth, to Egypt. When Burckhardt met him in Egypt, he found the sharif spoke boldly and with dignity, his spirit unbroken. He spent most of the day playing chess. In the summer of 1816 he was transferred to Salonica, where a residence was specially prepared for him, and the Sublime Porte provided a handsome monthly pension. He 'arrived with an entourage of forty and was treated with the greatest honour: he lasted a few years before succumbing to the plague. His son and successor, Abdul Muttalib – "a grand old man of sixty, of very brown colour, almost black, fine skin, a long blue robe, a Kashmir turban" – eventually followed in his father's footsteps and even erected a domed tomb in his father's memory which survived into the early twentieth century.'[27]

In Mecca, meanwhile, Muhammad Ali was still eager to secure thousands of camels, needed to march against the Wahhabis, a task that was proving particularly elusive.

8

Camels, Indians
and Feudal Queens

Most Meccans, who desired only peace and stability in their city, were not overly concerned about the capture and exile of their leader Sharif Ghalib. It was a different matter, however, for the Bedouins, for the sharif's clan and for their supporters – all of whom feared for their lives. All of Ghalib's family, along with many of the powerful families that supported the sharif, left the city immediately, taking refuge amongst Bedouin tribes in the vicinity. They no longer regarded the Turks as the Servants of the Holy Sanctuaries. Whereas in former times they had appealed to Istanbul for protection against external threats, now they saw the Ottomans as invaders determined to impose their rule on the Holy City. In this age of shifting alliances they openly sided with the Wahhabis. Some relatives of Ghalib went to Dariyya, the Wahhabi capital, to join the Wahhabi-inspired leader of the Saud clan, ibn Saud. They were received with open arms and given a great deal of financial support. Ibn Saud lavished them with impressive titles, but in keeping with Mecca's long history it was just another example of the city's elite swapping one protector for another.

The Bedouin tribes in the Hijaz quickly coalesced into an alliance against the Ottomans. The coalition was focused on the Baqoum Arabs, one of the strongest tribes in the region, which had fought and defeated the Turks on a number of occasions. The Baqoum, who were shepherds and cultivators, were based at Taraba, a small town east of Mecca, about a hundred miles from Taif. The tribe was unique for being led by a heroic woman, Ghalia, who displayed the determination and fierceness of Hind, the arch-enemy of the Prophet Muhammad. Ghalia's husband had been one of the chiefs of the tribe, and after his death she inherited his wealth. Although the Baqoum had a nominal male leader, it was Ghalia who mattered, and her ideas and opinions always carried in the council. The Turkish army had tasted her anger and feared her; they even circulated rumours that she was a sorceress who had bewitched the Wahhabi leaders and made them invincible.[1] Ghalia embraced the refugee sharif family and Bedouins from Mecca, distributed money amongst them, and encouraged them to prepare to fight against the Turks.

Muhammad Ali, the Ottoman governor of Egypt, keen to secure Arabia as part of the empire he was building for himself within the Ottoman lands, was well aware that an alliance of sharifs and Bedouins was being formed against him. He appointed Yahya ibn Sarur, a nephew of Ghalib, as the sharif of Mecca. Yahya was not the best person for the job, but the pasha wanted someone he could control and manipulate with ease. And he ordered Tousoun Bey to march against the newly formed sharif–Wahhabi alliance. The devoted son obliged and left Taif at the beginning of November 1813, with 2,000 troops and thirty days' supplies. He hunted down various tribes en route and subjugated them. By the time he reached Taraba, the headquarters of the sharif–Wahhabi alliance, he had only three days' supplies left.

He ordered his troops to attack Taraba at once. The Bedouin alliance, urged on by Ghalia, defended their city valiantly and the first attack was easily repulsed. The Turks attacked again the second day but were forced to retreat, leaving their baggage, tents, arms and limited provisions behind. The Bedouins gave chase, ambushed them at several places, and fell on them with ferocity, leaving the corpses of more than 700 slaughtered men to mark the line of their retreat. What remained of the Turkish army returned to Taif exhausted and wrecked; many who had survived the slaughter later died of hunger and thirst. Other expeditions against the sharif–Wahhabi alliance suffered a similar fate. In the port of Qunfidha, the Turks were surprised by the sudden appearance of some 10,000 Wahhabi soldiers. The fort was overcome; the Wahhabis entered the town, killing hundreds of soldiers. Fleeing troops tried to escape by jumping into the sea, but the Wahhabis followed them into the water with swords in their teeth.

Having suffered a humiliating defeat, Muhammad Ali changed tactics and opted to devote more time to planning and winning Meccan hearts. He abolished or reduced many customs duties, particularly on coffee; he paid attention to the needs of scholars and jurists, giving them generous donations; and he devoted much time to repairing the Sacred Mosque. He punished Turkish soldiers found insulting the Meccans or heard using abusive language when talking to them. And even though he was a declared sceptic, he spent much time in prayer and gave special attention to performing Islam's proper rituals. During the Hajj season, pilgrim caravans arrived loaded with gifts and commodities for the city. Even the Syrian caravan, suspended since the previous decade, was allowed through, although to pass through Bedouin territory it had to pay a toll not only for 1813, but also for the previous ten years. The citizens cheered at the sight of so many pilgrims in the Holy City. When the pasha decided to open his purse to citizens and pilgrims alike there was universal rejoicing. Fear of the Wahhabis momentarily abated and the pasha spent the following few months contemplating his next step.

An opportunity presented itself finally; or perhaps it was that Muhammad Ali's devotion and prayers paid off. Ibn Saud, the great Wahhabi patriarch, died in May 1814. As he lay on his deathbed, suffering from fever, he is said to have whispered his final advice to his son, Abdullah bin Saud: 'Never engage the Turks in the open plains.'[2] Abdullah succeeded his father, though not without dispute, which was eventually settled by the Wahhabi scholars. Although a man of considerable skill and courage, he could not manage the Bedouin tribes as well as his father. Many began to act independently, and disputes arose amongst tribal chiefs. The southern tribes, the nearest target for Muhammad Ali, ceased to receive support from their northern allies and the pasha knew he could pick them off one by one.

However, there was still a paucity of camels required to carry supplies over the vast desert tracks. The caravan to Mecca from Cairo brought several thousand camels and fresh horses for the troops, but they were far from enough. The roads from Jeddah to Mecca and Taif to Mecca were 'literally strewed with the carcases of dead camels, showing that a continual renewal of the baggage train was absolutely necessary'.[3] The city itself had so many dead camels that the stench of their rotting flesh and bones made it difficult for the inhabitants to carry on their daily business. The citizens petitioned the sharif to clear the city. Bands of poor pilgrims were drafted for the job. They brought dry grass from the mountains and used it to burn the carcases, a task that took several days to complete. An estimated 30,000 camels had perished in and around the Holy City since the arrival of Muhammad Ali.

The pasha increased his efforts to acquire more camels. He sent Sharif Yahya on expeditions outside Mecca with the specific aim of securing them. The sharif returned with a few hundred. Tousoun Bey confiscated the camels of passing caravans. Muhammad Ali himself purchased 3,000 camels from Syria. In November 1814, the pilgrim caravans from Syria and Egypt arrived safely in Mecca. Muhammad Ali's wife, and mother of Tousoun, arrived by sea to perform the Hajj. She brought 400 camels with her – mostly to carry her baggage. After the Hajj, which was performed by 80,000 pilgrims, Muhammad Ali secured the camels from both caravans. The Egyptian caravan was deprived of 2,000 camels, and the pilgrims sent back by sea through Jeddah. The Syrian caravan had over 12,000 camels. The pasha asked the pilgrims to extend their stay in the city to allow their camels to carry provisions for his troops.

Finally, Muhammad Ali, with sufficient camels at his disposal, was ready. On 7 January 1815 he led his 20,000 troops from Mecca and headed towards Taraba. He had twelve heavy field-guns, over 500 men with axes ready to chop down the trees that blocked the approach to Taraba, and numerous masons and mine layers who were to be employed in blowing up the walls of the enemy town. In addition, there was the unusual cargo of several camel-loads of watermelon seeds, gathered by the citizens of Mecca from Wadi Fatima, which Muhammad Ali intended to sow on the site of Taraba once he had obliterated the town.

The Wahhabis too were prepared. Led by Faisal, brother of Abdullah, and the redoubtable Ghalia, their forces were 25,000 strong, with 5,000 camels – the sharif–Wahhabi alliance had now expanded to include all the tribes of southeastern Arabia as well as many tribes from Yemen. They decided, in keeping with ibn Saud's advice, to engage Muhammad Ali outside Taraba in an area where level ground was encircled by a natural rampart of hills through which narrow defiles gave entrance to the city. The Wahhabis deployed on the mountains and waited. When the pasha's army approached they held their ground. Then, when the Ottoman army attacked, they used their elevated positions to advantage and forced it to retreat. On the plain, the Ottoman cavalry could be picked off: the Wahhabis made deadly forays at lightning speed, returning rapidly to their positions on the mountains. To give confidence to his troops, Muhammad Ali decided to plant the melon seeds he had brought with him, and a whole day was spent on this futile exercise. The Wahhabis used the opportunity to mount further raids against the Ottoman soldiers – so swift and lethal were their sorties that terror spread amongst Muhammad Ali's soldiers and those Bedouins who were fighting with him. The Wahhabis were elated and began to talk of victory, and once again the Ottoman soldiers despaired and started to think defeat was looming. Some deserted and fled back to Mecca.

In Mecca, the deserters spread a rumour that Muhammad Ali had been killed and that the Wahhabis had won. 'The terror caused by these reports', says Burckhardt, the Swiss traveller in the service of Britain, 'can scarcely be imagined. I resided there myself at that time, and can speak of it as an eye witness. Numerous stragglers belonging to the army, and Turkish hadjys preparing to go home; also Turkish merchants and such soldiers as were in the town, all expected to suffer death on the first arrival of the victorious Wahhabis.'[4] There was a scramble to leave the city. Many people decided to walk to Jeddah and left that very evening. Some put on Bedouin clothes to disguise themselves. Others sought refuge in the castle at Abu Qubays. Even though he had not received any official reports, Sharif Yahya made plans for a quick exit to Jeddah. Burckhardt himself joined those who had decided to hide in the Sacred Mosque, though no one believed that the victorious Wahhabis would regard it as sacred. All feared that death was on its way.

Back on the battlefield near Taraba the situation was not as bad as the rumours suggested. Muhammad Ali realized he could not defeat the Wahhabis as long as they remained on the mountains. Somehow they had to be coaxed to level ground. After some reflection, he took a leaf from Islamic history: namely from the Battle of Uhad fought in the year 625 between the Prophet Muhammad and the Quraysh. The Muslims lost the battle because they thought they had won; abandoning their protected position on Mount Uhad they came down to secure the booty. Once on level ground they were attacked from two sides and victory turned to serious defeat. Muhammad Ali used the same tactic. He spent a day withdrawing a sizable proportion of his army and placing these troops in strategic locations at the rear. Early next morning, he ordered his remaining officers to advance their columns towards the Wahhabi position, get much closer than they had managed so far, and after firing their guns, retreat. But they had to appear to retreat in a state of rout. The plan was put into practice. The Wahhabis, seeing the Ottomans retreat in what looked like total disarray, thought they had won and decided that it was time to annihilate their enemy. They came down from the mountains and pursued the fleeing Turks over the plain. It was at this point that the pasha's forces executed their plan to perfection: once the Wahhabis were some distance from the mountains, they were surrounded by the troops Muhammad Ali had held back.

The pasha now selected a little level spot, 'commanded his carpet be spread there, and calling for his pipe and seating himself, said that from that ground he would not move but there await victory or death as a result of his actions'.[5] He offered a reward of six dollars for every Wahhabi head presented to him. The battle was won in less than five hours. Some 5,000 heads were piled up in front of him: 'in one narrow valley fifteen hundred Wahhabis had been surrounded and cut to pieces'.[6] The whole of the plain was littered with the bodies of Wahhabi fighters. Only 300 Wahhabi troops survived, but among them both Faisal and Ghalia the warrior queen managed to escape.

After capturing Taraba, Muhammad Ali decided to take the battle to the enemy and marched against a number of Wahhabi supporters, including the port of Qunfidha. The treks across the desert, however, took their toll. Hundreds of horses and camels died every day, and the troops suffered from hunger and exhaustion. When he finally returned to Mecca on 21 March, only 1,500 Turkish soldiers and fewer than 300 camels were still alive – a pale shadow of the magnificent army that had left the city just ten weeks earlier.

The Wahhabis had been considerably diminished. Their rout near Taraba was announced as a major victory to the Porte. The 300 Wahhabi prisoners were paraded in Mecca – a city that had trembled at the very mention of their name. Fifty were impaled before the various gates of Mecca; twelve in front of the coffee houses and other places where the citizens gathered; the rest in front of the main gate of Jeddah. The bodies were left to dogs and vultures.

On arriving in Mecca, Muhammad Ali assembled all the scholars, jurists and nobles of the city. A letter addressed to Abdullah ibn Saud was read out to the assembly. It urged the Wahhabi leader in Dariyya to surrender and offered terms for peace. A few months later, the pasha returned to Cairo.

The governing structure of Mecca was now changed. The Egyptians were represented in the city by a *mahafiz* – literally a guardian. The Ottomans had a *wali* or governor in Jeddah. Sandwiched between the two was Yahya ibn Sarur, the sharif of Mecca. He was now merely a ceremonial titular leader who played no part in administration and had little influence on the affairs of the Holy City. The Meccans looked towards the Egyptian *mahafiz* – who ensured that the Sanctuary had enough corn and wheat to make bread – to maintain law and order in the city. From the *wali* they looked for generous donations and gifts. The arrangement was accepted by most of the inhabitants, who carried on their business happily.

Sharif Yahya however was less than satisfied, and he took his anger out on the messenger who brought communiqués and orders from Muhammad Ali for the citizens of Mecca. In 1827, while the messenger was reading a dispatch from the pasha, Yahya had him assassinated. He decamped at once for the castle and prepared to defend it, but the Egyptian guns were already trained towards him. He surrendered, and promised to present himself to Muhammad Ali in Cairo, though actually he took refuge with the Harb tribe. He was eventually captured by Egyptian soldiers near Taif and taken to Egypt, where he died in 1838.

A new sharif was needed in Mecca. At first, Muhammad Ali supported the candidature of Abdul Muttalib, the son of Ghalib, who had been exiled along with his father to Salonica in 1815. He was the popular choice of the Meccans and returned to rule for a year. But after further reflection, the pasha changed his mind. A better and more capable ruler would be his old comrade in arms Muhammad ibn Abdul Moin ibn Aun, who had helped the pasha with his campaigns in the Hijaz. Ibn Aun duly replaced Abdul

Muttalib in 1828. Over the next three decades, power swung like a pendulum between ibn Aun and Abdul Muttalib, each becoming sharif on no fewer than three occasions.

As usual, ibn Aun had to go through the traditional struggles with his relatives. However, he was a worthy choice, although not in the way Muhammad Ali intended. Eyewitnesses describe him as 'wise and moderate, of diplomatic character, five foot seven inches, good-looking, with a prominent chin and fine teeth, his curls very long'.[7] He was renowned for his sense of dress and is said to have worn brightly coloured tunics, huge white turbans with colourful bands, muslin shirts and embroidered trousers, and he always carried a gold dagger, a flashy Persian sword and a camel stick. All those who met him were astonished, even overwhelmed, by his dignity, pleasant demeanour, and the easy manner with which he conducted his business. But behind his agreeable exterior there was a steely determination to secure independent governance for Mecca. Muhammad ibn Aun considered his first task, now that the Wahhabis were no longer a threat, as ridding the Holy City of Egyptian troops. He began, like his ancestors, by making alliances with the Bedouin tribes in the Hijaz, particularly the Harb. But his efforts raised the suspicion of the Egyptian *mahafiz*, and the trouble between the two led to the removal of both to Cairo in 1836.

Ibn Aun returned to his position and rank, thanks to his diplomatic skills, in 1840. A treaty between Muhammad Ali and the sultan in Istanbul had again placed Mecca under the direct control of the Porte. The Sublime Porte was reasserting its position after the debacle of the war for Greek independence, a cause supported by various European powers. Ibn Aun's second term as sharif of Mecca lasted twelve years. During that time Istanbul was becoming known as 'the sick man of Europe', increasingly prey to the machinations of European powers that would eventually result in the Crimean War (1853–6). It was an appropriate time for the sharif of Mecca to attempt to manoeuvre to secure more independence for the Holy

City. His efforts, once again, generated friction: this time with the *wali* of Jeddah, Osman Pasha.

Osman Pasha was a friend of Muhammad Ali, and he used his friendship with the pasha to undermine the diplomatic efforts of the sharif. Osman Pasha had been a distinguished administrator in Medina and the sultan looked on him with favour. He had also gained good will in Istanbul through his numerous expeditions against the Wahhabis, who had established a new capital in Riyadh. Osman Pasha's raids in southern Arabia had also paved the way for Ottoman rule in Yemen. He was thus in a much stronger position than the sharif, who ploughed an isolated furrow.

The matter came to a head when the Harb revolted. Their anger was directed at Osman Pasha, who had failed to give them the subsidy due for providing safe passage to the pilgrims. Led by their sheikh, ibn Rumi, they attacked a small Turkish garrison near Medina to show their displeasure. The pasha acted in accordance with what had become an Ottoman tradition. He invited ibn Rumi to come for negotiations and a lavish dinner was organized for the sheikh, who was met with great pomp and ceremony. A special tent was erected where clowns were laid on to entertain him. During the entertainment Osman Pasha excused himself, soldiers cut the ropes of the tent, and the sheikh and his men were trapped like fish in a net. The inevitable butchery followed. Everyone was beheaded; even the twelve-year-old younger brother of Sheikh ibn Rumi was killed. Their heads were impaled on pikes and sent to Mecca to be displayed.

Sharif ibn Aun had been working hard to develop cordial relationships with the Harb, and Osman Pasha's action was a major setback to this policy and a serious blow to his prestige amongst the Bedouin tribes. Not surprisingly, the Harb now saw the Turks as their arch-enemies and began to harass the pilgrim caravans. During the next two decades – 1850s and 1860s – there were numerous incidents on the pilgrim routes and the Harb would only allow the caravans to pass on payment of heavy duties.

There was now open conflict between the sharif and the pasha, but it was an uneven contest. Osman Pasha convinced the sultan to replace ibn Aun, and received orders for his arrest in August 1852. The same day, without any notice, the sharif's palace was surrounded. Ibn Aun could have put up some resistance. However, with artillery in position in front of his palace he thought it wise to quietly surrender. Abdul Muttalib ibn Ghalib, now reaching sixty, was reappointed as the ruler of Mecca.

His days at the Ottoman court in Istanbul had had a profound impact on Abdul Muttalib. A tall, slender man with a dark complexion, he dressed in the manner of court officials: a Kashmir turban topped his long blue robe, and a splendid dagger with shining diamonds graced his waistband. He made good use of his friends in the sultan's court, particularly the grand vizier, and tried to provide Mecca with some peace and stability. But his second reign, like the first one, was short-lived.

His second tenure began when the city was going through one of the most shameful episodes in its history. A series of edicts from Istanbul banning slavery incensed the Meccans. The Sublime Porte, in common with European and other nations, was wrestling with the demands of modernization in an age that had become aware of civic rights, or perhaps more correctly the great lack of civic rights for the majority of people. France had been first to declare the abolition of slavery in 1794 in the first flush of its Revolution. It was restored in 1802 and not definitively ended until 1848. Britain abolished the slave trade in 1807, though slavery in the British Empire was not abolished until 1834 – with the exception of Ceylon and the territories administered by the East India Company. America would face the great question in the 1860s, when it was resolved only through a bloody civil war. Russia emancipated the serfs in 1861.

Europe had also been struggling with granting rights to religious minorities. France led the way with the Declaration of the Rights of Man and the Citizen by the first revolutionary assembly in 1789, resulting in the emancipation of the Jews in 1791. Holland followed, emancipating its Jews in 1796. In Britain Catholic emancipation was enacted in 1829 and the emancipation of the Jews was established by 1858. Turkey was no sicker than the rest of Europe, its problem with unreconstituted conservative elements no less thankless, most particularly and depressingly in Mecca.

In 1830, Sultan Mahmud II (r. 1808–39) issued a *firman* to give freedom to white slaves. His son and successor, Sultan Abdal Majid I (r. 1839–61), thought it was 'a shameful and barbarous practice for rational human beings to buy and sell their fellow creatures',[8] and issued another *firman*, in October 1854, abolishing the trade of Circassian children. And on 18 February 1856 came the edict known as *Hatti-Humayun*, 'the Turkish Magna Carta of the nineteenth century',[9] which gave equality to Jews and Christians before the law and contained strong anti-slavery measures. However, slavery was part of, and seen as, the natural order in Mecca. It was integral to the economy of the Holy City. Black slaves served as bodyguards and soldiers. Circassian children were used as domestic servants. Female slaves were considered concubines and served, as Burckhardt had noted, as mistresses for most rich merchants. Many pious Meccans actually believed that the Qur'an and the Prophet Muhammad sanctioned slavery. They were appalled at the very suggestion that slavery should be abolished. Since slavery was mentioned in the Qur'an, which was timeless and eternal, they argued, so slavery too had to be eternally present. Furthermore how could one be virtuous, as the Qur'an commended, by freeing slaves if there were no slaves to free?

Equally unpalatable was the fact that *Hatti-Humayun* allowed the testimony of Jews and Christian in Muslim courts and gave them equal opportunity and access to government and administrative positions. In fact, the edict abolished the traditional notion that Jews and Christians were *dhimmis*, or protected minorities required to pay a special tax (*jizya*). The Ottomans now saw them as citizens equal before the law and with all the rights and privileges of all citizens. The Meccans took this as a direct assault on Islamic law.

The whole of Mecca rose up against the *Hatti-Humayun* edict. There were violent demonstrations in the city. Scholars and jurists urged the citizens, natives and foreign, to stand up against the violation of God's law. Turks were attacked in the streets, and it became impossible for them – residents, pilgrims and soldiers – to move freely within the town. Sharif Abdul Muttalib tried to restore order but failed. He thought of asking the sultan for help but realized that Turkey's involvement in the Crimean War meant he could not expect much response from that quarter. He decided to organize his own troops and impose order on the city by military means. But the move was misread by the Turks, who saw it as a preparation against them. The matters were not helped when the Turkish official in the city was hit in the face by a stone hurled during a demonstration. Within weeks Abdul Muttalib was on his way back to Salonica, and ibn Aun in power for the third time. His efforts to restore order in Mecca were not exactly successful either. By now he was too old to wield meaningful influence in the city. The Meccans refused to name the sultan in Friday prayers. Turks continued to feel unsafe in the town. Ibn Aun died in March 1858 at the age of ninety.

In 1858, ibn Aun was succeeded by his son Abdullah ibn Muhammad ibn Aun. Like his father, Abdullah had spent considerable time in Istanbul and was a member of the sultan's Council of State. But unlike his father, Abdullah realized that times were changing. The British and the French had now established consulates in Jeddah, and he had to do business with European powers. Mecca had also become connected to the rest of the world via telegraph. Abdullah tried to adjust to the changing circumstances. After restoring a semblance of order in the Holy City, he used two British steamers to carry his supplies and led a successful expedition to Qunfidha in 1869.

The opening of the Suez Canal in the same year also had a profound impact on Arabia. The idea of the Canal had been discussed both by the Mamluks and, more particularly, the Ottomans when faced with the arrival of Portuguese forces in the Indian Ocean in the sixteenth century. Then the problem had been how to transfer Ottoman naval power from the Mediterranean to the Red Sea. It is one of those seminal 'what if' moments that I hate but cannot help thinking about. Armed with a canal, would the Ottomans have remained engaged with the Indian Ocean world they made such efforts to acquaint themselves with? Would they, rather than Europe, have reaped the benefits of realigning the trade routes of the world? And how might that have shaped the course of history? When a Suez Canal did materialize it was the work of a French engineer, Ferdinand de Lesseps, and French finance. It succeeded in entrenching European oversight of Egyptian affairs where Napoleon had failed, a case of finance being mightier than the sword. Since the Canal represented a vital link between Britain and the jewel in its imperial crown, India, it also made Egypt the site of continuing rivalry between Britain and France, as they contended with each other to manipulate and direct the country's domestic affairs. For Mecca the Canal meant that Turkish armies, which previously took months to reach the Holy Land and arrived exhausted after their long march through the desert, could now reach Jeddah speedily, and be reinforced just as rapidly. Global trends were beginning to have an impact on the Holy City itself.

The social makeup of Mecca changed considerably. Almost 20 per cent of the city's inhabitants, the largest single majority, were now of Indian origins – people from Gujarat, Punjab, Kashmir and Deccan, all collectively known locally as the Hindis (from Hindustan, the original name for India). The bulk of the pilgrims also came from India, travelling by ship to Jeddah. And India provided the largest financial contribution to Mecca. In fact, the city's economy was increasingly tied up with Indian trade – particularly from Surat, the capital of Gujarat, which was devoted almost exclusively to the 'Red

Sea run' through which shiploads of textiles, spices and other goods arrived not just in the Hajj season but all the year around. In the Hajj season itself, ship after ship brought pilgrims as well as goods and provisions from India. Mecca thus acquired a distinctively Indian character during the second half of the eighteenth century, and its economy and financial well-being became dependent on the Muslims of India.

But the relationship between the sharifs and the Hindis was not always cordial, and indeed started rather badly under the Emperor Babur (1483–1530), who established the Mughal Empire in the Indian subcontinent in 1526. Unlike the Abbasid caliphs and the Ottoman sultans, the Mughals did not send regular treasures to the Holy City. No caravans came from India, though they did maintain ships that carried pilgrims to Arabia. And the Mughals never came to the aid of Mecca's rulers. Moreover, up to the later eighteenth century pilgrims from India were few in number, not significant compared with pilgrims from Egypt, Syria or Turkey. The relatively small numbers of Indians might have been because many did not consider Hajj binding on them. Such a perception was based less on theology than on geopolitics, as the journey from India to Mecca in those days could only be undertaken by sailing through the Portuguese-dominated seas, or travelling overland through Shia Persia. The Mughal Emperor Akbar 'the Great' (1542–1605) floated the idea that a caravan should be sent from Hindustan, like the caravans from Egypt and Syria, but the suggestion was never put in practice. Instead, the Mughal emperors sent copies of the Qur'an, which they wrote by hand themselves, as gifts to the Holy City. Babur, not known for his piety, was the first to send such a handwritten copy. The Meccan leaders, more interested in hard cash, looked at these gifts with derision, and the relationship between the sharifs and the Mughals suffered accordingly.

In 1659, the Emperor Aurangzeb (1618–1707) sent a gift of 660,000 rupees to the Holy City. The sharifs rejected the donation as insignificant and even refused to recognize Aurangzeb, perhaps the most devout of all Mughal emperors, as a legitimate king. The donation was indeed rather small compared with others, but it was a deliberate act on the part of Aurangzeb, who, like his predecessors, regarded the sharifs as thoroughly corrupt. He was concerned that his gifts, rather than benefiting the people of Mecca, would be pocketed by the sharifs, and thus arranged to bypass the sharifs altogether and distribute his donations directly to the scholars, jurists and citizens of the Holy City. His stratagem only further increased the sharifs' ire.

While the Mughals had a rather low opinion of the sharifs, initially they saw Mecca itself in utopian terms. It was an honest and pure city, a place for redemption. Consequently, they exiled discredited and dishonoured nobles to the Holy City: 'to go off to Mecca, on a journey lasting probably at least a year and often longer, was in political terms a grave punishment, and one from which it was difficult to recoup one's fortunes.'[10] All sorts of misbehaviour could lead a noble or a courtier to Mecca. Sometimes just the threat of being sent there was enough to change unruly behaviour. But where the threat did not bring the desired results, nobles were actually shipped off to the Holy City to cool down. Akbar sent two religious leaders to the Hajj because they kept quarrelling publicly. Losing a battle could also result in a pious journey. In 1690, one of Aurangzeb's generals performed poorly on the battlefield. He was sacked and sent off to Mecca. The object of the exercise was to reform and enlighten the individuals concerned, though this didn't always happen. Some returned with stories of mistreatment at the hands of the Meccans; others came back as hardened criminals. Not surprisingly, the Mughal emperors' opinion of the Meccans slowly changed. In the end, they had virtually no interest in the Holy City – except as a destination of last resort for their troublesome aristocrats.

In contrast to the Mughal emperors, the rulers of India's principalities had a deep love for the city. The rajas, sultans and nawabs devoted considerable time and resources to looking after their pilgrims in Mecca. Sultan Muzaffar II of Gujarat (r. 1511–26), who sought to make common cause with the Ottomans against the Portuguese, for example, also arranged for housing to be constructed in Mecca for poor Indian pilgrims, and paid for a ship to carry the poor to Mecca free of charge. Another ruler of Gujarat, Sultan Mahmud II, reserved the revenues of some villages in his principality as a trust to be distributed in the Holy City and to build various religious buildings in Mecca. Rulers of Bengal, and other regions, followed his example.

The troubled history of Mecca and the Hindis had consequences for the Indian inhabitants of the city. The shift in its financial dependence from Egypt and Turkey towards India was not welcomed by the Meccans. For one thing, the British East India Company was now making its presence felt in the Indian Ocean, and the Indian pilgrims were carried to their destination by British merchant shipping. This considerably reduced the sharif's overland taxes and lightened the purse assigned to him by the Porte. At the same time, the Meccans regarded the Indians as none too generous towards them, and both rich and poor Indians were treated equally badly. This left the Indians quite vulnerable, as unlike the Turks, who made up only 5 per cent of the city's population, the Indians had no army to protect them. In fact, the Indians suffered at the hands of both the Arabs and the Turks. Only the Malays and Indonesians, who constituted around 5 per cent of the inhabitants and were known collectively in Mecca as 'the Jawah', were treated worse. The very word 'Hindi' had derogatory connotations.

It was against this background that Nawab Sikandar Begum (1838–1901) came to Mecca when Sharif Abdullah was still in power. Feisty, self-reliant and sophisticated, the begum was the hereditary ruler of the princely state of Bhopal, the second-largest Anglo-Indian principality on the subcontinent. Sikandar Begum never observed purdah, was trained in martial arts and even led her troops into combat on a number of occasions. She was an immensely wealthy woman, with a keen sense of business and an intellect to match.[11]

She inherited the rule of Bhopal from her mother, and was one in a line of four female rulers of the state. Female rule was hardly an oddity on the world stage when Victoria was on the throne of Britain. I am always struck by the marked resemblance between the begum and the woman who in 1876 was to be declared the queen empress of India. In photographs Sikandar Begum looks quite as unlikely to be amused as Queen Victoria, and just as portly. The begum was intensely loyal to Britain, and controversially stood alongside the Raj through the first Indian war of independence, also known as the Indian Mutiny of 1857. She countermanded the religious leaders in her territory who wanted to declare the uprising as a jihad. Most assuredly this endeared her and her descendants to the British and put her foremost in line for rewards, including insignia and letters after her name. As the *London Illustrated News* reported in 1863,[12] Sikandar Begum KSI was the only woman member of the Order of the Knights of the Star of India – apart from Queen Victoria. It was all part of the great show of pomp and ceremony that reigned in the heyday of the British Raj, when rules of precedence among the ranks of Indian rulers were graded to a nicety and demonstrated in the number of times cannon roared in the salute appropriate to each ruler. Courtly etiquette, deference and elaborate formal ritual, supplied courtesy of the British, was the cover for the lack of independence and autonomy the indigenous rulers enjoyed.

In making the Hajj the begum was following a tradition, going back to Emperor Babur, of noble Indian women coming to Mecca with their entourages. One of her predecessors was Gulbadan Begam, Babur's daughter, and aunt of Emperor Akbar. She came to Mecca in 1575 with an entourage of several hundred, consisting, apart from servants and attendants, almost entirely of women. They all remained in Mecca, performed the Hajj several times and returned, seven years later, in 1582. In 1660, the dowager queen of Bijapur brought another entourage of women to the Holy City. The princesses and noble women of the Deccan came regularly to Mecca throughout the seventeenth century. The begum was thus following in the footsteps of independent and urbane, albeit excessively wealthy, Indian women who visited, unaccompanied by their husbands, and overcame all the hazards and dangers of their journeys.

The begum arrived in Jeddah in January 1864 with shiploads of gifts and donations that she intended to distribute in Mecca, and as a ruler of an Indian state, she expected to be treated with the protocol that she believed her position deserved. And yet both the Arabs and the Turks treated her appallingly. Sharif Abdullah did not even bother to greet or meet her although he expected her to show due regard and follow his protocol. At the same time her wealth, well displayed, became a magnet for the robbers and brigands of the Holy Land, Arab and Turkish. Her baggage was broken into the moment her ship docked in Jeddah. The pasha in Jeddah also mistreated her and extorted criminal levels of tax. Her caravan of eighty camels was attacked several times by robbers on its way from Jeddah to Mecca. In Mecca, the place she was going to stay, and had reserved, was sublet in front of her. In short, the Holy City bestowed every indignity it could on the dignified nawab from India.

She reacted to every humiliation by firing letters to the sharif and the Turkish officials. The account of her visit to Mecca, written in Urdu and published in two copies – one for her, one for Queen Victoria, her co-regent, published in an English translation in 1870 – consists largely of these letters and the replies she received. One particular incident in *The Princess's Pilgrimage* captures the essence of the relationship between the Meccans and the Hindis.

On arriving in Mecca, the begum, following convention, went straight to the Sacred Mosque. As she walked to her residence after finishing the rituals she was accompanied by her personal attendant Molvi Abdul Kaium (the title 'molvi' signified that he was a religious scholar) and a Turkish official, Jafir Effendi. Four slaves of the sharif of Mecca ran after the molvi, pushed him against the wall, and started hitting him:

> The Molvi called out in a loud voice, 'Look, Madam! One of the Sharif's slaves is beating me shamefully', I said to the man, '*Bhai* [lit. Brother], why are you beating the Molvi who is one of my people?' He replied: 'You are to come to our Sharif's house, and eat the dinner he has prepared for you.' I answered: 'The Sharif has not invited me; I will come back when I have made my offering'. After this, I again proceeded on my way, when a slave, who was with Jafir Effendi, a very tall, powerful man, drew his sword and began to attack the Molvi. The later called out to me as before; and I remonstrated with the man who had assaulted him, saying the Molvi, in obedience to my order, was showing me to my house. The slave replied: 'My master the Sharif's feast, which cost him 5000 rupees, is all getting spoilt, and his money is being wasted'. Jafir Effendi then said, 'Your highness had better go to the Sharif's otherwise he will be very angry, and his anger is certainly not pleasant'.[13]

The begum was forced to go the sharif's house. But there was no Sharif ibn Aun to greet her, only a dinner table with the dinner laid out. 'The repast consisted of about five hundred specimens of Arabian cookery, some of the dishes savoury, some sweet. They said to me, "Eat your dinner." I excused myself by replying that I had had no invitation.' But the begum was forced to sit and eat the cold, flavourless food; and stay the night. Next morning she woke up to find 'a carpet, richly embroidered with gold, had been laid down' in front of her room.[14] Like most Indian nobles, the begum was very fond of *paan*, the betel leaf concoction that contains areca nuts, slaked lime and spices. One consequence of chewing the *paan* is the necessity of having a spittoon handy. Thinking that eating the *paan* in the vicinity of or on the carpet might spoil it, the begum asked for the carpet to be folded up. Even before the task was completed, Jafir Effendi arrived with twenty-five trays of food.

'I partook of his dinner last night,' the begum said, 'why has he sent me more this morning? It is not customary to feast a guest after the first day.' He replied: 'It is our custom in this country to send travellers meals twice a day for three days.' She replied: 'How can I partake this repast, without having been informed regarding it, without any invitation from the sharif?' He said: 'You *must* keep it; it is impossible to return it, for by so doing you would make the sharif very angry.' To this she said: 'If according to the etiquette of this country, the sharif intends feasting me for three days, let him do so when the ship arrives with all my retinue. I arrived here with only twenty or twenty-five people in my suite, and the sharif has sent me enough food for one or two hundred people. Among whom can I distribute it? The sharif's entertainment is being wasted.' The Turks who brought the food became very angry, and said: 'You are disobeying the sharif's orders, and treating him with disrespect.'[15]

Once again, the begum was forced to take the food, and it kept on coming during the day. Early next morning, armed and uniformed soldiers burst into the house. They seized the sharif's embroidered carpet, beat the begum's female attendants with sticks, ransacked the kitchen and threatened the begum.

Not surprisingly, the begum did not think highly either of the sharif or his city. She found Mecca to be 'wild' and unfriendly and its citizens to be insincere. Both men and women of Mecca, she declared, 'are worthless people'. 'Everyone is well off,' she writes, 'but they are miserly and covetous, it is no disgrace for anyone to beg; high and low, young men and old, women, boys and girls of all grades, are more or less beggars. Give them what you will, they are never satisfied. Even when work-people are paid for their labour, they do nothing satisfactorily, and demand their pay before their work is complete. The employers also, on their part, cheat as much as they can.'[16] Everyone, 'nobles as well as plebeians', clamours 'obstinately and violently for "bukhsheesh"'.

'In Mecca, people can neither sing nor dance,' says the begum, who in her court encouraged poetry, singing, dance, art and high culture. She also disliked the tendency of Meccan women to whistle, which perhaps says more about her prejudice than about Meccan women. 'On occasion of weddings, ladies sing comic songs and dance, but they do it so badly, that one has not the slightest pleasure in hearing or seeing them, but is rather disgusted.'[17] She was even more revolted at the frequency with which the Meccan women contracted marriages. Up to ten marriages were not uncommon, 'and those who have only been married twice are only a few in number. If a woman sees her husband growing old, or if she happens to admire anyone else, she goes to the sharif, and after having settled the matter with him, she puts away her husband, and takes to herself another, who is perhaps young, good-looking, and rich. In this way, a marriage seldom lasts more than two years.'[18] Not a recommendation to the begum, a widow, though she did not maintain permanent widow's weeds like her fellow monarch Queen Victoria, who was surely the most famous grieving widow in history. Almost all the bad characters, the begum concludes, 'that have been driven out of India, may be found in Mecca',[19] which housed more people from Delhi, she observed, than any other place outside India. But they were badly treated and not feared. She witnessed many incidents of the Bedouins treating Indian pilgrims violently.

Mecca may have been a 'wild', dreary', 'repulsive' place, as the begum suggests,[20] but it was still relatively safe. Life outside the city was precarious and hazardous. The journey for pilgrims from Mecca to Medina was now almost as dangerous as during the times of the Qarmatians in the tenth century. The begum wisely decided not to go to Medina, citing a long list of reasons, among them that 'the roads are very bad', 'I have very few troops', 'the Bedouins demand *bukhsheesh* at every step', and 'the local authorities do not exert themselves to protect pilgrims'.[21] The Meccans themselves tried to discourage the pilgrims from going to Medina, but the pious and zealous, many of whom had come from distant shores, often insisted on undertaking the hazardous journey. Where possible, the sharif tried to provide protection for the pilgrim caravans leaving for Medina.

Just how dangerous was the journey from Mecca to Medina is well illustrated by Hafiz Ahmad Hassan, who performed the Hajj a few years after Begum Sikandar. The hafiz was one of those who decided to follow the age-old tradition of visiting the Prophet's City after a sojourn in the 'House of God'. The hafiz (the title refers to someone who has memorized the Qur'an), an official of the nawab of Tonk in Rajasthan, India, came to Mecca with a party of 150 men in 1871. Like the begum, he was also loyal to the British Crown. As the title of his book, *Pilgrimage to the Caaba and Charing Cross*, suggests, his pilgrimage ended in London, but unlike the begum, he managed to make friends with the sharif, who agreed to provide him with an escort to Medina.

The hafiz found Sharif Abdullah to be 'an exceedingly polished gentleman' and 'a very fine looking man'.[22] Despite that, the hafiz shared the begum's aversion for the Meccans. He claimed that most of them were ignorant, uncultured and greedy. 'The people are very fond of wearing silk and woollen clothing of gay and gaudy appearance,' he wrote. 'The articles of dress are supplied from the manufactories of England and France, but the ignorant people believe that they are all of Istanbul manufacture, and will not be persuaded that they come from other countries, even though the manufacturer's name and place where they were made be written on them.'[23] This is an interesting example of convergent practice. Of course it was Indian textiles that changed the face, or more precisely the undergarments, of Europe. However, numerous new fashions and exotic products arriving in Europe with the opening of the Americas and the Indian Ocean were considered to be à la Turk, products of the

Ottoman lands wherever they originated. Thus did that sacrificial bird get its name – the turkey. Both the begum and the hafiz considered the Bedouins – both inside and outside the city – to be uncouth, unpleasant and 'violent plunderers'; not surprising, given the treatment they received.

While preparing for his journey to Medina, the hafiz discovered that many camel-drivers in Mecca were in league with Bedouin robbers and bandits. They led the pilgrims directly into well-established traps and pre-planned butchery. The sharif promised an escort of ten reliable camel-drivers, well armed, and a party of slaves: 'strong, stout men on whom he could rely'. The following day, 'some ten ill-favoured, ugly, misshapen wretches, of most villainous appearance, wearing long loose garments made of old blankets or strips of old carpet, were presented to me by the Sharif. They were armed with heavy flint matchlocks and daggers, and looked in every way the most abandoned and desperate characters.'[24] The hafiz took them for robbers, but was assured that they were to be his escort. Even after he had mustered a strong party, 'quite capable of giving a good account to any body of Bedouin plunderers', the hafiz still believed he didn't have enough protection. So he looked elsewhere for further security.

Not too far from the Sacred Mosque, the hafiz encountered a man described by local Indians as the Sheikh al-Haramme, or 'the prince of thieves and robbers'. *Haramme* is the Urdu word for bastards, a term, I suspect, that was generically used by the Hindis to describe all Bedouins. 'It is said,' the hafiz wrote, 'that he belongs to the noblest of the robber tribes, and that his influence was so great that the mere fact of his presence with our caravan would be sufficient to ensure our immunity from attack.'[25] The ageing Sheikh al-Haramme was duly hired – a good move – and the hafiz and his entourage set off from Mecca.

Despite all the precautions and security, the hafiz's caravan was still raided on the first night. Some of his camels were stolen and a number of his party attacked. The next day they encountered another caravan that had been attacked and several of its members badly wounded. 'I saw myself one man,' the hafiz wrote, 'he was a native of Kashmir, with fair complexion and well-built frame. His eyebrows and cheeks had been shockingly cut by the robbers.' The favourite tactic of the robbers was to attack the pilgrims from behind, slicing their eyes with their daggers, and slashing their cheeks. 'The Kashmiri's case appeared to me to be hopeless, so badly had he been sliced about face and eyes.' There was another disturbing incident: 'One of the party, a Turkish gentleman, had gone out of his mind, owing to the shock occasioned by the fact of five of his party having being carried away with their camels while they were asleep in the shugdoffs, by the brigands. The unfortunate men were carried off to a remote spot and there mercilessly butchered.'[26]

The Bedouins kept on attacking the hafiz's caravan. Even though the Sheikh al-Haramme was very vigilant, showed himself to and repeatedly addressed the Bedouins, several members of the hafiz's party, particularly the old and the weak who trailed behind, were grabbed and mercilessly butchered. Indeed, but for the Sheikh al-Haramme, the whole caravan would have perished.

It was not just pilgrims who were being badly treated and systematically robbed both in Mecca and beyond in the Hijaz. The city seemed to be in the grip of xenophobia. There was a mad campaign against Jews and Christians. As there were no non-Muslims in Mecca itself, the Meccans thus went to Jeddah, where Christians and Jews lived, to vent their anger. There were numerous attacks on Christians in Jeddah, mostly planned and carried out by Meccans. Indeed, troubles between Arabs and Europeans had now become a constant feature of life in the port, culminating in the murder of the French consul.

In Mecca itself, xenophobia forced Sharif Abdullah to accept a municipal reorganization of the city, which reduced his autonomy, and made law enforcement almost impossible. The Arabs refused to be tried by the Turks and submit to the modernized reformulations of Ottoman law, which they now considered against the Shariah, or Islamic law. So the Arabs had to be tried by the sharif himself, except where a case demanded trial by the Shariah court of the city. The Turks were tried by the *wali* or Turkish judges. The Indians and other nationalities sought out their own jurists. The convention that Bedouins and native Meccans – that is, Meccans born in Mecca – could only be judged by the sharif, however, had its limitations. A man tried by the sharif could be arrested or set free by the *wali*, and vice versa. Thus, confusion reigned.

It was Abdullah's successor, Sharif Hussain ibn Muhammad ibn Aun, who became the victim of the Meccans' wrath. Sharif Hussain took over from his brother in 1877, and continued his policies. A mild and liberal man, Hussain thought that the rising influence of European powers on the Hijaz could not be ignored. To the Meccans, it was nothing less than treachery, an act of collaboration with the Christians.

We have been provided with two, albeit brief, accounts of Sharif Hussain's looks and demeanour. The first comes from the pen of John F. T. Keane, an Anglo-Indian adventurer who lived in Mecca for six months in 1877–8. Born in Kipling's India, the son of a canon at Calcutta's Anglican cathedral, he ran away to sea as a boy. Keane, however, displays all the attention to detail and stereotypes typical of white administrators during the Raj. He spoke excellent Urdu and was so at home with the Indian Muslims that his white skin and English accent attracted no attention in Mecca – many of the inhabitants probably thought he was a Kashmiri. He travelled to Mecca in the entourage of an Indian prince who was doing the Hajj in style. Keane mixed and moved freely throughout the city. While the city was too crowded for his taste, he was fascinated by its racial mix, of which he provides a detailed breakdown. This was the true reflex and reflection of the habits of British India, which was codified, delineated and ruled as an ethnographic state. It was a wonderful trick of knowledgeable ignorance that the British fashioned in India and exported everywhere else they went. Keane notes that apart from the Indians, Arabs and Turks, who constituted the main inhabitants of the city, Mecca had small but equal proportions of Africans, Persians and people from the Maghreb, as well as Syrians, Tartars and Bedouins. Amongst other notable minorities were Chinese, Russians and 'wild Dawaysh-looking savages from God knows where'.[27] For Keane, Mecca was an exciting place, and there was fun to be had if one knew where to look.

Keane's secret source of fun was an English woman who had lived in Mecca for twenty years. He learned about her from a local Hindi barber, whom he seems to have frequented regularly and often, in the course of being shaved. Keane called her 'Lady Venus' (née Macintosh, Devon) and had several secret rendezvous with her during his stay in the Holy City. He fantasized that the totally veiled woman was ravished and forced to convert to Islam – not surprising for a man who had lived a life of 'wildest adventure' and who dreamed of rescuing maidens in distress. The more probable truth is that she was taken prisoner at the siege of Lucknow during the Mutiny of 1857 and added to the harem of one of the rebels. When the rebels were defeated the British put a price on the man's head, and in keeping with the old Mughal tradition the man sought refuge in Mecca, where he would be beyond the reach of the Raj. The husband had died, and although a bit lonely, she was content as who she was and where she lived.

Keane encountered Sharif Hussain in Arafat, during the Hajj that he performed for his own interest. During the ceremony, the sharif came riding on an iron-grey horse, 'dressed in the costume of Bedawi Sheikhs; light blue mantle worked in gold about the shoulders and collar; on his head the ordinary silk-dress of the Badawi; kept on by a camel's-wool ring around the top of the head'[28] – Keane was the ethnographic observer par excellence. The sharif was said to be 'a slight, wiry, well-made man, below the medium height; his complexion would be considered very dark even for a Badawi, almost black. He has a small round bullet head, and that particular cast of countenance which provokes you to say he has a face like a monkey, notwithstanding his very shrewd intelligent expression. His beard and moustache are short and scrubby.'[29] Keane also had some fun guessing the age of the sharif: 'I should guess him at under forty years of age. His years, however, are hard to judge, and he might be any age from twenty-four to forty, or older if he uses hair-restorer, as is the custom of many Meccans.'[30] And he provides us with a key observation: the sharif 'was mounted in an English saddle, doing the Great Pilgrimage in the pig's skin, happy and unconscious! The soul of that porker, wherever it is, must be grunting triumphant hallelujahs.'[31]

Keane's description contrasts sharply with that of Charles Doughty (1843–1926), the second Englishman to meet Sharif Hussain. Doughty, an eccentric, poet, geologist and traveller, was as much a religious fanatic as anyone to be found in the Holy City. He wandered in search of adventure around the Hijaz in 1870s, dressed as 'a Syrian of simple fortune' called Khalil. He joined the Hajj caravan from Syria, and travelled at the back of the caravan with the despised Persian Shias, who were spat upon by the Sunni Bedouins as they walked along. He found Sharif Hussain to be 'a man of pleasant face, with a sober alacrity of eyes and humane demeanour', who spoke with 'a mild and cheerful voice'. Doughty had no doubts about his age: around forty-five. Unlike Keane, who saw him only from a distance, Doughty had a face-to-face encounter with the sharif and writes about it in his typically ornate style, modelled on the King James Bible:

he seemed, as he sat, a manly tall personage of a brown colour, and large of breast and limb. The Sherif was clad in the citizen-wise of the Ottoman towns, in a long blue *jubba* of pale woollen cloth. He sat upright on his diwan . . . with a comely sober countenance; and smoked tobacco in a pipe like the 'old Turks.' The simple earthen bowl was set in a saucer before him: his white jasmine stem was almost a spear's length – He looked up pleasantly, and received me with a gracious gravity.[32]

Shortly after this meeting, the sharif was brutally murdered in Jeddah. Doughty provides a precise account of the assassination, tucked away as an entry to the index of his *Travels in Arabia Deserta*:

The Sherif Hoseyn was stabbed in the bowels at half-past six o'clock in the morning of the 14th March, 1880, as he entered Jidda, by one disguised as a Persian derwish. The wounded Prince was borne into his Agent's house; and in the next hour, feeling himself little the worse, he made light of the hurt; and sent comfortable tidings of his state to the great ones and to his kindred in Stambul. But an intestinal hemorrhage clotted in the bowel; and Haseyn, who lived through that night, was dying toward morning; and he deceased peacably [*sic*], at ten o'clock, in the arms of his physicians. The assassin, who had been snatched by the police-soldiery from the fury of the people, was cast into prison: but nothing is known of his examination. Yet it was whispered, among the Ottoman officers, that the Sherif had been murdered *because he favoured the Engleys!*[33]

In came Sharif Abdul Muttalib for his third, even shorter, term as the ruler of Mecca. By now the city, as Keane reports, was in the grip of cholera. The pilgrimage ended with the city awash with the carcasses of sacrificed animals. The cadavers lay rotting in and all around the city. An epidemic spread and quickly engulfed the city. According to Keane, sixty-three people died on the first day. Nevertheless, the citizens came out to applaud the arrival in Mecca of Sharif Hussain, impressed more than anything else by his determination and great age. But there was something else. Perhaps it was his survival instinct. Or maybe it was that he personified conservative tradition. Whatever it was, the Meccans now saw a mysterious quality in him; the citizens gathered around Sharif Hussain as though he was their last great hope. His eccentric, and sometimes cruel, actions only enhanced his reputation amongst the Meccans. He cancelled various trade licences awarded by his predecessors and then sold them by auction. He arrested three respectable and innocent people in the middle of the night, for no other reasons than he suspected their motives, and had them flogged in front of the Sacred Mosque until two of them died. For the Meccans, this was a demonstration of the power and autonomy of the city. He demolished the palace built by one of his relatives opposite his own house. A group of Bedouins who complained to the *wali* about his cruel treatment were raided and a number of them brutally killed. This act too enhanced his reputation not just amongst the Meccans but the Bedouin tribes as well.

It was as though madness had once again descended on Mecca. But within a year, the government of the zealous old man became intolerable even for his most ardent admirers. Secret petitions against him, drawn up largely by members of his own family and members of the sharif clan, were submitted to the sultan. Orders for his replacement came in November 1881. He could not be allowed to escape under any circumstances. A large proportion of the city's inhabitants still revered him and Istanbul feared they might gather around him and fight the Turks. The *wali* surrounded the sharif's house without warning in the middle of the night; guns, positioned on a nearby hill, were trained on it. A number of sharif leaders, who had quietly prepared their men, stood nearby to block all escape routes. At sunrise, the edict from Istanbul with the orders to depose him was read out, and he was taken prisoner. He was allowed to live out the rest of his life near Mecca, in Muna, where he died in January 1886.

The whole of Mecca attended his funeral, with the locals and Bedouins crying as though they had lost a beloved relative. In a way they had. The long line of sharifs had almost come to an end. Shortly

Mecca was to have a new set of rulers. The city the sharifs had marshalled, whose character and history they so often embodied, was no longer so enclosed, a forbidden city that was not as forbidding a place as it had been. It was now open to the outside world.

European colonialism was pressing ever closer to the Hijaz. Doughty had been preceded by and would be followed by a string of European travellers in the employ of European powers. Some travellers had converted to Islam, others merely pretended and came disguised as Arabs. The intriguing city closed to non-Muslims would become a central interest in the intrigues of the European powers that ruled over more and more Muslim peoples around the globe. Their agents and adventurers would publish more and more accounts of journeys to the Holy City. Whether written to whet the fascination of the public or fill the archives of learned societies, all these accounts had political implications for the way in which Mecca, Islam and Muslims were understood in Western capitals, where in future the fate of Arabia would be determined. The fortunes of Mecca would continue to rise and fall according to the interests of those who exercised power. The more Mecca opened up to the world, the more the world came to Mecca. And it would come in ways and numbers unimaginable during the reign of the sharifs. Indeed, it was as if an entire era in the history of the city was buried along with Sharif Hussain.

9

Western Visitors, Arab Garb

A panoramic photograph of Mecca, taken from the fort on Mount Abu Qubays in 1880, shows the city in its full traditional splendour. The prime focus is the Kaaba within the open courtyard of the Sacred Mosque. The houses around the Sanctuary, up to five floors high with *mashrabiya*, wooden fretwork window screens, facing outward and with internal courtyards, are elegantly spread out over the sharp-peaked hills bristling around the Haram. Within the Haram itself, dome structures designated for the four schools of thought – Hanafi, Maliki, Shafi and Hanbali – are plainly visible; as are the Haram library and the clock house used for determining the times of prayer. The city is clearly in a bad state of repair: the houses adjacent to the Abu Qubays fort are either derelict or in ruins, and there are not many people in the Sacred Mosque. Photographs depicting the main congregational Friday prayers around the Kaaba show that it is far from crowded. This is not surprising. Given the political turmoil in the city, with the mass exodus of the inhabitants a regular occurrence, the population was fluctuating wildly. During the closing decades of the nineteenth century, Mecca's population had fallen to fewer than 40,000 inhabitants. It would rise only slowly during the next decades, moving up to 60,000 – still considerably fewer than the 150,000 reported in previous centuries.

The photograph is part of an enormous collection (around 36,000) known as the *Yildiz Albums*.[1] Among the first photographs to be taken of the Holy City, the albums were commissioned by the opera-loving Ottoman Sultan Abdulhamid II (r. 1876–1909), whose hobbies also included carpentry – he made his own furniture, which I admired on a visit to Istanbul's Dolmabache Palace. The sultan assigned military officers to photograph buildings, schools, castles, forts, military barracks, government offices, Mecca and the Kaaba to provide a record of the entire journey undertaken by the pilgrims coming from Istanbul via Lebanon to Mecca. The photographs depict the routes that the pilgrim caravans traversed, the towns and cities they visited, the guesthouses where they stayed, and notable natural, cultural and military locations from Beirut, Medina and Mecca to all the ritual sites (Arafat, Muna, Muzdalifah) of the Hajj.

One could buy such pictures of the city, and the Sacred Mosque, in the bazaars in Mecca. Also available in the city's bookshops were postcards of the Hajj, scenes at Arafat, Muna, and the Stoning of the Devils, as well as of the royal *surre* caravans. The bookshops in the Holy City offered almost exclusively books printed in and imported from Egypt. The works on offer were largely theological, commentaries on the Qur'an, the life of the Prophet, works of canon law, along with calligraphy and Arabic poems and literature. *The Arabian Nights*[2] was widely available and very popular. Another regular bestseller was *The Assemblies of al-Hariri*.[3] This eleventh-century text, which contains fifty 'encounters' or short stories each with a particular moral, accompanied by well-known proverbs, phrases and segments of classical poems put into the mouths of characters, was partly or wholly committed to memory by more educated Meccans. Also available were a few works by Meccan writers, among them the popular text the *Six Discourses* by Sheikh Haqqi, printed in Cairo in 1882. The sheikh's warning against infidel modern culture echoed the tenor of general thinking in Mecca. Western culture, he wrote, has placed 'on all wares that are used by men pictures of living creatures so that there is now hardly a house, shop, market, bath, fortress or ship without pictures'. This is surely a sign of the Devil and of 'things that lead into Hell'.[4]

Books on science and arts, even those written by Muslims, seldom survived the censor's wrath. The bookshop also stocked a couple of local newspapers. *Al-Qibla*, the official gazette, started appearing in 1885 when Osman Nuri Pasha, the Ottoman *wali*, established a printing press in the city. A weekly newspaper consisting of four sheets half in Turkish (then written in Arabic script) and half in Arabic called *The Hijaz* was also available. These local newspapers seldom reported news of the outside world.

The photographs, printed books and newspapers were all harbingers of the arrival of modern communications in the Holy City. A new age was dawning, and the new sharif tried to reflect the spirit of the times. He was Aun-al-Rafiq, son of Sharif Muhammad ibn Aun. He became the ruler of the Holy City in 1882, after the death of Sharif Abdul Muttalib, at the age of fifty. Amongst his first actions, to the surprise of his citizens, was to have himself photographed. What was a passion for the sultan was good enough for the sharif.

The picture appears in the annexe to *Mekka in the Later Part of the 19th Century* by the respected Dutch Orientalist Christiaan Snouck Hurgronje (1857–1936).[5] While the photographic record of the Hajj and Mecca was being made in 1880, Hurgronje was receiving his doctorate at Leiden University for a dissertation on 'The Festivities of Mecca'. The Dutch government ruled over a large Muslim population; its East Indies colonies comprise what is today the most populous Muslim country on earth, Indonesia. Seeking a suitable agent to study the problem of rebellious natives, they lighted upon Hurgronje, a scholar of Islam with an expert's command of Arabic. He set off for Arabia in the pay of the Dutch government, though the money was channelled through the Royal Institute for Linguistics and Anthropology in a classic demonstration of the relationship between 'scientific investigation', 'intelligence-gathering' and 'covert operations' that runs through the history of Western colonialism in general, and attempts to penetrate the forbidden city of Mecca in particular.

Hurgronje based himself at the Dutch consulate in Jeddah for some months while he made useful contacts before moving to spend six months in Mecca during 1884–5. He assumed the Muslim name Abd al-Gaffar and intended to perform the Hajj – a desire that remained unfulfilled, as he was expelled from the Holy City by the Ottoman *wali*. The story of his exit has more than a touch of the Indiana Jones about it. Hollywood's popular hokum about the archaeologist, adventurer and covert agent Dr Jones are nostalgia for and ostensibly pastiche of a certain kind of film-making. Nevertheless, beneath all the pizzazz they do reflect something authentic about the interconnections that existed in the late nineteenth century between the scramble for knowledge and artefacts and the scramble for empire. Hurgronje's misfortune was the result of a little malicious activity on the part of the French vice-consul in Jeddah. Two scientists, one German and one French, had come across a fascinating stone inscription in South Arabia. The Frenchman was then promptly assassinated, and questions arose about repatriation of their possessions, including the enigmatic inscription, which had been left in Jeddah. Hurgronje merely translated the correspondence for the French vice-consul, who was conversant in neither Turkish nor Arabic. In the process the vice-consul conceived the notion that Hurgronje was trying to gain possession of the artefact at the heart of the matter, the Taima Stone, for Germany and denounced him in an article that appeared in a French newspaper, and that quickly came to the attention of the Turkish and Meccan authorities. Until that point Hurgronje had been accepted in good faith as a scholar and a convert to Islam. The newspaper article made everyone think they had been cruelly used, betrayed, taken for a ride. Hurgronje was immediately *persona non grata*. Though he was later exonerated by the Turkish authorities of any wrongdoing in the affair, he never sought to return to Arabia. He himself went to great philosophical and philological lengths to maintain ambiguity about the true meaning and nature of 'conversion', while making it evident that he had not actually converted to Islam.

While in Mecca Hurgronje enjoyed total freedom and the confidence of the citizens, and learned first hand how they taught and learned, talked politics and discussed issues of faith in mosques, divans, coffee houses and living-rooms. He married a Meccan woman and devoted a great deal of time to extensive research on the daily life of the citizens. When he was ordered to leave, he left his wife behind. Like any good anthropologist, or agent, what Hurgronje needed was a reliable informant who could be an effective research assistant. The wife would have been invaluable in that respect. And so was a young Javanese student, who, tellingly, was desperate for a sponsor to help him get a job with the Dutch administration in his homeland. Hurgronje found that he would do anything asked of him and go to inordinate lengths to satisfy the research agenda of his employer. We have no knowledge of what happened to the wife or the student once Hurgronje left the city.

His unceremonious expulsion from Mecca did nothing to dim Hurgronje's career. He became a policy adviser to the Dutch government in the East Indies. His principal advice was remarkably similar to the infamous Education Minute provided to the British in India in 1835 by the colonial governor and historian Thomas Babington Macaulay. Macaulay advocated Western education to build a compliant class of natives who would be clones of the Raj, capable of administering the empire on its behalf. Hurgronje advocated Western education to bypass Islamic religious education and advance compliant peaceable governance through indigenous elites to serve and preserve the purposes of empire. After his time in the East Indies Hurgronje returned to the Netherlands, where he became a noted academic, and was among the founders of the modern discipline of Islamic Studies.

The photographs Hurgronje amassed of Mecca are not without their own frisson of empire. Divided into three parts – 'Views of Mecca', 'A Gallery of Mecca's People' and 'Portraits of Pilgrims' – his book contains exquisite and remarkable pictures. A panoramic photograph, much sharper than that in the *Yildiz Album*, shows a well-planned city nestling in a valley between mountains, with handsome, evenly distributed houses surrounding the Sacred Mosque. The Meccans, mostly sitting and in formal dress, look serious but elegant. The pilgrims, photographed in groups and in their national costumes, appear tired, but happy to be photographed.

The photograph of Sharif Aun-al-Rafiq in the collection has him standing looking away from the camera. He has a stylish moustache, a small beard and a smooth, dark complexion. Clearly he has abandoned the huge turban and gold gowns of his predecessors, and is wearing a small, undistinguished white turban and a black, richly embroidered dress, with a light black *shash*, a scarf, with white borders holding the dress together. A large star hangs from the button of his robe. On his travels, the sharif was even more simply dressed, often like a Bedouin. He made it his policy to avoid talking politics in public. This seemed strange to the Meccans, but on the sharif's part it was an attempt to deflect the attention of Turkish agents and a cover for his intense hatred of Ottoman rule. He did not have the support of the Turkish *wali*, Osman Pasha, who has his portrait over the page in Hurgronje's album. The pasha wears a similar dress but with a fez in place of a turban. Full-bearded, with a stern face, he stands on a carpet grasping the sword that hangs by his side. A man of immense energy and capability, he was appointed at the same time as the sharif. The two seem to be eyeing each other warily, suggesting that trouble was in store.

They had similar administrative powers and clashed frequently. Osman Pasha tried, and succeeded, to reduce the sharif's power by virtue of his control of the customs duties from Jeddah. The sharif's share was now paid not as a right but as a salary. The pasha paid the sharif's guards directly, and took over the administration of justice, allowing the sharif to hear only the cases concerning his own family and clan and those of the indigenous Meccans. Moreover, the *wali* also took charge of public works in the Holy City. He improved the water supply, repaired the Zubaidah aqueduct, and built a new government office, new barracks and guard houses. This was a direct encroachment on the sharif's territory; and Aun-al-Rafiq saw this as an affront to his office and dignity. He would not see his authority eroded further; decisive action against the *wali* had to be taken.

Sharif Aun-al-Rafiq decided to follow the example of the Prophet Muhammad. There was to be a *hijra* – a migration from Mecca to Medina. One night he quietly slipped out of the city, along with his family and most of the jurists, scholars, and the nobles and merchants of Mecca. In the morning the Turks found themselves alone in the city, apart from pilgrims and visitors. Most of the houses in Mecca were empty and locked. Some had placards reading: 'Entrance to Paradise, without payment of bribe, for he who rids Mecca of its cursed and corrupt Wali'.

In Medina, the sharif wrote letter after letter to the sultan complaining about the excesses of Osman Pasha. Eventually Istanbul conceded, and Osman Pasha was dismissed in 1886. The sharif and his people returned triumphantly to Mecca. A new stone was now erected in front of his palace. The carving in large letters on the stone announced: 'Office of the Noble Emir and of his Glorious Government'. A string of *walis* now came and went. The sharif, however, always managed to keep them in their place and/or have them replaced. Only those who turned a blind eye to his dealings, or were satisfied with a bribe or two, could keep their appointments.

After his death in 1905, Aun-al-Rafiq was succeeded by his nephew, Ali ibn Abdullah ibn Muhammad ibn Aun. He emerged on the recommendation of Ahmad Ratib Pasha, the *wali* of Mecca at the time. The two were friends and mutual admirers and were able to administer Mecca jointly for four years. But a revolution was brewing in Istanbul. It had become obvious that the ageing and tottering Ottoman Empire – with its centralized bureaucracy, suppression of all opposition, obsession with spying on its citizens, together with loss of territory and prestige – was reaching its final stages. There was unrest and rebellion throughout the Empire. In Istanbul, the conviction that the economic penetration of foreign powers could only be checked by the dissolution of the Empire had taken hold. The Young Turks, leaders of the reform movement, were agitating against Sultan Abdulhamid II and campaigning for parliamentary government under their control. The success of their movement provided a certain symmetry to the reign of Abdulhamid II. He became sultan when his brother was deposed, and was succeeded by another brother when he too was deposed in 1909. There was, however, one major difference: when Mehmet V became sultan he was a mere figurehead with no powers, thanks to the new Turkish Constitution, which was proclaimed in late 1908. Ahmad Ratib Pasha, the *wali* of Mecca, was considered by the Young Turks to be incurably loyal to the old regime, so he was summarily dismissed. When Sharif Ali met a similar fate he sought refuge with the British in Egypt.

The British had effectively become the pre-eminent power in Egypt when they bought out the khedive's shares in the Suez Canal in 1875 under the noses of the French. It took decades before Britain and France eventually settled the equivocal status of the country between themselves. It was never a formal colony, but in constructing the *Entente Cordiale* the French agreed that Egypt was to be in the British sphere of influence while they had free rein in Morocco, Algeria and Tunisia. For Egyptians it made little practical difference: the administration of their lives remained under foreign 'guidance'. With Sharif Ali gone, his replacement was to be Abdilla, brother of Aun-al-Rafiq, who was as old and ailing as the Sublime Porte. Overjoyed by his appointment as sharif of Mecca, Abdilla decided to visit the grave of his son to say farewell. While saying his prayers at the gravestone, he had a massive stroke and died on the spot.

The news of his death in Mecca brought the old rivalries between the two branches of the sharif clan, Dhawi Zaid and Dhawi Aun, to the fore. Dhawi Zaid put forward Ali Haider, grandson of Ghalib, as their candidate. Haider, a cultured, moderate man who abhorred violence, had spent most of his life in Istanbul. Although highly respected and trusted by the Ottomans, he was generally seen by the Meccans as pro-British, a view reinforced by the fact that he was married to an English woman. Hussain, the Dhawi Aun candidate, too had spent a long time – around fifteen years – at the court of the sultan in Istanbul. Self-obsessed, cantankerous and expert at politicking, he outmanoeuvred the gentle Haider with relative ease, won the support of the Porte and became the sharif of Mecca in 1908. He was to be the last sharif to rule Mecca.

Sharif Hussain took over Mecca at the same time as the Hijaz railway was being inaugurated. It was to be a major turning point in pilgrim travel. The train from Damascus to Medina and then on to Mecca was to replace the Syrian caravan. For the Ottomans the project had additional significance: a cheap and convenient way of supplying and reinforcing their garrisons in the Hijaz. They presented the project not as an imperial Ottoman activity but as an Islamic endeavour, a service for the pilgrims to carry them to their spiritual journey's end – Medina and then Mecca. The railway was financed as a *waqf*, or Islamic endowment, and Sultan Abdulhamid II sought donations for the project from all over the Muslim world. In return, he promised that the railways would be built solely with workers and material from Muslim lands. And with the exception of a German engineer and tracks and cars from Europe, he lived up to his promise. The bulk of the labour was supplied by the Turkish army; other work was carried out using Egyptian and Indian workers. After eight years of effort, the first part of the project, Damascus to Medina, was complete. For the small cost of a third-class ticket, £3.10s, the pilgrims could travel over a thousand miles in relative comfort and safety.

On board the train on its inaugural journey from Damascus to Medina was Arthur J. B. Wavell, a twenty-five-year-old soldier in the Welsh regiment. Wavell was but the latest of the explorer-spies to arrive in Mecca. Trained at the Royal Military College, Sandhurst, he had already fought in the Boer War and served

British intelligence in his travels in southern Africa (Swaziland, Tongaland and parts of Zululand) and later in East Africa, travelling to Mombasa. Wavell was one among many British spies roving around Arabia, gathering information and intelligence. The British had serious interest in the region, both to gain a foothold in the Muslim Holy Lands and to undermine the Ottoman Empire. The Middle East in general was of interest to the British, being a vital link in the chain of communication and connection to India. Galvanized by Napoleon's foray into Egypt and resolute after the opening of the Suez Canal, they bolstered their efforts throughout the region. They had interests in Kuwait, Persia, and with the sheikhdoms around the Persian Gulf; and what happened in Istanbul and Mecca mattered to them, just as it did to the Dutch authorities. The British ruled over a vast Muslim population across the Indian subcontinent as well as in the Malay states.

The British also funded John Lewis Burckhardt's travels. He was followed by the most famous, and flamboyant, Englishman to visit Mecca: Sir Richard Burton. Burton arrived in Mecca in 1853, aged thirty-two, after spending seven years in India (in the province of Sind) as a soldier for the East India Company, where he acquired a well-founded reputation for spying. His decision to visit Mecca, and perform the Hajj, was in fact a smart career move. The point of the journey, he told his supporters at the Royal Geographical Society, was to further scientific knowledge and provide the East India Company with valuable information on Arabian trade routes. With precocious talents as a linguist, Burton travelled in disguise, switching his initial false persona of a Persian to that of an Afghan once he appreciated the hostility faced by Shia pilgrims. However, he had little to add to Burckhardt's descriptions of Mecca, so little in fact that he contents himself merely with quoting what Burckhardt had written. Burton was nevertheless the Victorian adventurer par excellence. After Mecca he accompanied John Hanning Speke on the expedition to identify the source of the river Nile. Always wayward and truculent, his manner caused squabbles, and Burton felt under-appreciated for his achievements. He turned his attentions from exploration to translation, notably of *The Arabian Nights*. When he realized that it was not so much the ancient tales of Sheherazade that titillated the British public as his raunchy footnotes, he gave them the exotica of the Orient in full measure with his translation of *The Perfumed Garden*.[6] It was a fitting culmination in many ways, the sexual laxity and appetites of the Meccans having been a consistent theme of so many travellers' tales.

Another probable spy was Eldon Rutter, who performed the Hajj in 1925, and also provided one of the most comprehensive and detailed accounts of life in Mecca. The unique selling point of his two-volume account was that he travelled to Mecca from the south, something entirely new in the annals, since all other visitors had arrived from the north.

These non-Muslim English visitors to the Holy City spoke excellent Arabic. Many were highly knowledgeable about Islam and Muslim customs, and entered the city in Arab garb with Muslim pseudonyms. Burton used various disguises; Wavell travelled with a black-market Turkish passport and two travelling companions, a Swahili-speaker from Mombasa called Masaudi, and an Arab, Abdul Wahid, from Aleppo, who had lived in Berlin. Rutter became a Syrian and took the name of Salah ed-Din. The British were by no means the only nation sponsoring such visitors. Apart from Hurgronje on behalf of the Dutch, the French, with increasing colonial responsibilities for Muslim populations across north, west and central Africa, were also in the game. Ten years after Hurgronje's visit, the French dispatched Gervais Courtellemont on a secret commission to the Holy City. The mystique of Mecca added to the challenge faced by these explorers and spies. It was absolutely essential to be inconspicuous in a city forbidden to non-Muslims. Courtellemont, even by his own admission, seems to have violated this prime directive by being almost unbelievably tactless and awkward. His travelling companion, Ali, was frequently at his wits' end and called upon to rescue the situation by placating the authorities. But for all his misadventures Courtellemont was a skilled photographer, and in a period that seems dominated by the urge to take pictures he provided a number of excellent photographs of Mecca.

Wavell was the first who did not have to endure extreme privations on the journey. After arriving in Medina on the Hijaz railway, he made his way to Mecca, where he spent several months. During the Hajj of 1908, he came across Sharif Hussain's camp. It stood, he wrote,

> on an artificially raised platform, [and] comprised four high marquees and many smaller tents. Lines of troops formed a passage and kept back the crowd. Bands paraded up and down the empty spaces between them. The various grandees present arrived one after the other with their proper escorts and were received by the Shareef seated on a dais at the far end of the largest marquee . . . [after the grandees had left the Sharif held] a sort of levee to which everyone was admitted who cared to go . . . While quite alive to the dignity of his position, he endeavours to revive the old traditions of the Prophet and the earlier Caliphs, who were accessible to all and sundry, and put into actual practice the theory of equality and fraternity inculcated by the Koran.[7]

In Mecca itself, Wavell discovered that not all postcards in the bookshops depicted innocent scenes of the city and the Hajj. In a bookshop in the short street leading to the main gate of the Haram, he was shown a few postcards that, 'in England at any rate, it is not advisable to use for correspondence'. Thinking that he was interested in more saucy illustrations, the proprietor, a Meccan by birth, ushered him into 'the darker recesses at the back of his shop and brought out an album of pictures, the nature of which need not be indicated more particularly'.[8] The customers of the bookshops were almost exclusively foreigners, pilgrims and visitors like Wavell, as the Meccans themselves were hardly interested in reading.

The only book that most Meccans themselves read was the Qur'an. An educated person in the Holy City was someone who had memorized the Qur'an and could write its verses elegantly. Consequently, children's education was focused solely on the art of recitation and calligraphy. At the tender age of three or four, children would be marched to traditional Qur'anic schools, known as *kuttab*, where memory was considered the only important human faculty. Pupils were treated harshly and the most sadistic teachers were held in highest esteem. The Saudi journalist and social critic Ahmad Suba'i (1905–84) was taken by his father to the *kuttab* of al-Shish Alley near the Mudda quarter. 'Sir,' his father told the teacher, 'the flesh and sinew are for you and the bones for us. Sir, you are entitled to break his bones and we will fix them.'[9] Consequently, Suba'i tells us in his autobiography *My Days in Mecca*, the teachers showed neither tolerance nor kindness to the children under their control. They 'regularly disciplined us by generously thrashing us with a *falagah*, a big stick with a knotted rope at the end – part and parcel of the kuttab system'.[10] There were no breaks during the classes; children had to sit all day memorizing the Qur'an verse by verse. After three years memorizing the Qur'an, he moved on to memorize the *Book of Grammar*, and the works and biographies of famous poets.

Suba'i, the first modern historian of Saudi Arabia, grew up in Mecca during the days of Sharif Hussain. Like all children in the Holy City, he was raised with draconian discipline. Children had to strictly follow the rules of public dress: a turban with the regional *igal* (headband), a belt around the robe, and traditional shoes – all were required. Children had to show utmost respect to their elders, particularly their fathers. When he sat in front of his father, Suba'i had to sit in a way that showed absolute respect and submission. He was not allowed to utter a single word in front of his father. Failure to comply would result in a severe thrashing. Indeed, frequent beating was the norm at any perceived misdemeanour: 'whether I was guilty or innocent, the beating would take place anyway'.[11] He saw so much cruelty in the city – both to humans and animals, especially the abuse of donkeys – that he became traumatized, and rebelled. As a teenager he was desperate to read anything other than the Qur'an or works on grammar and theology. But a young boy with an inquiring mind could find little to read in the Holy City. He read stories of Sufis and jinn, and books of dubious science, with such titles as *The Beauty of Flowers*, *The Wonders of the World* and *Mysteries of the Sea*. 'I had to learn about seven different levels of the earth and the different jinn population of each level. I also read about the sources of the Nile and how it originally flowed from paradise.'[12]

Despite its anti-intellectualism, the Holy City was a magnet for international students, mostly from India, Africa and southeast Asia. These students did not attend the *kuttab* but studied under noted scholars and jurists. The most prestigious place to learn and teach was the Sacred Mosque, where professors vied for students. Spaces were reserved for various distinguished teachers throughout the Mosque, and classes were held, between prayers, throughout the day and at night between evening and late-night prayers. The lectures were free and anyone from the age of sixteen to sixty could attend the classes. Apart from classical commentaries and books of Islamic law, the basic text was *The Revival of Religious Science* by the twelfth-century theologian and jurist Imam Abu Hamid al-Ghazali (1058–1111).[13] Even though al-Ghazali was a philosopher, philosophy itself was prohibited. Indeed, the ideas and works of the rationalist school of Islamic thought, the Mutazilites, who were regarded as heretics and compared to ignorant heathens, were strictly forbidden. All students needed to know, the professors would announce, was that 'the Mutazilites were stupid pigheads who held human reason to be the measure of truth – a terrible superstition'.[14]

The professors had to pass an examination before they could teach and receive a stipend. The potential candidates applied to the sheikh of the *ulamas*, the scholars, who was usually appointed by the government. When the sheikh decided that the candidate was suitable and prepared for the examination – a decision that required some persuasion, representations from established scholars and perhaps even a bribe – the candidate would be called. The examination usually took place in the afternoon, at a specific spot in the Sacred Mosque, and in public. The sheikh and his assisting deputies would sit in a circle, with the candidate sitting in front of them, while the candidate's friends and members of the public sat in the background. A small group of professors, there to witness the proceedings, sat at a distance. The examination consisted of a single question: the candidate was required to provide a commentary on *bismillah* ('In the name of God'), the prayer uttered before reading any verse of the Qur'an or at the commencement of any undertaking. Through the exegesis provided by the candidate, the examiners could judge his knowledge of Arabic language and grammar, logic and theology, the classical commentaries on the Qur'an and canonical texts of Islamic law, and therefore his ability to pass judgements on issues of faith.

There was fierce competition amongst the scholars and professors. Those from the Shafi school of thought and educated at Al-Azhar University in Cairo were held in the highest regard. The scholars from India and southeast Asia were seen in a less favourable light, and few were able to teach in the Sacred Mosque itself. Normally they held classes in their own houses, teaching mostly students from their own backgrounds, and survived on donations from pious foundations funded by Indian princes. It was not uncommon for one scholar to denounce another, perhaps from a different school of thought, or to write tracts denouncing certain practices. There were frequent clashes between sheikhs of Sufi groups, who wrote tracts denouncing each other's mystical practices as un-Islamic. Hurgronje reports one such incident between a learned scholar and the Sheikh of Ulama. The scholar, the son of a converted Copt, circulated amongst his followers a treatise that argued against smoking and suggested that it was an un-Islamic practice. The Sheikh of Ulama, who enjoyed his *shisha*, immediately wrote a counterblast. 'If tobacco smoking was unholy,' he argued, 'the smokers, that is to say nearly all Mekkans, were, from their unholiness, unfit to be witnesses to marriages, and therefore most of the Mekkan marriages were invalid.'[15] Hence the original contention must be wrong, absurd and itself un-Islamic. In disagreements between scholars, custom and orthodoxy, rather than arguments, often prevailed. And not infrequently such clashes led to the banning or burning of books, even to the imprisonment of the authors, labelled as heretics.

Given the emphasis on reciting and memorizing the Qur'an, those who recited were naturally held in high esteem. They regarded themselves not as scholars but as artists akin to opera singers, and commanded high fees for reciting the Qur'an at formal and informal gatherings. On the whole, and much like some opera singers, many were also often vain and jealous of their competitors. When paid what seemed to them too low a fee, they deliberately performed below par, to the displeasure of the audience.

When not reading or listening to the Qur'an, or attending to pilgrims during the Hajj season, the Meccan men had little else to do. An average day in Mecca was a leisurely affair for its male citizens. The Meccan would wake up an hour and a half before daylight on hearing the *Azan*, the muezzin's call to morning prayers. He would perform his toilet and ablution in a little stone closet, and with a twig-style toothbrush known as a *miswak* in his mouth, run to the Haram to offer his prayers. (The *miswak* remains popular today and is made from a shrub called arak: the end of the shoot is chewed to separate the fibres, which function as a toothbrush to rub the teeth, using the sap of the branch as toothpaste.) After morning prayers, he would go home for breakfast, which usually consisted of bread, a bowl of beans, some eggs and several glasses of sweet tea. After breakfast, a few hours would be spent discussing domestic matters and smoking the *shisha*. A visit to the bazaar to buy meat and vegetables and other provisions for the day would follow. The main chore of the day complete, it was time to sit in the *mogo'od*, one's favourite sitting place – usually a small room on the ground floor, or a raised platform at the entrance hall – where friends and guests would be received and entertained and more *shisha* would be smoked, till the call came for midday prayer. After the midday prayer, the Meccans would rest or sleep until the *Asr* or afternoon prayer. The main meal of the day would normally consist of boiled rice mixed with lentils, a dish of stewed sheep or goat meat, with a few tomatoes and onions added for flavour, and a dish of vegetables, which were usually boiled marrow or spinach or eggplant. The meal would be followed by some more rest and a bit of sleep until sunset. Then, after the evening prayers, it was time to go out in the cool twilight air to chat and smoke the *shisha*.

Not surprisingly, most Meccans did not want the outside world interfering with their idyllic existence. The Hijaz railway was thus seen as an intrusive nuisance shedding unwanted attention on the Holy City. Sharif Hussain had another concern: he saw the railway as a direct threat, as it could bring the Turkish army to Mecca more easily and rapidly. For his Bedouin allies it represented a loss in revenue: the pilgrims did not have to cross their land and hence they could not impose any taxes, nor could they be easily robbed. Thus all concerned, the sharif, the citizens and the Arab Bedouins, were strongly against the project being completed.

The consensus in the city was to prevent the extension of the Hijaz railway from Medina to Mecca. Fortunately for the Meccans, Turkey was now embroiled in the First World War; the Ottoman passion for the railway had evaporated. In the game of shifting international alliances that had bedevilled the Ottomans throughout the days of their slow decline, they had opted to enter the war on the side of Germany. Sharif Hussain was faced with two stark options: to stand by Turkey at this key moment in its history and thus earn its grateful recognition; or to seek freedom for Mecca and the Arabs in open revolt. Although Sultan Mehmet V was merely a figurehead, he was notionally still a caliph, successor to the Prophet and commander of the faithful. His last notable action was to declare jihad against the allied forces ranged against Germany and its Turkish ally. The declaration was clearly designed to rouse the Muslim subjects of France, Britain and the Netherlands against their imperial masters.

The call to jihad would have greater force with the support of Mecca. Sharif Hussain received numerous communications from Istanbul asking him, as ruler of the Holiest City of Islam and the religious leader of Muslims, to join in this call for jihad. It was the religious duty of all Muslims, the Turks argued, to join them in their battle against the 'infidel' Europeans. The sharif gave enthusiastic replies: he was with Turkey in spirit, he wrote back, he prayed for their success, gave them all his blessings. But the situation on the ground, as the sultan in his infinite wisdom knew well, prevented him from publicly declaring jihad. The Red Sea was dominated by the British and they could blockade its ports, starving Mecca and the people of the Hijaz. His hands were tied. In fact, secretly the sharif was communicating with the British, who were seeking his support against the Turks. He was also in touch with clandestine groups in the Middle East, especially the 'Union' society in Mesopotamia and the 'Freedom' society in Syria, who advocated open rebellion against the Turks. He liked the idea of Mecca as an independent city state, and began to dream about becoming the king of Arabia.

However, the sharif feared that an open revolt might fail and thus lead to dire consequences. He was also convinced, with good reason, that Britain and France had designs on acquiring further territory in the region such as Iraq, Lebanon and Syria. Preventing the colonization of more Arab land meant that, initially at least, he would have to stand by Turkey. If the war ended with victory for Britain and France, he feared, these Arab territories could suffer the same plight as those of Turkey.

He decided to provide enough encouragement to keep the British interested, and sent emissaries to Arab rulers in the region to discover if they were fully prepared for a revolt. He received emphatic replies. Still he hesitated. If you want me to remain quiet, he wrote to a Turkish commander in the region, you must recognize my independence – not just in Mecca but the whole of the Hijaz. And, he insisted, establish me as a hereditary king. The Turkish response was muted.

In contrast, the British policy towards Mecca was more obvious. It was made clear in a letter to Sharif Hussain from Lord Kitchener, the secretary of state for war. The letter

contained a definite promise to Hussain, that if he and his followers were to side with England against Turkey, the British government would guarantee his retention of the dignity of the Grand Sharif with all the rights and privileges to it and would defend it against all aggression. It held out a promise of support to the Arabs in general in their endeavours to secure freedom, on condition that they would ally themselves to England. It concluded with a hint that, in the event of the Sharif being proclaimed Caliph, he could count on England's recognition.[16]

It was a reassuring message. The sharif entertained the idea of being a caliph. Moreover, the British were happy to hand over unlimited amounts of gold to the sharif, through Colonel T. E. Lawrence of the British military mission. A wonderful self-publicist, much in the mould of the travellers who had ventured into Arabia before him, T. E. Lawrence was not the romanticized figure portrayed in the 1961 film *Lawrence of Arabia*. After graduating from Oxford, Lawrence had spent much time travelling in the Middle East ostensibly as an archaeologist. Indeed his first assignment of the war, along with the noted archaeologist Leonard Woolley, for whom he had been working, was an intelligence mission in the guise of an archaeo-logical survey of the Negev desert. In war even more than in peace, the interconnection between 'scientific' inquiry and politically and militarily significant intelligence was self-evident.

Lawrence had a delusional sense of self-importance. Englishmen, he wrote, were always 'sure of their own absolute excellence'. They had 'a collective sense of duty towards the state' and a 'feeling of individual obligation to push struggling humanity up its road'. He had come to Arabia, he declared, to set things right.[17] He became a close friend of the third son of Sharif Hussain, Faisal, who tried to convince his father that the revolt could succeed with British help. Faisal was also president of several secret Arab societies, and reliably informed the sharif that preparations for the revolt throughout the region were at an advanced stage. If the sharif still had any doubts, they were dispelled when he heard that a Turkish expedition was about to march from Medina to Yemen. He realized that it could make a detour to Mecca and depose him. Finally, he made a decision.

On 5 June 1916, Sharif Hussain made a unilateral declaration of independence and entered the war on the side of the Allies. Turkish troops were besieged in their Meccan stronghold and invited to surrender. They refused. The ensuing fight was intense, and focused on the government office where the *wali* had entrenched himself with a garrison. After three days, the sharif's army was able to storm the palace and force the garrison to surrender. Other officers holding out in different parts of the city refused to lay down their arms. Fighting even took place in the Sacred Mosque, where shots were fired towards the Kaaba. The total surrender of the Turks was only achieved on 4 July, after heavy guns, brought from Jeddah, came into play. The entire city was cleansed of Turks. It was exactly 400 years since they had assumed sovereignty of the Holy City. While Mecca was still in the grip of battle, on 22 June 1916, Sharif Hussain declared himself king of Arabia, the liberator of Arabs, and the caliph of all

Islam. He denounced the tyranny of the Turks, and asked all Muslims to follow his example and fulfil their obligation towards him as the sharif of Mecca and their caliph.

The British and the French were quick to recognize Sharif Hussain as the 'king of Hijaz'. Faisal, aided and encouraged by Lawrence, managed to unite different tribes, largely through bribes with gold supplied by the British, and lead them against the Turks. In September, British naval vessels were used for the first time to bring ceremonial material for the Hajj. Sharif Hussain thought that his ambitions were being realized.

The news of the revolt caused alarm in Turkey. The Young Turks were shocked to hear that a sharif supported and appointed by them, someone whose failings and shortcomings they had consistently overlooked, had rebelled against the sultan. The news of the revolt was kept from the public for several weeks. Istanbul now turned to the Dhawi Zaid candidate, Ali Haider. He was appointed as the new sharif of Mecca and dispatched to the Hijaz. Haider only managed to get as far as Medina, where he remained for several months, while Faisal and his troops laid siege to the city. The sharif designate repeatedly asked Istanbul for troops and ammunition, but his pleas were never answered. After eighteen months, Haider gave up the struggle to defend Medina and was forced to return to Turkey. Soon afterwards, Sharif Hussain, with the active support of the British, had most of the Hijaz under his control.

The end of the First World War revealed the existence of the secret Sykes-Picot Treaty of 16 May 1916 by which the British and French had agreed on the distribution of territories of the defeated Ottoman Empire. Mandated territories were a polite fiction for colonial rule and the wholesale remaking of lands and their peoples towards the interest of the European powers. Arab independence had been gained from the Ottomans, only to become mortgaged to Britain and France. In such a context Hussain's claim to be 'king of Arabia' was as bizarre as the man himself. Most of the principalities and

295

sheikhdoms in Arabia were now entirely independent. The sheikh of Kuwait, a long-time British client, was recognized as an independent ruler, as was the sultan of Muscat, who had a treaty with France and the US. Bahrain and Yemen too were now independent states. And Najd, the biggest territory in Arabia, was ruled by a totally independent Wahhabi king: Abdul Aziz ibn Saud.

After their attempts to take over Mecca were thwarted by Muhammad Ali, the Wahhabis had concentrated on building a viable state in Najd. In 1902, King Abdul Aziz captured Riyadh from the Rashidi emirs who had established, in 1891, a state in central Arabia stretching from Hali in the north to Qasim in the centre and Riyadh in the south. After Riyadh, the Wahhabis moved to Qasim. The Ottomans came to support the Rashidis with troops and ammunition, while the British backed Abdul Aziz, who succeeded in capturing Qasim in 1906. But despite their support for him, the British regarded King Abdul Aziz as an Ottoman sympathizer. The Ottomans in turn entered into a treaty with him and recognized him as de facto ruler of Najd. Hostilities between him and the Rashidis continued during the war – with Abdul Aziz making expedient alliances with both the Ottomans and the British. After the war, in 1921, Abdul Aziz succeeded in the capture of Hali, with the support of British ammunition and subsidies. His control over Najd almost complete, Abdul Aziz was, unlike Sharif Hussain, a king with real power. And like his Wahhabi forefathers, he was now keenly looking towards the Hijaz.

King Abdul Aziz was quite stunned at Sharif Hussain's rebellion. The family of Hussain, he declared, had produced nothing but injury and discord by their rebellion. He was further incensed by Hussain's claim to the Caliphate. Nevertheless, he sent Hussain several invitations to meet him and discuss their differences amicably. Hussain declined. He even refused to attend a conference in Kuwait, planned for 1925, where various leaders were to meet to settle issues of national boundaries. The British tried hard to mediate between the two, but Hussain remained intransigent. A Wahhabi invasion of the Hijaz now looked imminent.

In August 1924, as the Wahhabi forces moved towards the Hijaz, the sharif of Mecca wrote to the British prime minister. He wanted troops and ammunition, and asked that the guarantees given to him during the war – that his rights and privileges would be retained and defended against aggressors – should be fulfilled. By now Hussain had become an object of ridicule at the Foreign Office. He was generally regarded as a demented megalomaniac, and stories about his erratic behaviour, true and fabricated, circulated amongst the civil servants. He received no reply. In September, the Wahhabis invaded Hijaz and captured Taif.

Hussain had little to defend Mecca. His 20,000 Mauser rifles had no cartridges, the artillery had no shells, and his aeroplanes lacked bombs. The inhabitants of the city fled on foot to Jeddah. Shops were closed. The sharif emptied his already depleted treasury, and moved his family and officials to Aqaba. On 13 October 1924 Mecca was once again occupied by the Wahhabis. The long line of sharifs had ended.

The sharif's son, Ali, returned to Jeddah, hoping one day to recapture Mecca and continue the dynasty. King Abdul Aziz besieged the port as well as Medina for a year, trying to avoid bloodshed and complications with European powers. Both cities surrendered in December 1925. In Aqaba, Hussain made a last-ditch appeal to the Russians to restore him as sharif of Mecca. He died a broken man in exile in Amman on 4 June 1931 – claiming his divine right to rule Mecca to his last breath.

King Abdul Aziz now controlled an area far larger than the sharifs ever ruled, and possessed strength not seen in Arabia since the end of the Abbasid power. He moved fast to consolidate his position by maintaining strict discipline amongst the Bedouins, creating a military police, employing the *mutawwa* (religious ritual specialists) to impose religious order and improve security for the pilgrims. He was also concerned to assure the Muslim world that shrines and cultural property in Mecca were safe in his hands. He toyed with the idea of installing another sharif in the Holy City. Newspapers in Istanbul, Damascus, Baghdad, Hyderabad and New York even reported that plans were afoot to recall Sharif Ali Haider. Yet, in the end, Abdul Aziz decided that his best option was direct rule of the Holy City; he appointed his son Faysal as the new governor. Sharif Haider was refused permission to perform the Hajj in 1926; he was not even allowed to disembark from his ship, even though a large party of Meccans had gathered to welcome him.

The city waited nervously for the changes the Wahhabis would introduce, but King Abdul Aziz seemed to be in a conciliatory mood. He called a conference of the chief scholars from the different schools of thought and asked them to debate and settle their differences with Wahhabi *ulama*. Eldon Rutter, who was among the first outsiders to visit the city after the Wahhabi takeover, witnessed the meeting. There was a general consensus at the conference, he reports, that Wahhabi practice was not all that different from other schools of thought. The consensus had a radical effect on how prayers were organized in the Sacred Mosque. Up to now, there were different prayer stations in the Haram for different schools of thought: one each for Imams Shafii, Malik, Hanbal and Abu Hanifah. The followers of each imam prayed behind their own imam at slightly different times. Why was it necessary, the Wahhabi scholars asked, for different schools of thought to occupy different parts of the Sacred Mosque and perform their prayers under different imams, at different times? As the call to prayer is one, these scholars suggested, would it not be better for all worshippers, no matter which school they followed, to perform their prayers together under one imam and at the same time? The argument won the day. By order of the king, the stations of different schools of thought were removed, and prayers were now led by a single Wahhabi imam.

There was one issue on which there was a serious disagreement at the conference. The scholars from the different schools of thought suggested that the Wahhabis hated all Muslims who did not belong to their own community. King Abdul Aziz tried to assure the gathering that this was not the case. The Wahhabi scholars stated they hated only those Muslims they considered were observing practices contrary to Islam. The non-Wahhabis were not convinced. As Rutter puts it:

> if one party of men cry 'God is One', and they meet another party, different in speech, in dress, and in manners, to themselves, but whose members also cry 'God is One', then the two parties ... may do one of two things. The first of these is that they may disregard the differences of customs, of speech, and of dress, and join fraternally in the united cry of 'God is One'. That was Muhammad's way. The second is that each may loathe the other and, if they be strong, shun them; or if they be weak, annihilate them. That is the way of the ignorant Wahhabis, and most of the Wahhabis are ignorant.[18]

And the ignorant were in power. So difference of religious practices, as well as different schools of Islamic jurisprudence, were rapidly eradicated in Mecca.

Throughout the nineteenth century the possibilities of long-distance travel had been improving with the coming of railways and, especially from the 1850s onwards, of coal-powered steamships. By the 1920s, in the wake of the Great War, the age of mass transportation was dawning. It was easier than ever for Muslims to make their way to Mecca, and the influx of noted Muslim pilgrims increased several-fold. One noted visitor, for example, was the celebrated Muslim scholar Muhammad Asad, who visited the Holy City in 1927. An Austrian Jew (his original name was Leopold Weiss), he converted to Islam and travelled extensively in the Hijaz as a journalist for *Frankfurter Zeitung*. Asad, who stayed in Arabia for six years and became a friend and confidant of King Abdul Aziz, describes his adventures in *The Road to Mecca*[19] – which, incidentally, contains virtually nothing about the Holy City itself. There were many other visitors who, like Asad, were converts to Islam, and quite a few were English.

There was a good reason for this. During the early decades of the twentieth century, there was a thriving community of white Muslims in Britain. The ports of Britain with their worldwide trading links had long been home to lascars, sailors recruited from the colonies to work on British ships. Many were Muslims who came ashore and founded their own small communities in the cosmopolitan enclaves around the harbours. Yemenis were notable among them, since Aden was a principal coaling station for all the ships plying the Suez Canal route to the East. The British converts were a different class of people. They were led by Lord Headley, the 5th Baron of Headley (1855–1935), who had converted to Islam in 1913. A first-class mathematician as well as a heavyweight and middleweight boxing champion, Lord Headley was an influential man. He led a campaign to establish a central mosque in London's Regent's Park. Lord Headley, who performed the Hajj in 1923 and 1927, was also the president of the British Muslim Society. The society had such notable members as Muhammad Marmaduke Pickhall, the celebrated translator of the Qur'an,[20] the feisty aristocrat Lady Evelyn Cobbold, who took the name Zainab after conversion, and Mahmoud Mobarek Churchward, an artist and theatre painter. As the establishment looked on Muslim converts with suspicion, many remained secret believers for some time. However, the desire to visit Mecca was immense; and without declaring their conversion to Islam, openly performing the Hajj was not possible. Lady Evelyn Cobbold came out in early 1915. Shortly afterwards, during dinner at Claridge's, she tried to persuade Pickhall to declare himself a Muslim in public – with two waiters as witnesses. Both Lady Cobbold and Churchward performed the Hajj and wrote notable accounts of their experiences.

However, the fact that they were Muslim did not afford them an easy passage to Mecca. Their European complexion mattered more in a city where reservations about and suspicions of outsiders were as natural as the landscape. Moreover, by now the Meccans had become wise to European non-Muslims who came in Arab garb and later wrote disparaging accounts of their beloved city. Churchward was accused of being a Christian, a spy, and arrested. He had to appear in the court of the *wali* and was only acquitted when he produced a certificate of conversion signed by the *qadi* of Egypt. While Churchward arrived in Mecca as a regular pilgrim, Lady Cobbold, a socialite of considerable beauty and elegance, arrived as the member of the landed aristocracy she was. She was already widely travelled, but travelling alone to Mecca presented particular difficulties: even today a woman on her own cannot enter the Holy City without a male escort. That, however, was not too great a problem for someone who enjoyed a reputation as a first-class angler, rifle shot and deer-stalker, and was the first British woman to shoot a fourteen-point stag. She had spent her childhood in North Africa, where she made many famous friends who knew her as someone who was naturally sympathetic to Arabs. They would help her get an invitation from none other than King Abdul Aziz ibn Saud himself. She relied heavily on one particular friend: Harry St John Bridger Philby, the father of the famous Soviet double agent Kim Philby, and a close adviser of King Abdul Aziz ibn Saud.

Philby senior, known locally as Sheikh Abdullah, was the most noted foreign resident in Mecca. He was an explorer, a writer, and an intelligence officer in the British Colonial Office. He was amongst the first socialists to join the Indian Civil Service and spoke Urdu and Arabic as fluently as English. He was sent as head of a mission to King Abdul Aziz in November 1917. The two became friends and Philby, contrary to British policy, secretly supported the Wahhabi king and passed on intelligence regarding Sharif Hussain of Mecca to him. He was made chief of the Secret Service for the British Mandate of Palestine in November 1921. But Philby saw the Balfour Declaration, adopted by the British during the First World War and committing them to the establishment of a national home for the Jews in Palestine, as a betrayal of the Arabs. When King Abdul Aziz invited him to become his adviser, Philby converted to Islam and settled in Mecca.

He lived in an opulent house in the Jarwal quarter of the city, next to the king's palace. The house was a gift from the king on the occasion of his conversion. The king also presented him with a slave girl. While his wife, Dora, lived in Jeddah, Philby spent most of his time in Mecca, tending the garden he had lovingly created, recounting his adventures in *The Empty Quarter*[21] and writing a biography of the Abbasid Caliph *Harun Al Rashid*.[22] He maintained a cordial relationship with his wife but, as a non-Muslim, she was unable to visit Mecca, where Philby was ideally placed as an intermediary between the court of King Abdul Aziz in Riyadh and his son Faisal, the governor of Mecca. This made his other job as a representative of Standard Oil of California that much easier. It also meant that Philby was well placed to get permission for Lady Cobbold to visit Mecca.

Lady Evelyn duly arrived in the Holy City on 26 March 1933. Philby organized suitable accommodation and a car for the woman he described as 'Gertrude Bell in figure and mannerism, slim, active, rather snobby and full of quite entertaining chatter'.[23] She travelled from Jeddah to Mecca by car: a journey that normally took two days by caravan was accomplished in two hours. She became not only the first British woman on record to visit Mecca, but also the first foreigner to make the pilgrimage by car, the first to report on the new pilgrim buses, and the first pilgrim to record the trip by car from Muna to Arafat – a string of spiritual firsts for a woman who was also, as she claimed, the first woman to travel by air to Africa. She arrived in Mecca, according to the frontispiece photograph of the 1934 edition of her book *Pilgrimage to Mecca*, in her pilgrim clothes: dressed in two pieces of cloth in white, her face covered with a netted veil. It is evident that Philby soon found that a little of Lady Evelyn was quite sufficient. And that seems to have been the attitude of the

British establishment as well. Despite her achievements, the book received a chilly reception from the Foreign Office and the Royal Geographical Society. Her friendship with Philby and her sympathetic portrait of the Meccans and the Wahhabis was not appreciated.

The English visitors to Mecca, Muslims and non-Muslims alike, describe the city in similar terms. Wavell found the city had several good cafés – which he frequented – and a main market that was roofed and had very good shops. But it was not as pleasant as Medina, and rather unworldly, too immersed in obscurantist religious practices. Rutter thought Mecca was an ugly old Arab town, with no ornaments or gardens, but fascinating.

The fascination of the city was due largely to the Sacred Mosque and the Hajj. Everyone is awestruck by the sight of teeming humanity, all dressed simply in white, prostrating and performing various rituals en masse. Wavell was overwhelmed by the spectacle of prayers inside the Sacred Mosque:

the Friday prayer in the Haram was really a most imposing sight. Scarcely a square yard of the great space remained unoccupied. The uniform movement of this vast concourse during the prayer, and the strange stillness that pervades, appeal strongly to the imagination. During the *sijda*, that phase of the prayer when the forehead is placed on the earth, not a sound but the cooing of the pigeons breaks the silence; then, as the hundred thousand or more worshippers rise to their feet, the rustle of garments and clink of weapons sweeps over the space like a sudden gust.[24]

Lady Cobbold thought she needed a 'master plan' to describe the scene at Arafat:

poignant in its intensity of that great concourse of humanity of which I was one small unit, completely lost to their surroundings in a fervour of religious enthusiasm. Many of the pilgrims had tears running down their cheeks; others raised their faces to the starlit sky that had witnessed this drama so often in the past centuries. The shining eyes, the passionate appeals, the pitiful hands outstretched in prayer moved me in a way that nothing had ever done before, and I felt caught up in a strong wave of spiritual exaltation.[25]

She had a similar experience when she first entered the Sacred Mosque and came face to face with the Kaaba: I was 'lost to my surroundings and in the wonder of it'.[26]

Rutter entered the Sacred Mosque early in the morning and stood in front of the Kaaba pondering its significance:

I walked forward to the edge of the cloisters, and looked out across the wide court of the Mosque towards the great black-draped cube – that strange building, in the attempt to reach which tens of thousands, perhaps millions, of human beings have prematurely forfeited their lives; and seeing which, unnumbered millions have felt themselves to be on the very threshold of Paradise. It stood, with the simple massive grandeur of a solitary rock in the midst of the ocean – an expressive symbol of the Unity of God Whose house it is. Aloof and mysterious it seemed, reared up majestically in the centre of the great open quadrangle: while round and round its base the panting Hajjis hurried eagerly, uttering their pitiful supplications – 'Oh God! grant us in the world, good; and, in the hereafter, good; and save us from the punishment of fire.'[27]

But outside the Sacred Mosque and the Hajj, Mecca was a different place. The Meccans themselves had few redeeming features. Burton, who arrived in September 1853 just in time for Hajj, thought the inhabitants of the Holy City were somewhat coarse and lymphatic:

The Meccan is a covetous spendthrift. His wealth, lightly won, is lightly prized. Pay, pension, stipends, presents and the *Ihram* (meaning pilgrims) supply the citizen with the means of idleness. With him everything is on the most expansive scale, his marriage, his religious ceremonies; entertainments are frequent, and the junketings of his women make up a heavy bill at the end of the year. It is a common practice for the citizen to anticipate the pilgrimage season by falling into the hands of the usurer. If he be in luck, he catches and skins one or more of the richest Hajis.[28]

He found their pride, particularly their sense of superiority at their language and their lineage, most unpleasant and annoying. They see themselves as 'the cream of the earth' and resent even the slightest criticism of the Holy City. 'They plume themselves upon their holy descent, their exclusion of Infidels, their strict fasting, their learned men, and their purity of language. In fact, their pride shows itself at every moment.'[29]

Rutter agreed. Meccans assume the traits of pride and meanness, prodigality and greed, from childhood, he wrote. They are intrinsically xenophobic, 'impatient of the intrusion of foreigners in their midst', and total hypocrites. The most objectionable characteristic of the Meccans, he suggested, was their sense of 'belonging to a superior race', which was a product of the fact that they considered themselves to be 'neighbours of God'[30] and teachers to visiting pilgrims. 'The absorption of all classes in matters of profit and loss, and their lack of precision in discussing any useful matter, not excepting their religion, created an atmosphere of discomfort and hopelessness,' he wrote.[31] 'Sometimes life in Mecca seemed to take on a strangeness of insanity. Mentally comparing manners of many of my companions with those of the dwellers in more fortunate countries, I found them repulsive. Sometimes I have felt, when they joked together, that laughter like theirs belonged within the walls of a mad-house, and that the counterpart of their grimacing faces and staring eyes could only be seen through the aperture of a padded cell.'[32] Wavell echoed these sentiments. He found the citizens of the Holy City to be 'the demurest of hypocrites'.[33]

In contrast to these harsh assessments of the Meccans, Muslim Europeans, for whom the city had sublime significance, saw its citizens in a more favourable light. But words such as pride, bigotry, greed, ostentation and hypocrisy occur frequently enough in their descriptions of the Meccans.

Muslim pilgrims were enchanted by Meccan houses. Churchward was more than happy at the guest house where he stayed. It was a seven-floor building, with 'a square, flagged courtyard surrounded by seven tiers of galleries. Most of these were closed off by *mushrabiehs*, lace-like screens of twisted wood which enable women to see men but prevent the latter, while standing below, from discovering a single female face'. He had an agreeable time sitting beside the fountain, 'pleasantly shaded by the tall façades' of the veranda.[34] When Lady Cobbold, who had unprecedented access to women, visited a harem she was totally delighted. It was a beautiful, large house where women lived in splendour, in the company of goats, and everything was provided for:

> the rooms are bright with Eastern rugs and divans covered in silk, a small cage holds a bulbul. The largest room opens on to a flat roof which is now a garden of flowers . . . Several ladies are squatting on the divans, the older ones smoking narghilehs. In the women's quarters there was a bakehouse for baking bread, a great kitchen, the laundry room, and a work room where they sit sewing and gossiping. Everything necessary for running the home is done within the harem and the flat roofs are utilized for airing and drying, while all have their own roof to sleep on in the spring, when the rooms are uncomfortably hot. Nor must we forget the goats who have also their own roof and are plentifully fed with

bunches of burseem [clover] brought from Wadi Fatima, an oasis on the hill to the West.[35]

But the delights of Meccan houses were not enough. Churchward was particularly disturbed by a city where laughter and music were conspicuously absent and women were invisible on the streets, and on those rare occasions when they ventured out were veiled in 'a wide thickly starched linen covering that stood out several inches around their shapeless persons and touched the ground about their feet'.[36] The streets were quite filthy and an alarming number of poisonous reptiles infested the town. The Holy City always smelled a bit foul. Both Churchward and Rutter attribute this to its primitive sewage system – 'a large and deep hole is dug in the street before the house, and the refuse conduit is led to it'[37] – and the existence of innumerable cesspools that are emptied out at dead of night on a definite date each year. Churchward counted himself fortunate to miss the event, but Rutter witnessed it. A group of poor pilgrims, mostly Malays and Indians, were hired to open the sewers, load the effluent on donkeys, and carry and dump it outside the city boundaries. One also had to be careful of what one ate. It wasn't just the flies, the dirt and the debris that were apparent everywhere – there were hidden dangers too. Churchward was particularly keen on kebabs sold by a butcher near his guest house at much below the market price, but then his Meccan friends, watching the butcher's abattoir from the roofs of their houses, noticed that he was luring street dogs into his den. The tasty kebabs were dog meat. The butcher was arrested, lashed, and driven out of the Holy City sitting backwards on a donkey.

The few modern amenities in the city were also distinctively backward in nature. Although Meccans showed, as Churchward notes, 'the utmost broad-mindedness' in terms of currency, and coins and notes circulated from almost everywhere in the world, there were no banks. Wavell had an exceptionally hard time cashing cheques. The

Holy City had one post office, but letters were not delivered. One had to go to the whitewashed building, be interviewed by the post-master, and wrestle one's post out of the robed officials' hands. It took an eternity to buy a stamp, and if one wanted more than one, the stock must be carefully checked before it could be ceremoniously handed over.

When Churchward had had enough of countless prayers and visits to the Sacred Mosque, he ambled through the city on a donkey in search of mirth. He found some, he notes, at the markets, where white-robed merchants sat smoking long hookahs or water pipes. One cried: 'Good watches, by Allah.' Another yelled: 'Pearls, pearls of paradise.' A third man sold lemons: 'Lemons for True Believers!' The half-naked, muscular water-carriers, with sewn goatskins of liquid round their hips, who ran hither and thither delivering water, were also a sight to behold. But eventually Churchward learned that there was some laughter to be had in Mecca. It resided in the cafés on the outskirts of the city where the inhabitants argued over chess, their favourite game, and in listening to storytellers regaling the citizens with tales from *The Arabian Nights*.

There was also some joy to be had from feeding the pigeons in the Sacred Mosque. Burton, Wavell, Rutter, Lady Cobbold – all were charmed by the pigeons and lavished praise on them. 'There are as many pigeons here as in the square of St Mark's at Venice,' Wavell announced, 'and they are nearly as tame.'[38] But they get so much food that they can seldom be induced to feed off one's hand. Rutter points out that the pigeons, of 'a pretty blue-grey colour', are looked after by an endowment fund that exists only to supply them with grain and look after their needs. 'Two little stone troughs, sunk in the ground of the open quadrangle, are constantly kept filled with water for their use. One man holds the office of dispenser of the grain to the pigeons, while another holds that of waterer to them.' The Meccans, Rutter suggests, regard the birds as sacred; and they never perch on or spoil the roof of the Kaaba. To prove the assertion he slept every night for some months on a roof over-looking the Kaaba, and was delighted to report: 'I have repeatedly searched the roof of the sacred building, and have never seen there either a bird or any other living thing. At times when the roofs . . . and the ground below them, were covered with myriads of pigeons, I have constantly seen the Kaaba's roof bare and silent.'[39] Lady Cobbold too observed that the pigeons are 'too well behaved ever to sully the Haram'.[40]

All visitors to the Holy City, Muslims and non-Muslims alike, found two facets of Meccan society particularly disturbing: slavery and ignorance. Slavery prospered in Mecca. It was common for households to have several slaves, and for Meccan men to have African slave girls as concubines. The slave market thrived, and was an essential port of call for all visitors. Wavell made several visits. He believed that the Holy City was:

one of the few places remaining where the trade is carried on thus openly. The slaves, who are kept in special show rooms, sit, as a rule in a row on a long bench placed on a raised platform. They were all women; male slaves or eunuchs may be bought by private treaty, but are not exposed in the market. One is ushered into each room by the proprietor, who expatiates the while on the points of his wares, and the phenomenally low price he is asking for them. One may, if so disposed, prod them in the ribs, examine their teeth or otherwise satisfy oneself that they are sound in wind and limb, which their owner is usually prepared to guarantee if desired. It is not unusual, however, to warrant them free from vice – which would, moreover, merely have the effect of depreciating their value . . . The usual price of a female slave ranges from £20 to £100.[41]

Burton thought that Meccans were generally much darker than other Arabs of the Hijaz because of 'the number of female slaves that find their way to the market' and because 'most Meccans have black concubines'.[42]

Many poor students, particularly Indian and Malay, who wanted to settle in Mecca and study Islam ended up marrying slaves. Too poor to buy the freedom of their wives, their children were born in slavery and became the property of the woman's owner. 'A master may marry his slave,' writes Rutter, 'one to another, at his will. Frequently, the male slave of one owner was married to the female slave of another, and the offspring of the union was considered to belong to the woman's owner.'[43] Rutter discovered many ageing slaves in the city, freed or abandoned by their owners because they were no longer fit to work. 'Several of these poor creatures, some of them women, were living in the Haram during my stay in Mecca,' surviving on begging.[44]

Rutter had studied the Qur'an and was an expert in Islamic law. He could not reconcile the teachings of Islam with the prevalence of slavery in the Holy City. If the injunctions of Islam were 'rightly practised', he observed, it would lead to 'the complete cessation of slavery in the Islamic state . . . again and again, the Koran reiterates the teaching that one of the most acceptable acts in the sight of God is the liberation of a slave. In an ideal Muslim community, therefore, slavery must soon cease to exist.'[45] Churchward was given a bath by several black Sudanese slaves immediately after his arrival in the city and was appalled to discover that two-thirds of the resident population of Mecca were in bondage. Having studied at the famous Al-Azhar University in Cairo, he was able to put the Islamic case against slavery quite strongly to his Meccan friends and acquaintances, but his objections were brushed aside: 'all of them thought it a perfectly natural and harmless institution'.[46] Lady Cobbold was equally astonished to see that every household in Mecca had several slaves. While arguing that Islam does not permit slavery, she tried to underplay the tradition by pointing out that the slaves themselves seem 'perfectly happy' with their lot. They were mostly treated as part of the family. 'One jet-black old lady is a great character and rules the roost. I saw her try to box the ear of Abdullah, a youth who is twice her size, so he lifted her off the ground and kissed her, when she ran away laughing and shaking with a withered finger.'[47]

Stories about the ignorance and prevalence of superstitions in Mecca abound in all accounts. In cases of sickness, Rutter reports, Meccans believe that the most effective treatment is to write a verse from the Qur'an on a piece of paper, soak the paper in water until the ink is washed off, and then drink the inky water. While in Mecca, Rutter witnessed an eclipse of the moon. Most of the city rushed to offer special payers for the eclipse. After the lengthy prayers, he was asked: 'Which is brighter? Your moon in Damascus, or this our moon?' 'The moon is one,' he replies. 'This moon which we see here is the same moon which the Syrians see, and the Egyptians, and the Indians, and all the world.' When his answer was dismissed, Rutter tried to convince the Meccans by providing evidence from the Qur'an. In the Qur'an, he told them, 'we find Chapter *The Moon*. Had there been more than one moon, would not this have been called Chapter *A Moon* or Chapter *The Moons*?'[48] After some discussion, the Qur'anic confirmation was finally accepted.

By a strange coincidence, Churchward arrived in Mecca when Halley's Comet was visible in the sky – indeed, he could easily see it against the roofline of his guest house. The Meccans thought he was an exceptionally lucky man 'to have come with such a star'. Churchward suggested that it was purely a coincidence. 'Men can calculate when a comet becomes due.' His answer elicited an angry response. He was told to repent. 'It is a work of God and you must not say that people know when it is coming.'[49]

Churchward also relates the story of an Indian pilgrim who brought a phonograph to Mecca with the aim of earning some money to pay for his pilgrimage. He placed the instrument in the Bazaar and started to play a few tunes. A crowd gathered, and the Indian pilgrim asked for some donations for the pleasure of listening. But to his shock the crowd turned on him. 'Evil spirits have entered the City of God,' they shouted. The phonograph was confiscated; the pilgrim arrested and marched to the *qadi*. He was asked to provide a demonstration. The pilgrim played a religious song in praise of the Prophet, hoping that it would impress the judge, but the *qadi* was disturbed, and a little afraid of the musical instrument. 'It is against the rules of Mecca to possess such devices,' he thundered. The *qadi* called for a hammer, and in the presence of a large crowd, the talking machine was smashed to pieces. The pilgrim received a severe sentence.[50]

But the Meccans could not keep technology at bay. Soon the onslaught of technology would transform their city beyond recognition.

10

Mecca Under the Saudis

By the time he died in 1953, King Abdul Aziz ibn Saud had introduced noticeable trappings of modernity in Mecca. As had happened so often in the past, the Holy City's new overlords had stamped their imprint. However, the new rulers, unlike the sharifs, came without ties of blood or lineage to Mecca. Both would in time become the main tools through which the House of Saud would exert control.

The changes ushered in by King Abdul Aziz had less to do with a return to tradition or accommodation of modernity than with fidelity to the Wahhabi worldview.[1] In future the fate of the Holy City would be determined by the complex and frequently contradictory relations between the House of Saud and its expanding oil wealth, and the Wahhabi clerics that helped to confer legitimacy on the ruling family. At the outset, despite the assurances of Abdul Aziz and protests from other Muslim countries, all the mausoleums in the city, including those of the Prophet's family, were demolished. Sufi shrines, for which the Wahhabis had a particular hatred, were bulldozed. The curriculum in schools was radically changed: only the books of Muhammad ibn Abd al-Wahhab and some traditional literature could be taught.

The discovery of oil in Saudi Arabia in March 1938 initiated a major development programme in the Kingdom, and Mecca benefited from the new-found wealth. At the same time the city became zealously puritanical and its religious diversity virtually disappeared. Ironically, the character of Mecca as the metropolis of Islam was actually enhanced. There was an influx of new settlers from else-where in the Middle East, most notably Egyptians, Hadramis from Yemen, people from Central Asia, and a further increase in its resi-dent population of Malays and Indonesians. The Saudis, however, considered themselves superior to all others and looked down on all non-Wahhabi inhabitants of the city as lesser and inferior Muslims.

Abdul Aziz was succeeded by his son, Saud, the designated crown prince, who ruled from 1953 to 1964. Saud lacked the political and administrative skills of his father. His squandering of the Kingdom's wealth generated resentment and feuds within the royal family. To consolidate his position, he went on a spending spree to buy the loyalty of certain tribes, and built an immense army of palace sentries known as 'the White army', since the guards wore traditional Arab dress instead of military uniform. Saud's troubled and strife-ridden reign is known for only one thing: the first Saudi extension to the Sacred Mosque.

The influx of Saudis from the rest of the country increased the population of the Holy City. It now had a settled population of 150,000. During the pilgrim season, the city catered for 200,000 visi-tors, and found it hard to cope.[2] Travel to Mecca was becoming relatively easy. Most of the pilgrims now arrived by sea, disembarked at Jeddah, and used buses and cars to travel to Mecca as well as within the city and its sacred environment. The advent of air travel was about to swell these numbers dramatically. In 1953, Abdul Ghafur Sheikh, a student at Harvard Business School, was amongst the first to travel by this means, as he recorded in a cover story for the *National Geographic Magazine* entitled 'From America to Mecca on Airborne Pilgrimage'.[3] Soon chartered flights were bringing in more and more pilgrims. It was evident that the existing Sacred Mosque had to be enlarged to cater for the surge in their numbers.

The decision to expand the Mosque was originally taken by King Abdul Aziz himself. He appointed his son Faisal to undertake and supervise the task, which began in 1956. It was carried out in four phases. During the initial stage, work was concentrated around the hills of Safa and Marwah. Nearby houses were demolished, the area where the pilgrims ran between the two hills was paved, a barrier added to separate pilgrims travelling in opposite directions, and a second storey was added making it possible for pilgrims to perform this ritual on two levels. The Sacred Mosque was opened up with new doorways and entrances: eight doorways on the ground floor on the eastern façade overlooking the main road, and two entrances to the first floor on the side of the Haram, one each at Safa and Marwah, were added. The Mosque itself was paved with white marble. A new and even bigger doorway was added during the second phase, from 1961 to 1969. The wide entrance gateway, which enclosed three existing smaller doors, was named after the new ruler – the King Saud Gate.[4]

King Saud was deposed by Faisal in 1964, as soon as the new gate in his honour adorned the Sacred Mosque. Faisal, a charismatic and highly accomplished administrator, continued the work of expanding the Sacred Mosque.

During the third phase of the first extension, houses on the western side of the Sacred Mosque were demolished to make way for a new western arcade. In the fourth and final phase, two new minarets were built and all the gates of the Sacred Mosque were renovated in a similar style to give the building some visual coherence. The Haram area had now been expanded sixfold and had seven minarets and two balconies with parapets. Pilgrims could be transported rapidly from Jeddah via a new four-lane highway to Mecca; they could move on to Muna and Arafat via new roads and flyovers. In the Jamarat, where the pilgrims stoned the Devils, a two-storey arrangement was built to enable more pilgrims to perform the ritual.

When the African-American activist Malik al-Shabazz, better known as Malcolm X, performed the Hajj in April 1964, it took him only a couple of hours to travel from Jeddah to the Sacred Mosque in Mecca by car. At first he faced difficulty with immigration officials who wanted proof that he had genuinely converted to Islam, but once this little matter was cleared up he was treated as an honoured guest of Faisal. 'A well-lighted, modern turnpike highway made the trip easy.' When he entered Mecca, he found it 'as ancient as time itself. Our car slowed through the winding streets, lined by shops on both sides and with buses, cars and trucks, and tens of thousands of pilgrims from all over the earth were everywhere.' He was thrilled to see the building work on the extension to the Sacred Mosque. 'When it is finished,' he wrote, it 'will surpass the architectural beauty of India's Taj Mahal.'[5]

Mecca may have looked 'ancient' but it had changed radically. The city had grown informally in all directions, and new buildings appeared wherever there was space within the mountainous natural barriers. New quarters had been constructed on its western, eastern and southern borders, mainly to house pilgrim guides and to offer low-cost lodgings to the pilgrims. Noticeably there were few high-rise buildings which, many citizens argued, would violate the sanctity of the Sacred Mosque and the Kaaba. Indeed, regulations had been introduced to limit the height of the buildings in the Holy City. New houses had to adopt a vernacular architectural style and form in keeping with the heritage of Mecca. The new buildings had whitewashed walls with lattice screens and windows both to preserve privacy and to trap cool air in hot and humid Mecca. The area around the Sacred Mosque was restricted to pedestrians. There were even plans to renovate the remaining historical buildings and cultural property (mainly old mosques), preserve the urban environment and open spaces, and control development in the city to ensure continuity and compatibility with tradition and heritage. Mecca never looked better: a cosmopolitan metropolis that was both 'ancient' and 'modern'.

But Faisal had much bigger ambitions. He saw the Holy City as a symbol of Muslim unity and Saudi Arabia as the hub of the Muslim world. To reform the international Muslim community – the *ummah* – Saudi Arabia itself had to change and modernize. As soon as he took the reins of the Kingdom, he announced a ten-point plan for reform. The Kingdom would have a new constitution, an independent judiciary with both secular and religious judges, power would be devolved to local government, and there would be a string of social reforms including provisions for social security, unemployment benefit, and free education for both men and women. Faisal's first act of reform was, at long last, to abolish slavery in 1962.

In the same year Faisal organized a major international conference in Mecca of Muslim leaders. Delegates from a number of countries gathered to hear him argue for more cooperation and solidarity amongst Muslims. More especially, the king wanted to establish a Muslim organization on the model of the United Nations. Now he embarked on an extensive tour of Muslim capitals to rally support for an Islamic Summit that would bring 'the supreme powers in the Islamic world to discuss Muslim affairs and by God's will, take decisions in their interest'.[6] Faisal wanted the Islamic Summit to be held in Mecca in 1965, but the Summit actually took place, after the disaster of the 1967 Arab–Israeli war, in September 1969 – in Rabat, Morocco. The permanent Secretariat of the OIC, Organization of Islamic Cooperation (later changed to Organization of Islamic Conference and since renamed to its original title), was established in Jeddah in 1970. Despite all his efforts, Faisal could not bring the Second Islamic Summit Conference to Mecca either – it was held in February 1974 in Lahore, Pakistan. Indeed, the passionate and captivating Faisal, who had become the most popular leader in the Muslim world of his time, did not live to see his dream realized.

In March 1975, King Faisal was assassinated by a nephew in an apparently isolated act of revenge. He was sitting in open court receiving visitors and citizens who had come to petition. The murderer, Prince Faisal bin Musaid, the son of the king's half-brother, walked calmly to the monarch. As the king leaned to kiss him on his cheeks, the prince shot him twice. His successor and younger brother, King Khalid, buried Faisal's reforms along with him.

Khalid was more interested in falcons than in ruling the Kingdom, and during his tenure from 1975 to 1982 the country was effectively ruled by Crown Prince Fahd, an extreme modernizer, with a particular dislike for things that looked old, traditional and ancient. Conservation was an idea as alien to the new king as paganism. He wanted Mecca to look ultramodern, like a typical American city – Houston, Texas, for example. A fitting choice: one hub of an oil state designed to resemble another. And it is hard not to see parallels with *Dallas*, the American television series that launched in 1978 and became a global cult, with all the twists and turns of its machinations, family intrigue, the curious interweaving of nouveau riche glitz and glamour with a certain unschooled old-fashioned homeliness – the Ewings for all their wealth lived in one house. But outside everything in Dallas city had to look new, big, high-tech, and advertise modernity as loudly as possible.

In the same way, Mecca began to change rapidly. Ugly high-rise buildings, spaghetti junctions and high-mast lighting appeared overnight. The little that remained of historic value in the city was bulldozed. Planning restrictions were eased, property speculators moved in with the inevitable consequence of urban decay and severe social problems. The holiest city of Islam was now ugly, noisy, dirty, smelly, and crowded with modern architecture that was as appalling as it was out of human scale. There were virtually no green areas in the city – trees were conspicuous by their absence, and the few landscaped areas lacked imagination. The entire city was handed over to cars, with virtually no provision for pedestrians. And there was a new god in town: money. The Holy City seemed to be consumed by the new-found oil wealth. Mecca had indeed been transformed, almost overnight; it was modern, but without redeeming qualities. Only the beauty of the Kaaba in the Sacred Mosque and the solace and community spirit of Mecca's villages on the outskirts gave a glimpse of what the city had been like just a couple of years earlier.

Not surprisingly, enlightened established citizens of Mecca, who had lived there for generations, were concerned about their city. The young felt alienated by what was happening around them. Senior citizens lamented the loss of their neighbourhoods and the ties that bound them – the traditional communal activities, economic patterns and architecture.[7] The established families of the city traced their ancestry to the sharifs of Mecca, and beyond to the Prophet Muhammad, and were proud of being Hijazis, people of the Hijaz. They considered themselves to be, and indeed were, quite different from the Najdis, people from the northern province of Najd, the homeland of the Saudi rulers. The far-reaching economic, social and religious changes ushered in by the Wahhabis had altered their status and identity. The Hijazis liked music and *malud*, the celebration of the Prophet's birthday, and leaned towards Sufism, drawing on an urban tradition of religious mysticism.[8] These things were anathema to the Najdi puritans, and the Hijazis were forced to hold their traditional ceremonies in secret within the four walls of their homes. Their honoured traditional occupations had now become redundant; even their religious scholars had been usurped by the State. They felt marginalized and oppressed. They despised the uncouth Najdi families that had taken over the city and risen to prominence through access to oil money. For the Hijazis, Mecca was not just the centre of Islam, it was also a source of their identity. Its cultural heritage and sophisticated traditional architecture were intimately connected to their genealogies, essential to their survival as Hijazis. During the more enlightened reign of King Faisal, in the 1960s and 1970s, they had engineered a small boom in traditional architecture and built many magnificent traditional Hijazi houses and buildings, mixing the Hashemite style with old Turkish, Egyptian and Moorish designs. All this was now threatened. Hushed murmurs spread through the city: the Sanctuary had to be saved from the onslaught of rampant development, and the obsession with technology and modernity of the despised Najdis.

But few had the courage or the ability to do anything. The sole exception was Sami Angawi, a Meccan architect from a distinguished Hijazi merchant family. He was educated in Britain and in the United States, and was passionately devoted to the traditional architecture and cultural property of the Holy City. Angawi oozed charm, and many in Mecca saw him as the undeclared leader of the Hijaz. When I first met him in 1974, he reminded me of Faisal, son of Sharif Hussain, as played by Omar Sharif in David Lean's *Lawrence of Arabia*, the character who ultimately becomes the moral conscience of the film in his nuanced reflections on the challenge of change. Angawi believed that the indiscriminate use of technology was radically transforming Mecca. Astronomical sums of money were being poured into making Mecca look like Houston, where many of the government ministers had spent time pursuing higher studies. There was a 'Master Plan of the Holy City of Mecca',[9] but it was never adhered to as a guide for developers, and Western consultants were producing ever more grandiose plans of a damaging nature. If implemented, these plans would level the mountains, introduce skyscrapers, and rip apart the very fabric of the Sacred City. The challenge facing Mecca, Angawi declared, was to synthesize tradition and modernity, and thus to 'fit the variables into the constants'.[10] That task, he concluded, could only be accomplished through 'interdisciplinary research'.

Angawi formed an alliance with another Hijazi, Abdullah Naseef. He had just returned from Britain after completing a PhD in geology and landed the job of secretary-general of the King Abdul Aziz University in Jeddah. Naseef belonged to a distinguished Jeddah family of scholars and merchants. His grandfather, Omar Naseef Effendi, had been the governor of Jeddah when Sharif Abdullah ibn Aun and his various successors from the Aun family ruled Mecca during the second half of the nineteenth century. Effendi was a passionate bibliophile and spent most of his life collecting precious manuscripts and rare books. To accommodate his collection of 6,000 volumes, he built a magnificent house in the Ottoman style right in the centre of Jeddah on its main street, Suq al-Alawi. With 106 rooms, numerous halls, elaborate and intricate woodwork, and exquisite *rawashins* (traditional bay windows), the house took almost a decade to build; it was completed in 1881. Effendi himself was not a scholar, but he made sure that his orphaned nephew, Muhammad Naseef, whom he looked after from the age of three, immersed himself in scholarly pursuits. Muhammad Naseef grew up to be a noted scholar of religion, law and linguistics. In his later years, after the death of his uncle, he withdrew from public life and devoted most of his time to managing the book collection, which had grown to 16,000 volumes. By now Naseef House had become an intellectual and social magnet, a rendezvous for scholars, intellectuals and artists.[11] King Abdul Aziz stayed at the house when he first entered Jeddah in December 1925.

Like Mecca, Jeddah too had been transformed by rampant and uncontrolled development. Numerous traditional buildings, characterized by their carved doors of teak wood and ornate verandas and bay windows, became victims of the bulldozers. There was, however, an intense campaign to save Naseef House as the symbolic representative of Old Jeddah. In 1975, Muhammad Naseef turned it into a public library. This act and Muhammad Naseef's own reputation saved the historic building, together with the magnificent centuries-old tree, the only one in Jeddah inside a house, that adorns the courtyard of Naseef House.

Abdullah Naseef was thus a natural ally for Sami Angawi. Both had a passion for conservation and traditional architecture, and were determined to save Mecca from the onslaught of naked modernity. Angawi established the Hajj Research Centre in September 1974, and Naseef invited him to locate it at the King Abdul Aziz University in Jeddah. Six months later, at the request of Angawi and Naseef, who had become a friend from my student days, I joined the Centre and moved to Jeddah.

We functioned as a semi-autonomous unit within the University. Or at least we thought we did. But the University bureaucracy, which consisted largely of Najdis, resented both Naseef and Angawi; they saw the Centre as an illegal Hijazi enclave. Almost every bureaucratic hurdle imaginable was thrown at the Centre and its half a dozen researchers. But motivated by a higher goal – to save Mecca from destruction – we persevered. We collected data on the history and cultural property of Mecca, its traditional neighbourhoods and social structures, its geography and geology, its urban problems and new buildings, and on every aspect of the Hajj from pilgrim accommodation to movements, congestion to pollution, health issues to supplies of provisions. We photographed, filmed (documentary, aerial and infrared) and documented almost everything in the Holy City and the Hajj environment. And we made a computer simulation model of the city and the Hajj.

Our research showed that Mecca was really a conglomerate of village units that were either nestling in the small valleys or were perched on mountain tops. Behind the façade of a metropolis, Mecca functioned as a network of villages. It provided the economic opportunities of a big city and the social security of a village. And our interrogation of the Master Plan for the Holy City of Mecca pointed to a single, unavoidable conclusion: it would destroy the unique patchwork character of the Holy City, level its contours, flatten its hills and mountains, and marginalize its inhabitants in favour of the car. The Centre stressed that two features inherent in the Holy City, 'the quality of beauty' and 'the quality of timelessness', would disappear under the onslaught of 'modern planning'. 'Large ugly buildings would flourish in a concrete jungle fed by the fertilizer of greed.'[12] No one seemed to understand that Mecca had natural boundaries, that it could not go on growing indefinitely. On the contrary, various government bodies involved in the development of the city, along with their Western consultants (who could not actually visit the Sanctuary and had to imagine it from a distance), had no notion of limits to growth. We feared not just for the natural environment of the Holy areas and the erasure of its history, but also for its inhabitants. Our research showed that family units and associations necessary for social and psychological security would be broken, mental illness would increase and the traditional characteristics of the Hijazis would disintegrate. Mecca would become an inhuman concrete jungle where grotesque steel and glass buildings would jostle for attention.

There were also urgent and immediate problems. The number of international pilgrims coming to perform the Hajj had increased fourfold within two decades – from around 200,000 in the late 1950s to over 800,000 in the mid-1970s.[13] Add the local pilgrims to these figures, and the number crossed the million mark. Our projections suggested that the next decade would see pilgrim numbers rise to 2 million. There were immense health and safety issues in accommodating and moving such numbers rapidly from one ritual point to another. This became quite evident in 1975, when 200 pilgrims were killed in Mina's tent camps in a fire that started when a gas cylinder exploded; it happened during my first Hajj, while we were engaged in a field-research exercise at the site.

During the 1976 Hajj, I recorded that it took, on average, over nine hours for a pilgrim to travel by bus from Mina to Arafat – a distance of less than nine miles. Parts of Mecca, most of Mina and the area around Arafat were in permanent gridlock. The air was so foul that it was difficult to breathe. We calculated that 80 tonnes of exhaust fumes were being generated during the peak period every day.[14] The lethal effects of exhaust fumes, heat and exhaustion were all too evident: I saw a number of people collapse and die. Some 800,000 sheep, goats and camels were being sacrificed; one could walk for miles on top of the carcasses.[15] The slaughterhouse area was blocked with pile upon pile of carcasses and it was not possible for workers to get in; emergency gates had to be opened with bulldozers. It took days to bury the carcasses in prepared pits. People were falling off the bridges in the Jamarat area, where the Devils are stoned – but fortunately no one was killed that year.

It was obvious to the Hajj Research Centre team that major disasters were probable during the Hajj if the current situation continued. Indeed, thanks to our computer models, we could visually demonstrate what could happen in the Jamarat area, inside the Sacred Mosque, to pollution and traffic congestion if the trends persisted. We recommended that fireproof tents should be introduced at once, and shaded pedestrian areas built where the pilgrims could sit and rest. And, where possible, everyone should be encouraged to walk to Mina, Arafat and Muzdalifah. We asked for the use of private vehicles to be banned except for emergency and essential services. The Centre also urged the government 'to freeze all demolition and construction projects because of their far reaching and irreversible character'.[16] Beyond that we had a highly developed critique of the Master Plan and a host of alternative policies and methods for more environmentally friendly ways of developing Mecca and the Hajj environment. The Saudi government paid scant heed to our proposals. The Centre, and its persistent director, Sami Angawi, were seen as an irritating boil that had to be lanced – sooner rather than later.

Meanwhile, the Kingdom was distracted by more immediate issues. Islam was nearly 1,400 years old and arrangements were being made to mark the arrival of the new century with suitable celebration. In Mecca there was a great deal of talk about 'Islamic revival'. The beginning of Islam's fifteenth century, it was being suggested in Muslim intellectual circles, would herald the return of Islam as a force in world affairs and as a power in Muslim societies. The Saudis would be in the driving seat, ready to fuel the resurgence with their petrodollars. Mecca might have failed to hold an Islamic Summit, but it had now become the capital of Muslim conferences. In 1976, the city was host to the First International Conference on Islamic Economics, which established the newly emerging discipline of 'Islamic economics' and later led to the formation of a host of Islamic banks, financial institutions and Islamic economics departments in universities throughout the world.[17] The following year, the city was welcoming the delegates to the First World Conference on Muslim Education.[18] This led directly to the formation of an Islamic Academy in Cambridge, UK, and generated an international debate on how higher education could be infused with Islam. I attended both conferences, the first as an observer, the second as a participant. Numerous other conferences on a whole range of subjects were planned, and vigorous efforts were being made to bring the main Islamic Summit of heads of state to Mecca. Preachers and teachers from Mecca were dispatched to mosques and universities all over the world to spread the message of Wahhabism and to help usher in a revival of Islam. And where clerics were unable to go, hundreds of millions of Wahhabi books and pamphlets were showered like confetti in their place.

Early in the afternoon of Wednesday 19 November 1979, on the eve of the new Islamic century, I travelled from Jeddah to Mecca to visit the campus of Umm al-Qura University. It was the first Saudi institution of higher education to be established in the Holy City, set up as a College of Islamic Law in 1949 by King Abdul Aziz. Umm al-Qura was loosely attached to King Abdul Aziz University. A royal decree had just been issued announcing that, within a year or two, it would become an independent university in its own right and all ties to Jeddah would be severed. That was a cause of concern for us; we feared that the Hajj Research Centre too would be absorbed by this ultra-conservative institution. A shrewd move, we thought, to domesticate and zip the voice of dissent.

After I finished my brief business at Umm al-Qura, I walked towards the Sacred Mosque to join my colleagues from the Centre. We planned to measure the flow of worshippers around the Kaaba. There was a joyous atmosphere and the streets and alleyways of Mecca were so crowded that it was difficult to negotiate one's way. Many inhabitants of the city, who normally avoided going to the

Sacred Mosque during festivals because of overcrowding, were making their way towards it. Inside the Mosque was jam-packed. Not surprising, we thought, given that the Hajj had only finished ten days ago and it was the eve of Islam's fifteenth century. However, the presence of a curiously large contingent of students from Medina University holding meetings in the compound was a bit unusual. We knew them well. During the Hajj seasons, we would employ hundreds of them to collect data for our research. We joked about them, their irrational beliefs and obscurantist views, and carried on with our work. I stayed to offer the evening prayer and then left to spend the night in the house of a friend, on the outskirts of the city. Most of the congregation remained in the Sacred Mosque, reading the Qur'an all night.

The following morning, I was looking for a taxi to return to Jeddah when I noticed an armed vehicle speeding towards the Sacred Mosque. I could also hear gunshots coming from the direction of the Mosque. I ran there to see what was happening, only to be stopped by a cordon of policemen. They were instructing everyone to leave the area immediately and get as far away as possible. A group of heavily armed men had taken over the Sacred Mosque and trapped over 100,000 worshippers inside. Mecca was under siege.

By the time I got back to Jeddah, all communication links to the Kingdom were cut off. Saudi Arabia is a police state and bad news is buried quickly and permanently. There was a total blackout and no one had any idea what was happening. Jeddah was full of rumours. Mecca was under attack by Zionist and American imperialist plotters, said some. The Sacred Mosque had been taken over by renegade Shia from Ayatollah Khomeini's Iran, others speculated. A third theory postulated a split in the royal family, with Crown Prince Fahd's men trying to overthrow King Khalid.

Outraged Muslims held violent demonstrations at the desecration of their sacred city in front of American and European embassies in various Muslim capitals. In Islamabad, six people were killed when a mob of 20,000 stormed the American embassy. Militant crowds demonstrated outside the embassies in Turkey, Bangladesh and India.

When the truth began to emerge it was even more unsettling. A five-kilometre ring of roadblocks was set up around the Mosque. People living within the circle were asked to leave, and tens of thousands of pilgrims were airlifted to Jeddah. We were able to piece together a rough story of what was happening by talking to eyewitnesses, residents and pilgrims who had come from Mecca.

Gunshots were first heard in the Haram area immediately after the early morning prayer was completed. Hundreds of Bedouins brought out sub-machine guns, rifles and revolvers concealed beneath their robes and fired into the air. The insurgents used coffins to smuggle a huge cache of arms and ammunition inside the Mosque and were carrying, we heard, 'mostly Kalashnikov assault rifles' of Soviet manufacture and 'Israeli-made Uzis'. The armed guards within the Mosque, posted on each of the main doors and by the side of the Kaaba near the Black Stone, were outnumbered and quickly overpowered. Three were shot dead. The insurgents took over the Sacred Mosque, and announced that 'the Mahdi' (redeemer) had arrived to purify Islam. Their leader demanded that the imam and the clerics inside must recognize and accept him as the Mahdi, and read out his denunciations of the royal family's corruption and religious deviation. His demand was rejected. The insurgents bolted all thirty-nine doors to the Mosque from inside and started shooting, killing at least a dozen civilians and a cleric. The trapped pilgrims panicked; some were able to escape through narrow holes in the walls of the Mosque. Once the panic had subsided, the insurgents permitted the foreign pilgrims to leave freely. They urged the Saudis to remain in the Mosque but made no attempt to restrain them. By late afternoon, the compound of the Sacred Mosque was clear and the insurgents had taken up positions on the minarets and the covered arches of the upper gallery.

They were led by a Bedouin preacher, Juhayman al-Uteybi, and his brother-in-law, the twenty-seven-year-old Muhammad Abdullah Qahtani, the alleged Mahdi. The rebels included Egyptians, Pakistanis and American converts, but most were Saudi from the Oteiba tribe. This tribe had actively supported King Abdul Aziz in his wars against the Rashidi emirs in the capture of Riyadh in 1902. After Saudi Arabia was established, the Oteiba were largely employed as royal security guards, a highly prestigious post, and lavished with royal subsidies. By 1930, however, they were already rebelling against the Saudi family. The Saudi Wahhabi reforms were not Wahhabi enough for the Oteiba tribe. Now they saw the royal family as utterly corrupt, the state as promoting heresies, the religious scholars as collaborating with the royal family in spreading immoral practices, and Saudi Arabia as a Kingdom obsessed with money and consumerism. In particular, they saw the modernization of Saudi Arabia and the holy cities of Mecca and Medina, promoted by the royal family, as sacrilegious. The Oteiba were as puritanical as the Kharijites in the early history of Mecca and as vehement as the Qarmatians of the tenth century. Moreover, modernization threatened the nomadic lifestyle of their Bedouin tribe.

Juhayman and his band were followers of the blind scholar Sheikh ibn Baz (1910–99). Ibn Baz, a major architect of contemporary Saudi Wahhabism, held several influential positions. He was appointed vice president of the Islamic University of Medina in 1961, and went on to become its president and chancellor. He was the chair of presidency for Scientific Research and Religious Edicts (Dar al-Ifta), the Kingdom's main institution for issuing fatwas. He went on to become, in 1992, grand mufti of Saudi Arabia and head of the Council of Senior Scholars. At the Islamic University of Medina he indoctrinated thousands of students with his firebrand puritanism. More devout followers were invited to desert retreats for special attention – Juhayman was one of them. I would frequently encounter ibn Baz in the Sacred Mosque. He would always be surrounded by his students – ushering him from place to place, kissing his hand, and lauding him with praise. Frequent conversations with the students convinced me that they were, without exception, irrational zealots. Largely tribal people, they had replaced fierce tribal loyalty with loyalty to their brand of Islam. And Islam, as far as they were concerned, was how they defined it – with greater emphasis on rather dubious and historically questionable traditions of the Prophet Muhammad than on the teachings of the Qur'an. They saw themselves as the only authentic guardians and defenders of Islam. Everyone outside the bounds of their sacred territory was, by definition, an unbeliever and hostile to Islam. This included the Shia, the Sufi mystics and liberal folks like me. The students would often tell me that my association with unbelievers was nothing but apostasy. That the students from Medina University would eventually do something drastic was taken for granted by myself and my colleagues. It was indeed as if history was repeating itself as lethal parody.

The Saudi authorities were slow to realize what had happened. It was only when the first batch of police and security officials were gunned down that the state moved reluctantly into action. National guardsmen were summoned, but even backed by tanks and a helicopter their first efforts were unsuccessful. The insurgents had occupied prime sites on the nine minarets of the Mosque and were able to pick off anyone who approached the site. Army marksmen targeted the snipers in the minarets, but fears of damaging the Sacred Mosque limited the counter-assault. A number of assaults, involving police, National Guard and the army, ended in bloodbaths.

In dealing with this act of insurrection the authorities showed not only that they were totally incompetent, but shockingly that they had no architectural plans of the Sacred Mosque. The three security forces had different commands, did not trust each other, and were unable to communicate with each other as they used different radio systems. There were only two institutions in the whole of the Kingdom with detailed plans of the Mosque. One was the Bin Laden

Construction Company, which enjoyed a close relationship with the royal family, and had built the new extension to the Sanctuary. The other was my own Hajj Research Centre. For the past four years we had measured, calibrated and photographed almost every inch of the Mosque. At considerable risk to himself, Sami Angawi, our director, delivered the plans to the frontline troops.

The original strategy was to starve the insurgents out, but on the night of Saturday 22 November 1979 King Khalid ordered his National Guard to take the Mosque. One of the gates was identified as the entry point for this new offensive. It was blown up with a massive charge of explosives. Paratroopers, backed by armoured personnel carriers (APCs), stormed in only to walk into an ambush. Another bloodbath ensued. It seemed that the insurgents had an answer to whatever the army threw at them. Even blowing up the minarets of the Mosque did not help much. Eventually, using heavy artillery and scores of APCs, the army and the National Guard fought their way, step by bloody step, to the centre of the compound, where the Kaaba is located. Qahtani, the self-claimed Mahdi, who fought with exceptional daring, was killed.

This victory, however, was only partial. The rebels retreated to the Mosque's underground section. Known as the Qaboo, it is a labyrinth of rooms and alleys, a mini-city where the insurgents had stowed the bulk of their weapons. Once again, the army's attempt to enter proved futile and deadly.

After a week of horrendous bloody combat, it was clear that the Saudis needed help. They turned to their foremost allies: the US and the CIA. In his painstakingly researched account of *The Siege of Mecca*,[19] the investigative journalist Yaroslav Trofimov reports that a host of CIA operatives were quickly converted to Islam, so that they could enter the Holy City and assess the battlefield for themselves. It was decided to use chemical warfare. Potent tear gas was pumped into the Qaboo through its various entrances, but the exercise turned to fiasco. Hardened rebel fighters were able to shield themselves with mattresses, cardboard and cloth and prevented the gas spreading into narrow underground corridors. Their water-soaked headdresses protected their breathing. The gas had a natural tendency to rise and came up into the compound of the Mosque. The Saudi soldiers were ill prepared to use gas masks. Equipped with generous facial hair, their bushy beards prevented the masks from sealing on the skin. The gas seeped through their beards and knocked out a large contingent. Then it made its way to the surrounding areas – so the remaining inhabitants of Mecca had to be evacuated.

The grapevine in Jeddah suggested that the Qaboo was eventually flooded and the rebels who escaped drowning were forced to the surface and captured. But Trofimov discovered that the Saudis were forced to call on the French Foreign Legion. According to his account, Paris dispatched Captain Paul Barril, a mercenary commando with expertise in such situations, on a 'provost mission' to the Kingdom. Barril recommended another dose of gas – indeed, a whole ton of CS gas, enough to poison a small city. However, the entire French stock of CS gas came only to 300 kilograms, so the operation was limited to this amount. This time the gas was to be used with a particular cunning. Countless holes were bored from the surface of the compound right down to the Qaboo, and the gas pumped in through these holes. At the same time, battalions of the army entered the Qaboo from two points, in a pincer movement. They succeeded in overpowering the insurgents and capturing Juhayman. It took two full weeks to liberate the Sacred Mosque.

Juhayman was tried in a religious court and brought in front of his teacher and mentor, Sheikh ibn Baz. The Mufti – who had provided the religious sanction for the military assault on the Sacred Mosque – sympathized with the insurgents. When their accusations were read out in full, he endorsed most of them. The insurgents were correct, he said, in pointing out that a true Wahhabi state should not associate with unbelievers, that heresies and deviation from pure Islam should be eliminated, that images of all kind were forbidden, and consumerism and worship of money had become the norm in Saudi Arabia. The Najdis in Mecca, and virtually all the religious establishment in Saudi Arabia, concurred. But the insurgents, ibn Baz declared, were wrong on two counts: in challenging the royal family and in announcing the arrival of the Mahdi. Like the Meccan judges of the past, there was only one decision he could reach: 'the judgement of God'. His judgement was duly carried out. Juhayman was publicly beheaded.[20]

Why did Juhayman, an arch-Sunni, claim that his brother-in-law was the Mahdi? While most Muslims loosely hold such beliefs, it is an article of faith for the Shia. The Mahdi is supposed to be the long-lost Twelfth Imam, who disappeared in 869, and will reappear sometime in the future as the ultimate saviour of humanity. Perhaps it was a kind of millenarian fever, which gave rise to such fervour to coincide with the beginning of the fifteenth century of Islam, that led Juhayman to hold such a belief. But it was this claim that initially led many in Mecca, and more broadly in Saudi Arabia, to suspect that Shia militants, eager to spread their revolution, were behind the siege of the Sacred Mosque. The timing also suggested a Shia conspiracy. The Shia mourn the death of the Prophet's grandson Hussain at Kerbala in Iraq during the first ten days of the first month of the Islamic calendar. Indeed, the Saudis had been preparing for such an attempt, and arrested a group of Iranian pilgrims for distributing revolutionary pamphlets. A fleet of C-130 Hercules transport planes were on red alert in case the Saudi authorities were forced to ship out Shia agitators by the thousands. Even when the identity of the insurgents had become clear, many in Mecca continued to believe that the Iranian Shia were up to no good and that the age-old Shia–Sunni rivalry was coming to a head.

The Iranians did not take kindly to such slurs. Ayatollah Khomeini, the spiritual and political leader of the Iranian revolution, issued suitable retorts to early news bulletins suggesting the insurgents were Shia. The 1980 Hajj saw relatively few pilgrims from Iran, as war had broken out between Iraq and Iran. By 1981 the relationship between the Kingdom and the Islamic Republic had grown openly hostile. King Khalid urged Saddam Hussain to crush the Iranians. Iranian pilgrims retaliated by organizing a huge demonstration in front of the Sacred Mosque, where pro-revolution slogans were chanted. King Khalid wrote a letter to Ayatollah Khomeini suggesting that the Iranian pilgrims had defiled the sanctity of the Haram with their blasphemous slogans. While performing the circumambulation of the Kaaba, claimed the king, the Iranian pilgrims were chanting 'God is Great, Khomeini is Great'. This was a calculated attempt to portray the Shia as polytheists in the eyes of the Sunni world. In fact, the Iranian pilgrims were chanting 'God is Great, Khomeini is our leader'. In his reply, the Ayatollah asked a question for which the king had no reply. 'How is it', Khomeini wrote, 'that the Saudi police attack Muslims with jackboots and weapons, beat them, arrest them, and send them to prison from inside the Holy Mosque, a place which according to the teaching of God and the text of the Qur'an, is a refuge for all, even deviants?'[21] The mention of 'deviants' was clearly a reference to Juhayman and his followers.

There was little doubt that Iran saw the Hajj not just as a spiritual event but also a political one. Revolutionary Iran viewed the Saudis as corrupt and unfit to look after the holiest city of Islam. Tensions between Iran and Saudi Arabia dominated the Third Islamic Summit, which was finally held in Mecca in January 1981. However, the city, still recovering from the siege, was in no position to host a major event. After an opening session, the Summit was moved to the nearby city of Taif. Its final communiqué came to be known as the 'Mecca Declaration'; it urged 'solidarity' between brother Muslims, and asked them to 'overcome rifts and divisions and to settle in a peaceful manner all disputes that may arise amongst us on the basis of covenants and the principles of brotherhood, unity and inter-dependence'.[22] It had the intended effect, and for a time at least, it seemed the dispute over Mecca and the Hajj between Iran and Saudi Arabia had been resolved. The Ayatollah instructed Iranian pilgrims to pray behind the Sunni imams in the Sacred Mosque and temper their political activism. In return, the Saudis allowed these pilgrims to hold their demonstrations in specific places in Mecca, under their strict supervision and specific rules. The demonstrators could shout slogans against the US and Israel but not against other Muslim governments or their hosts. And they were not allowed to bring posters and propaganda material from Iran for distribution in Mecca. Both sides stuck to the agreement for the next few years.

The situation changed drastically in 1986, when the Saudi authorities caught a group of Iranian pilgrims, opposed to the modernization of Mecca and the destruction of cultural property, trying to smuggle large qualities of explosives in their suitcases. Over a hundred Iranian pilgrims were arrested. The Saudis were now convinced that the Iranians were plotting to take over the Sacred Mosque. The following year, 1987, Saudi security was on full alert. Armed soldiers virtually took over the city during the Hajj season. Every entrance to the Sacred Mosque was guarded and, for the first time, everyone entering the Sanctuary was subjected to a full body search. No one was allowed to take anything into the Mosque. On 31 July, the day when the Iranian demonstration was planned, the city woke up to a charged atmosphere. The residents expected something to happen.

The demonstration started in the afternoon with customary speeches and slogans. Then the demonstrators, led by women in black chadors, started to march; they were kept to the planned route by Saudi police and the National Guard. Towards the end of the route, the demonstrators met a cordon of police and soldiers who blocked their path and asked the protesters to turn back. The demonstrators demanded that the procession be allowed to enter the Sacred Mosque. While the exchanges between Iranian pilgrims and security forces were going on, someone started throwing bricks and stones towards the demonstrators. Their targets fought back. Skirmishes broke out between the police, who were armed with truncheons and electric prods, and the demonstrators, who grabbed whatever they could to fight back. For a moment it seemed that the Saudi police would not be able to contain the protesters, who surged forward like a tsunami. The police summoned reinforcements. Soon a fresh contingent of National Guards arrived and fired gas shells at the surging protesters. Then they opened fire. According to official Saudi figures – always to be taken with caution – 402 people were killed, including 275 Iranian pilgrims, 87 Saudi policemen and 42 pilgrims from other countries; 649 people were wounded.[23]

The carnage appalled Muslims everywhere. Both countries hurled insults at each other. The Saudis accused the Iranians of 'sedition' and defiling the Haram. The Iranians declared that Mecca was in the hands of 'a band of heretics', the 'evil clique' of 'Wahhabi hooligans' who would not stop to 'commit any crime'.[24] Both countries took their case to the broader Muslim public – in the time-honoured way. The Saudis organized a conference in Mecca in October 1987 and spent several hundred million dollars to fly over 600 of their support-ers – mostly first class – from all over the world. It was opened by King Fahd, who had come to power in June 1982 after the death of his brother. The well-paid delegates did not mince their words in condemning the Shia Iranians who fanned 'the fires of wickedness' and had become 'accustomed to terrorism and a thirst for Muslim blood'. The Iranians responded the following month with their own 'International Congress on Safeguarding the Sanctity and Security of the Great Mosque'. Their delegates called for the 'liberation' of Mecca from the 'claws of al-Saud', and an international Muslim alli-ance to govern the Holy City as an independent city-state.[25]

The Saudis now moved on to a second line of attack. They proposed that the number of Iranian pilgrims, running to around 150,000 per year and constituting the largest group, should be pruned to no more than 45,000. There was another genuine concern. By 1987 the number of international and local pilgrims had exceeded over a million. There was talk of a 'two million Hajj' within a decade. King rand, who styled himself 'Custodian of the Two Holy Mosques', thought that the problem of the escalating numbers of pilgrims, not solely the Iranians, could be solved at a stroke. The Saudis took their case to a meeting of the Organization of the Islamic Conference in Amman in March 1988. It was suggested that a quota system, pegged to each country's population, should be introduced to reduce the overall number of pilgrims performing the Hajj. Each country would be allowed to send one person per 1,000 of population in any given year. The Saudis at first saw this move as a three-year interlude, and argued that it would give them enough time to improve the facilities in Mecca and modernize the city. Even though they dominated the Organization, the Saudis did not control it totally. There was much debate and resistance from Iran and its supporters. But eventually the Saudis carried the day. Indeed, the quota system was adopted as a permanent feature of Hajj organization. Based on their 1988 population of 51 million, Iranian pilgrims were reduced to 50,000. The Iranians reacted by announcing a boycott of the pilgrimage. The Saudis closed their embassy in Tehran, making it impossible for any pilgrims from Iran to perform the Hajj. No pilgrims came from Iran between 1988 and 1990.

The dispute continued and took a few years to resolve – with both sides conceding considerable ground. Iranian pilgrims returned in 1991 but, under a special dispensation, their quota was allowed to increase to 115,000 by mutual agreement. However, mutual suspicion between Iran and Saudi Arabia continued to fester.

Throughout this period of discord between Saudi Arabia and Iran, the Saudis continued work on the Sacred Mosque. The initial priority was to repair the damage done by the siege of 1979. The Mosque's basic structure was intact and the Kaaba was untouched by the gunfire. But the Sai area – the long covered corridor that runs along one side of the Mosque, containing the area between the hills of Safa and Marwah – had sustained serious damage: many of the doors and the marble walls had to be repaired, and long rows of chandeliers had to be replaced. Five minarets were badly damaged and had to be rebuilt. The mosaics within the building were pockmarked with bullet holes and required extensive work, and the scores of priceless carpets from all over the world were so damaged that they had to be replaced. The repair work took just over a year.

Once the Mosque had been repaired, work started on the second Saudi extension in 1982, the year King Fahd came to power. Naturally the first item to be built was the King Fahd Gate, on the new wing of the western side of the Mosque. Another fourteen gates and entrances were added to the basement of the Mosque, along with three new domes and two new minarets, and the roof of the Mosque was modified so that worshippers could pray on top. Five escalators were located around the Sacred Mosque to take worshippers to the first floor and the roof. An outdoor prayer area, in white marble, was built next to the Mosque on the western side, sited at the bottom of Abu Qubays mountain.

The shining new Haram bore little resemblance to the historic building. It now had four main gates and fifty-four smaller doors, in addition to six entrances to the basement and more entrances to the second level. The Sacred Mosque could accommodate 820,000 worshippers on ordinary days and a million during the Hajj season. New roads and tunnels were built to take the pilgrims directly from the Haram to Mina and other sites of ritual.

While some of the recommendations of the Hajj Research Centre were accepted during the second extension, most of our worst fears were realized. Legislation was introduced banning private vehicles from the Hajj environment. Footways were built between Mina and Arafat, making this area one of the safest and pleasantest parts of the Hajj environment. But the Mosque and the accompanying palace were eyesores. It was grand, but it had none of the beauty that Malcolm X imagined.

Our Hajj Research Centre, which was finally given formal and legal recognition by King Fahd in 1980, vigorously opposed the building of tunnels. We argued that they were 'death traps': crowds of fervent pilgrims leaving the Sacred Mosque and surging through the tunnels towards Mina were bound to cause a fatal accident. It was as though football crowds from thirty major stadiums all left at once and simultaneously surged towards a bottleneck. As usual, the Centre's objections were brushed aside. The Saudis now embarked on a third extension of the Holy Sites.

It began during 1988, soon after the quota system was established, and continued till 2005. The Sacred Mosque was further extended, more minarets were added, and the Mosque was provided with air-conditioning for summer and heated floors for chilly nights. Muna, Arafat and Muzdalifah were also extensively developed. The Jamarat area was expanded from two to five storeys; it now consisted of a permanent structure 950 metres long, with eleven entry and twelve exit points, and the capacity to handle 300,000 pilgrims per hour. The Centre had always considered the Jamarat area as a black spot, and saw the new extension as a major accident waiting to happen. When the third extension was completed in 2005, King Fahd, obsessed with building palaces, could look down on the Kaaba from the bedroom of his new residence in Mecca. The palace was located on the eastern side and overshadowed the whole of the Sacred Mosque. For security reasons, the historic Bilal Mosque, dating back to the time of the Prophet Muhammad, adjacent to the palace, was demolished. The development took care to ensure that the king had a full view of the worshippers in the compound of the Haram; hence no minarets were built facing the palace. However, the king spent little time in his new place, as he died in the same year.

By now the hazardous nature of the ill-conceived grandiose developments in Mecca were becoming obvious as a series of major accidents broke out. In 1990, 1,426 pilgrims died during a stampede inside the Al-Ma'aisim tunnel.[26] As pilgrims were making their way from the Haram to Mina, a power failure cut the air-conditioning and lighting system of the tunnel. The pilgrims panicked, thousands were trapped inside and suffocated to death. The tunnels were closed. The next major accident, not surprisingly, was in the Jamarat area: here 270 pilgrims were trampled to death in 1994. Indeed, it is not unusual for crowds to surge and pilgrims to be crushed or trampled, or ramps to collapse under the overwhelming weight of multitudes, at the Jamarat, and accidents have occurred with mundane regularity: 118 people died from overcrowding in 1998, 35 were crushed to death in 2001, 14 died in 2003, 251 in 2004, 346 in 2006. During the last accident, pilgrims were killed when a pilgrim bus discharged its passengers on the eastern access ramps to the Jamarat Bridge. The pilgrims emerging from the bus rushed towards 'the Satans' – the symbolic masonry pillars – tripped, and caused a lethal crush. The same year, the Al Ghaza Hotel, located near the Sacred Mosque, collapsed. An estimated seventy-six pilgrims who were staying in the hotel, or eating at its restaurant and shopping at its convenience store, were killed. The Jamarat area was redeveloped after each accident, but the basic design, and hence the risks, remained the same.

I left Saudi Arabia and the Hajj Research Centre towards the end of 1979, after five years.[27] It was obvious to me that nothing would stop the Saudis from turning Mecca into Disneyland, their nightmare vision of modernity. That the Holy City would be a permanent site of accidents – I predicted a major one every three years – was also evident. I admired the passion and perseverance of Sami Angawi but did not share his optimism. When, in 1993, the Centre was transferred out of King Abdul Aziz University in Jeddah to Umm al-Qura University in Mecca, the struggle to save Mecca was truly over. The Centre was turned into a statistical bureau, reminiscent of the practices of the Soviet Union, under the guardianship of an ultra-conservative body. Angawi himself was labelled a dissident and confined to virtual house arrest for the rest of his life.

I felt guilty. Guilty for throwing in the towel too early. Guilty for abandoning a man who had sacrificed everything to rescue from the clutches of rampant, ugly modernity a city that all Muslims allegedly revere and regard as sacred. I wanted – needed – a second chance.

It presented itself in 1987. The Muslim world was still recovering from the shock of the massacre of Iranian pilgrims in Mecca. I was asked to organize a conference of Muslim thinkers and intellectuals in Mecca to explore viable and sustainable ways forward and try to develop common ground between Sunnis, Shias and other varieties of Muslims. There was considerable support for such a conference, and we managed to raise over a million dollars for the event from Malaysia and Pakistan, and Muslims in the US and Britain, as well as from Saudi businessmen. To play to the religious sensibilities of the Saudis as well as to thwart them, I came up with an unusual title: '*Dawa* and Development in the Muslim World: The Future Perspective'. *Dawa* is a technical term in Muslim theology, usually translated as 'preaching' by those who espouse it, and 'evangelism' by those who don't. The Saudis take pride in sending *dais*, evangelicals or preachers, as paid employees to spread the Wahhabi faith throughout the world. However, *dawa* also means 'invitation'. Prophet Muhammad asked his followers to invite others 'to all that is good'. Surely, I argued, *dawa* must include good ways of managing change.

'Change', I argued, 'must be studied with reverence and humility and ushered in, in a planned, systematic way, with imagination and with total participation and complete consensus of the community.'[28] Planning, I suggested, is a form of *dawa*. It is not concerned simply with getting from A to B, a succession of short-range steps made in reaction to rapid changes. It is more concerned with what would be a good point B to choose, which strategy would get us there in a good way. It requires thinking consciously and rationally, looking after the environment as well as historic property, and operating within certain values and norms. I hoped, along with my colleagues organizing the Conference, that the powers that be would listen to an influential gathering of Muslim intellectuals who used Islamic terms to argue for a more human-scale, cultural and environmentally sound development of the Holy City.

The conference, held during October 1987, was a total disaster. It started well, with many young Saudi intellectuals agreeing with much that was being said. Then, a group of heavyweight Saudi scholars arrived halfway through the five-day meeting, and at once began to argue that good *dawa* can only be based on good, correct, faith. People with faulty, heretical or contaminated faith could not perform good *dawa*. The implication was quite clear: as people of 'correct' faith, the Saudis were the only people who could do good; indeed, everything they did was intrinsically good. Heated arguments followed, leading to the premature exit of Shia and many other scholars.

There was one unexpected outcome. Aware that they had disrupted the conference and were openly being criticized and shunned by most of the 400 international participants, the Saudis offered a special concession. They announced that the gates of the Kaaba would be opened and all the participants invited to go inside. This was a rare privilege, one reserved throughout most of history for a chosen few – caliphs, Ottoman sultans and pashas, and other high-level dignitaries. Almost instantly criticism evaporated; praises were heaped on the benevolence and kindness of the Saudis. At the appointed time, all the participants, their special badges in hand, went to the Sacred Mosque and queued to go inside the Kaaba.

During all the numerous days and nights I had spent in the Haram, I had never seen the door of the Kaaba open. Unless it is being repaired or cleaned, there is no real need to open the door; the cleaning takes place only twice a year. There is nothing inside. It is simply a dark room, with three pillars and no windows – much as it was described by Naser-e-Khosraw in the eleventh century. Participants were allowed to enter the Kaaba in groups of forty. But I was not amongst them. I had politely declined the invitation, much to the astonishment of friends and colleagues.

The function of the Kaaba, a cuboid structure made of brick and mortar and draped in black cloth, is to provide Muslims with a sense of direction. Wherever they may be on God's benevolent earth, Muslims turn towards the Kaaba during their five daily prayers. They walk around it seven times when they are performing the Hajj, or Umra, the lesser pilgrimage. It is a symbol, a sign of direction for Muslims to turn towards and inculcate a sense of unity amongst themselves. When seen from the outside the Kaaba draws attention both to the representational drama around it and to the plight and disunity amongst Muslims. Within the Kaaba, there is no sense of direction, and hence no purpose. That is why it is empty. To be inside the Kaaba is to lose all sense of direction and purpose. I did not need to confront this moral within the confines of the Kaaba when it was so obviously and ubiquitously advertised wherever one looked around the redeveloped and modernized environs of Mecca. The Holy City reduced to a vapid space, shorn of identity and meaning.

I found it hard to fight off the feeling that Muslims had been living inside the Kaaba for centuries. What was meant to be symbolic had to all intents and purpose been transformed into a literal monolith. The Saudis seem to have little regard for anything other than the purity of their literalism, no concern for the history, cultural property, art and culture, debate and dissent, and the diversity and plurality of what Mecca ought to be. The Sacred City is a microcosm of the Muslim world. What happens in Mecca not only reverberates throughout Muslim societies, it actually defines the state of Muslim civilization. Mecca was making a categorical statement: the Muslim world is in a dire and perilous state.

11

The Reconfigured Utopia

It all began, I suppose, with a desire to walk into the past. Nearly four decades ago, I set off with my good friend Zafar, a tour guide called Ali and our rebellious donkey Genghis. Our collective aim was a kind of oneness with the history of the city of our hearts. Foot-slogging through the desert all those years ago we experienced the welter of contradictions surrounding Islam's Holy City. Since then it has taken me numerous visits to the Sanctuary to unravel the enigma of Mecca. In the process I have found one can learn as much about the world from reading and reflection in the comfort of one's armchair as from a trek through the desert.

On foot, I found the dream I took with me to Mecca had to contend with a growing array of jarring irritants, the disruptive intrusions of unwelcome realities. My transcendent ideal of Mecca existed at a place of all-too-human habitation caught in the throes of rampant modernization. The more I have explored this other Mecca, the city where history has been lived, the more it disturbs me. This other Mecca makes no claim on my heartstrings. It is the Mecca we all forget to remember, the Mecca that has escaped close scrutiny cloaked behind the façade of the most observed, most revered place in Muslim consciousness. What is not acknowledged, what could and should be known, reveals a great deal about the relationship Muslims have with history. And the concluding question I have to confront is: what should Muslims do when faced with the complete eradication of respect for the traces of their history at the very place where their identity begins?

'Mecca calls to you till you have gone there,' says an old Moroccan proverb, 'then you cry out for Mecca to return.' My concern is with the unrequited return of reality and the reality of history being unmade in Mecca in our time. It seems that the more Muslims cherish an idealized, almost idolized, Mecca, the more their sense of collective history is romanticized. Mecca is not just a symbol, the encapsulation of religious aspiration; it is and has always been a place where people lived amidst all the unflattering man-made vicissitudes that constitute history. Could it be that the more we disregard the grit and gore of history, the more unearthly, less engaged in the problems of human life, becomes the spiritual dimension of Mecca?

The annals of Mecca's history reveal a city where pilgrims thronged for spiritual enlightenment but sanctity was largely a sideshow for the ruling elite and most of the city's inhabitants. Most Muslims know little of this history because their romantic attachment to their own past is increasingly selective and selectively self-serving when not entirely apologetic. The need to assert that once, long ago, Muslim civilization was great, that there was a 'Golden Age', easily becomes the proposition that it was always good, and leads to the obligation to suspend judgement on virtually the entirety of what happened in history. What is done with one's vision of the past has enormous implications for how present realities are handled and the quality of idealism that can be applied to shaping the future.

The factionalism, dissension and violence that Mecca has witnessed are integral to Muslim history from its beginning. It was the first generation of Muslims, known as the 'Companions of the Prophet', who created the internecine conflict over the meaning, interpretation and implementation of religion. It was these same companions who initiated the power struggles for control of what in short order became an imperialist project. How benign can an empire be? The companions of the Prophet have been idealized, just as miracles have been attributed to the Prophet even though Muhammad himself, as well as the Qur'an, insists that he is only human: 'Am I anything but a mortal'? (17. 93). The reality of their lives and actions has been all but obliterated, not because the facts are not known but for the even more perverse reason that no critical reflection, no questioning of the sanctified status of the companions, is permitted. All must be for the best in the best of all possible histories, otherwise there might be some problem with Islam itself.

It is a familiar category mistake, blaming revelation, the Divine, for the failings of the human beings who so imperfectly adhere to its word. The long, frequently inglorious, history of what happened in Mecca is a necessary riposte to what are conventional attitudes. The lived history of this place of human habitation is a necessary restorative, a place to begin operating a critical and more informed consideration of the meaning and understanding of what it means to be human and Muslim in the twenty-first century.

I heard Mecca calling one morning in September 2010. I was performing my usual rituals of drinking coffee and reading the *Guardian*. As I turned the pages of the newspaper, I came across a full-page advertisement. 'Live a few steps away from the holy heart of the universe' it said, underneath a large photograph of the Sacred Mosque. 'When you look for residence in Makkah, the first thing you seek is how close you'll be to the holy mosque', the advertisement said, inviting the reader to buy a property at the 'Emaar Residences at the Fairmont Makkah'.[1]

These residences are located within the Royal Makkah Clock Tower, which at 1,972 feet is the world's second-tallest building after Dubai's Burj Khalifa. It is part of a mammoth development of skyscrapers and includes shopping malls devoted to luxury goods and seven-star hotels catering exclusively to the obscenely rich. The Clock Tower, as the photograph accompanying the advertisement made clear, dwarfs the Kaaba and soars above the Sacred Mosque. The skyline above the Sacred Mosque is no longer dominated by the rugged outline of encircling mountains. It is surrounded by the brutalism of hideously ugly rectangular steel and concrete buildings, built with the proceeds of enormous oil wealth that showcase the Saudi vision for Mecca. They look like downtown office blocks in any mid-American city. The advertisement invites you not to live 'a few steps' from the Sacred Mosque but to live over and above it.

What the advertisement does not tell you is that this grotesque metropolis is built on the graves of houses and cultural sites of immense beauty and long history. An estimated 95 per cent of the city's millennium-old buildings, consisting of over 400 sites of cultural and historical significance, were demolished to build this eruption of architectural bling. Bulldozers arrived in the middle of the night to demolish Ottoman-era town houses. The complex stands on top of the bulldozed al-Ayad fort, built in 1781 and no longer able to perform its function of protecting Mecca from invaders. At the opposite end of the Grand Mosque Complex, as it is now called, the house of Khadijah, the first wife of the Prophet Muhammad, has been turned into a block of toilets.[2]

The Royal Makkah Clock Tower is not the only building to hover above the Sacred Mosque. There is the Raffles Makkah Palace, a luxury hotel, with round-the-clock butler service. Add to that the Makkah Hilton, built over the house of Abu Bakr, the closest companion of the Prophet and the first caliph. Along with the Intercontinental Mecca they all vie for prominence on the skyline. There are numerous other five-star hotels and high-rise apartment blocks. Within the next decade there will be a ring of 130 skyscrapers looking down upon the Sacred Mosque.

There are spectacular plans to further redevelop the Sacred Mosque so that it can accommodate up to 5 million worshippers. With a seemingly casual disregard for history, the Saudis are rebuilding the Ottoman-era section of the Haram, the oldest surviving section of the Sacred Mosque. The interior, of exquisite beauty, with intricately carved marble columns, built by a succession of Ottoman sultans – Sultan Suleiman, Sultan Salim I, Sultan Murad III, and Sultan Murad IV – from 1553 to 1629, will give way to series of multi-storey prayer halls, eighty metres high. The columns, which are adorned with calligraphy of the names of the Prophet's companions, will be demolished. Indeed, the whole of the old Sacred Mosque will be bulldozed. History stretching back to Umar, the second caliph of Islam, ibn Zubair, who sacrificed his life to rebuild the Kaaba, and to the Abbasid caliphs, will be replaced by an ultramodern doughnut-shaped building. The new Jamarat Bridge will ultimately be twelve storeys high, so pilgrims will be able to 'Stone the Devils' on even more multiple levels.

It seems only a matter of time before the house where Prophet Muhammad was born, located opposite the imposing Royal Palace, is razed to the ground, and turned, probably, into a car park. During most of the Saudi era it was used as a cattle market; the Hijazi citizens fought to turn it into a library. However, even to enter the library is apparently to commit an unpardonable sin – hence no one is allowed in. But even this is too much for the radical clerics who have repeatedly called for its demolition. Also in their sights is Jabal al-Nur, the mountain that contains the cave of Hira, where the Prophet used to retire for meditation and reflection and where he received his first revelations.

What I find particularly troubling is how few are willing to stand up and openly criticize the official policy of the Saudi government. Turkey, and the arch-enemy of the Kingdom, Iran, have raised dissenting voices about the erasure of history, but most Muslim countries are too fearful of the Saudis. There is real fear that their pilgrim quota will be cut – just as the Saudis refused to give visas to the Iranian pilgrims during the late 1980s. Popular vituperative complaint between consenting adults in private, though it is the norm in Muslim circles, is, as it always has been, inconsequential and irrelevant. Far from cautioning the Saudis, architects, including some who are Muslim, are actively colluding with the destruction of Mecca. Peace activists and archaeologists have raised concerns in newspapers and in the pages of learned journals, but the mass of believers are silent. Archaeologists fear that access to the few remaining sites open to them will be blocked. Would-be pilgrims understandably worry that they may be barred from performing a compulsory sacred ritual. Everything else for believers comes secondary to Mecca's place as the destination for one of five 'pillars' of the practice of faith.

Mecca today is a microcosm of its own history replayed as tragedy. The city that has serially been remade in the image of the wealth and imperial splendour of whatever power was dominant is the plaything of its latest masters – who happen on this occasion to be lacking any aesthetic sensitivity, so that the underlying theme of naked power and wealth-driven consumer excess is brazenly exposed for all to see, devoid of saving graces.

Modern Mecca is a city of contradictions. And the contradictions start with the name itself. Mecca, the name of the Holy City, is the original transliteration of the Arabic name. But in English Mecca is used more widely as a generic term, meaning ultimate destination; a magnet that attracts people in large numbers; or an activity centre for people with a common interest – we refer to Los Angeles, for example, as the Mecca of show business, to Paris as the Mecca of chic fashion. Saudi officials have complained at such 'derogatory' usage. They see the name of the Holy City in such labels as 'Mecca Bingo', 'Mecca Motors', and worse, Mecca as the name for loosely clad American girls, as sacrilegious. So, in the 1980s, the Saudi government officially changed the spelling from 'Mecca' to 'Makkah', the old spelling, to emphasize the uniqueness of its holy and traditional character. Makkah, or more fully *Makkah al-Mukarramah* (Mecca the Blessed), is now used by Saudi government institutions as well as international organizations such as the United Nations, the US Department of State and the UK Foreign and Commonwealth Office.

'Makkah' may be blessed, but the more spiritually oriented Meccans, the descendants of the old and established families of the city, find nothing particularly 'holy' in the recycled designation of 'Makkah'. What is evident to them is a city of proliferating bling, a haven of consumerism and opulent tourism that have usurped spirituality as the city's raison d'être. They call it 'Saudi Las Vegas'.

Like the American city famed for its gambling casinos and gaudy architecture, Mecca has become a playground for the rich. For most of the year, it plays host to religious tourists who arrive partly to pray in the Sacred Mosque but also to shop in its countless opulent malls. Many have bought property around the Sacred Mosque not just as a financial investment but in the hope that it will translate into real estate in paradise. For rich Muslims the world over – most notably the Gulf, Malaysia, India, Turkey, and among the diaspora in Europe and the US – a quick visit to Mecca for Umra (the lesser pilgrimage) or *ziyarat* (the religious term for visit) has become routine. Indeed, for many it's a badge of prestige: the more visits you make to Mecca the more pious and dedicated you appear. The poor arrive only during the Hajj seasons, and are packaged and processed speedily, without much dignity, from entry to exit in the space of less than two weeks. Yet even the relatively poor are incited to shop at every available moment. Wherever you look in the city, someone close is selling something. Beyond the expensive shopping malls, there are numerous markets, such as Souk Gaza or Souk al-Lail, where only one manner of existence is possible: the shopping mode. The markets are full of stalls, hawkers and street vendors selling everything from fake watches to plastic bottles of 'holy Zamzam water', from perfume to cheap prayer rugs and plastic trinkets. The ethos is clear: no one should leave Mecca without some memento.

It was ever the way that souvenirs from Mecca had special value, and carried an aura of the sacred. I just cannot see how this sentiment attaches to a cheap plastic replica of the Kaaba or an outrageously expensive perfume inside a Kaaba-shaped bottle. Muslim historians insist that Mecca was an important trading city time out of mind before the era of the Prophet. Revisionist Western historians argue it was the coming of Islam that required the invention of Mecca as a trading city. Well, look at it now: the city is the acme of selling with the addition of the manufacture of consumer goods. On its outskirts a vast network of cottage industries produce or import consumer products to service and supply the markets for all grades of tourist tat: warehouses for storing electronic goods, bottling plants for soft drinks and Zamzam water, vegetable oil extraction establishments, poultry farms, ice-cream factories, factories for manufacturing trinkets, photography-processing plants, and the like. Mecca was always, as we have seen, a trading place, and pilgrims would buy and sell merchandise in its markets. But a subsidiary activity has now become ubiquitous and omnipotent.

Apart from the Kaaba and the Sacred Mosque, there is nothing that remains in Mecca that is unique to the city – it is a focal place with no sense of its own history or its place in the world. Nor is it any longer attuned to its own geography and ecology: it is air-conditioned and air-polluted in spite of its location in the Arabian Desert. There are no monuments, no relics, no culture, no art, and no architecture worthy of the name. In contemporary accounts of Hajj, such as Michael Muhammad Knight's *Journey to the End of Islam*, there is no sense of the city of Mecca, largely because there is nothing special about the city itself.[3] Knight, an American Muslim with a punk background who has evolved an eclectic Islamic liberation theology, found the Holy City 'homeless'. Beyond the 'immaculate' Haram, the city was utterly mundane. The Moroccan anthropologist Abdellah Hammoudi, who performed the Hajj in 1999, found Mecca 'to be hesitating between the sublime and a film set'.[4] Michael Wolfe, the American poet and film-maker, who converted to Islam in the 1980s after extensive travels in the Muslim world, thought – appropriately given the inspiration for its contemporary redevelopment – 'that the streets of Mecca resembled Houston'.[5]

Like Houston, on which it was modelled, Mecca loves its wealth. Throughout history, it has used its special status as the 'House of

Allah' to gain riches it did not earn, the largesse of others from Abbasid caliphs to Ottoman sultans. Whatever has been best in Muslim civilization has had to be brought to Mecca, and has had a transitory acquaintance with the Holy City, but has not taken root there. Surely this is why Mecca has succumbed so easily to a theology that assigns no value to history or culture. The great scholars and thinkers who abound in Muslim history paid their visit to Mecca and left to do their thinking elsewhere. Muslim writers insist that faith without reason is deficient, yet the epicentre of religion has become a place where sensation, emotion and fervour are all and reason is not required. Indeed it would be fair to acknowledge that no great ideas about Islam or anything else have come out of Mecca since the Prophet migrated from the city to Medina. All efforts to reason out contemporary relevance, all strategies for rethinking and reforming Islam in the last two centuries, have occurred at a far remove. In Mecca itself such efforts have been met with denunciation, excoriated to the echo rather than given serious critical consideration.

In truth, this is not a product of the Wahhabi rise to prominence. It is a pre-existing state of affairs: a predilection for conservative obscurantism is original and authentic to the way Mecca as a centre of religious learning developed over centuries. Worse, the defiant rejection of critical thinking goes hand in hand with strenuous objection to advances in human knowledge and understanding. Everything about the modern world, except the creature comforts of consumerism, is anathema to the generality of clerics in Mecca. Ignorance is holy. And with this comes open denigration of all people and things non-Muslim. Such attitudes, characteristic of and emanating from the Holy City, have offered aid and encouragement to the abominable ideologies that extremists have fashioned into instruments of hatred and indiscriminate slaughter. Where in Mecca today is the dream of peace, tolerance and humane, respectful, mutual understanding? It can be found in the hearts of pilgrims, but where else does it reside in the Holy City? A simplistic distinction is drawn nowadays between the people of Najd, who flooded in with the Wahhabi ascendancy, and the Hijazis, who are the historic people of Mecca. It is suggested that the Hijazis are gentle, more enlightened and conservation-oriented compared with the harsh and violent Najdis. This is a myth. The sharifs, who shed so much blood in the Sanctuary, were Hijazis after all. History suggests that while there may be differences of degree and style in substance, little separates the essential stance of the religious worldviews that both Hijazis and Najdis have propounded.

The Prophet Muhammad himself knew that many of his fellow Meccans loved money above all else, as illustrated by a telling event in his life. It happened in the year 630 at the Battle of Hunayn, where the Muslims acquired considerable booty. The Prophet distributed the booty amongst his followers, who included many new converts, Meccans, who had joined the army of the Prophet after the fall of the city a month earlier. The Prophet assigned the lion's share of the spoils, some several hundred camels among them, to the Meccans. His followers from Medina received virtually nothing. This upset the Ansar, the Helpers, as the people of Medina were known. These were the loyal supporters who had followed him unconditionally ever since he was driven out of Mecca and had to migrate to Medina to save his life. Rumours began to circulate amongst the people of Medina. Muhammad was from Mecca, and now he was back with his people; this was why he was showing clear bias towards them. 'By God, the apostle has met his own people,' they said. Eventually, one of them went to the Prophet to report what was being said. 'And where do you stand on this matter?' the Prophet asked him. 'I stand with my people,' he replied. 'Then gather your people,' Muhammad asked him.

When all the people from Medina had been ushered in front of him, the Prophet asked the crowd: did you not believe in me when I came to you discredited? Did you not help me when I was deserted? Did you not take me in when I was a fugitive? Did you not comfort me when I was poor? They all shook their heads in agreement. Are you upset now, the Prophet continued, because of the good things in life that I give to Meccans? 'Are you not satisfied that [Meccan] men should take away flocks of herds while you return with the Prophet of God? By Him in whose hand is the soul of Muhammad, but for the migration I would not be one of the Ansar myself. If all men went one way, and the Ansar another, I would be with the Ansar.' The gathering fell to its knees, and the 'people wept until the tears ran down their beards'.[6]

Whether Hijazis or Najdis, in history many of the people of Mecca have only had one true love: material wealth, the pilgrims their 'flocks of herds'. With a few notable exceptions, the citizens of the Holy City have been greedy and money-grabbing.

In the midst of garish skyscrapers, and the manic consumption that envelops Mecca, stands the Kaaba, which is intended as a symbol of equality. But equality is conspicuously absent in the Holy City. Mecca has always been a closed city, enclosed by its own sense of historic importance – the importance of lineage and blood. It has guarded the prerogatives of this unearned inheritance down the centuries with tenacity. The aura of religiosity cannot be inherited. However, this is not an impediment to the ethos of lineage and blood, rather it is its stock in trade. In consequence, Mecca is a place riddled with racism, bigotry and xenophobia. The Najdis regard the Hijazis as inferior for their lack of ethnic purity and keep them at respectable distance. The Hijazis have compromised their cosmopolitanism and cultural openness for the sake of a stake, and status, in the power structure. The Saudis, the Najdis and Hijazis together, are a society apart from the rest of Mecca's inhabitants – a kind of 'no-go area' for ordinary mortals. In Mecca, as in the rest of Saudi Arabia, the Saudis are superior to everybody; but this superiority has its own gradations.

The most 'superior' Saudis belong to the royal family, the rulers of a quasi-totalitarian dynastic state based on the absolute supremacy of a single clan, the Al Saud. Next in the pecking order after the royal family, and often quite indistinguishable from them, are the wealthy families such as the Bin Ladens, who are responsible for most of the construction in Mecca and elsewhere in Saudi Arabia;[7] the al-Shaikhs, descendants of Muhammad ibn Abd al-Wahhab, the eighteenth-century founder of Wahhabism, who dominate the religious institutions of the Kingdom; the al-Turkis, who own several investment and development companies; and the Rajhis, owners of several banks. Most wealthy families, as well as a string of billionaires, are related to the royal family through marriage or connected to it in some convoluted way involving business deals, loyalty oaths and other tribal rituals. Today, as through much of its history, status in Mecca is demonstrated by the size and location of one's property around the Sacred Mosque. With a palace towering over the Kaaba, the king is obviously pre-eminent. The bottom layers of social strata comprise the poor Bedouins, who are travellers and refuse to settle and are denied citizenship by Saudi Arabia, and the even poorer Yemenis, who want to be Saudis.

After the Saudis, the scale of superiority moves, still in careful gradation, from Arabs to non-Arabs, taking race and wealth into full consideration. At the top, a few notches beneath the privileged Saudi families, stand European and American converts to Islam. The Saudis see them as demonstrating the innate superiority of Islam as a living and expanding faith. The next rung is Arabic-speaking Muslims. Since they speak the 'language of the Qur'an', the Saudis see them as superior to all other Muslims who do not have Arabic as their mother tongue. Then come the Pakistanis, Indians, Malays and Turks. If they are wealthy, they will be treated with some respect. And finally, right at the bottom of this unsubtle Meccan hierarchy, are the Africans – Sudanese, Ethiopians, Somalis – who came initially for pilgrimage and stayed, often illegally. As anyone who has been to Mecca for the Hajj can testify, black skin tone is not appreciated in the Holy City. One can see black African men and women being treated abominably by the local citizens in front of the Sacred Mosque. The expatriate Muslims, who work and live in the city and have actually built the gigantic structures surrounding the Haram, are treated with equal contempt. Slavery may have been abolished, but in Mecca it is alive and well, although now it goes under the rubric of 'labour laws'. These define 'foreigners' as intrinsically untrustworthy people who cannot be allowed to travel freely in the Kingdom, and have to be watched at all times. Thus the racial and ethnic divisions in the Holy City have remained intact since it was first visited by Naser-e-Khosraw and ibn Jubayr in the eleventh and twelfth centuries.

Before an expatriate can work in Mecca, he or she has to be tied to a *vakeel*, ostensibly a 'sponsor' to look after their interests in the kingdom, but in essence a master with full control over their life and movements.[8] The foreign employees have virtually no rights: they can be and usually are exploited in every possible way. The 'sponsor' holds the passport of the employee, and can prevent him from travelling, bringing his family, or visiting his relatives even within the Kingdom. And there is no appeal to a higher authority: the utterance of the Saudi *vakeel* is sacrosanct. Many poor labourers in the Holy City lead a miserable, slave-like existence. It is not unusual to see labourers crying and pleading with their *vakeels* simply to be allowed to visit their families back home after years of service. Scalding, abusing and beating of domestic Asian workers as though they were slaves are not uncommon. The brotherhood and sisterhood of a community, an *ummah* beyond differences of race, colour, languages, cultures and ethnicities, seeks to find a focus in Mecca – Mecca's rulers seek to hold fast to the distinctiveness of lineage and blood.

The oneness of the *ummah* is what pilgrims come to Mecca to experience. Yet even this most noble and uplifting ideal has been afflicted by the mentality of lineage and blood. It came out of Mecca to stamp itself on the thinking of the Umayyad dynasty, scions of the Meccan elite, in much the same way as it is evident in the quasi-caste system to be found in today's Mecca. It was the Umayyads who declared Mecca closed and forbidden to all non-Muslims. The original *ummah*, the community that gathered around the Prophet in Medina, was not exclusively Muslim, but a social compact among people of different faiths, including pagan polytheists. The sense of community as a moral entity working together despite and through their differences to better collective human welfare and well-being is an original Islamic motif. However, it is a concept alien to Mecca – one that its people never could or can implement. This Holy City forbidden to all but Muslims outlaws the practice of a precept original to the religion it proclaims and so desperately needed in our time. There is much food for thought and self-critical reflection for all Muslims in this. It fascinates me that so many Muslims have no idea why non-Muslims are denied access to Mecca, nor when, why and how this came about. A cursory glance at the strings of comments on the internet suffices to show that most put it down to the Crusades – making it someone else's fault and Muslims the victims. It is a common enough reaction. What would be the result if Muslims actually started to wrestle with the reality – that it was a choice of Muslim imperialism, a statement of superiority and specialness enacted by a product of Meccan elitism?

In a city that owes its existence and survival to two women – Hagar, wife of Abraham, whose search for and eventual discovery of water first established the city in the 'Barren Valley'; and Zubaidah, wife of the Abbasid Caliph Harun al-Rashid, who first provided the city with the supply of usable water that sustained it for centuries – women are treated as chattels. They have to be shrouded and hidden, if they go out they must be accompanied by a male guardian, and under no circumstances can they drive any of the motor vehicles to which the city and its environs have been given over. Foreign maids, from Southeast Asia, Indonesia or African countries, employed by many Meccan households are considered fair game for everything from incarceration to beatings to sex.

Mecca is about religion. One would expect a city devoted to monotheism to be free of superstition and idolatry. The Wahhabi clerics justify the demolition of historical sites and shrines because, they argue, they promote *shirk* – the sin of polytheism. Yet Mecca is knee-deep in *shirk*. It is manifest not just in the worship of money, wealth and consumerism. It can be discovered in the Sacred Mosque itself. During the late 1990s, I was in the Haram when there was a call to prayer. The evening prayer had already concluded, so I was rather surprised. Nevertheless, I joined the congregation. The imam started reading the second, and longest, chapter in the Qur'an; I soon realized that this was going to be a very long prayer. I noticed that some members of the congregation were looking towards the sky. I followed their gaze and realized there was a partial eclipse of the moon. The congregation was performing *Salat-ul-Kasuf*, special prayers to diffuse the 'darkness' of the lunar eclipse. I was aghast – what could be closer to *shirk* than this? I left the prayer – which went on for over three hours – but was stopped by members of the *Mutawwa*, the religious police force that enforces the moral code and strict observance of rituals. I pointed out to the *Mutawwa*, like my predecessors Mahmoud Mobarek Churchward and Eldon Rutter, who visited the Holy City at the dawn of the twentieth century, that eclipses and other stellar events are a natural phenomenon, as it is clearly stated in the Qur'an: 'the sun, too, runs its determined course laid down for it by the Almighty, all Knowing. We have determined phases for the moon until finally it becomes like an old date-stalk. The sun cannot overtake the moon, nor can the night outrun the day: each floats in its own orbit' (36. 38–40). I also told them the story of the death of the Prophet Muhammad's infant son, Ibrahim. It coincided with an eclipse of the sun. Muslims at that time took it as a miracle, a sign from God. A rumour spread throughout Medina that even the heavens were crying for the deep sorrow and loss of the Prophet. But Muhammad was not consoled; he was angry at this gossip. 'The sun and the moon are signs of God,' he announced.

'They are eclipsed neither for the death nor the birth of any man.'[9] The *Mutawwa* answered by saying that the prayer was a requirement of the Shariah, Islamic law, and forced me back towards the congregation.

The Prophet, of course, removed all the idols from the Sacred Sanctuary. Today the walls of the city are full of advertisements featuring people missing an eye or a female hand or with a foot painted over. These have been disfigured by the *Mutawwa* to avoid adulation of the graven images. Yet Meccans venerate the wonders of technology as sacrosanct, revere opulence, and worship insatiable desire. Contemporary Mecca has reverted to its old self and become the pagan heart of Arabia.

Mecca is a city where rituals reign supreme but there are no ethics. One of the most common sights in the city is to see a Saudi man emerging from the Sacred Mosque after prayer, worry beads in hand. He is approached by *takruni* (black African) women, covered head to toe in a black *abaya* in scorching heat, who beg outside the Haram. Far from giving them charity, the Saudi treats them with utter contempt, cursing as he goes along. It is not unusual for pilgrim guides to take the money of the poor pilgrims and leave them lost and confused, without provision, to manage on their own. The *Mutawwa*, *Mukhabarat* (intelligence forces) and the Bedouins of the National Guard are often aggressive and hostile towards female worshippers, as I have observed on many occasions. And if a visitor or a foreign worker is arrested for some reason, he can easily end up by being tortured – innocent or guilty. One of the noted spectacles of the city is the Friday executions, often carried out in a shroud of secrecy, where mostly poor foreign workers – marginalized labourers from Pakistan, Bangladesh and Africa – are beheaded.[10]

On the surface Mecca is changing rapidly. But it is also frozen in a time when cultural diversity, religious pluralism, political dissent, art and music, intellectual accomplishments, academic freedom, political dissent and bridges across gender and nationalities do not exist.

Visually the city looks like an amalgam of two film sets, one part 'Arabian Nights', the other a science-fiction saga. Minarets jostle with skyscrapers; motorways and towers align to face the Kaaba. Monorails take pilgrims from Mecca to Mina (initially only the Saudis and Gulf Arabs). But look beneath the ground and all the ultramodernity dissolves into sewage. The city has no new sewage system; dig anywhere around the Sacred Mosque, and you will hit sewage after three metres. The Saudis could demolish the Ottoman buildings and town houses, but they could not build a sewage system, which has remained much as it was described by Churchward and Rutter. And, of course, the city's effluence – much like its affluence – is way past the carrying capacity of the old network. The famous cemetery of Al-Muala, where many members of the household of the Prophet Muhammad are buried, is drowning in sewage. On the outskirts of the town, sewage oozes from the houses.

The Muslim novelist and poet Ahmad Kamal described Mecca as 'not so much a geographical location' but 'a frame of mind'. Kamal, a cosmopolitan writer of Turkish origin, had lived in Baghdad and Bandung, Indonesia, before performing the Hajj in 1953. He was troubled by the schisms and sectarianism he saw in the city. His response was *The Sacred Journey*, a lyrical guide to performing the Hajj that transcends all sectarian boundaries. 'So long as we remain intolerant of one another,' he wrote, and will not recognize that different schools of thought such as 'Hanafi and Maliki, Shafi and Hanbali – Shia and Sunni – are nothing and Islam is everything, none of us deserve to be free'. Do not go to Mecca, he advised potential pilgrims, 'in search of aspiration', but because you 'are inspired'. 'Pilgrims will discover in Mecca only what they take to Mecca.'[11]

Kamal seems to suggest that there is nothing that has happened in Mecca after the time of the Prophet that makes any difference to the life and faith of Muslims. This is a shibboleth, a hoary old myth that, like so many, contains only the merest grain of truth. Muslims have and do listen to Mecca. In so many ways, what is happening in and to Mecca in our time is an extreme encapsulation of the condition of Muslims everywhere, the challenges they face and the failings they are heir to. What Mecca does is echoed throughout the Muslim world. When Mecca, the heart of Islam, is defiled, polluted, culturally arid and surrounded by corruption, the rest of the Islamic world hardly fares better. Everything that has happened in Mecca since the time of the Prophet tells us a great deal about Muslims themselves. The city is not just a symbol, it has been part and parcel of the history of Muslim civilization. Throughout its bloody history, Mecca has been the centre of religion writ small: narrow, enclosed and indifferent to the changing realities of the wider world. This has been the essence of the influence Mecca has exerted upon the Muslim world, most perniciously in the days when most of the Muslim world was colonized. Mecca was the redoubt that withstood history. It is timeless and caught in time like no other place on earth. The export model Mecca provided was and is one of detachment from the world, retreat into prurient pieties as the bastion of traditionalism. The Meccan model is not exactly how its citizens led their lives; it is much more the ethos it disseminated as fit for purpose everywhere that is not Mecca. And that is a problem. Mecca retains an almost invincible aura of authenticity that Muslims frequently find difficult to shed, even when they disagree. In seeking to assert a contemporary identity in a rapidly changing world the Meccan model seems like a benchmark, an enduring reference point – just what the home of the Kaaba should be. By placing Mecca in history, by revealing the people and pressures that shaped its character and outlook, I hope it becomes easier to think about what Mecca should mean. How should our understanding of Mecca, the experience it offers, operate in the real world today and for the future? How do we take possession of Mecca as an ideal that is humane, tolerant, open, welcoming and forgiving?

For the majority of Muslim believers, Mecca is the ideal city. Yet the ideal has little historic warrant. When I lived in Malaysia I remember being fascinated and bemused by the formality and gravitas I witnessed at a friend's office. One of his colleagues came to see him. There were formal handshakes, copious greetings and well wishes, and then we sat quietly for quite some time before the visitor departed to the sound of even more earnest well wishes. I could not wait for an explanation of what I had witnessed. 'Oh, he's going on Hajj,' I was told, as if the answer was self-explanatory. I made further inquiries and discovered that it was a Malay custom to take formal leave of everyone one knew before departing for Hajj. The custom evolved in the days when it took months, possibly even years, to go to Mecca, with the likelihood that a large proportion of the pilgrims would never return. It survives in the days of air travel, inoculations, and the best organization and administration of Hajj in the history of Islam. Do we ever stop to think that in history the greatest hazard for the pilgrim was of being robbed, tortured or killed by one's own co-religionists who saw the Hajj as a charter of criminal entitlement? Where does that factor into the ideal of Mecca – or more importantly, why does it not factor at all?

All Muslims know that the Hajj is one of the five pillars, the central tenets, of Islam, an obligation to be undertaken once in a lifetime, if one is able. History argues that most Muslims who have ever lived have not been able. Pilgrim numbers have fluctuated wildly, reflecting the political and economic conditions of the Muslim world as sensitively as a finely tuned barometer. Even at the best of times the opportunity to complete the Hajj has been the privilege of only a small proportion, usually the most affluent and educated, of any population. The idea of Mecca, the history of its elevation and idealization in Muslim consciousness, is a function of the rarity of the experience. It was something to long for and dream about. Every other element of the five pillars could be accomplished in the comfort of one's own home. Going to Mecca was something quite different.

Not surprisingly it is the journey, the enormous effort of getting there, that predominates in all the books written down the centuries by pilgrim travellers. When so few Muslims could ever realistically conceive of performing the Hajj it is little wonder Mecca became the concern of the dominant powers, the imperial courts, those who wished to publish and broadcast their credentials as guardians of Muslim existence. In an age of increasing ease of global travel, do we not need to unpick this historic connection? When the bulk of the world's Muslims can realistically plan for and look forward to going to Mecca not once in a lifetime but whenever they want, should the focal point of religious consciousness, the lodestone of Muslim identity, not acknowledge and be answerable to all those whose lives it informs and enriches? How would it be possible to make the transformation from beacon to the world to the place that belongs to the whole world? Could Mecca ever become truly an international city, the heart that belongs to the whole body of believers, rather than the Arabian backwater compliant with the grand imaginings of its chance rulers? I have heard people assert as much. The question is what would such a transformation consist of, and what kind of difference would it make in Mecca and throughout the Muslim world? The factionalism and dissension, the intolerance of differences, so prevalent in history have by no means disappeared from Muslim existence. Yet to internationalize Mecca would be a grand idea. All the grander for requiring urgent and informed thought about what it means to be Muslim now and wherever one happens to live in this all too real world.

In all my travels, actual and literary, the city of my heart remains secure. Nothing could change my relationship to the Mecca I first encountered as a child. I have dreamt of Mecca, loved Mecca, longed for Mecca and found Mecca. This Mecca has always been more than a geographical location: it is a state of consciousness, the focus of prayer, the signifier of aspiration for the Divine. It is the place where I experienced the most profound moments of my life. This is not to say that my ideas have not been changed by travelling to Mecca and through the annals of its history. I have found a great deal more than

I dreamed of, much of it a nightmare. I have concluded that dreams are not enough. Our dreams, like everything else, must be subject to critical scrutiny and objective judgement if they are to be worthwhile ideals to help negotiate the realities of this world. Mecca exists to shape us, not to be shaped by an unchallenged parade of human follies and foibles.

Nevertheless, my last best hope for myself and everyone is to know the timeless peace of Mecca I met in the eyes of one old man, the Pakistani peasant who had come to the Holy City to die. For believers like him, Mecca is a place of eternal harmony, something worth living for and striving to attain. It has always been. And it will always be.

Chronology

c. 1812–1637 BCE	Prophet Abraham builds the Kaaba, assisted by his son Ishmael.
c. 100 BCE	The Greek historian Diodorus Siculus mentions the Kaaba in his *Bibliotheca Historica*.
90–168 CE	The Egyptian Roman citizen Claudius Ptolemy mentions Mecca in his *Geography*.
100–250	The Yemeni tribes of Jurham rule Mecca.
250–380	The tribe of Khuza rules Mecca.
400	Qusayy unifies the Quraysh tribe and establishes a hamlet around the shrine.
552	Abrahah attacks Mecca (probably).
570	The Prophet Muhammad is born.
605	The Quraysh rebuild the Kaaba, assisted by the young Muhammad.
610	Muhammad receives the first revelation, and becomes the Prophet of Islam.
613	The Prophet begins preaching in Mecca.
622	The Prophet Muhammad is forced to migrate from Mecca to Medina.
630	The Prophet Muhammad captures Mecca.
632	The Prophet Muhammad performs his first and only Hajj and gives his 'Farewell Pilgrimage' at Arafat, near Mecca.
632	Death of the Prophet Muhammad in Medina.
646	Othman, the third caliph of Islam, enlarges the Sacred Mosque to accommodate the growing number of pilgrims.
656	Battle of the Camel between Caliph Ali, the cousin of Muhammad, and Aisha, the Prophet's youngest wife.
661	Muawiya, the governor of Syria, establishes the Umayyad dynasty and reigns from Damascus.
661	Urban development of Mecca begins.

680	In the Battle of Kerbala, the Prophet's grandson, Hussain, is killed.
681–92	Ibn Zubair leads a resurrection against Umayyad rule, becomes the leader of Mecca and restores the Kaaba.
692	Mecca comes under siege from the Umayyad General al-Hajjaj bin Yusuf. Ibn Zubair is killed defending the Sacred Mosque single-handed; his restoration is destroyed and the Kaaba is reconstructed.
747–50	Construction of a gallery in the Great Mosque.
749	The Abbasids overthrow the Umayyads. The capital shifts from Damascus to Baghdad.
767–820	Muhammad ibn Idris Shafii is born, studies in Mecca, establishes his School of Islamic Law and dies in the city.
768	Death of ibn Ishaq, the author of *The Life of Muhammad*, the first biography of the Prophet.
779–85	A major extension of the Sacred Mosque by the Abbasid Caliph al-Mahdi begins and is completed by his son and successor, Caliph Musa al-Hadi; the Sanctuary now has 484 columns and 19 gates, and is decorated with most elaborate and beautiful works.
785–6	A permanent shrine at the Station of Abraham is constructed.
786	Shia insurrection in Mecca.
786–809	The Abbasid Caliph Harun al-Rashid visits Mecca. His wife Zubaidah installs water conduits in the Holy City.
833–48	The Abbasid Caliph al-Mamun initiates the *Mihna*, the trial on the created nature of the Qur'an, leading to the imprisonment of the jurist ibn Hanbal.
848–55	Ibn Hanbal in Mecca, where he establishes his School of Islamic Law, and dies.
865	Al-Azraqi publishes *Akhbar Makkah*, the first history of Mecca.
890	The emergence of the fanatical sect the Qarmatians.
894–5	Al-Mutadid, Abbasid caliph, demolishes the buildings around the Sanctuary and extends the Sacred Mosque towards the west, repairs walls and adds new gates.
918	Al-Muqtadir, Abbasid caliph, extends the Sacred Mosque further, adding new doors.
923	Death of the historian al-Tabari, author of *The History of al-Tabari*.
930	The Qarmatians enter Mecca, slaughter a great many pilgrims, loot the Kaaba and carry off the Black Stone.

950–1	The Qarmatians return the Black Stone to Mecca.
960	The sharifs establish themselves as local rulers of Mecca.
1046–52	The Persian poet, philosopher and Ismaili scholar Naser-e-Khosraw visits Mecca.
1181–3	The French knight Reynaud de Châtillon threatens Mecca; Reynaud's forces raid the Hijaz; the Franks are hunted down and killed or captured.
1183–5	The Andalusian geographer and poet ibn Jubayr visits Mecca.
1201–20	Qitada sharif of Mecca.
1202	Ibn Arabi's sojourn in Mecca and the publication of *The Meccan Revelations*.
1220–1	Hassan ibn Qitada sharif of Mecca.
1221–54	Rajih ibn Qitada sharif of Mecca, sporadically losing and regaining power.
1236–40	Ibn al-Mujawir, a trader from Khorassan with literary ambitions, visits Mecca.
1253–4	Idris ibn Qitada sharif of Mecca.
1254–1301	Muhammad Abu Nomay sharif of Mecca, with intervals of absence.
1260–1517	Mecca comes under the control of the Mamluk sultans of Egypt and Syria.
1269	Baybars, Mamluk king of Egypt, makes the Hajj.
1301–44	Rumaitha bin Abu Nomay sharif of Mecca, with intervals of absence.
1325–54	Ibn Battuta, the traveller and adventurer from Tangiers, visits Mecca five times during his travels around the world.
1325	Mansa Musa, the emperor of Mali, performs the Hajj in Mecca and brings camel-loads of gold to the Holy City.
1344–75	Ajlan bin Rumaitha rules Mecca, with a few co-rulers.
1360–86	Ahmad ibn Ajlan sharif of Mecca.
1387–94	Ali ibn Ajlan sharif of Mecca.
1394–1425	Hassan ibn Ajlan rules Mecca, with co-rulers, losing and regaining power a few times.
1399	The western side of the Sacred Mosque burns down in a fire, and part of the ceiling collapses.
1425–55	Barakat I rules Mecca, with intervals of absence.
1455–95	Muhammad ibn Barakat sharif of Mecca.
1468–96	Sultan Qu'it Bay of Egypt builds a theological school in Mecca.
1481–1512	Ottoman Sultan Bayezid II establishes the institution of

	the *surre* of the Holy Cities, which sends official gifts to Mecca.
1495–1524	Barakat II sharif of Mecca, with intervals of absence.
1517	Mecca comes under Ottoman rule.
1520–66	Sultan Suleiman the Magnificent repairs and extends the Sacred Mosque.
1524–84	Abu Nomay II sharif of Mecca.
1533	The Indian painter Muhi al-Din Lari publishes *kitab futuh al-haramayn*, the first paintings of Mecca.
1551	Sultan Suleiman has the roof of the Kaaba rebuilt.
1566–74	Sultan Selim II extends and rebuilds the foundation of the Sacred Mosque.
1574–95	Pilgrimage of Gulbadan, consort and aunt to the Mughal ruler Akbar the Great.
1584–1601	Hassan ibn Abu Nomay sharif of Mecca.
1595	The Ottoman artist Abdullah Lutfi publishes miniature paintings of Mecca, illustrating *The Life of Muhammad* (*Siyer-I Nebi*) by the blind Sufi scholar Mustafa Dariri Erzeni.
1601–24	Idris ibn Hassan rules Mecca with co-rulers.
1611–12	The architect Mehmed Aga repairs the Kaaba.
1624–31	Mecca has a string of different sharifs.
1629	The Kaaba is flooded, and is rebuilt by Sultan Murad IV.
1630–1	Mutinying Ottoman troops occupy Mecca; Kaaba is destroyed by a flash flood.
1631–66	Zaid ibn Muhsin rules Mecca, with intervals of absence.
1666–87	A number of sharifs fight for power in Mecca.
1671	Evliya Celebi, the refined Ottoman traveller, performs the Hajj in Mecca.
1687–1716	Said ibn Saad rules Mecca, with many intervals of absence.
1703	Muhammad ibn Abd-al Wahhab, the founder of the Wahhabi movement, is born.
1716–34	Mecca has a string of rulers, all fighting each other for power.
1734–52	Masoud ibn Said sharif of Mecca for the second time.
1756–70	Masaad ibn Said sharif of Mecca for the third time, with an interval.
1770–3	A number of sharifs fight for power.
1773–88	Sarur ibn Masaad becomes ruler of Mecca.
1747	Muhammad ibn Saud, ruler of Najd, enters into a

religious and political alliance with Muhammad ibn Abd
al-Wahhab, the founder of the Wahhabi movement.

1788–1813   Ghalib bin Masaad the sharif of Mecca.
1790   Outbreak of hostilities between the Wahhabis and the
sharif of Mecca.
1791   Death of Muhammad ibn Abd al-Wahhab.
1803   Sharif Ghalib cedes Mecca to the Wahhabis, but the
Wahhabis are unable to hold the city and Ghalib regains
it.
1805   Wahhabis besiege Mecca.
1806   Mecca surrenders to Wahhabis.
1807   Ali Bey Abbasi, the Spanish noble Domingo Badia y
Leyblich, visits Mecca for Hajj and witnesses the arrival
of the Wahhabis.
1813   Mecca falls to Tousoun, son of Muhammad Ali, the
pasha of Egypt, in January.
1813   Muhammad Ali arrives in Mecca in November.
1813–27   Yahya ibn Sarur is appointed sharif by Muhammad Ali,
the pasha of Egypt.
1814   The Swiss explorer John Lewis Burckhardt spends some
time in Mecca, meeting Sharif Ghalib.
1815   Muhammad Ali leads his troops to Taraba and defeats
the Wahhabis.
1827–8   Abdul Muttalib ibn Ghalib is appointed sharif for the
first time; returns as sharif for the second time in 1852–6;
and again in 1880–1.
1828–36   Muhammad ibn Abdul Moin ibn Aun becomes sharif of
Mecca for the first time; in 1840–52 for the second time;
and in 1856–8 for the third time.
1851–3   The British explorer Richard Burton visits Mecca, travelling in disguise with Indian pilgrims.
1854–6   The Ottomans abolish slavery, leading to riots and uprising in Mecca.
1858–77   Abdullah ibn Mohammad ibn Aun the sharif of Mecca.
1864   Nawab Sikandar Begum, the hereditary ruler of the
princely state of Bhopal, performs the pilgrimage to
Mecca and describes the city as a 'wild', dreary', 'repulsive' place.
1870   Hafiz Ahmad Hassan, an official of the nawab of Tonk in
Rajasthan, India, visits Mecca and finds the people of
Mecca to be 'ignorant, uncultured and greedy'.
1877–80   John F. T. Keane, Anglo-Indian adventurer, in Mecca.

1880	The Ottomans photograph Mecca for the *Yildiz Albums*.
1882–1905	Aun-al-Rafiq ibn Muhammad ibn Aun rules Mecca.
1884–5	C. Snouck Hurgronje, Dutch Orientalist and adviser on native affairs to the colonial government of Netherland East Indies, in Mecca, where he photographs the city's inhabitants.
1905–8	Ali ibn Abdullah ibn Muhammad ibn Aun the sharif of Mecca.
1905	Eldon Rutter, English traveller, disguised as a Syrian, performs the Hajj.
1908–24	Hussain ibn Ali becomes sharif of Mecca, proclaims himself the 'king of Hijaz' in 1917.
1908	A. J. B. Wavell, British soldier, in Mecca; meets Sharif Hussain.
1910	Mahmoud Mobarek Churchward, an artist and theatre painter, and convert to Islam, performs the Hajj.
1924	Hussain abdicates as king of the Hijaz; Wahhabis occupy Mecca.
1925	Harry St John Bridger Philby, the father of the famous Soviet double agent Kim Philby, becomes adviser to ibn Saud and settles in Mecca and Jeddah.
1926	The Wahhabi leader Abdul Aziz bin Saud declares himself king of the Hijaz.
1932	The Kingdom of Saudi Arabia is established by King Abdul Aziz bin Saud.
1933	Lady Evelyn Cobbold, Scottish noble and convert to Islam, becomes the first British woman to perform the pilgrimage to Mecca.
1953	King Abdul Aziz bin Saud dies.
1955–64	The first Saudi extension to the Sacred Mosque: the basement and the ground and first floors of the Mosque are repaired, with walls faced in marble and the arches in artificial stone; the distance between the hills of Safa and Marwah (the *sai* area) is covered, many buildings of historic significance are demolished.
1964	The American Black Muslim leader Malcolm X visits Mecca to perform the Hajj.
1973	'Master Plan for the Holy City of Mecca' is launched.
1974	The Hajj Research Centre is established at King Abdul Aziz University in Jeddah by the Saudi architect and dissident Sami Angawi.
1975	Fire kills at least 200 pilgrims in the camp in Mina.

1979	On 20 November, a group of fanatics invade and take over the Sacred Mosque, trapping tens of thousands of worshippers in the Sanctuary. The insurgents, whose leader declares himself to be the Mahdi, control the Sacred Mosque for two weeks. The siege ends after the death of 255 pilgrims, insurgents and military personnel.
1982–8	The second Saudi extension to the Sacred Mosque: a new wing on the western side of the Haram Mosque is built, supplemented by a new gate, King Fahd Gate, and four-teen minor gates and entrances to the basement of the Sacred Mosque, which also acquires three new domes and two new minarets. The entire roof of the Mosque is modified to enable worshippers to pray on top; in addi-tion five escalators are distributed around the Haram and the new extension, and an outdoor prayer area, on the western side of the Mosque, located at the bottom of the famous Abu Qubays mountain, is built next to the Mosque; tunnels are also built to take worshippers direct from the Sacred Mosque to Muna; all remaining cultural property and buildings of historic significance are bulldozed.
1987	A violent clash between Shia pilgrims from Iran and Saudi security forces in front of the Sacred Mosque; 402 pilgrims are killed.
1989	Terrorists set off two bombs in Mecca, killing one and wounding sixteen.
1990	1,426 pilgrims die in the tunnel connecting the Sacred Mosque to Mina.
1997	A fire kills 343 pilgrims in Mina.
1988–2005	The third Saudi extension to the Sacred Mosque: palaces are built, a clock tower is added, and shopping malls incorporated within the precinct of the Sacred Mosque.
2004	251 pilgrims are killed in a stampede during the stone-throwing ritual.
2006	345 pilgrims are crushed to death during the stone-throwing ritual.
2011	Plans announced to extend the Sacred Mosque to accom-modate 2 million worshippers.

Notes

INTRODUCTION

1 Some of the work I did on Mecca is reported in Ziauddin Sardar and M. A. Zaki Badawi, *Hajj Studies* (Croom Helm, London, 1978).

2 Ibn Battuta, *Travels in Asia and Africa: 1325–1354* (Routledge and Kegan Paul, London, 1929); trans. Ross E. Dunn, *The Adventures of Ibn Battuta* (University of California Press, Berkeley, 1989). Tim Mackintosh-Smith has retraced the journeys of Ibn Battuta in *Travels with a Tangerine* (2001), *The Hall of a Thousand Columns* (2005) and *Landfalls: On the Edge of Islam with Ibn Battutah* (2010), all published by John Murray, London.

I THE VALLEY OF WEEPING

1 Psalms 84: 5–6, New International Version, 2011.

2 Martin Lings, *Mecca* (ArchType, Cambridge, 2004), p. 5.

3 The main proponents of this thesis are Patricia Crone and Michael Cook, *Hagarism: The Making of the Islamic World* (Cambridge University Press, Cambridge, 1980); Tom Holland's controversial book *In the Shadow of the Sword* (Little Brown, London, 2012) draws heavily on the work of Crone.

4 See, for example, W. F. Albright, *Archaeology and the Religion of Israel* (Johns Hopkins University Press, Baltimore, MD, 1946); Israel Finkelstein and Neal Asher Silberman, *The Bible Unearthed: Archaeology's New Visions of Ancient Israel and the Origins of its Sacred Text* (Free Press, New York, 2001); and Jonathan Kirsch, *King David: The Real Life of the Man Who Ruled Israel* (Ballantine Books, New York, 2002).

5 Edward Gibbon, *Gibbon's Decline and Fall of the Roman Empire*, Introduction by Christopher Dawson, vol. V (Everyman's Library, London, 1994), pp. 223–4.

6 *Diodorus of Sicily*, trans. C. H. Oldfather, vol. II (William Heinemann Ltd., London & Harvard University Press, Cambridge, Mass., 1935), p. 217.

7 D. G. Hogarth, *The Penetration of Arabia* (Alston Rivers Limited, London, 1905), p. 18.

8 G. E. von Grunebaum, *Classical Islam: A History 600–1258* (George Allen & Unwin Limited, 1970), p. 19.

9 E. Dixon, J. R. Cann and Colin Renfrew, 'Obsidian and the Origins of Trade', in *Old World Archaeology: Foundations of Civilization* (W. H. Freeman and Company, San Francisco, 1972), p. 87.

10 Jack Turner, *Spice: The History of Temptation* (Arnold Knopf, New York, 2004), p. 145.

11 Richard W. Bulliet, *The Camel and the Wheel* (Columbia University Press, New York, 1990).

12 Fred M. Donner, *Muhammad and the Believers at the Origins of Islam* (Harvard University Press, Cambridge, Mass., 2010).

13 Genesis 21:15–19.

14 Genesis 21:20.

15 Shaikh Safiur Rahman Mubarakpuri, *History of Makkah* (Darussalm, Riyadh, 2002), p. 32.

16 'Hagar is seen as a victim, a lascivious sinner, an abused slave, or as strong, nurturing mother of Ishmael. Sarah is painted either as a jealous wife, a Jewish prophet, or mother of all true Christians. Abraham is generally regarded as the obedient servant of God, the embodiment of a one-dimensional faith, rather than a complicated, multi-layered individual who suffers greatly during this episode in his life.' Charlotte Gordon, *The Woman Who Named God* (Little, Brown, London, 2009), p. xiv.

17 Kamal Al Salibi, *The Bible Came from Arabia* (Jonathan Cape, London, 1984).

18 'They are sagas which were handed down orally long before they were fixed in writing. Sagas are not fairy tales, as a rule they have a historical nucleus, for all their brevity, simplification and concentration on a few persons.' Hans Kung, *Islam* (OneWorld, Oxford, 2007), p. 45.

19 Heinrich Schliemann, *Troja und seine Ruinen* (1875), trans. into English by L. Dora Schmitz as *Troy and its Remains*, reissued by Cambridge University Press, Cambridge, 2010.

20 Al-Azraqi, *Akhbar Makkah* (2 vols, Dar al Andalus, Beirut, 1983); see also Abu al-Walid Muhammad bin Abdullah bin Ali al-Azraqi, *Kitab Akhbar Makka*, ed. F. Wustenfeld as vol. I of *Geschichte der Stadt Mekka* (Leipzig, 1858; reprint Georg Olms, 1981).

21 Oleg Grabar, 'Upon Reading Al-Azraqi', in *Muqarnas III: An Annual of Islamic Art and Architecture*, ed. Oleg Grabar (Brill, Leiden, 1985).

22 Al-Tabari, *The History of al-Tabari*, ed. Ehsan Yar-Shater, various transla-
   tors (40 vols, State University of New York Press, New York, 1988–2007).
23 Ibn Saad, *Kitab al-Tabaqat*, trans. Moinul Haq (Kitab Bhavan, Delhi,
   1986).
24 Ibn Ishaq, *The Life of Muhammad*, trans. A. Guillaume (Oxford
   University Press, Oxford, 1955).
25 The Qur'an 2. 130.
26 Ibn Kathir, *The Life of Muhammad*, trans. Trevor Le Gassick (Garnet,
   London, 1998), vol. 1, pp. 38–40.
27 Ibn Ishaq, pp. 46–7.
28 Ibn Hisham, *Al-Sirat al-Nabawyah* (Cairo, 1936), vol 1, p. 116, quoted
   in Emel Esin, *Mecca the Blessed, Madinah the Radiant* (Elek Books,
   London, 1963), p. 37.
29 Ibn Ishaq, pp. 24, 35, 39.
30 Esin, p. 41.
31 Hisham ibn-al-Kalbi, *The Book of Idols*, trans. Nabih Amin Faris
   (Lahore, 1952), p. 17.
32 *The History of al-Tabari*, vol. VI, p. 54.
33 Ibn Saad, pp. 63–74.
34 Esin, p. 59.
35 Marshall Hodgson, *The Venture of Islam* (Chicago University Press,
   Chicago, 1974), vol. I, p. 156.
36 *The History of al-Tabari*, vol. VI, p. 10.
37 For a full account of Abrahah's attack on Mecca see ibn Kathir,
   pp. 20–8.
38 Ibn Ishaq, p. 25.
39 Ibid., p. 67.
40 Ibid., p. 82.
41 Ibid., p. 85.
42 Ibid., p. 86.
43 Ibid.

2 'I LOVE THEE MORE THAN THE ENTIRE WORLD'

1 Al-Tabari, *The History of al-Tabari* (State University of New York
  Press, New York, 1988), vol. VI, p. 71.
2 The Qur'an 96. 1–5.
3 T. S. Eliot, *Four Quartets* (Faber and Faber, London, 1944).
4 W. Montgomery Watt, *Muhammad At Mecca* (Oxford University Press,
  Oxford, 1953), p. 55.
5 The Qur'an 111. 1–3.
6 The Qur'an 106. 1–3.
7 The Qur'an 93. 9–11.

8 The Qur'an 37. 22–3.
9 The Qur'an 89. 17–20.
10 The Qur'an 98. 6.
11 On the Hanifs, see Fred Donner, *Muhammad and the Believers* (Belknap Press, Cambridge, Mass., 2010); and Irving M. Zeitlin, *The Historical Muhammad* (Polity, Cambridge, 2007), pp. 50–63.
12 Ibn Ishaq, *The Life of Muhammad*, trans. A. Guillaume (Oxford University Press, Oxford, 1955), p. 119.
13 Ibid.
14 Ibid., p. 312.
15 The Qur'an 41. 68.
16 Ibn Ishaq, p. 133.
17 Al-Tabari, vol. VI, p. 112.
18 Ibid., p. 113.
19 *Sahih Bukhari*, vol. II, book 23, no. 442.
20 Ibn Saad, *Kitab Al-tabaqat Al-kabir*, trans. S. Moinal Haq and H. K. Ghazanfar (Kitab Bhava, New Delhi, 1986), p. 264.
21 Shibli Nomani, *Sirat-un-Nabi* (Kazi Publications, Lahore, 1979), p. 242.
22 The Qur'an 90. 1–2.
23 The Qur'an 95. 1–6.
24 The Qur'an 2. 150.
25 The Qur'an 3. 96–7.
26 The Qur'an 2. 150.
27 Ibn Saad, p. 12.
28 Ibn Ishaq, p. 374.
29 Ibid., p. 385.
30 Ibid., p. 386.
31 Ibid., p. 454.
32 Ibid., p. 460.
33 The Qur'an 2. 97.
34 Ibn Ishaq, p. 504.
35 Ibid., p. 505.
36 Ibid., p. 547.
37 Ibid.
38 Ibid., p. 553.
39 Ibid., p. 533.
40 The Qur'an 17. 81.
41 Ibn Ishaq, p. 553.

3 REBELLIONS AT GOD'S EARTHLY THRONE

1 Al-Waqidi, *The Life of Muhammad*, ed. Rizwi Faizer, trans. Rizwi Faizer, Amal Ismail and Abdulkader Tayob (Routledge, London, 2011),

p. 539. Classical sources give different versions of the 'Farewell Sermon'. The al-Waqidi version, for example, is rather different from ibn Ishaq's. While al-Waqidi has a section on wife beating, ibn Ishaq makes no mention of it. Tabari, on the other hand, does not report the Farewell Sermon at all!

2 Ibn Ishaq, *The Life of Muhammad*, trans. A. Guillaume (Oxford University Press, Oxford, 1955), p. 652.

3 *Al-Tabari, The History of al-Tabari* (State University of New York Press, New York, 1988), vol. XVII, p. 227.

4 Imam Ali, *Nahjul Balagha*, selected and compiled by as-Sayyid Abu'l-Hasan Muhammad ibn al-Husayn ar-Radi al-Musawi, trans. Syed Ali Raza (Ansariyan Publications, Qum, 1971).

5 Al-Tabari, vol. V, p. 27.

6 Fatima Mernissi, *Women in Islam: An Historical and Theological Enquiry* (Blackwell, London, 1991), p. 7. Mernissi looks at the Battle of the Camel in some detail to show how it has been used to promote misogyny by classical and modern conservative scholars.

7 Emel Esin, *Mecca the Blessed, Madinah the Radiant* (Elek Books, London, 1963), p. 127.

8 Ann K. S. Lambton, *State and Government in Medieval Islam* (Oxford University Press, Oxford, 1981), p. 27.

9 Al-Tabari, vol. XVII, pp. 109–10.

10 Ibid., p. 115.

11 Ibid., vol. XIX, p. 65.

12 Ibid., p. 67.

13 See Muwwafaq Khwarizmi, *Maqtal al-Husayn*, ed. Muhammad Samawi (Anwar al-Huda, Qum, 2003); Annemarie Schimmel, 'Karbala and the Imam Husayn in Persian and Indo-Muslim literature', in Muhammadi Trust, *Al-Serat: The Imam Husayn Conference*, vol. 12 (Muhammadi Trust, London, 1986). There is a full list of sources on Imam Hussain in Mohammad Ishtihardi, *Lamentations – Part II: The Tragedy of the Lord of Martyrs*, trans. Arif Abdulhussain (Al-Mahdi Institute, Birmingham, 2001).

14 Asma Afsaruddin, *The First Muslims: History and Memory* (One World, Oxford, 2008), p. 83.

15 Al-Tabari, vol. XXI, pp. 229–32.

16 Esin, p. 139.

17 Al-Azraqi, *Akhbar Makkah* (2 vols, Dar al Andalus, Beirut, 1983), vol. II, p. 79.

18 See M. A. Shaban, *The Abbasid Revolution* (Cambridge University Press, 1970); Jacob Lassner, *The Shaping of Abbasid Rule* (Princeton University Press, 1980); M. J. L. Young, J. D. Latham and R. B. Serjeant, eds, *Religion, Learning and Science in the Abbasid Period* (Cambridge

University Press, 1990); Franz Rosenthal, *The Classical Heritage in Islam* (University of California Press, Berkeley, 1975).

19 Louis Massignon, *The Passion of al-Hallaj*, trans. Herbert Mason (4 vols, Princeton University Press, 1982), vol. I, p. 5. This is a magnificent work, a product of forty years' labour of love, which offers not only a definitive account of al-Hallaj's life but also a vivid and detailed portrait of tenth-century Baghdad.

20 Cyril Glassé, *The Concise Encyclopaedia of Islam* (revised edition, Stacey International, London, 1991), p. 203.

21 Seyyed Hossein Nasr, *The Garden of Truth: The Vision and Promise of Sufism, Islam's Mystical Tradition* (HarperOne, London, 2008), p. 178.

22 See Margaret Smith, *Rabi'a The Mystic and her Fellow-Saints in Islam* (Cambridge University Press, 1984).

23 M. M. Sharif, ed., *A History of Muslim Philosophy* (Otto Harrassowitz, Wiesbaden, 1963), vol. I, p. 221.

24 Marshall Hodgson, *The Venture of Islam: Conscience and History in a World Civilization* (3 vols, University of Chicago Press, 1974), vol. I, *The Classical Age*, pp. 387–8.

25 Ibid., p. 386.

26 Walter M. Patton, *Ahmed ibn Hanbal and the Mihna* (Brill, Leiden, 1897), pp. 70–2.

27 Ibid., p. 57.

28 The Qur'an 17. 19.

29 The Qur'an 17. 20–5.

30 Al-Tabari, vol. I, p. 301.

31 Ibid., p. 294.

32 Ibid., p. 295.

4 SHARIFS, SULTANS AND SECTARIANS

1 Knut S. Vikor, *Between God and the Sultan: A History of Islamic Law* (Hurst, London, 2005), p. 91.

2 Maseeh Rahman, 'Among Many, Many Believers', *Time*, 4 March 2002.

3 Gustave E. von Grunebaum, *Medieval Islam* (2nd edition, University of Chicago Press, 1953), p. 197.

4 Marshall Hodgson, *The Venture of Islam* (3 vols, University of Chicago Press, 1974), vol. I, p. 490.

5 Ibid., p. 491.

6 For radical ideas during the English revolution of the mid-seventeenth century, see Christopher Hill, *The World Turned Upside Down* (Penguin, London, 2010).

7 Qutb al-Din, *Kitab al-I'lam bi a'lam bayt allah al-haram*, quoted in F. E. Peters, *Mecca: A Literary History of the Muslim Holy Land* (Princeton University Press, Princeton, 1994), pp. 123–4.

8 Ibid., p. 125.

9 On the science and learning of the 'Golden Age', see Jan P. Hogendijk and Abdelhamid I. Sabra, eds, *The Enterprise of Science in Islam* (MIT Press, Cambridge, Mass., 2003); Ehsan Masood, *Science and Islam: A History* (Icon Books, London, 2008); Michael Hamilton Morgan, *Lost History: The Enduring Legacy of Muslim Scientists, Thinkers and Artists* (National Geographic, Washington DC, 2007).

10 On Islam's contribution to European Renaissance and Western civilization see George Saliba, *Islamic Science and the Making of the European Renaissance* (MIT Press, Cambridge, Mass., 2007); Tim Wallace-Murphy, *What Islam Did for Us: Understanding Islam's Contribution to Western Civilisation* (Watkins Publishing, London, 2006); Jonathan Lyons, *The House of Wisdom: How the Arabs Transformed Western Civilisation* (Bloomsbury, London, 2009).

11 Al-Nadim, *The Fahrist of al-Nadim*, ed. and trans. Bayard Dodge (2 vols, Columbia University Press, New York, 1970).

12 *The Collected Poems of W. B. Yeats* (Wordsworth Editions, Ware, 2000).

13 George Makdisi, *The Rise of Colleges: Institutions of Learning in Islam and the West* (Edinburgh University Press, Edinburgh, 1981).

14 Naser-e Khosraw, *Book of Travels*, trans. W. M. Thackston Jr. (Bibliotheca Persia, State University of New York, 1986), p. 69.

15 Ibid., p. 68.

16 Ibid., p. 80.

17 Ibid., p. 68.

18 Ibid., pp. 69–70.

19 Ibid., pp. 71–2.

20 Ibid., p. 76; the quotation from the Qur'an is 3. 96.

21 Ibid., p. 80.

22 Ibid., pp. 76–7.

23 In the *Chansons de geste*, the heroic poems of medieval France, Saladin is treated with some respect while 'Saracens' as a whole are demonized. See Norman Daniel, *Heroes and Saracens* (Edinburgh University Press, 1984). For a more general representation of Islam during this period, see Norman Daniel, *Islam, Europe and Empire* (Edinburgh University Press, 1966). For the Muslim view of the Crusades, see Nabil Matar, *Europe Through Arab Eyes* (Columbia University Press, New York, 2009), and Amin Maalouf, *The Crusades Through Arab Eyes* (Al Saqi Books, London, 1984).

24 *Travels of Ibn Jubayr*, trans. Roland Broadhurst (original 1952; Goodword Books, Delhi, 2007), p. 49.

25 Ibid., p. 71.
26 Ibid., p. 92.
27 Ibid., p. 71.
28 Ibid., p. 85.
29 Ibid., p. 87.
30 Ibid., p. 85.
31 Ibid., p. 80.
32 Ibid., p. 104.
33 Ibid., p. 174.
34 Ibid., p. 120.
35 Ibid., p. 117.
36 Ibid., p. 187. The 'Divine law' mentioned is the verse in The Qur'an that describes Joseph being sold as a slave: 'Some travellers came by. They sent someone to draw water and he let down his bucket. "Good news!" he exclaimed. "Here is a boy." They hid him like a piece of merchandise – God was well aware of what they did – and then sold him for a small price, for a few pieces of silver: so little did they value him' (12. 19–20).
37 Ibid., p. 91.
38 Ibid., p. 92.
39 Ibid., p. 93.
40 Ibid., p. 72.
41 Ibid., p. 147.

5 LOVE AND FRATRICIDE IN THE HOLY CITY

1 See, for example, Dan Bahat, *Atlas of Biblical Jerusalem* (Carta, Jerusalem, 1994).
2 See Stanley Lane-Poole, *Saladin and the Fall of Jerusalem* (Greenhill Books, Barnsley, 2002; original 1903). Lane-Poole, who worked at the British Museum and later became Professor of Arabic Studies at Dublin University, was a prolific historian with a passionate love for his subject, as demonstrated by his earlier work, *Saladin: All-Powerful Sultan and the Uniter of Islam* (1898). For a broader perspective on the Crusades see Jill N. Claster, *Sacred Violence: The European Crusades in the Middle East 1095–1396* (University of Toronto Press, 2009); and the classic work by Steven Runciman, the 3-volume *A History of the Crusades* (Penguin, London, 1990; originally 1951–4).
3 Steven Runciman, *The History of the Crusades*, vol. II, *The Kingdom of Jerusalem and the Frankish East 1100–1187* (Cambridge University Press, 1951), pp. 445, 450. See also Bernard Hamilton, 'The Elephant of Christ: Reynald of Châtillon', *Studies in Church History* 15 (Oxford, 1978), pp. 97–108.
4 Gary L. Rashba, *Holy Wars* (Casemate, Oxford, 2011), p. 116.

5 Joshua Prawer, *The Crusaders' Kingdom* (Phoenix, New York, 1972), p. 71.

6 *Travels of Ibn Jubayr*, trans. Roland Broadhurst (Goodword Books, Delhi, 2007), pp. 51–2.

7 For an abridged version, see Ibn Arabi, *The Meccan Revelations*, ed. Michel Chodkiewicz, trans. Michel Chodkiewicz, William Chittick and James Morris (2 vols, Pir Publications, New York, 2002).

8 *Ibn Al-Arabi, On the Mysteries of the Pilgrimage: From the Meccan Revelations*, trans. Aisha Bewley (Great Books of the Islamic World, Chicago, 2009), p. 121.

9 Ibid., p. 43.

10 Ibid., p. 104.

11 For the Arabic original see Ibn Arabi, *Tarjumān al-Ashwāq* (Dar Sadir, Beirut, 1966); for an English translation see Ibn Arabi, *The Tarjumān al-Ashwāq: A Collection of Mystical Odes*, ed. and trans. Reynold Nicholson (Royal Asiatic Society, London, 1911).

12 Quoted in Roger Allen, *The Arabic Literary Heritage* (Cambridge University Press, Cambridge, 1998), p. 194.

13 On the evolution of *ghazal*, see the excellent *The Penguin Anthology of Classical Arabic Literature* by Robert Irwin (Penguin, London, 1999).

14 For a recent translation, see *Poems from the Diwan of Umar ibn Abi Rabia*, trans. Arthur Wormhoudt (William Penn College, Oskaloosa, Iowa, 1977).

15 Allen, p. 175.

16 Ibid., p. 176.

17 On al-Farabi's *The Grand Book of Music* see Owen Wright, 'Music', in *The Legacy of Islam*, ed. Joseph Schacht and C. E. Bosworth (Clarendon Press, Oxford, 1974), pp. 489–505; H. G. Farmer, *The Sources of Arabian Music* (E. J. Brill, Leiden, 1965).

18 *Encyclopaedia Britannica*, http://en.wikipedia.org/wiki Encyclop%C3 %A6dia_Britannica, 'The Canon of Medicine', 2008; and Manfred Ullman, *Islamic Medicine* (Edinburgh University Press, 1978).

19 *Ibn al-Arabi, On the Mysteries of the Pilgrimage*, p. 253.

20 Ibid., pp. 282, 284.

21 Gerald de Gaury, *Rulers of Mecca* (Roy Publishers, New York, 1950), p. 84.

22 Takk-l-Din al Fasi, *Shifa al Ghuram bi Akhbar al balad al haram* (F. Wustenfeld, Leipzig, 1859), quoted in de Gaury, p. 84.

23 Ibn Khaldun, *The Muqaddimah: An Introduction to History*, trans. Franz Rosenthal (Routledge and Kegan Paul, London, 1967).

24 Ibn al-Mujawir, *A Traveller in Thirteenth-Century Arabia: Ibn al-Mujawir's Tarikh al-Mustabsir*, ed. G. Rex Smith (Hakluyt Society, London, 2008).

25 Ibid., p. 33.
26 Ibid., p. 36.
27 The Qur'an 24. 31.
28 Ibn al-Mujawir, pp. 34–5.
29 Ibid., p. 80.
30 Ibid., p. 79.
31 Ibid., p. 78.
32 See P. Thorau, *The Lion of Egypt: Sultan Baybars I and the Near East in the Thirteenth Century* (Longman, London, 1992).
33 See Elias N. Saad, *Social History of Timbuktu* (Cambridge University Press, 1983).
34 Marq de Villiers and Sheila Hirtle, *Timbuktu: The Sahara's Fabled God City* (Walker and Company, New York, 2007), p. 75.
35 There are several translations of *Rihlah*, from the classic *Ibn Battuta, Travels in Asia and Africa 1325–1354* by H. A. R. Gibb (Routledge, London, 1929, which incidentally does not give the name of the translator); to Ross E. Dunn, *The Adventures of Ibn Battuta* (University of California Press, 1989), which describes and paraphrases his journeys; and *The Travels of Ibn Battutah*, ed. Tim Mackintosh-Smith (Picador, London, 2002), which is an abridged version of the *Rihlah*. Mackintosh-Smith has retraced Ibn Battuta's journeys in three enthralling volumes: *Travels with a Tangerine*, *The Hall of the Thousand Columns* and *Landfalls* (John Murray, London, 2001, 2005 and 2010, respectively).
36 *The Travels of Ibn Battutah*, ed. Tim Mackintosh-Smith (Picador, London, 2002), p. 47.
37 Ibid., p. 48.
38 Ibid., p. 49.

6 THE CARAVANS OF PRECIOUS GIFTS

1 Emel Esin, *Mecca the Blessed, Madinah the Radiant* (Elek Books, London, 1963), p. 172.
2 Halil Inalcik, *The Ottoman Empire: The Classical Age 1300–1600* (Phoenix, London, 1973), p. 57.
3 Justine McCarthy, *The Ottoman Turks* (Longman, London, 1997), p. 89.
4 See C. R. Boxer, *The Portuguese Seaborne Empire 1415–1825* (Hutchinson, London, 1969); and Malyn Newitt, *The First Portuguese Colonial Empire* (University of Exeter, Exeter, 1986).
5 J. H. Parry, *The Age of Reconnaissance: Discovery, exploration and settlement 1450–1650* (Hutchinson, London, 1963).
6 Yolaç Afetinan, *The Oldest Map of America, Drawn by Piri Reis* (Türk Tarih Kurumu Basimevi, Ankara, 1954).

7 Translations of the notations are available at http://turkeyinmaps.com/piri.html

8 Piri Reis, *Kitab i Bahriye* (Historical Research Foundation, Istanbul Research Centre, Istanbul, 1988). See also Jerry Brotton, *Trading Territories: Mapping the Early Modern World* (Reaktion Books, London, 2003).

9 See A. J. R. Russell-Wood, *The Portuguese Empire, 1415–1808* (Johns Hopkins University Press, Baltimore, Md., 1988).

10 Suraiya Faroqhi, *The Ottoman Empire and the World Around It* (I. B. Tauris, London, 2011), p. 183.

11 See Chris Ware, *Admiral Byng: His Rise and Execution* (Pen and Sword Maritime, London, 2008).

12 Suraiya Faroqhi, *Pilgrims and Sultans* (I. B. Tauris, London, 1994), p. 58.

13 It was in fact a general practice for professors to sit on a chair, surrounded by their students sitting in a circle, throughout the Muslim world. See George Makdisi, *The Rise of Colleges: Institutions of Learning in Islam and the West* (Edinburgh University Press, 1981).

14 See Grace Martin Smith, *The Poetry of Yūnus Emre: A Turkish Sufi Poet* (University of California Press, Berkeley, 1993).

15 Esin, p. 171.

16 Faroqhi, *Pilgrims and Sultans*, p. 85.

17 Michael Axworthy, *The Sword of Persia: Nader Shah from Tribal Warrior to Conquering Tyrant* (I. B. Tauris, London, 2010), pp. 120–1, 125.

18 Ira M. Lapidus, *A History of Islamic Societies* (Cambridge University Press, 1988), p. 245.

19 Faroqhi, *Pilgrims and Sultans*, p. 68. See also Cafer Efendi, *Risāle-i Mi'māriyye: An Early Seventeenth-Century Ottoman Treatise on Architecture*, ed. Howard Crane (Brill, Leiden, 1987).

20 See Zeren Tanindi, *Siyer-I Nebi* (Hurriyet Vakfi Yayinilari, Istanbul, 1984). On Erzeni's life see Emel Esin, *Turkish Miniature Paintings* (Charles E. Tuttle Company, Rutland, Vt., 1960).

21 Muhi al-Din Lari, *kitab futuh al-haramayn*, Safavid Iran, dated 940AH/1533 CE. Leaves from the book are on display at various museums such as the Metropolitan Museum of Art, New York, and Chester Beatty Museum, Dublin.

22 Sheila S. Blair and Jonathan M. Bloom, *The Art and Architecture of Islam: 1250–1800* (Yale University Press, 1994), p. 145.

23 Esin Atil, *The Age of Sultan Suleyman the Magnificent* (National Gallery of Art, Washington, 1987), p. 64.

24 Gerald de Gaury, *Rulers of Mecca* (Roy Publishers, New York, 1950), p. 133.

25 Ibid., p. 135.

26 See Ali al-Kharbutli, *Tarikh al Kaabah* (Dar al Jil, Beirut, 1991), and Sayyid Abdul Majid Bakr, *Ashhar al Masajid fi al Islam* (Dar al Qiblah, Jeddah, 1984).

27 De Gaury, p. 142.

28 Faroqhi, *Pilgrims and Sultans*, p. 87.

29 Muhammad Haider al Hussaini, *Kitab Tandhid al Uqud* (Baghdad, 1750), quoted in de Gaury, p. 148.

30 De Gaury, p. 148.

31 The Qur'an 45. 3.

32 The Qur'an 29. 20.

33 Evliya Celebi, *Narrative of Travels in Europe, Asia, and Africa in the Seventeenth Century*, trans. Joseph von Hammer (abridged in 2 vols, Cambridge University Press, 2012).

34 *An Ottoman Traveller: Selections from the Book of Travels by Evliya Celebi*, trans. Robert Dankoff and Sooyong Kim (Elaand, London, 2010), p. 359.

35 Ibid., p. 361.

36 Evliya Celebi, *Travels*, quoted in de Gaury, p. 151.

37 Esin, p. 179. Evliya Celebi, *Travels*, quoted in de Gaury, p. 151.

7 THE WAHHABI THREAT

1 Gerald de Gaury, *Rulers of Mecca* (Roy Publishers, New York, 1950), p. 180.

2 Madawi Al-Rasheed, *A History of Saudi Arabia* (2nd edn, Cambridge University Press, 2010), p. 15.

3 David Cummins, *The Wahhabi Mission and Saudi Arabia* (I. B. Tauris, London, 2008), p. 11.

4 Muhammad ibn Abd al-Wahhab, *Kashf Ashubuhat*, trans. Mualafat Ash-Sheikh al-Imam Muhammad ibn Abdul Wahhab (Islamic University of Imam Muhammad ibn Saud, Riyadh, n.d.), p. 46.

5 John S. Habib, 'Wahhabi Origins of the Contemporary Saudi State', in Mohammad Ayoob and Hasan Kosebalaban, eds, *Religion and Politics in Saudi Arabia: Wahhabism and the State* (Lynne Reinner, Boulder, Colo., 2009), p. 58.

6 Hamid Algar, *Wahhabism: A Critical Essay* (Islamic Publications International, Oneonta, New York, 2002), p. 34.

7 De Gaury, p. 180.

8 John Lewis Burckhardt, *Travels in Arabia*, 1829 (reprinted, The Echo Library, Teddington, Middlesex, 2006), p. 149.

9 Natana J. DeLong-Bas, 'Wahhabism and the Question of Religious Tolerance' in Ayoob and Kosebalaban, eds. *Religion and Politics*, p. 12.

10 De Gaury, p. 182.

11 Uthman bin Abdullah bin Bishr, *Unwan al-Majid fi Tarikh Najd* (Riyadh, n.d.), p. 123, quoted in Algar, p. 26.

12 *Travels of Ali Bey*, vol. II (Longman, London, 1816; reprinted, Garnet, London, 1993), pp. 60–1.

13 Ibid., p. 61.

14 Ibid., p. 62.

15 Afaf Lutfi al-Sayyid Marsot, *Egypt in the Reign of Muhammad Ali* (Cambridge University Press, 1984), p. 21.

16 The title of the famous book by Henry Dodwell, *The Founder of Modern Egypt: A Study of Mohammad Ali* (Cambridge University Press, 1931; reprinted 2011).

17 Marsot, p. 198.

18 John Lewis Burckhardt, *Notes on the Bedouins and Wahabys* (Henry Colburn and Richard Bentley, London, 1831), vol. I, p. 345.

19 Marsot, p. 200.

20 Burckhardt, *Travels in Arabia*, pp. 64, 120.

21 Ibid., p. 79.

22 Ibid., p. 75.

23 Ibid., p. 73.

24 Ibid., p. 72.

25 Ibid., p. 110.

26 De Gaury, p. 204.

27 Mark Mazower, *Salonica* (HarperPerennial, London, 2005), p. 112.

8 CAMELS, INDIANS AND FEUDAL QUEENS

1 John Lewis Burckhardt, *Notes on the Bedouins and Wahabys* (Henry Colburn and Richard Bentley, London, 1831), vol. II, p. 269.

2 Ibid., pp. 287–8.

3 Gerald de Gaury, *Rulers of Mecca* (Roy Publishers, New York, 1950), p. 218.

4 Burckhardt, p. 314.

5 Giovanni Finati, *Narrative of the Life and Adventures of Giovanni Finati* (2 vols, John Murray, London, 1830), quoted in F. E. Peters, *Mecca: A Literary History of the Muslim Holy Land* (Princeton University Press, 1994), p. 320.

6 De Gaury, p. 227.

7 Ibid., p. 241.

8 Ehud R. Toledano, *Slavery and Abolition in the Ottoman Middle East* (University of Washington Press, 1997), p. 117.

9 Lord Kinross, *The Ottoman Empire* (Folio Society, London, 2003), p. 496.

10 M. N. Pearson, *Pious Passengers: The Hajj in Earlier Times* (Sterling Publishers, Delhi, 1994), p. 116.

11 For further background on Nawab Sikandar Begum, see Shaharyar M. Khan, *The Begums of Bhopal: A History of the Princely State of Bhopal* (I. B. Tauris, London, 2000).

12 'The Begum of Bhopal', *Illustrated London News*, 16 May 1863.

13 *A Princess's Pilgrimage: Nawab Sikandar Begum's A Pilgrimage to Mecca*, ed. Siobhan Lambert-Hurley (Indiana University Press, Bloomington, 2008), pp. 47–8.

14 Ibid., p. 49.

15 Ibid., p. 50.

16 Ibid., p. 60.

17 Ibid., p. 70.

18 Ibid., p. 72.

19 Ibid.

20 Ibid., p. 121.

21 Ibid., pp. 133–5.

22 Hafiz Ahmed Hassan, *Pilgrimage to the Caaba and Charing Cross* (W. H. Allen, London, 1871; reprinted Wirsa, Karachi, 2006), p. 68.

23 Ibid., p. 69.

24 Ibid., p. 96.

25 Ibid., p. 92.

26 Ibid., p. 109.

27 John F. T. Keane, *Six Months in Meccah* (Tinsley Brothers, London, 1881, p. 100; reprinted Barzan Publishing, Manchester, 2006).

28 Ibid., p. 140.

29 Ibid.

30 Ibid., p. 141.

31 Ibid.

32 Charles M. Doughty, *Travels in Arabia Deserta* (Dover Publications, New York, 1979), vol. II, p. 542.

33 Ibid., p. 673; Doughty's emphasis.

9 WESTERN VISITORS, ARAB GARB

1 Mehmet Bahadir Dorduncu, *The Yildiz Albums of Sultan Abdulhamid II* (The Light Inc., New Jersey, 2006). Only a small selection is included here. The landscapes of Mecca are on pp. 68–9, 70–1, 72–3 and 74–5.

2 *The Arabian Nights: Complete and Unabridged*, trans. Sir Richard F. Burton (Halcyon Press, 2010, Kindle Edition); *The Arabian Nights: Tales of 1001 Nights*, trans. Malcolm C. Lyons (Penguin Classic, London, 2010).

3 *The Assemblies of al-Hariri*, trans. Amina Shah (Octagon Press, London, 1981).

4 Quoted in C. Snouck Hurgronje, *Mekka in the Later Part of the 19th Century*, trans. J. H. Monahan (Brill, Leiden, 2007), p. 179.

5 C. Snouck Hurgronje published two volumes in German under the general title of *Mekka* in 1888–9. *Mekka in the Later Part of the 19th Century* is the second volume.

6 *The Perfumed Garden of Shaykh Nefzawi*, trans. Sir Richard Burton (HarperCollins, London, 1993; first published 1886).

7 A. J. B. Wavell, *A Modern Pilgrim in Mecca and a Siege in Sanaa* (Constable and Company, London, 1913), p. 167.

8 Ibid., p. 137.

9 Ahmad Suba'i, *My Days in Mecca*, trans. Deborah S. Akers and Abubaker A. Bagader (First Forum Press, Boulder, Colo., 2009), p. 19.

10 Ibid., p. 21.

11 Ibid., p. 39.

12 Ibid., pp. 86–7.

13 Abu Hamid al-Ghazali's *The Revival of Religious Science* consists of 4 parts, each divided into 10 chapters or 'books' – 40 volumes in all. A selection of individual books, such as the *Book of Knowledge*, *Foundation of Belief* and the *Book of Purity*, have been translated into English.

14 Hurgronje, *Mekka in the Later Part of the 19th Century*, p. 210.

15 Ibid., p. 191.

16 George Antonius, *The Arab Awakening* (Putnam and Sons, London, 1946), p. 133.

17 T. E. Lawrence, *Seven Pillars of Wisdom* (Jonathan Cape, London, 1926), p. 63.

18 Eldon Rutter, *The Holy Cities of Arabia* (2 vols, Putnam, London, 1928), vol. I, p. 190.

19 Muhammad Asad, *The Road to Mecca* (Simon & Schuster, New York, 1951).

20 Muhammad Marmaduke Pickhall, *The Meaning of the Glorious Koran* (A. A. Knopf, New York, 1930).

21 Harry St John Bridger Philby, *The Empty Quarter* (Constable, London, 1933).

22 Harry St John Bridger Philby, *Harun al Rashid* (P. Davies, London, 1933).

23 Cited in Lady Evelyn Cobbold, *Pilgrimage to Mecca* (Arabian Publishing, London, 2009), p. 41.

24 Wavell, p. 151.

25 Cobbold, p. 183.

26 Ibid., p. 182.

27 Rutter, vol. I, p. 108.
28 Richard F. Burton, *Personal Narrative of a Pilgrimage to Al-Madinah and Meccah* (Dover Publications, New York, London, 1964; first published 1855–6), vol. II, p. 191.
29 Ibid., p. 191.
30 Rutter, vol. II, p. 78.
31 Ibid., p. 77.
32 Ibid., p. 78.
33 Wavell, p. 137.
34 Eric Rosenthal, *From Drury Lane to Mecca: Being an Account of the Strange Life and Adventures of Hedley Churchward* (Howard Timmins, Cape Town, 1982), p. 151.
35 Cobbold, p. 192.
36 Rosenthal, p. 150.
37 Rutter, vol. I, p. 197.
38 Wavell, p. 151.
39 Rutter, vol. II, p. 70.
40 Cobbold, p. 187.
41 Wavell, p. 142.
42 Burton, *Personal Narrative*, vol. II, p. 190.
43 Rutter, vol. II, p. 92.
44 Ibid., p. 93.
45 Ibid., p. 90.
46 Rosenthal, p. 160.
47 Cobbold, p. 204.
48 Rutter, vol. I, pp. 204–5.
49 Rosenthal, p. 154.
50 Ibid., pp. 157–8.

10 MECCA UNDER THE SAUDIS

1 See William Ochsenwald, 'The Annexation of the Hijaz', in Mohammed Ayoob and Hasan Kosebalaban, eds, *Religion and Politics in Saudi Arabia* (Lynne Rienner, Boulder, Colo., 2009), pp. 75–90.
2 David Long, *The Hajj Today* (State University of New York Press, Albany, 1979), Appendix A, 'Hajj Arrival Figures for Selected Year: 1807–1942', pp. 127–8.
3 Abdul Ghafur Sheikh, 'From America to Mecca on Airborne Pilgrimage', *The National Geographic Magazine*, July 1953, pp. 1–62.
4 Muhammad Kamal Ismail, *The Architecture of the Holy Mosque Makkah* (Hazar Publishing, London, 1998), pp. 57–69.
5 *The Autobiography of Malcolm X*, with the assistance of Alex Haley (Penguin, London, 1968), pp. 449–50.

6 Ekmeleddin Ihsanoglu, *The Islamic World in the New Century: The Organisation of the Islamic Conference, 1969–2009* (Hurst, London, 2010), p. 22.

7 Mohammad Jamil Brownson, 'The Socio-Economic Dynamic of the Sacred City', in Ziauddin Sardar and M. A. Zaki Badawi, *Hajj Studies*, vol. I (Croom Helm, London, 1978).

8 For the difference between the Hijazis and the people of the Najd, who rule Saudi Arabia, see Mai Yamani, *Cradle of Islam: The Hijaz and the Quest for Identity in Saudi Arabia* (I. B. Tauris, London, 2009).

9 Ministry of Planning, 'Master Plan for the Holy City of Mecca' (Government of Saudi Arabia, Riyadh, 1973).

10 Sami Angawi, Preface, in Sardar and Badawi, p. 11.

11 On Naseef House and social life in Jeddah during this period, see Angelo Pesce, *Jiddah: Portrait of an Arabian City* (Falcon Press, Naples, 1974), pp. 101–48.

12 Hajj Research Centre, 'Mecca: Policy Framework and Future Development', Report MEC 2 77/96, King Abdul Aziz University, Jeddah, 1977.

13 Kingdom of Saudi Arabia, Ministry of Finance, General Statistics Department, *Pilgrim Statistics*, Riyadh, 1969, 1970, 1971, 1972, 1973, 1974 and 1975.

14 Hajj Research Centre, 'Atmospheric Quality in Muna During the Hajj Season of 1398 AH' and 'Air Quality in Mina: Microbial Content During Hajj Season 1398/1999 AH', King Abdul Aziz University, Jeddah, 1978.

15 Hajj Research Centre, 'A Quantitative and Qualitative Analysis of Holy Sacrifice', King Abdul Aziz University, Jeddah, 1977.

16 Hajj Research Centre, 'First Hajj Seminar: A Brief Report', Report SEM 1/95, King Abdul Aziz University, Jeddah, 1976.

17 See Khurshid Ahmad, ed., *First International Conference on Islamic Economics* (Amar, Karachi, 1984); see also Nejatullah Siddiqui, *Muslim Economic Thinking* (Islamic Foundation, Leicester, 1981), and Muhammad Akram Khan, *Islamic Economics: Annotated Sources in English and Urdu* (Islamic Foundation, Leicester, 1987).

18 See Syed Ali Ashraf, *The First World Conference on Muslim Education: A Review* (Muslim Institute, London, 1977); and S. S. Husain and Syed Ali Ashraf, *Crisis in Muslim Education* (Hodder and Stoughton, London, 1979).

19 Yaroslav Trofimov, *The Siege of Mecca: The Forgotten Uprising* (Allen Lane, London, 2007), p. 173. The involvement of the French Foreign Legion, and of Captain Paul Barril, is described on pp. 188–97 and 209–13.

20 See 'Juhayman's Sins', *Al Majalla*, Arab Press House, London,

21 November 2009, where one of Juhayman's followers, Nasser Al Huezzeimi, tells the background story of the movement.

21 Khalid–Khomeini correspondence, *Al-Nashra al-arabiyya lil-hizb al-jumhuri al-islami* (Tehran), 19 October 1981; and in *Sawt al-umma* (Tehran), 31 October 1981; quoted in Martin Kramer, *Arab Awakening and Islamic Revival* (Transaction, New Brunswick, 1966), p. 169.

22 http://www.oic-oci.org/english/conf/is/3/3rd-is-sum.htm

23 Robert Bianchi, *Guests of God: Pilgrimage and Politics in the Islamic World* (Oxford University Press, 2004), p. 11.

24 Quoted in Kramer, p. 174.

25 Ibid., p. 175.

26 Bianchi, p. 11.

27 It wasn't easy to leave Saudi Arabia due to 'exit visa' problems; see Ziauddin Sardar, *Desperately Seeking Paradise* (Granta, London, 2004), for the full story.

28 Introduction to *An Early Crescent: The Future of Knowledge and Environment in Islam*, ed. Ziauddin Sardar (Mansell, London, 1989), p. 2.

11 THE RECONFIGURED UTOPIA

1 *Guardian*, Thursday 23 September 2010, p. 14.

2 This has been widely reported. See, for example, Jerome Taylor, 'Mecca for the rich: Islam's holiest site turning into Vegas', *Independent*, 24 September 2011, and 'The photos Saudi Arabia doesn't want seen – and proofs Islam's holy relics are being demolished in Mecca', *Guardian*, 15 March 2013; Damian Thompson, 'The Saudis are bulldozing Islam's heritage: Why the silence from the Muslim World?', *Telegraph*, 2 November 2012; and Oliver Wainwright, 'As the Hajj begins, the destruction of Mecca's heritage continues', *Guardian*, 14 October 2013.

3 Michael Muhammad Knight, *Journey to the End of Islam* (Soft Skull Press, New York, 2009).

4 Abdellah Hammoudi, *A Season in Mecca* (Polity, Cambridge, 2005), p. 111.

5 Michael Wolfe, *The Hadj: An American's Pilgrimage to Mecca* (Grove Press, New York, 1993), p. 192.

6 Ibn Ishaq, *The Life of Muhammad*, trans. A. Guillaume (Oxford University Press, Karachi), p. 569.

7 See Steve Coll, *The Bin Ladens: Oil, Money, Terrorism and the Secret Saudi World* (Allen Lane, London, 2008).

8 For more details see Q. Javed Mian and Alison Lerrick, *Saudi Business and Labour Law: Its Interpretation and Application* (Graham & Trotman, 1982).

9 Muhammad Husayn Haykal, trans. Ismail R. A. al-Faruqi, *The Life of Muhammad* (American Trust Publications, Plainfield, Ind., 1976), p. 454.

10 On torture and legal representation in Saudi Arabia, see Anders Jerichow, *Saudi Arabia: Outside Global Law and Order* (Routledge, London, 1997); and for the alleged reforms see Joseph Kechichian, *Legal and Political Reforms in Saudi Arabia* (Routledge, London, 2012).

11 Ahmad Kamal, *The Sacred Journey* (Allen & Unwin, London, 1961), p. 6.

Acknowledgements

I am grateful, as usual, to my friend Merryl Wyn Davies for her invaluable help in researching and writing this book. Ehsan Masood provided beneficial advice on various drafts; and M. A. Qavi, apart from providing useful reference materials, gave constant (sometimes nagging) encouragement. Thanks are also due to all my former Hajj Research Centre colleagues: Sami Angawi, visionary architect and Director of the Centre; James Ismail Gibson, town planner; Mohammad Jamil Bronson, urban geographer; Bodo Rasch, world expert on 'tent cities'; Peter Endene, transport engineer; Zafar Malik, artist and designer extraordinaire; Saleem ul-Hassan (aka 'Tabligh'), statistician and data cruncher; and the late Zaki Badawi, the Centre's expert on theology and Shariah. Wasiullah Khan, Chancellor, East West Univsity, Chicago, kept me amused during more challenging days in the holy areas. Finally, special thanks to Abdullah Naseef, the former President of King Abdul Aziz University, Jeddah, for always being there.

Index

al Abaqla, 224
abaya, 157
Abbas ibn Abd al-Muttalib, 88
al-Abbasi, Ali Bey (Domingo Badia y Leyblich),
    226
Abbasid caliphate, xxxvi, 88–115, 297, 347
    decline of, 115–17, 121–3
    and descendants of the Prophet, 122
    and Islamic civilization, 112–14
    and music, 151
    Qarmatian threat to, 109–11
    and wearing of black, 94
Abd al-Malik ibn Marwan, Caliph, 85–6
Abd al-Muttalib (Shaybah), 25–9, 46, 94
Abd al-Shams ('the Servant of the Sun'), 25
Abdal Majid I, Sultan, 255
Abdilla, Sharif, 282
Abdilla bin Said, Sharif, 211–12
Abdulhamid II, Sultan, 275–6, 282–3
Abdullah (son of Abd al-Muttalib), 29
Abdullah ibn Ali, 89–90
Abdullah ibn Hussain, Sharif, 212
Abdur Rahman I, Caliph ('the Falcon of the
    Quraysh'), 90, 115
Abdur Rahman III, Caliph, 115
Abrahah, 27–9, 41, 224
Abraham (Prophet), xiv, 6–13, 38, 41, 48, 133,
    356
Abu al-Abbas Ahmad al-Nasir, Caliph, 137
Abu Aun, 195
Abu Bakr, Caliph, 38, 52–3, 69–71, 79, 82
    his house, 134, 346
    mosque dedicated to, 238
Abu Hanifa, 106
Abu Hashim, Sharif (Muhammad ibn Jafaar),
    126–7, 137, 140
Abu Jahl, 40, 44–7, 49–51

Abu Jandal, 58–9
Abu Lahab, 40, 44, 47
Abu Musa, 76
Abu Muslim, 88
Abu Nomay I, Sharif, 160, 162–3
Abu Nomay II, Sharif, 173, 183, 194–5, 229
Abu Nomay, Ahmad, 167
Abu Nomay, Sharif Hassan, 195
Abu Nomay, Sharif Idris, *see* Abu Aun
Abu Nomay, Sharif Rumaitha ('the Sword of
    Religion'), 162–5, 167
Abu Nomay, Sharif Utayfa ('the Lion of
    Religion'), 163, 165, 167
Abu Said Khurbandr, 163–5
Abu Sufyan, 40, 44, 47, 49–55, 60–3
    and Umayyad dynasty, 68, 71, 74, 79, 85, 105
Abu Tahir al-Qarmati, 111–12
Abu Talib, 39–40, 44–6
    his tomb, 239
Abukir, Battle of, 222
Abul Ghaith, 163
Abyssinia, 43–4
Acre, 161, 222
Adam, xiv, 61, 101–3
Aden, 129, 179–81, 300
Adhaan (call to prayer), 49, 126
Aga, Sedefhar Mehmed, 191–2
Ahmad Pasha, 195–6
Ahmad Agha Bonaparte, 229, 233–4
Ahmad Ratib Pasha, 281–2
Ain Jalut, Battle of, 162
Aisha (wife of the Prophet), 63, 71–3, 75, 77, 82
Ajlan, Sharif ('the Swift'), 167–9
Akbar 'the Great', Emperor, 258–9, 261
Al Ghaza Hotel, collapse of, 339
Al Hussainiya, 224
Al Qabil, Yusif, 212–13

395

Al-lah (Meccan deity, 'the god'), 24
Albuquerque, Alfonso de, 180
Aleppo, 174, 190
Alexandria, 144, 222–3
Algeria, 205, 282
Ali, Caliph (cousin of the Prophet), 38, 47, 52, 57–8
  his birthplace, 239
  descendants of, 79–80, 92, 106, 116, 121–2, 127
  moves capital to Kufa, 73–4, 79
  murder of, 78
  and succession dispute, 70–2, 75–8, 82
  his sword, 125
Ali (guide), xxiv–xxv, xxix–xxx, 343
Ali Bey, General, 199–201
Ali Haider, Sharif, 282–3, 295, 298
Alids, see Ali, Caliph, descendants of
Almeida, Francisco de, 179–80
Alp-Arslan, Sultan Adud ad-Dawla, 126–7
Amalik tribe, 14
Amer (Hisham) ('the bread breaker'), 25
America, slavery in, 254
Amina (mother of the Prophet), 29
  her tomb, 239
Amman, 297
Ammar, 43
Amr, 76–7
Anabaptists, 110
al-Andalus, 90
Angawi, Sami, 320–1, 324, 330, 339
Ansar (the Helpers), 61, 352–3
Antioch, 142, 161
Aqaba, 21, 46, 297
Arabian Nights, The, 276, 285, 308
Arabic language, 113–14, 354
Arabs, superiority of, 76, 354
Arafat, 19, 66, 93, 133, 172, 207, 209, 225, 270, 276, 315
  Adam's pilgrimage, 102–3
  development at, 337–8
  Lady Cobbold visits, 302–4
  and pilgrim numbers, 323–4
archaeologists, 347–8
Aribi, 2–3
Arish, 222
Asad, Muhammad, 299–300
Asma, 82, 86
Assemblies of al-Hariri, The, 276
astrology, 210, 213

astronomy, 205–6, 209–10
Aun-al-Rafiq, 277, 280–2
Aurangzeb, Emperor, 258–9
Awqaf al-Haramain (Pious Foundations for the Holy Cities), 184
al-Ayad fort, 346
Aydhab, 143
Ayyubid dynasty, 129, 139, 161
al-Azraqi, Meccan Reports, 12, 95

Bab al-Mandab, 143, 180
Babur, Emperor, 258, 261
Baca Valley ('Valley of Weeping'), 2–3, 8–9, 14–15, 28–9, 50
Badr, xiv, 231–3
Badr, Battle of, 49–51, 63
Baghdad, 95–7, 105, 154, 170
  and Abbasid caliphate, xxxvi, 113–14
  compared with Mecca, 159
  Qarmatians and, 109, 111
  sacking of, 160
  Wahhabis and, 218, 232
Baghdad caravans, 90, 93, 108, 111, 160
Bahrain, 109, 124, 181, 296
Bait al-Sade palace, 240–1
Balfour Declaration, 301–2
Balkh, 96
Bandar Shah, 181
Banu Asad, 54
Banu Bakr, 59–60
Banu Hashim, 39, 44–7, 63, 70, 81, 88
Banu Nadir, 54
Banu Qurayza, 55–6
Banu Sad, 54
Banu Sulaim, 54
Banu Umayya, 78
Baqoum Arabs, 244–5
Barakat I, Sharif, 169–71, 203
Barakat II, Sharif, 171–3, 183, 209
Barakat, Ali (son of Barakat II), 173
Barakat, Qu'it Bay (son of Barakat II), 172–3
Barakat ibn Muhammad, Sharif, 209–10
Barra bint al-Harith (wife of the Prophet), 171
Barril, Captain Paul, 331
Bashir Agha, 203
Basra, 71–2, 121, 181
Battle of the Camel, 72–3, 82
Battle of the Elephant, 27–9, 224
Battle of the Nile, 222
Battle of Trenches, 54–6

Bayazid Bastami ('the splendid beggar'), 96
Baybars al-Bandaqdari az-Zahir Rukn-ad-Din, Sultan, 161–2
Bayt al Hikma, 113
Bedouins
    allegiance to sharifs, 125, 127–8
    benefit from Ottoman largesse, 183
    discipline under Wahhabis, 297
    and Hajj pilgrims, 107–8
    Indians' experience of, 267–8
    and Islamist insurgency, 327–8
    living in Mecca, 236
    and resistance to Ottomans, 244–5, 247–8, 252–3
    and resistance to Wahhabis, 230, 232, 234, 240
    sharifs' bodyguards, 127–9, 139, 142
Beersheba, 11
Bhopal, 260–1
bida (innovation), 97, 100, 217
Bilal ibn Rabah, 43
Bilal Mosque, demolition of, 338
Bin Laden Construction Company, 329–30
Bin Laden family, 354
Black Stone, the
    and celestial myth, 102
    damaged, 83, 112, 132
    first set in place, 31
    kissing of, 133, 135, 137, 227
    and rebuilding, 198
    repaired, 132–3
    'the right hand of God', 147
Book of Genesis, 7
Book of Psalms, 2, 4–5
bookshops, 276, 286
Britain
    abolition of slavery, 254
    emancipation of minorities, 255
    Middle Eastern interests, 284, 292–6
    Muslims in, 300
    and Suez Canal, 257, 282
British African Association, 219
British East India Company, 204, 222, 254, 260, 284
British Muslim Society, 300
Bukhari, Imam, 94
Burckhardt, John Lewis, 219–20, 226, 243, 249, 255, 284
    his description of Mecca, 234–9
Burton, Sir Richard, 284–5, 304–5, 308–9

Buyids, 116–17, 124, 126
Byng, Admiral, 181
Byzantine Empire, 25, 41, 171–2

Cairo, 105, 116, 130, 144, 161, 170, 188, 234
    Al-Azhar University, 289, 310
    sharifs and, 167–8
Cairo caravans, 93, 108, 123, 164
Calicut, 179
camels, xxii, 6, 28, 188, 215
    and campaign against Wahhabis, 219, 240, 243, 247–8, 250
    sacrifice of, 29, 66–7, 85
capital punishment, 76, 238, 358
cartaz (Portuguese licence), 182
Celebi, Evliya, 206–8
Ceuta, 175
Ceylon, 254
Chaul, 180
chess, 197, 243, 308
China, 88, 93
cholera, 272
Christianity, and Meccan economy, 41
Christians, in Hijaz, 24
Churchward, Mahmoud Mobarek, 300–1, 306–8, 310–11, 357, 359
CIA, 330
Circassians, 255
Clermont, 128
Cobbold, Lady Evelyn, 300–3, 306, 308–10
coffee-houses, 237, 250
Columbus, Christopher, 177
comets, 205, 213
conferences, Islamic, 324–5, 335, 340–1
Constantinople, fall of, 171
Cordoba, 90, 105, 113, 115
'corsairs', 177
Courtellemont, Gervais, 285–6
Crimean War, 252, 256
Crusades, 128–9, 141–3, 161, 176, 222, 356
Ctesiphon, 109

da Gama, Vasco, 176, 178
Damascus, 105, 170, 185, 190, 210, 222, 311
    Umayyad caliphate and, xxxvi, 79, 83, 87
    Wahhabis and, 228, 232
Damascus caravans, 93, 108
Damietta, 161
Dar al-Nadwa (house of Qusayy), 46–7, 87, 90, 135

Dariyya, 218, 244, 251
David, King, 5
dawa, 340–1
Dawud Pasha, 186
Dawud ibn Ali, 90
'Day of Arafat', xxxiii
Daylam, 116
Declaration of the Rights of Man, 254
Dervish orders, 210
Dhawi Zaid
   dispute with Dhawi Aun, 282–3, 295
   dispute with Dhawi Barakat, 203–4, 210–13
dhimmis (protected minorities), 255
Diggers, 110
Diodorus Siculus, 5
Diu, 179–81
divining arrows, 29
Djinguereber Mosque, 165
dogs, 159–60, 307
donkeys, cruelty to, 288
Doughty, Charles, 271–2, 274
drum-beating, 210
Dutch East India Company, 204

eclipses, 311, 357–8
Edirne, 191–2
education, 169–70, 185–6, 287–9, 313
   see also madrassas
Egypt
   British influence, 282
   Fatimid conquest, 123–4, 126, 129
   grain supplies, 130, 139, 188, 205
   Muslim conquest, 69
   Napoleonic invasion, 222–3, 228, 257, 284
   Ottoman conquest, 173
   and succession dispute, 77–8
   under Muhammad Ali, 228–9, 239
Elat, 143
elephants, 27–8, 165
Eliot, T. S., 33
Emre, Yunus, 187
English Civil War sects, 110
Erzeni, mustafa Dariri, 193
Esin, Emel, 18
Euphrates, river, 7, 75
expatriates, Muslim, 260, 355

Fadak, 24
Fahrist of al-Nadim, 113–14
Faisal ibn Hussain, 294, 320

falagah, 287
al-Farabi, 151
Farah bin Barqaq, Sultan al-Nasir, 169
Fariskur, Battle of, 161
fashions, Turkish, 266–7
Fatima (daughter of the Prophet), 20–1, 60, 63,
   116, 122, 127
   her birthplace, 133, 238
Fatima bint Yunus, 152
Fatimid caliphate, 110, 115–16, 121, 123–4,
   126–7, 129
Fazara tribe, 54
Fezzan desert, 219–20
field guns, 220, 248
fiqh (jurisprudence), 100
firearms, introduction of, 198–9
firmans, Ottoman, 173, 210, 255
First World War, 291–5
fitna (rebellion and strife), 205
France
   ban on slavery, 254
   colonial expansion, 221–3
   and Egypt, 222–3, 257, 282, 284
   emancipation of minorities, 254–5
   Middle Eastern interests, 292–3, 295
Frankfurter Zeitung, 299
French Foreign Legion, 331
French Revolution, 254

Gabriel, Archangel, 33–4
Gallipoli, 178
Garden of Eden, 101
Gate of Bani Shayba, 165
Gate of Banu Jamah, 90
al-Gawri, Sultan Al-Asraf Qansuh, 178
Gaza, 25, 94, 208, 222
Genghis Khan, xxiv
Genghis (donkey), xxiii–xxx, xxxiii, xxxv–
   xxxvi, 131, 343
Genoa, 116
Ghalia, 245, 248, 250
Ghassani tribe, 27
Ghatafan tribe, 54–5
al-Ghazali, Imam Abu Hamid, 288
Ghifar tribe, 61
Gibbon, Edward, 5
Goa, 180–1
gold, 164–5, 175–6, 236
goldsmiths, 3, 24
Great Dam of Marib, 15

Grenada, fall of, 179
Groundhog Day, 110, 153
Gujarat, 179, 181
Gulbadan Begum, 261
Gulnus, Sultan, 183

Hadhramaut, 129
al-Hadi, Caliph Musa, 91
hadith, 94, 106, 216
'Hadith folk' (*Ahl al-Hadith*), 98
Hagar (wife of Abraham), 8–11, 104, 356
Haifa, 222
Hajj
    beginnings of, 64
    and criminality, 361
    and ibn Arabi's vision, 146–7
    Prophet's 'Farewell Pilgrimage', 65–7
    see also pilgrims
Hajj Research Centre, xvi–xvii, xxiv, xxvi,
    321–2, 325, 330, 337–9
Hajj tax, 171
Hajr, 109
al-Hakim, Caliph, 124–5
Hali, 183, 223, 296
al-Hallaj, Mansur, 95–6
Halley's Comet, 311
halqa (circle of listeners), 186
Hamdan Qarmat, 109
Hammoudi, Abdellah, 350
Hamud, 203–4, 208
Hamza (uncle of the Prophet), 43, 52–3, 62
Hamza ibn Muhammad, 172
Hanafi school of law, 106, 172, 275, 298, 359
Hanbali school of law, 95, 100, 106, 172, 216,
    275, 298, 359
Hanifs, 38
Haqqi, Sheikh, 276
al-Haramme, Sheikh, 267–8
Haran, 7
Harappa, 6
Harb tribe, 215–16, 230–2, 251–3
harems, description of, 306–7
Haret al-Jyat, 236
Haret Bab al-Umra, 236
Harun al-Rashid, Caliph, 92–3, 302, 356
Hashim dynasty, 126, 144
Hassan Pasha, 207–8
Hassan, Hafiz Ahmad, 266–8
Hassan ibn Ali (grandson of the Prophet), 122,
    126, 133

Hassan ibn Qatada, Sharif, 155
al-Hassani, Sharif Abdul Futuh ibn Jafar, 124–5
al-Hassani, Sharif Isa ibn Jafar, 124, 133
al-Hassani, Sharif Jafar ibn Muhammad, 123–4
al-Hassani, Sharif Muhammad Shukr, 125
Hatti-Humayun edict, 255–6
Hattin, Battle of, 144
Headley, Lord, 300
hijab, 156–7
Hijaz, The, 277
Hijaz railway, 283, 286, 291
Hind, 40, 51, 53, 71, 74, 78, 105, 245
    her conversion, 62–3
Hira, xiv, 24, 33, 88, 347
Hisham ibn-al-Kalbi, 19
History of al-Tabari, 12
history, cyclical theory of, 155–6
Holland, 255
Homer, 12
Hormuz, 180–1
hospitals, 113, 183
hotels, xxix, 346
House of Happiness, 195
House of Khayzuran, 134
Houston, Texas, 318, 320, 350
Hubal (deity), 17, 29
Hubba, 21
Hudhail tribe, 215–16
Hudhaim tribe, 61
Hulagu Khan, 160
Hulayl, 21
Humaidha, Sharif, 162–3
Hums, 41
Hunyan, Battle of, 352
Hurgronje, Christiaan Snouck, 277–80, 285, 289
Hussain Pasha, 208–9
Hussain, Sharif, 283, 286–7, 291–7, 301
Hussain, Saddam, 333
Hussain (judge), 191
Hussain ibn Ali (grandson of the Prophet),
    79–81, 122, 134, 167, 223, 332

ibn Ajlan, Sharif Ahmad ('the Meteor of
    Religion'), 168
ibn Ajlan, Sharif Ali, 168–9
ibn Ajlan, Sharif Hassan, 168, 170
ibn Ajlan, Sharif Muhammad, 168
ibn Arabi, Muhyi Din, 145–9, 151–2, 156
ibn Aun, Sharif Abdullah ibn Muhammad, 256,
    260, 262, 266, 268–9, 320

ibn Aun, Sharif Ali ibn Abdullah ibn
    Muhammad, 281–2
ibn Aun, Sharif Hussain ibn Muhammad,
    269–74
ibn Aun, Sharif Muhammad ibn Abdul Moin,
    251–4, 256, 263, 277
ibn Ayyub, Abu Bakr, 137
ibn Ayyub, Adil, 144
ibn Battuta, xxi–xxiii, xxvi, xxxiv, xxxvi, 165–7,
    207
ibn Ghalib, Sharif Abdul Muttalib, 243, 251–2,
    254, 256, 272, 277
ibn Hanbal, Ahmad, 95, 97–100, 106, 216
ibn Ishaq, *Life of Muhammad*, 13, 39
ibn Jafaar, Sharif Muhammad, *see* Abu Hashim,
    Sharif
ibn Jubayr, 130–9, 144, 166, 355
ibn Khaldun, 155
ibn Masaad, Abdul Aziz, 220
ibn Masaad, Abdul Muin, 224
ibn Masaad, Abdullah ibn Sarur, 219
ibn Masaad, Sharif Ghalib, 219–21, 223–5,
    228–30, 232–4, 237, 239–43, 282
  arrested by Muhammad Ali, 241–4
  exiled to Salonica, 243, 251
  his fortune, 243
  his garden, 238
  his house, 236
ibn Masaad, Sharif Sarur, 212–16, 219, 229, 241
ibn Masaad, Sharif Yahya ibn Sarur, 245, 247,
    249, 251
ibn Misjah, 151
ibn Muhriz, 151
ibn al-Mujawir, 156–60, 166
ibn Rumi, Sheikh, 253
ibn Saad, *Book of the Major Classes*, 13
ibn Said, Sharif Ahmad, 212–14
ibn Saud, King Abdul Aziz, 296–9, 301–2,
    313–15, 321, 325, 328
ibn Saud, Abdullah, 231, 246–7, 250
ibn Saud, King Fahd, 318, 326, 335, 337–8
ibn Saud, Faisal, 231, 248, 250
ibn Saud, King Faisal, 298, 302, 314–17, 319
ibn Saud, Prince Faisal bin Musaid, 317
ibn Saud, King Khalid, 317–18, 326, 330, 333
ibn Saud, Muhammad, 218
ibn Saud, Saud ibn Abdul Aziz Muhammad,
    223–6, 229–30, 244, 246, 248
ibn Saud, King Saud, 314–15
ibn Sina, 151

ibn Sulaiman Maghribi, Muhammad, 205–6,
    209–10
ibn Surayj, 151
ibn Talib, Sharif Ahmad, 195–7, 199
ibn Zola, 151
ibn Zubair, Abdullah, 79–89, 134, 144, 149,
    197–8, 208, 347
Ibrahim (son of the Prophet), 357
Ibrahim Bey, 190
Ibrahim bin Adham, Sultan, 96
ihram, xi, xxvii–xxviii
Ikrama, 51
Illustrated London News, 261
Indian Mutiny, 261, 270
Indians, 236, 257–68
Indonesia, Muslim population of, 277
Indus Valley, 6, 88
infanticide, 30
Inspector of the Holy Places, 171, 202
intelligence-gathering and spying, 283–5, 294,
    301
Iran, revolutionary, 326, 332–6
Iran–Iraq war, 333
Iraq, Wahhabi incursion into, 218–19
Iraqi caravans, 127–30, 153–4, 160–1
Isaac, 8, 11–12
Ishmael, xiv, 8–13, 20–1, 104
Ishmaelites, 13–16, 19, 21–2
al-Islam, Sheikh, 197, 206
Islam
  disinformation about, 162
  elite status of Arabs in, 76, 354
  fifteenth century of, 324–6, 332
  growing exclusivity of, 105
  spreads along sea routes, 175–6
  Sunni–Shia split, 188–9
  and Wahhabi reformation, 216–17, 225
'Islamic revival', 324–5
Islamic Summits, 317, 324, 333
Ismail I, Shah, 188–9
Ismailis, 108, 112, 115, 118, 129, 153
Istanbul
  Blue Mosque, 192
  and departure of *surre* caravan, 184–5
  Dolmabache Palace, 276
  and making of *kiswa*, 221, 223
  Muhammad Ali threatens, 234
  Suleymniye Mosque, 191
  Sultan Ahmad Mosque, 221

Jabal al-Nur (Mountain of Light), 6, 8, 13, 20, 29–30, 32–3, 347
Jabal Hindi, 241
Jaffa, 222
Jafir Effendi, 262–4
jahiliyya (pre-Islamic period), 66–8
Jamil (poet), 149
Jaqmaq, Sultan al-Zahir Sayf-ad-Din, 169–70, 172
Jazan ibn Muhammad, 172
Jeddah
    and arrest of Al Qabil, 212–13
    and arrest of Sharif Ghalib, 241, 243
    British and French consulates, 256
    customs duties, 229, 239, 280
    ibn Jubayr's description of, 131
    Jews and Christians in, 268
    King Abdul Aziz University, xvi, 320–2, 325, 339
    loss of Ahmad Pasha's belongings, 195–6
    murder of Ottoman inspector, 202
    murder of sharif, 272
    Naseef House, 320–1
    and Portuguese naval dominance, 180–1
    and rise of Wahhabis, 225–6, 229, 234, 239–40, 297
    sack of, 200
    Sharif Hussain flees to, 297
    Sikandar Begum's arrival, 262
    uncontrolled development under Saudis, 320–1
Jerusalem, 48, 70, 78, 87, 144, 210
    fall (liberation) of, 128, 141–2
    Jewish Temple, 5, 24
jewellers, 236
jizya (tax on minorities), 255
John the Baptist, 79
Judaida, 231–3
Juhaina tribe, 61
Jurham tribe, 14–16, 20

Kaaba
    Abbasid redevelopment, 90–2
    and arrival of paganism, 17
    ascribed magical powers, 104
    basis of Mecca's fame, 2–3
    building of, 10
    circumambulation of, 19
    conference delegates enter, 341–2
    enlargements, 70, 84–5, 90–2, 107, 191–2, 197
    etching of the Virgin Mary, 62
    and famine, 117
    fires and reconstruction, 30–2, 169
    guardianship of, 13–16, 21–3
    history, 4–5
    house-building around, 22–3
    and ibn Arabi's vision, 145–7
    ibn Battuta's description of, 166–7
    interior roofed, 172
    massacre of Khuza, 59–60
    Naser's description of, 118–21
    opening ceremony, 120–1
    Ottoman rebuilding, 197–8, 201
    paintings of, 194
    pigeons and, 308–9
    Prophet performs lesser pilgrimage, 59
    proscription document, 44–5
    Qarmatian assault on, 111–12
    risk of flooding, 70, 197
    Rutter's description of, 304
    as symbol of equality, 353
    Umayyads and, 82–3, 85–7
    Wahhabi occupation of, 227–8
Kabul, 93
kafirs (unbelievers), 217
Kaium, Molvi Abdul, 262–3
Kamal, Ahmad, 359
Kamaran islands, 180
Kavalla Volunteer Contingent, 228
Keane, John F. T., 269–72
Kerak, 142–3
Kerbala, 218, 223, 225, 332
Kerbala, Battle of, 81, 94
Khabban ibn al-Aratt, 43
Khadijah (wife of the Prophet), 6, 30, 36, 38, 63
    her house, 79, 133, 346
    her tomb, 239
Khaibar, 24
Khalid bin Walid, 52, 68
Kharijites ('the separatists'), 75–9, 82, 84, 86, 88, 94, 97, 108, 219, 328
Khaybar, 183
khila (robe of honour), 170–1
Khomeini, Ayatollah, 326, 332–4
Khorasan, 82, 88, 93, 119, 156
khutba (Friday sermon), 126, 136, 163, 166–7, 173
Khuza tribe, 16, 21–2, 59–60
al-Kindi, 151
King James Bible, 271

kiswa coverings, 91, 162, 170–1, 198, 221, 223
Kitchener, Lord, 293
Knight, Michael Muhammad, 350
kohl, 166
Korah, sons of, 5
Kufa, 73–4, 77–81, 109, 111, 154
kuttab (Qur'anic schools), 287
Kuwait, 284, 296

labour laws, 455
'Lady Venus', 270
Lahore, 317
Land of Canaan, 8
Lari, Muhi Al-Din, 194
lascars, 300
al-Lat (deity), 17
Latin Kingdom of Outremer, 142, 161–2
law, Islamic
    development of, 100
    and emancipation of minorities, 255–6
    four schools of, 94–5, 106, 148, 197–8, 275,
        298
    jurists and professors, 186
    opposed to Ottoman law, 269
    Shariah, 98, 269, 358
    and slavery, 310
Lawrence, Colonel T. E., 293–5
Lawrence of Arabia, 293, 320
Lesseps, Ferdinand de, 257
Levellers, 110
libraries, 113, 185
London Stock Exchange, 35
Louis IX, King of France, 161
Lucknow, siege of, 270
Luhayy tribe, 16–17, 20
Lutfi, Abdullah, 192–4

Mabad, 151
Macaulay, Thomas Babington, 279
al-Madhaifi, Othman, 223–4, 232–4, 240
madrassas, 186, 210
al-Maghribi, Abdul Qassim, 124–5
mahafiz (guardian), 251
al-Mahalib, 157–8
al-Mahdi, Caliph, 90–3
al-Mahdi, Caliph Ubaydallah ('the Mahdi'),
    110, 115–16
Mahmoud, General, 199–201
Mahmud II, Sultan, 255
Mahmud II, Sultan of Gujarat, 260

Mahmudiya, 186
Maimonides, 7
Makhzum tribe, 40
Malacca, 180
Malcolm X, 315–16, 337
Mali, 164–5
Malik, Zafar, xxiv–xxxiv, xxxvi, 131, 343
Malik bin Anas, 106
Maliki school of law, 106, 172, 275, 298, 359
malud (Prophet's birthday celebrations), 211,
    319
Mamluk sultans, 161, 169, 172–3
    armies defeated by Napoleon, 222
    and Portuguese naval dominance, 175,
        178–80
    and rise of Muhammad Ali, 228–9
    and Suez Canal, 257
al-Mamun, Caliph, 95, 97–9, 113, 216
Manaf (deity), 17
Manat (deity), 17
Manisa, Mosque of Murad III, 192
Mansa Musa, 164–5, 175
al-Mansur, Caliph, 90, 92–3
maps and map-making, 141, 176–8
Marrakesh, 105
marriage customs, 157–8, 265
Marwan ibn Hakim, Caliph, 85
Marwar II, Caliph, 88–9
mashrabiya (window screens), 275
al-Masud, Prince (Aqsis), 155
mathematics, 151, 210
mausoleums, destruction of, 313
Maymuna, 171
measurements, standards of, 159
Mecca
    Abbasid redevelopment, 90–3, 119
    absence of crime in, 134
    Burckhardt's description of, 234–9
    and celestial myth, 101–6, 114, 117, 153
    commercialism, 349–50
    competing sects in, 105–6, 121–2
    competition with Medina, 152–3
    daily life in, 290–1
    dead camels in, 247
    decline of, 64, 67–8
    economic hardships, 30
    Egyptian political influence, 169–72
    ethnic mix, 235–6, 269–70
    European visitors and, 300–12
    execution of mufti, 196

expansion under Saudis, 314–16
expulsion of foreigners, 211–12
expulsion of Turks, 294–5
fame based on Kaaba, 2–3
famine in, 117
geographical situation, 24–5
histories and historians, 12–13, 68, 95
history and archaeology, 4–6
house-building in, 22–3
ibn Battuta's description of, 165–7
ibn Jubayr's description of, 131–7
ibn al-Mujawir's description of, 156–60
impact of the Prophet's preaching, 36–7
increasing wealth, 26–7
introduction of sharifate, 122–3
Jews and Christians in, 24, 104–5, 255–6, 268
Jurham rule, 14–15
merging of cults, 23–4, 26
names for, 2, 348
Naser's description of, 117–21
neutrality, 23–5
official spelling of the name, 348
oral history of, 20
Ottoman conquest of, 69
paganism and economy, 17–19, 26–7, 41, 68
persecution of Banu Hashim, 44–7
persecution of Muslims, 42–4
as place of sanctuary, 79–80
population under Ottomans, 188, 275
population under Saudis, 314
and Portuguese naval dominance, 174–82
praying in the direction of, 48
Prophet enters, 61–2
prosperity under Ottomans, 182–92
prosperity under Qatada, 145
Qarmatian assault on, 111–12
rebellion and conflict under sharifs, 203–5,
   207–16
repair and reconstruction under sharifs,
   170–2
resistance to modernity, 307–12
return of Ishmaelites, 21–2
risk of flooding, 107
sacked by Ottoman generals, 200
saved from Abrahah's army, 27–9
seeks independence from Ottomans, 252–3
Sikandar Begum's visit, 260–5
and succession dispute, 70–2, 74
traditionalism and anti-intellectualism,
   97–100, 287–8

Umayyad redevelopment, 79, 86–8
Umayyads besiege, 82–3, 85–6
uncontrolled development under Saudis,
   318–19, 322–3, 337–40
uniformity of religious practice, 298–9
village and family networks, 322–3
Wahhabi prisoners paraded in, 250
Wahhabis and, 219–34, 297–9, 313–14, 352
war with Medina, 49–62
water supplies, 93, 107, 119, 167, 190–1, 225
'Mecca Declaration', 333
Medina (Yathrib), 25–6, 29–30
   Aun-al-Rafiq's *hijra*, 281
   as capital of Muslim state, 64, 67–8, 73, 121
   competition with Mecca, 152–3
   Jews and Christians in, 24, 104–5
   murder of Ottoman *qadi*, 202
   pilgrim journey to, 265–6
   Prophet arrives in, 47–9
   Prophet returns to, 64
   Reynaud advances on, 143–4
   rise of, 56
   Shia insurrection, 92–3
   and succession dispute, 70–2
   tomb of the Prophet, 107
   Wahhabis and, 216–17, 226, 230–4, 297
   war with Mecca, 49–62
Medina, emir of, 129, 145, 160
Medina University, 326, 328–9
mehalabye (jelly), 237
Mehmet II, Sultan, 171–2, 177
Mehmet V, Sultan, 282, 292
mehndi ceremony, 158
melon seeds, 248
Meri (pilgrim ship), sinking of, 178
Mihna (testing or trial), 97–9
Mikhthar bin Isa, Sharif, 129–31, 139, 145
Mina, 66, 323–4, 337–8, 359
Mina, Battle of, 21–2
missionaries, Christian, 162
miswaks (toothbrushes), 290
Mohenjo-Daro, 6
Mohsin, Sharif, 195–6
Mombasa, 179
Mongol horde, 160, 162
Mongols, converted to Islam, 163
months, Islamic
   Dhu al-Hijjah, xix, xxiv, xxxiii, 65–6
   Rabi al-Awwal, 133
   Rajab, 144, 184

Ramadan, xix, 33, 120, 185
Shaban, 120
Shawaal, 120
Montréal, 142
Morocco, 116, 175, 205, 214, 282
Mount Abu Qubays, 10, 14, 16, 22, 91, 103, 119, 133, 208, 337
fort on, 128–9, 139, 241, 249, 275
Mount Budh, 101
Mount Marwah, 56, 62, 65, 119, 134, 147, 237, 336
Mount Safa, 56, 62, 65, 119, 134, 147, 237, 336
Mount Sinai, 48
Mount Uhad, Battle of, 51–3, 62, 249
Mountain of Light, see Jabal al-Nur
Al-Muala cemetery, 359
Muawiya, Caliph, 68, 71, 74–6, 78–9, 82
Mudad ibn Amer, 15–16, 20
Muggletonians, 110
Mughal emperors, 182, 222, 258–9
gifts to Mecca, 258–9
al-Mughammas, 27
al-Mughirah bin Abdullah bin Umar bin Makhzum, 31
Muhammad, Prophet
and Ansar, 352–3
appearance, 1–2
arrives at Mecca, 1–2, 6–8, 20, 30–2
artistic representations of, 193
his birthday, 211, 319
his birthplace, 183, 211, 238, 347
conception, 29–30
and conversion of Hind, 62–3
death, 67
denunciation of Mecca, 36–8
divine revelation, 33–6
education, 20
enters Mecca, 61–2, 171
'Farewell Pilgrimage', 65–7
leaves Mecca for Medina, 44–8
marriage with Khadijah, 30
mortal nature of, 344–5
'Night Journey', 144
and rebuilding of Kaaba, 31
relationship with Abu Talib, 39–40, 45-6
returns to Medina, 64
his tomb, 107, 178
and Treaty of Hudaybiya, 57–60
and war with Mecca, 49–62
Muhammad IV, Sultan, 183, 207

Muhammad Ali, Khedive, 228–9, 232, 234, 239–53
arrest of Sharif Ghalib, 241–3
defeat of Wahhabis, 244–51, 296
Muhammad Bey Akmal Zadi, 191
Mukhabarat (intelligence service), 358
Mukthir, Sharif, 130, 133, 137–9
Muna, 144, 168, 207–9, 273, 276, 302, 315, 338
attacks on pilgrims, 153–4
al-Muqtadir, Caliph, 126–7
Murad III, Sultan, 193–4, 346
Murad IV, Sultan, 198, 200–3, 346
Murcia, 145
Murray, Bill, 110
Murut II, Sultan, 186
Muscat, 179, 181, 296
mushrabiehs (wooden screens), 306
mushrikin (polytheists), 218
music and musicians, 151–2, 195, 307, 319
al-Mustakfi, Caliph, 116
al-Mutadid, Caliph, 107
al-Mutasim, Caliph, 99
al-Mutawakkil III, Caliph, 174
mutawwa (religious police), 297, 357–8
mutawwafs (pilgrim guides), 236
Muttalib, 25–6
Mutzalites, 288
Muzaffar II, Sultan of Gujarat, 260
Muzdalifah, xi, xv, xxxiv, 19, 66, 172, 276, 324, 338
mystics and ascetics, 95–6, 153, 187

Nabateans, 21
al-Nadim (bookseller), 113–14
Nadir Shah, King of Persia, 189
Nahrawan, 75, 78
Najd, 183, 194, 200, 216, 226, 233, 239, 296, 319
Najran, 24
Napoleon Bonaparte, 222–3, 257, 284
Naseef, Abdullah, 320–1
Naseef, Muhammad, 321
Naseef Effendi, Omar, 320–1
al-Nasir Nasir-ad-Din Muhammad, Sultan, 163–4, 167
Nasr (deity), 17
Nasr-e-Khosraw, 117–21, 130, 132, 341, 355
National Geographic Magazine, 314
National Guard (Saudi), 329–30, 334–5, 358
Negev desert, 294

Negus, King of Abyssinia, 44
Nelson, Admiral Horatio, 222
newspapers, 277, 298
Niger, river, 219
Nile, river, 284, 288

Organization of Islamic Cooperation (OIC), 317, 336
Osman Pasha, 253–4, 277, 280–1
Oteiba tribe, 328
Othman, Caliph, 70–2, 77, 84, 115, 122
    prayer niche of, 202
Ottoman dinar, devaluation of, 204
Ottoman Empire, 171–4
    ban on slavery, 254–5
    decline of, 204–5, 252
    and era of prosperity in Mecca, 182–8
    etiquette and protocol, 185, 242
    and First World War, 291–5
    and French colonialism, 221–3
    and Portuguese naval dominance, 174–82, 260
    and Suez Canal, 257
    and Sunni–Shia split, 188–9
    and Wahhabis, 219–21, 228–34, 244–51
    and Young Turks, 281–2

paan, 263
painters, Islamic, 71, 192–4
Palestine, 69, 124, 301–2
paper-making, 113
Paran desert, 11
passion plays, 81
Perfumed Garden, The, 285
Periplus of the Erythean Sea, 6
Persian Gulf, 284
Petra, rediscovery of, 220
Philby, Harry St John Bridger, 301–3
Philip III, King of Spain, 205
philosophy, 97–9
phonographs, 311–12
photographs, 275–7, 279–80, 286
Pickhall, Muhammad Marmaduke, 300
pigeons, 308–9
pigs, 271
pilgrim buses, 302
pilgrims
    and air travel, 314
    Alids provide security for, 121–2
    attacked in Muna, 153–4

attacks on, 108, 111, 116, 139, 215
and car travel, 302, 314–16
economic and religious importance of, 106–7, 117
exploitation of, 127–8, 130, 138–9
Indian, 257–8, 260, 265
Iranian, 332–6, 340, 347
journey to Medina, 265–6
killed in accidents, 338–9
numbers of, xvi, 70, 84, 188, 191, 314, 323, 335–6, 361–2
photographs of, 276, 280
pilgrim girls and love poetry, 150
quotas for, 336, 347
and railway travel, 283
and rise of Wahhabis, 221, 226, 234, 246–7
and sea travel, 175–6, 204, 299, 314
Plessey, Battle of, 222
poetry, 114–15, 125, 148–52, 195
    ghazals (love poetry), 149–51
    and music, 151–2
    qasidahs (epic poems and odes), 17
    rajaz (short verses), 17
    Urdu, 149
pollution, 323–4, 350
Portuguese naval dominance, 174–82, 204, 257–8, 260
Potosí, 204
press censorship, 276–7
Ptolemy, 5
public baths, 238

Qaboo, the, 330–1
qadis (judges), 97, 188, 197, 206, 219
Qahtani, Muhammad Abdullah, 328, 330
al-Qalis, 27
Qarmatians, 108–10, 114–17, 121, 124, 132, 153, 219, 265, 328
Qarqar, Battle of, 2
Qasim Bey, 191
Qasim, Sharif, 127
Qasim, 296
Qatada ibn Idris, Sharif, 144–5, 153–5
Qatar, 181
Qatura tribe, 14
Qibati (Egyptian cloth), 84
Al-Qibla, 277
Qu'it Bay, Sultan al-Asharaf Sayf-ad-Din, 172
Qunfidha, 199, 224, 246, 250, 256
Qunsowa Pasha, 196–7, 199

Qur'an
    created or uncreated nature of, 98–9
    and natural phenomena, 311, 357–8
    and Prophet's mortal nature, 344–5
    reading and recitation of, 287–9
    relationship to Mecca, 35, 48
    revelation of, 33–4
Quraysh tribe, 20, 22, 26, 30, 37, 87, 235
    hostility to Muslims, 38–47
    and succession dispute, 71, 76
    war with Medina, 49–62
    women at war, 51–3
Qusayy (Zayd bin Kilab), 20–5, 30
    his house, see Dar al-Nadwa
Qutb al-Din, 111
Quzah (deity), 17

Rabat, 317
Rabia Khatoon, 153–4
Rabiah al-Adawiyah, 96
Rajhi family, 354
Ramses II, Pharaoh, 6
Reis, Kemal, 177
Reis, Piri, 176–9, 181, 204
Reynaud de Châtillon, 142–5
Rijal, Sharif, 154–5, 160
Riyadh, 253, 296
Romans, 25
Royal Geographical Society, 284, 303
Royal Makkah Clock Tower, 345–6
Russia, emancipation of serfs, 254
Rutter, Eldon, 285, 298–9, 304–5, 307–8,
    310–11, 357, 359

Saad, Sharif, 203–5, 207–9
Saad tribe, 61
Saba, 15
Sacred Mosque, siege of, 326–32
Safavids, 188–9
as-Saffah, Caliph Abu al-Abbas Abdullah,
    88–90
Safra, 231
St Paul, 12
Salah-ad-Din, al-Malik an-Nasir (Saladin),
    129–30, 137–9, 141–4, 153
Salat-ul-Kasuf, 357
Salim I, Sultan, 346
Salma, 25–6
Salonica, 243, 251, 256
Sanaa, 27, 29, 129

Sarah (wife of Abraham), 8, 10–11
Sassanian Empire, 24, 74, 109
Saudi Arabia
    distrust of history and archaeology, 4
    founding of state, 296–7
    modernization and development, 316–19
    oil wealth, 313, 318–19, 324, 346
    tensions with Iran, 332–6
Saudis, sense of superiority, 353–4
Sayf al-Islam, Sultan (Taghtakin), 138–9
Sayl Wadi Ibrahim, 70
scholars, Islamic, xxxvii, 93–5, 100
schools, see education
secret societies, 292, 294
Selim I, Sultan, 173–4, 176–7, 183, 190, 197
Selim II, Sultan, 192–3
Seljuks, 117–18, 126–7
Seth, 103
Seville, 145
sewage system, 359
Shafi school of law, 94, 106, 168, 172, 188, 275,
    289, 298, 359
Shafii, Imam Muhammad ibn Idris, 94–5, 106
Shah of Persia's caravan, 207
al-Shaikh family, 354
Shalmanesar III, King of Assyria, 2
Shariah, see law, Islamic
sharifs
    definition of, 122–3
    end of line of, 273–4, 297
Sheikh, Abdul Ghafur, 314
Sheikh ibn Baz, 328, 331–2
Shias
    and coming of the Mahdi, 332
    and descendants of the Prophet, 122
    and expulsion order, 201–2
    insurrection in Medina, 92–3
    and rebuilding of Kaaba, 197–8, 201
    religious practice, 81
    and rise of Wahhabis, 218–19, 223
    and split in Islam, 188–9
    weakening of ulama, 189
    and wearing of black, 94
    see also Alids
shirk (polytheism), 357
shisha pipes, xxiii, 225
shuras (representative councils), 71
Sicily, 116
Siffin, 75
Sikandar Begum, Nawab, 260–7

silver, 204, 236
Sinan (Mi'mar Sinân Ãğâ), 186, 191
slavery, 254–5, 309–11, 317, 355
slaves, Abyssinian, 236–7
smallpox, 28
smoking, 212, 217, 225, 290
Spain
    and Arabic love poetry, 114–15
    expulsion of Muslims, 179
    and Fatimid threat, 116
    Muslim conquest, 88, 90, 97
Spanish Inquisition, 97
Speke, John Hanning, 284
spice trade, 175–6
Spring of Hunayn, 93
Standard Oil, 302
Station of Abraham, 10, 65, 92, 106, 133, 135,
    137
steamships, 299
Suba'i, Ahmad, 287
Sudan, 234
Suez, 178–9, 181
Suez Canal, 257, 282, 284, 300
Sufi mystics, 187, 289, 329
Sufi shrines, destruction of, 313
Sufism, 96, 216, 218, 319
Suhayl ibn Amr, 57–8
al-Sulaihi, Muhammad, 125–6
Sulaim tribe, 61
Suleiman 'the Magnificent', Sultan, 186, 190–1,
    198, 346
sundials, 205–6
Sunnah (example), 115
Sunnis
    definition of, 115
    and split in Islam, 188–9
superstitious practices, 311–12, 357–8
Surat, 236, 257
surre caravans, 184–5, 187, 276
Sykes-Picot Treaty, 295
Syria
    British and French interests in, 292
    Fatimid conquest, 124–5
    Hellenistic culture, 109
    Muslim conquest, 69
    and succession dispute, 71, 74–5, 78
Syrian caravans, 246–7, 258, 283

al-Tabari, Abu Ja'far Muhammad ibn Jarir,
    12–13, 70, 101

Taif, 3, 17, 93, 121, 145, 214–15, 241, 251, 333
    Wahhabis and, 224, 233–4, 240, 244–5, 297
Taima, 24
Taima Stone, 278
taqlid (imitation), 100
Taraba, 244, 248–50
Tariq bin Amr, 86
tattoos, 235
tear gas, 330–1
Tehran, 105
telegraph, 256
al-Thaqafi, Al-Hajjaj ibn Yusuf, 85–7, 134
Thompson, E. P., 83
Tibet, 93
Tigris, river, 7
Tihāmah, 129
Timbuktu, 113, 164–5
Tonk, 266
Topkapi Palace, 177, 185
Tousoun Bey, 229–34, 242, 245, 247
Treaty of Hudaybiya, 57–60
Treaty of Tordesillas, 177
Tripoli, 161
Trofimov, Yaroslav, 330–1
Troy, 12
Tunca, river, 192
Tunisia, 205, 282
tunnels, accidents in, 338–9
turkeys, 267
al-Turki family, 354
Turkish Constitution, 282
Turkoman soldiers, 127

Ukaz poetry competition, 17–18
Umar, Caliph, 43, 52–3, 70, 73, 84, 107, 122,
    347
Umar ibn Rabia, 149–52, 157
Umayyad caliphate, xxxvi, 78–88, 109, 355–6
    and closing of Mecca, 104–5
    and music, 151
    revolt against, 88–90
Umm Hakim, 51
Umm Kulthum, 73
Umm al-Qura University, 325, 339
ummah, and ideal of oneness, 355–6
Umra Gate (al-Zahir Gate), 131, 154
'Unity of Being' philosophy, 147–8
universities, European, 113–15, 161
Ur of the Chaldees, 7
Urban II, Pope, 128

Urfa (Edessa), 7
al-Usfan, Battle of, 127
Utba (Quraysh commander), 49–51
Utba bin Rabia, 42
al-Uteybi, Juhayman, 328, 331–3
Uyayna, 218
al-Uzza ('the she devil'), 17

vakeels (sponsors), 355
Valley of Nakhla, 17
vegetarianism, 109
Venice, 179
Victoria, Queen, 261–2
Vienna, Battle of, 182, 205

Wadi al-Abar, Battle of, 199–200
Wadi Fah, 208
Wadi Fatima, 238, 248, 307
Wadi al Marr, 213
Wadi al Minhana, Battle of, 213
al-Wahhab, Muhammad ibn Abd, 216–18, 220,
   223, 313, 354
Wahhabis
   beginnings of movement, 216–19
   and *dawa*, 340
   defeated by Muhammad Ali, 244–51
   establish capital in Riyadh, 253, 296
   establish independent state, 296–7
   and Mecca, 219–34, 297–9, 313–14, 352
   and uniformity of religious practice, 298–9
Wahriz (Persian general), 29
Wahshi (Ethiopian slave), 52
al-Walid bin al-Mughirah, 31
War of Greek Independence, 252
water-carriers, 308
al-Wathiq, Caliph, 99
Wavell, Arthur J. B., 283–7, 306, 308–9
'White Army, the', 314
Wolfe, Michael, 350
women
   appearance and attire, 156–7, 166–7, 206–7
   Indian, 261–2

jurists and law professors, 186
large buttocks, 157, 166
sex workers and concubines, 236–7, 255,
   309–10
status in Islam, 72–3, 82
status in Mecca, 63, 72–3, 306–7, 356
use of perfume, 166, 207, 210
at war, 51–3
and whistling, 265
Woolley, Leonard, 293
wudu (ritual washing), 107

Yanbu, 155, 203, 215, 230, 232, 234
Yathrib, *see* Medina
Yazid I, Caliph, 79–83, 85, 149, 172
Year of the Elephant, 29
Yeats, W. B., 114–15
Yemen
   Ayyubid invasion, 129
   gains independence, 296
   under Ottoman rule, 181, 253
   Zaidi dominance in, 167–8
Yildiz Albums, 275, 279
Young Turks, 282, 295

Zab, river, 89
Zab, Battle of, 88
al-Zahir Gate, *see* Umra Gate
al-Zahiri, al-Amir Bist, 169
Zaid ibn Ali, 167
Zaid ibn Muhsin, Sharif, 198–203
Zaidis, 167–8
zakat (poor tax), 171
Zamzam (well of Ishmael), xx, 9, 15, 22, 26,
   104, 194, 225, 228
   bottles of water from, 238, 349–50
   ibn Jubayr's description of, 133, 137–8
   Qarmatian assault on, 111–12
Zoroastrians, 24
Zubaidah aqueduct, 93, 190, 280, 356
Zuhrah, 20–1

A NOTE ON THE AUTHOR

Ziauddin Sardar was born in Pakistan and grew up in Hackney. A writer, broadcaster and cultural critic, he is one of the world's foremost Muslim intellectuals and author of more than fifty books on Islam, science and contemporary culture, including the highly acclaimed *Desperately Seeking Paradise*. He has been listed by *Prospect* magazine as one of Britain's top 100 intellectuals. Currently he is the Director of the Centre for Postnormal Policy and Futures Studies at East West University, Chicago; co-editor of the quarterly *Critical Muslim*; consulting editor of *Futures*, a monthly journal on policy, planning and futures studies; and Chair of the Muslim Institute in London.

ZiauddinSardar.com

A NOTE ON THE TYPE

The text of this book is set in Linotype Stempel Garamond, a version of Garamond adapted and first used by the Stempel foundry in 1924. It's one of several versions of Garamond based on the designs of Claude Garamond. It is thought that Garamond based his font on Bembo, cut in 1495 by Francesco Griffo in collaboration with the Italian printer Aldus Manutius. Garamond types were first used in books printed in Paris around 1532. Many of the present-day versions of this type are based on the *Typi Academiae* of Jean Jannon cut in Sedan in 1615.

Claude Garamond was born in Paris in 1480. He learned how to cut type from his father and by the age of fifteen he was able to fashion steel punches the size of a pica with great precision. At the age of sixty he was commissioned by King Francis I to design a Greek alphabet, for this he was given the honourable title of royal type founder. He died in 1561.